JUN 29 2014

OTHER ROUTES

"For far too long we have been trained to see the world through the eyes of a handful of Western travellers. *Other Routes* is a first step in establishing a new perspective, demonstrating, as it does, that the history of Eastern culture has also been marked by the intellectual curiosity and passion for discovery which characterises the literature of travel. This is a long overdue anthology that will be of interest to students of history, postcolonialism and literature, as well as readers of travel writing and any Asian or African who wants to know his or her own history as it has seldom been written."

> Mike Phillips, novelist, critic, author of *Windrush: The Irresistible Rise of Multi-Racial Britain*

"*Other Routes* opens the reader to a world of alternative traditions to European travel writing and the pieces it contains offer alternatives to the European traveller's gaze. The editors of this imaginative and broad anthology expand the concept of 'travel writing' to include journeys such as spiritual journeys that are written about in poetry; extracts include the personal, ethnography, natural history, geography, cartography, navigation, politics, history, religion, diplomacy, politics, pilgrimage and culture(s) in general."

> Garry Marvin, editor, *Journeys: The International Journal of Travel and Travel Writing*

OTHER ROUTES

1500 YEARS OF AFRICAN AND ASIAN TRAVEL WRITING

Edited by
Tabish Khair, Martin Leer,
Justin D. Edwards, and Hanna Ziadeh

Foreword by Amitav Ghosh

Indiana University Press
Bloomington & Indianapolis

This book is a publication of
Indiana University Press
601 North Morton Street
Bloomington, Indiana 47404-3797 USA

http://iupress.indiana.edu

Telephone orders 800-842-6796
Fax orders 812-855-7931
Orders by e-mail iuporder@indiana.edu

The paper used in this publication is acid-free.

Manufactured in India

Cover design: Devdan Sen
Photographs: Devdan Sen

Cataloging information is available from the Library of Congress.

ISBN 0-253-34693-2 (cl.)
ISBN 0-253-21821-7 (pbk.)

1 2 3 4 5 10 09 08 07 06 05

CONTENTS

CONTENTS

COPYRIGHT ACKNOWLEDGEMENTS

The editors and Signal Books (UK) would like to express their appreciation to the following authors and publishers for their generous permission to reprint copyright material.

Matsao Basho (Nobuyuki Yuasa, trans.), *Narrow Road to the Deep North and Other Travel* Sketches (London: Penguin, 1967)

Li Chi, *The Travel Diaries of Hsü Hsai-K'o* (Hong Kong: The Chinese University of Hong Kong, 1974)

P. M. Holt, *The Memoirs of a Syrian Prince* (Wiesbaden: Franz Steiner Verlag Gmbh, 1983)

Nabil Matar, *In the Lands of The Christians: Arabic Travel Writing in the Seventeenth Century* (London and New York: Routledge/Taylor and Francis Books, Inc, 2003)

John Meskill, *Ch'oe Pu's Diary: A Record of Drifting across the Sea* (Tucson: University of Arizona Press, 1965). Copyright held and granted by the *Association for Asian Studies, Inc.*, Ann Arbor, USA.

Ivan Morris, *The Pillow Book of Sei Shonagon* (New York: Columbia University Press, 1967)

Edwin O. Reischauer, *Ennin's Diary: The Record of a Pilgrimage to China in Search of the* Law (New York: The Ronald Press Company, 1955)

G. R. Tibbetts, *Arab Navigation in the Indian Ocean before the Coming of the Portuguese* (London: Royal Asiatic Society of Great Britain and Northern Ireland, 1971)

As specified in the concerned sections, some entries to *Other Routes* were requested from and have been contributed by:

Dr Lene Sønderby Bech, East Asian Department, Institute of History and Area Studies, University of Aarhus, Aarhus, Denmark

Professor Kaiser Haq, Professor of English, Dhaka University, Bangladesh

Dr Pekka Masonen, Senior Assistant Professor in General History in the Department of History at the University of Tampere, Finland.

Professor Nabil Matar, Professor of English and department head of Humanities and Communication at the Florida Institute of Technology, USA.

Dr Prem Poddar, Associate Professor, Department of English, University of Aarhus, Aarhus, Denmark.

Professor Sadik Rddad, Assistant Professor of Travel literature at Sidi Mohammed Ben Abdellah University, Faculty of Letters, Dhar Mehraz, Fez, Morocco.

FOREWORD

Amitav Ghosh

If the phrase "Book of Wonders" was a favoured title among Arab travellers of the Middle Ages, it was not because those learned wanderers could not distinguish between wonderment and make-believe. As these excerpts demonstrate, the true corollary of a genuine sense of wonder is not fancifulness but, on the contrary, a certain meticulousness. When the Chinese traveller Zhou Daguan relates that young Cambodian mothers use poultices of hot rice and salt to restore their maidenhood, he is not necessarily buying the story ("when first informed of this, my credulity was severely taxed" (p. 147)); he repeats the story because he feels he owes it to his reader. There is a recognition here that what is common sense for him need not be so for the rest of the world. For this recognition to exist there has to be a certain openness to surprise, an acknowledgement of the limits of the knowingness of the witness. This is why so many apparently trivial details find their way into these narratives: because these travellers feel obliged to record what they see and what they hear. They do not assume a universal ordering of reality; nor do they arrange their narratives to correspond to teleologies of racial or civilizational progress.

For me, it is this openness, this sense of wonderment, that sets these accounts apart from travel writing of the kind that is guided by notions of "discovery" and "exploration". In that tradition, travel is a means of laying claim to the world, imaginatively in the first instance, but also politically. Often there is an intricate braiding of the two, so that the imaginative claim becomes, as it were, a fact realized by political means.

There is perhaps no more egregious example of this than the mythology of "discovery" that surrounds the monument of Angkor Wat in Cambodia. I remember very well my first encounter with this monument in January 1993. The country was then still convulsed by the death throes of its long civil war. The guns of the Khmers Rouges could be heard from within the monument and the grounds were littered with mines and explosives. Half-reclaimed by the jungle, the state of the site was such as to evoke memories of Henri Mouhot's discovery of it in the nineteenth century.

I remembered Mouhot's account of his find: in this telling, the temple was said to have been abandoned to the jungle after being sacked by a Thai army in 1431; thereafter it had lain hidden from the world until its veil of greenery was parted by the Frenchman in 1860. The site itself offered no contradiction of Mouhot's account—or so it seemed at first. Despite the moss and greenery, there was a splendidly beguiling consistency to the monument: it had nothing of the haphazard, improvised feel of such medieval remains as the complex of Pagan, in Burma, or the Cities of the Dead in Cairo. It was all of a piece, conceived in its entirety: like a body recovered from a glacier, it looked as though it had been flash-frozen at some distant point in time.

Imagine my surprise then when, right in the main courtyard, I came upon two small wooden temples whose appearance was a visual affront to the consistency of the whole. Hidden by screens of trees, these temples did not immediately catch the eye. But on closer scrutiny it quickly became evident that they were of much more recent provenance than the main complex, being built in the same style as most contemporary Thai and Cambodian shrines. Presently I noticed that a few worshippers were making their way into these temples bearing flowers and offerings. This too was a surprise: so far as I knew, the complex of Angkor Wat had ceased to be a site of devotion several centuries ago. Why were these worshippers visiting a lapsed temple?

Intrigued, I made my way into one of the temples, in the company of a Cambodian archaeologist called Im Phally. Inside the shrine room, we encountered an elderly Buddhist monk and a few visitors—a woman with her mother and baby daughter, a couple of newlyweds. After attending to the devotees, the monk—the Ven. Luong Chun—made time to speak to us. The story he told was entirely at odds with the tale of exploration, discovery and restoration that surrounds the monument of Angkor Wat.

The Ven. Luong Chun was skeletally thin, with a long, gaunt face and a sparse few teeth. He had been in this monastery since his adolescence, he said. He had been drawn to it because of his grandfather, who had spent a part of his life there, before leaving the order to raise a family.

Monks had lived in Angkor Wat for centuries before Mouhot's discovery, said the Ven Luong Chun. Although the site had indeed ceased to be a great centre of kingly ceremony and power, it had never been completely abandoned. Through the centuries monks had continued to use it as a place of worship. Until his grandfather's time their shrine was located in the very heart of the temple. It was only after the monument's "discovery" by the French that it was truly abandoned: when archaeologists took possession of the complex, they forced the monks to move their shrine out of the temple's interior and into the adjoining courtyards. They would have liked to evict them from the complex altogether, but the monks had resisted. The most senior monk of the time had led a delegation to King Monivong (d. 1941) in Phnom Penh. The king could not prevent their being moved out of the temple's interior, but at his intercession they were allowed to build their pagoda where it now stands.

The broad outlines of the Ven. Luong Chun's story were quickly confirmed by a Cambodian archaeologist who was then working at Angkor. He told me that the monks had indeed maintained a continuous presence in the temple complex since at least the sixteenth century.

So to whom then was the monument "lost"? Certainly the Buddhist Sangha was well aware of its existence, as were the ruling powers in Thailand and Cambodia: indeed Thai and Khmer kings fought a centuries-long struggle for possession of the complex (this conflict remains a sensitive issue to this day: in 2002 Phnom Penh was convulsed by riots after a Thai princess said in public that Angkor Wat had once been in her country's possession). Anyone who is in doubt of Thailand's links with Angkor Wat need only visit Bangkok's Wat

Phra Kaeo, the eighteenth-century shrine complex that houses the Emerald Buddha: a miniaturized scale model of Angkor Wat has long stood near this famous image.

It was only to Europeans, then, that Angkor was a "discovery", but as the colonial masters of the country they were able not only to re-write the complicated narrative of the monument's past, but also to recast the actual structure to accord with their telling of the tale. Had the archaeologists had their way the complex would have been purged of all "accretions" and every trace of continuous occupation would have been erased. Mouhot's claim would then have been realized retrospectively, by an act of power, and the monument would have been forcibly re-modelled to conform to the myth of its discovery. It was the Sangha's resistance that prevented them from achieving their aim in its entirety.

Unfortunately there is little chance that the Ven. Luong Chun's version of the story will ever gain widespread acceptance. The truth is that the myth of discovery is much more saleable than the story of the tenacious persistence of a small group of Buddhist monks. Being well aware of this, the tourist industry in today's Cambodia is heavily invested in the selling of Mouhot's version: the legend of the monument's rescue and restoration by French explorers and archaeologists has thus been given a new lease of life by a post-colonial state. The irony, of course, is that this version of the tale reduces the role of Angkor Wat to a prop in a story already written. With a few tweaks, the same tale could be—and is—told of Mayan, Incan, Egyptian, Sumerian, Trojan and Greek monuments.

What sets apart the narratives in *Other Routes* is that the writers who feature in it are not seized by a compulsion to fit what they see into familiar narratives—thus their meticulousness in noting details and noticing the unfamiliar. And this too is why this collection is so timely and necessary: because it reminds us of the spirit in which we undertake our most instructive and pleasurable journeys.

Kolkata
24 January 2005

African and Asian Travel Texts in the Light of Europe:
AN INTRODUCTION

Tabish Khair

Travel! Set out and head for pastures new –
Life tastes the richer when you've road-worn feet.
No water that stagnates is fit to drink,
For only that which flows is truly sweet...

> [Attributed to al-Imam al-Shafi'i (orthodox Sunni–Muslim
> scholar of the eighth century)[1]]

They travel in a manner over the whole world to trade. For they are
continually to be seen in Egypt, in Ethiopia, in Arabia, Persia, India,
and Turkey: and whithersoever they go, they are most honourably
esteemed of: for none of them will possess any art, unless he has attained
unto great exactness and perfection therein.

> [Leo Africanus, 1526, on West Africans/Moors.]

If religions are not seen as false consciousness or sacred knowledge but
as particularly rich repositories of human hopes and fears, failures and
achievements, then surely it is significant that travel seems to mark the
beginning of all major religions. The epic exiles of the Pandavas in the
Mahabharata and of Ram, Lakshman and Sita in the Ramayana;
Siddhartha, the Buddha's wanderings after leaving behind palace and
progeny; the wayfarers of Daoism; Abraham and the fall of Babel;
Moses' return from Mount Sinai bearing the ten commandments; the
journey that ended in the birth of Jesus and Jesus' later wanderings; St
Paul's travels; Mohammed's journey before revelation: always a
movement away and a return that is never to the same place (even
when it is to the home town). It is pertinent that so many religions
begin with a movement that is either both physical and mental, or that
is later supplemented with mental travel as well. The lines between the
two are difficult to define. As Justin Stagl puts it in *A History of*
Curiosity,

> Real or imaginary travelling is… frequently connected with extraordinary states of consciousness, for example initiation, the quest for visions, ecstasy, shamanism and pilgrimages. A homecomer from a real or imaginary journey is expected to have changed. Like a visitor from abroad he thus becomes a menace to the identity of his group. (Stagl, p. 12)

Travel, then, is not just a matter of going away. It is also a matter of coming back, even when the return never takes place in person. It is this Janus-faced aspect of travel that makes it impossible to separate the "imaginary" elements of travel from the "real" elements.

Contrary to the common stress on the secularity of travel writing, it can be argued that "travel writing" grew in and from the "spiritual space" that, according to Ratzel (1897, p. 263 ff), surrounds every society—the space narrated in the "imaginational" and actual travel reports available to that society—and that travel tales in ancient epics or folk stories are the earliest extant definitions of this spiritual space in that particular society. In contemporary terms, one may wish to call this space "discursive" (in a broad sense that locates discourses in society and not only in language) rather than "spiritual"—but the argument would retain its power.

Not surprisingly then, the first accounts of travel known to humankind are largely "fanciful". The demons and flying chariots of the *Ramayana* and the *Mahabharata*, the Cyclops and Circe of the *Odyssey*, the talking animals of folk collections like the *Panchatantra*… one can extend the list to fill an entire book, especially if one considers the fanciful "travels" of the medieval ages and the early centuries of European colonization. By contemporary standards, these texts would not be considered travel writing. Bound as we are by contemporary standards, we have left out such travel accounts from this anthology. And yet, it would be an error to ignore them. One comes across their influence not only in the mixture of fact and fiction that often distinguishes travel writing down to the twentieth century,[2] it might also be necessary to consider them as offering early prototypes of travel and travel writing, and discursive maps of the "self" and the "other", "home" and "foreign lands". The earliest such epic of travel can be traced back 5,000 years: *The Epic of Gilgamesh*, incidentally a text from outside Europe. But, of course, other records of "travel" predate this long poem. These records do not exist in writing: they exist in the form of shards of pottery, items of exchange, early coins or their equivalents. And they also exist in what we have been able to unearth about the history of human movements: those prehistoric waves or groups of human beings traversing entire continents, sometimes in a generation or two, sometimes over centuries.

Gilgamesh, and the texts that followed it, also shatter the common myth that travel writing was in the past—because it is today—largely a prose genre. Apart from the travel in epic poems like the *Ramayana* and the *Mahabharata*, we have texts like Kalidasa's long poem *Meghadutam* (fifth to seventh century AD) that revolve around real or fictional travel. Around the same time in China, we also had Tang poetry, which contains poems that can only be read as descriptive and, in all likelihood, actual travel accounts. One can also claim that some Bhakti and Sufi poets in medieval times wrote travel-based poems. A separate anthology can be made of such early and poetic accounts, which have been left out of this book.

Recognition of this heritage of "travel poetry" is necessary not only because poetry creeps into various Chinese, Arabic, Persian and Japanese travel texts of later centuries, but also because it enables us to highlight: (1) the antiquity of human travel, (2) the fact that much of early literature presents actual experiences of travel in "symbolic" or even "spiritual" forms, (3) the fact that much of the earliest travel writing existed as poetry (not least in oral forms), (4) the intermingling of "fact" and "fiction" that was and remains (in more self-conscious forms) an aspect of much of travel writing, and (5) the fact that such works created the necessary vocabulary, different in different cultures, that would be employed to record first-hand experiences of travel in later centuries.

In yet another sense, travel writing goes back to the earliest of writing. The written script is always an indicator of movement across space and time. In that respect, the meagre difference between the

Arabic word for "travel" (*safar*) and that for "writing" (*sifar*) is full of significance.[3] This anthology does not employ travel in such a wide manner as to encapsulate all writing, or vice versa, but the connections between writing and travelling are worth recalling even when both, singly and together, need to be defined further.

I

If we choose not to bother with the definition of "writing", we are still left with two vital questions: what is "travel" and what, above all, is "travel writing"? Both are difficult questions, and made even more difficult if you are an Asian or an African writing in the language of the (neo-)colonial empire.

In the sense in which the word is used here, "travel", the *Concise Oxford Dictionary* informs us, means "go from one place to another; make a journey, esp. of some length or abroad" and "a journey along or through (a country)". Immediately, what is highlighted is the late nature of the definition: it implies the prior definition of a "country" and/or a "nation" (abroad). Both these definitions either were not available to most peoples until fairly recently or kept on changing from period to period for the same people. Travel, it appears, consists of going from place to place. But the distance that separates one place from another place is measured not so often in kilometres as in languages and discourses, so that some movements might not get registered as travel.

In this anthology, we are primarily concerned with travel in the sense of spatial movement and, hence, with travel writing in the delimited meaning ascribed to it by Roy Bridges: Travel writing is "a discourse designed to describe and interpret for its readers a geographical area together with its natural attributes and its human society and culture." (Hulme and Youngs, p. 53) To this I would add that travel writing also entails defining, consciously or unconsciously, the writer's relationship to a geographical area, its natural attributes and its society and culture; and, just as significantly, the writer's relationship to his or her own society and culture.

However, until recently, (European) discussions of travel writing often carried an assumption that mere movement across space was not enough to qualify any trajectory as travel or its account as travel writing: the distance travelled has to be large enough or there ought to be "an express commission for exploration." (Stagl, 1995, p. 11) The largeness of the distance travelled was, obviously, a relative matter and, in practice, it depended on the distinctiveness of the space left (and also sometimes the distinctiveness of the other distance entered). In that sense, travel was and is also a matter of self-definition. As James Clifford puts it, travel is a "range of practices for situating the self in a space or spaces grown too large, a form both of exploration and discipline." (1998, p. 177) "Exploration", in both the quotations above, highlights how current definitions of both travel and travel writing are embedded in a distinctive cultural and historical experience: that of the European age of expansion and colonization stretching from the fifteenth century to the twentieth. It is not surprising, then, that much of what is considered travel writing is attributed to Europeans writing in exactly that period.

Padmini Mongia has pointed out in an essay on Amitav Ghosh that "the geographical spaces to which one travels by traversing space are peopled already—always—and always with lives and histories more textured than one could imagine." (Mongia, in Khair, 2003, p. 75) Employing Syed Manzurul Islam's convenient (and, to my mind, emblematic) distinction between sedentary travel and nomadic travel,[4] Mongia notes that travel is not just "about physical movement and the journey from here to there" but that it is also—primarily, she claims— "a figure for different modes of stasis, movement, and knowledge." It is true that when one employs the word "travel" in an Anglophone context, one is struck by the extent to which it represents not sight but blindness. The travels of entire peoples (sometimes within Europe, but more often outside European and Eurocentric spaces) have been erased. Some have been easy to erase, as they left few or no written records. The Inuit, for instance, travelled for years by sledge or boat and the knowledge they accumulated was used by European travellers to "discover" their regions: the former narrative has largely disappeared; the latter has usurped nearly all tropes of discovery and travel in those regions. Similarly with the Gypsies or the slaves of the Atlantic Trade or with the Ayahs and the Lascars from India[5] or with the Black sailors who accounted for a quarter of the British navy by the middle of the colonial period (Gilroy, p. 13). These travellers often *appear* to have left nothing or little in writing. Hence, the feeling grew—and it persists in the present—that until recently non-Europeans did not travel or hardly travelled. If many historians in the past and even some "post-colonial" writers today are to be read (or read between the lines), it would appear as if Africans and Asians simply stayed at home discoursing about karma or Allah, shorn of curiosity and enterprise.

Of course, the matter in the past was always more complex than is indicated by popular reports of it in the present. Non-European peoples travelled too—that, after all, is the justification for an anthology like this. Even Europeans travelled in ways other than those covered by the notion of "exploration" or the otherness of sufficient distance. For instance, if there is exploration in the narratives of Christian pilgrimages—which, revealingly, are hardly ever seen as travel writing today—it is primarily the exploration of the soul, based on traversing a trajectory that in both spiritual and physical senses had already been mapped and traversed (by Jesus, St Paul and other pilgrims).[6] One can talk of the "pilgrim paradigm", as Ian Richard Netton does (1993, p. 57), as involving a "search" for the shrine, knowledge and (spiritual) power, but this involves a very different kind of exploration from the colonial one of new "discovery", "authentic" mapping and a definitive claim to control/possess as well as a very different attitude to curiosity (Melman, in Hulme and Youngs, p. 108).

And yet, in the centuries of European colonization, even European pilgrimage came to be informed—and (travel) writing about it changed—by the presence of or desire for (colonial) power: In Africa and the East Indies, one can say, there arose the trope of European "discovery"; in the Middle East, the Holy Land, there arose the trope of European "re-discovery": "Palestine, it may be said, was rediscovered by Edward Robinson in 1841." (Elliott-Binns, 1956, quoted in Lock, 2003, p. 112)

In this sense, travel and travel writing were (and are) about the gaze of power. It is this that helps explain how the movements of some (non-European) peoples were effectively frozen under that narrative gaze, even when European travellers noted the presence of non-European travellers in the margins of their texts.[7] In spite of African and Asian travellers who actually left behind accounts of their experiences and thoughts, today erudite scholars who might know of medieval Japanese travellers are often unaware of equivalent Arabic ones and vice versa. The kind of "general knowledge" that enfolds the travels of Columbus or Cook or Marco Polo never extends to Asian or African travel narratives.

I do not mean to deny that the "discovery" of the Americas and Australia must have added to the self-perception of Europeans as great sailors and discoverers, thus creating an appetite for travel writing and obscuring the achievements of, say, the Arabs and the Chinese. By the nineteenth century, in Albert Hourani's words, "the growth of large-scale factory production and changes in methods of communication—the coming of steamships, railways and telegraphs—led to an expansion of European trade" (263) – and hence, probably, documented travel. Though even here the word "probably" should be kept in mind: recent research (Markovits) indicates that Indian merchants, to take only one example, continued to operate in a "global world" in the eighteenth and nineteenth centuries as well.

It is also true that various factors, as noted by Giovanni Arrighi among others, ensured that (to quote just one example) Cheng Ho's navy chose not to sail around Africa and "discover" Europe a few decades before the Portuguese rounded the Cape (Arrighi, 33-36).[8] There can, again, be a difference between the survival of travel accounts in societies with a high use of printing[9] and those in which printing is new, underdeveloped or unknown. However, even keeping in mind these qualifications, one is faced with the fact that human mobility came to be seen and continues to be seen as a predominantly European prerogative.[10] Even the recent post-war visibility of Third

World immigration is premised upon the discourse of a Euro-colonial bridge, linguistic and political, linking the "wild and sullen" peoples of the rest of the world (and to the world).

In short, by the twentieth century, human movement in the past came to be seen as a predominantly European characteristic. This was perhaps connected to the fact that colonial discourses tended to deny rational agency to colonized people. In other words, Europeans and their descendants had a monopoly on both history and agency in many accounts of the recent centuries.

No wonder Europeans and their descendants appeared to have "traveled", "discovered", "settled" etc—and, thus, made possible the modern world that, it was widely agreed, existed in the twentieth century. The editors of this anthology have been motivated by a shared conviction that aspects of this general perception have remained largely unchanged even in recent decades, and in spite of the fact that travel writing, long ignored, has finally gained some academic attention.

II

After centuries of academic neglect and public avidity that counterpoised occasional accusations of lying with much gullibility about distant places and peoples, travel writing has come to be taken seriously by at least a circle of scholars and intellectuals. This has partly reflected, for better and for worse, a postmodernist reversal of the hitherto privileged "relations of dwelling over relations of travel" (Clifford, 1997, p. 22). Evidence of the changing status of travel writing is the rise of journals such as *Studies in Travel Writing* and *Journeys: The International Journal of Travel and Travel Writing*, as well as special issues of general journals, such as *Wasafiri*, devoted to travel writing.[11] Travel writing—along with "travel", as indicated above— has been redefined in recent years, and the travel journals mentioned above are both the location and the result of such redefinitions.

Earlier on, factual or fictional travel was often seen and read as entertainment (sometimes along the lines of "tall tales"), with or without a moral and/or Christian undertone—Sir John Mandeville's creative *Travels* (1357-57 in French; 1375 in English) is an early example and William Beckford's novel *Vathek* (1786), which presents both a journey of the imagination to a magnificent and depraved "Orient" and a journey within the narrative, is a late one.[12] On the other hand, as an Enlightenment philosopher like Locke saw it, travel was also considered predominantly a matter of data-collection. Both these perceptions of travel and writing about it—"entertainment" and "science", literature and ethnography—have survived in more self-conscious forms into the present.

Perhaps the one great change is that travel writing and the act of reading critically about travel have become more opaque and self-conscious today than they used to be. In the past, if not neglected, travel writing was often considered—like language in general—to be transparent. It purported to describe a place and/or a people and neither the description nor the position of its enunciation or inscription was interrogated along lines other than those of veracity.[13] All this has changed in recent decades under the impact of, to start with, Marxism, Freudianism, Anti-colonialism and Feminism in their structuralist versions and, later, of Post-colonialism, Post-structuralism, Post-modernism, Deconstruction.

Travel texts continue to be read by scholars in the light of the "romance origins" of the genre: "The romance origins of the genre preclude any simple opposition." (Clark, 1999, p. 2) This reading often stresses the commonalities of vision or of human curiosity. But often they are also informed by another critical mode that reads travel texts in relation to some version of colonial/imperial otherness, often permeated by class and gender differences as well. This mode often sees dominant definitions of "travel writing" as evolving, locally in England, in a complex class-cultural phenomenon: "The rhetoric and discourse of European travel was an eighteenth-century construct that began with the Grand Tour that young men of the English aristocracy undertook as part of their education, a mode of travel that was central to class and gender formation." (Grewal, 1996, p. 1) It also sees these dominant definitions as embedded in British empire-building and

European colonization. In *Imperial Eyes*, for instance, Mary Louise Pratt sees (European) travel and travel writing as deeply complicit in colonial subject formation and imperialism: "...travel books by Europeans about non-European parts of the world went (and go) about creating the 'domestic subject' of Euroimperialism." (p. 4)

III

Travel and travel writing remain sites of discursive contention, and it is not my aim in this introduction or my brief as an editor to provide an exhaustive description of the battles that are being fought over (and within) these sites or to resolve the matter. What I and my co-editors have tried to do is to provide readers with extracts from some significant accounts left behind by people travelling and writing: whether all these extracts qualify as travel writing *per se*, within or without Eurocentric paradigms, is a debate we intend to fan but not to settle in these pages.[14]

However, some of the recent tendencies in this interesting and ongoing redefinition of travel writing (which is also a discussion of criteria for evaluating non-European agency) can be highlighted with relevant quotes from scholars in the field. A number of recent works, as Grewal notes, problematize travel and travel writing "as a consolidation of stable unitary identities of nation, class, sexuality or gender, and suggest forms of Selfhood that evade such consolidations." (1996, p. 3) Clark states that, in response to earlier ways of seeing travel and travel writing, "less authoritarian models of transit have been proposed by recent criticism: mobility within European world systems (Abu-Lughod, 1989); transnational movements such as the Atlantic triangle resistant to the gravitational pull of the metropolitan centre (Rediker, 1987); reconstitution of a female politics of the local (Kaplan, 1996); and the phenomenology of diaspora and other forms of enforced migrancy (Brah, 1996)." (1999, p. 3)

It is in this context that we have included texts that cover ethnography, natural history, geography, personal writing, cartography, navigation, politics, science, history, religion, philosophy, diplomacy, pilgrimage, gender debates and culture(s) in general.[15] While the bulk of the texts fit the general (Europeanized) definitions of "travel writing" today, we have also included examples that call into question some assumptions of these definitions.

The contestation of the meanings of the sign "travel writing", as illustrated above, is often part of a larger attempt to reformulate identities and recover histories in Asia and Africa in the wake of European colonization. Even the term "travel"—not to mention "travel writing"—is considered suspect in this context:

> That this [European/Colonial] mode of travel became and is hegemonic to this day is revealed by the deployment of the term travel as a universal form of mobility. Such a use erases or conflates those mobilities that are not part of this Eurocentric, imperialist formation, while including some, like the trope of exile, that reinscribe European hegemonic aesthetic forms. For instance, migration, immigration, deportation, indenture, and slavery are often erased by the universalising of European travel. (Grewal, 1996, p. 2)

Grewal's observation explains why we need to cast our net of *travel* over a large and at times loosely segregated textual area, especially when we are dealing with Asian and African (rather than European or dominantly settler-European, such as American or Australian) travel texts.

So prevalent is the perception of travel as European(ized) travel that even an erudite scholar like Clark, well-versed in post-colonial perceptions, feels compelled to note that "to a certain extent, however, travel writing is inevitably one-way traffic, because the Europeans mapped the world rather than the world mapping them." (1999, p 3). However, this anthology sets out to illustrate that the world was "mapped" by non-European peoples as well, and that many of these peoples left behind travel accounts. When I use the word "map", I do not use it in a light-hearted manner. At least some of the Asian and African travellers included and/or mentioned in this anthology, did draw actual maps—sometimes maps that were used by European travellers to "discover" the world.[16]

One may or may not agree with Gavin Menzies that the Chinese circumnavigated and discovered the world—including the Americas, Australia and the Antarctica—in the year 1421, seventy year before Columbus. One may or may not agree with some (Islamic) scholars who locate the "discovery of America" in, say, the claim of the Muslim historian and geographer Abul-Hassan Ali ibn Al-Hussain al-Masudi (871–957) that during the rule of Abdullah ibn Muhammad in Spain, a navigator, Khashkhash ibn Saeed ibn Aswad of Córdoba, crossed the Atlantic and reached an unknown territory ("Ard Majhoola").[17] One might or might not accept the evidence that Leo Weiner offers in *Africa and the Discovery of America* or Van Sertina in *They Came Before Columbus* to suggest that Africans had sailed—among others, via the Moorish connection—and settled on the continent long before Columbus "discovered" it.[18] There are other similar claims that Asian and Africanist scholars have advanced, with varying degrees of documentation, to decentre the myth of the European "discovery" of the world.

Whatever the veracity of such counter-claims, there is hardly any denying the extensive—and overlooked—textual and cartographic evidence of vast parts of the world being navigated and traversed by Asians and Africans before, during and after Europeans set out on their post-Enlightenment voyages, regardless of who got to a particular place first. However, the dominant and multi-faceted focus on European or European-settler travel lends weight to the impression that the contours of our world have been mapped exclusively by such travellers. By drawing attention to Asian and African travellers from before 1900, we suggest that there have been alternative traditions to European travel writings and these too have contributed vitally to contemporary spatial definitions. (For proof, the reader is invited to trace for him/herself the different referents of the signifier "West"— also as "Maghrib"—or of the signifier "white" in the travel extracts included in this anthology.)

The fact that this anthology brings together lengthy extracts from a number of selected texts—ranging across time and space—has to be seen in the light of this almost total erasure of non-European travel accounts. The nature and extent of this erasure should not be underestimated, for it conditions not only European but also non-European perceptions. In the only area of this anthology where this editor can claim to exercise some expertise—that of travel writing from South Asia—we come across the belief that travel writing is "a new genre of narrative that emerged in Indian Literature during *the last two decades of the nineteenth century* mostly under the influence of contemporary English writings." (stress added) (Das, p. 186) This perception is at least partly flawed. Travel writing about "India" and by "Indians" draws on traditions that are not only "English"[19] or even confined to the late nineteenth century. Even in the eighteenth and the (*early*) nineteenth century, travel books like Sheikh I'tesamuddin's *Shigurf Nama-e-Vilayet* (1765), Mir Izzatullah's *Masir-i-Bukhara* (1813) and Abu Taleb's *Lubbu-s Siyar* (1803) were written in Farsi (Persian) and had their roots in non-English literary traditions.

From the eighteenth century onwards, there was a proliferation of travel books by Indians—penned not only in English, but also in other Indian languages like Malayalam, Bangla (Bengali), Urdu, Hindi, and, in the past, Persian. However, the eighteenth century also marked a proliferation of travel writing in Europe. While the European proliferation has been thoroughly studied and variously explained, no book length comparative study has been made of analogous travel writings in different Indian languages, even though some interesting lines of similarity and difference might exist. This dearth, as well as the extent and suddenness with which English took over as the language of the Indian elite in the late nineteenth and the twentieth century, has consolidated the myth of the centrality of Anglophone/European travel writing—and world-architectonics[20]—even in the work of scholars who are interested in retrieving Indian, rather than European, travel texts.

IV

Given the above-mentioned context, this anthology is obviously "interventionist" and, as such, perhaps unfortunately, sometimes informed by European discourses even as it sets out to map their limits. It intervenes in discourses of European centrality and it reacts against the supposed paucity of Asian and African travel narratives by making a number of them available. While the first characteristic imposes on it a degree of contentious "Eurocentricity"—most obvious in its collection of such varied Asian and African texts under one heading—the other characteristic, permitted partly by virtue of the first, at least invites the readers to attempt to exceed or break out of that Eurocentricity. These two aims (intervention and extension)— and the fact of much cultural transaction between Asia and Africa (and, for that matter, parts of Europe, as indicated by some of the extracts) that *did not* require the bridge of European colonization— explain why diverse texts by Asians and Africans needed to be collected into one anthology.

And, of course, another reason why this anthology is necessary is the fact that most of these texts are not easily available to the general reader—the most famous of these non-European writers, ibn Battuta, according to a recent article in *The Times* (London), is not familiar to a "wider European audience"—and even scholars in one field often remain unaware of analogous travel texts in another field.

Some of the lack might have had to do with the paucity of attention paid to travel writing in general by scholars in the past. However, this is no longer true. Travel writing, as indicated earlier, has been in focus in recent years. But this dramatic increase in academic interest in travel writing over the past ten years has been dominated by critical readings of the accounts of white men (and, less often, white women) from Europe travelling through the world. (There have been individual exceptions to this—some exceptional translations, such as that of Lady Nijô's book by Karen Brazell or studies by Bernard Lewis, Nabil Matar and other scholars as well as the seminal and enabling work of organizations like the Royal Asiatic Society, but these have not been generally accessible to students and ordinary readers. European travel accounts of the world have, on the other hand, not only received much serious scholarly attention, they have been made available to a wider public in various forms—ranging from comics and films to popular anthologies.) Finally, such has been the centrality of later European Self-Other perception that even obvious facts—like the porous borders between Asia, Africa and Europe from prehistory through the Greek civilization and the Moorish era in Spain to the present times—have been overlooked outside specialist circles. For instance, it is common—and not unjustified—to claim that Herodotus (fifth century BC), more famous as the "father of history", was the "first travel writer" (Casson, 95-96). But how often do we recall that Herodotus was born in *Asia Minor*, in a state that was under the control of the great *Persian empire* whose defeat at the hands of the Greek city states was to be rather gleefully described by him in later years?[21] The purpose of such an anthology is then not very different from the uses to which the best accounts of travel can be put: it dismantles the borders of our perception within and without. The people who travel in this anthology and narrate their travels are difficult to straitjacket into Eurocentric discourses, whether colonial or post-colonial.

V

This anthology stops with the year 1900, which like any boundary is a partly arbitrary demarcation. It was selected simply because twentieth-century travel accounts by Asians and Africans—or people of Asian and African origin—are somewhat more visible. Even here, one can claim that travel accounts written and published before 1950s are less visible than those—by V. S. Naipaul, Salman Rushdie, Vikram Seth, Amitav Ghosh—published later. While this may be so, the fact remains that twentieth-century travel accounts by Asians and African can be obtained from ordinary public libraries. Moreover, we did not feel that, in terms of ideas, positions and approaches, there was much in colonial travel texts from the *first half* of the twentieth century that was not already covered in late nineteenth-century travel texts, also colonial, included in this anthology. Both these sets of travel texts seemed to be informed by the colonial experience and/or anti-colonial sentiment. Malabari's text, for instance, is a good example of many later texts written by Indians in the 1930s and 40s. Actually some of the elements that one can identify in texts like that by Malabari (but not in all the texts of the period) point in the direction of (non-European) travel texts from the *second half* of the twentieth century as well.

In selecting extracts for this anthology—whenever possible by inviting contributions from scholars who had worked on a particular text—we had about a hundred texts to choose from, and we had not even come close to exhausting the sources. Our actual selection was influenced at times by extraneous factors, like space, availability and reproducibility. We do not claim that we have included all the best or most significant travel texts written by Asians and Africans before 1900, though we do claim to have included a fair many important (though, at times, invisible) texts. Analogous texts have been usually left out—these include many Chinese pilgrim and Arab merchant accounts in the early centuries (fourth to tenth century), dozens of memoirs, travel-based histories and autobiographies, and all except one of the many extant English-language travel books by Indians in the nineteenth century. Of the fascinating sixteenth- and seventeenth-century Arab travel texts discussed or translated by Nabil Matar, we have selected and included extracts from only one—a seventeenth-century account of travel in South America (and Europe).

Medieval and later pilgrimages have been toned down to a bare minimum: again partly because of the above-mentioned considerations and partly because many pilgrimage accounts are not available in translation.[22] The eighteenth and nineteenth centuries, with their plethora of travel books, have suffered because of editorial contingencies: lack of space has made us leave out major nineteenth-century travel books by Asians and Africans, including one that is central to any understanding of what is being called Islamist revivalism today.[23]

Some accounts, like Wang Lü's "Mt Hua Album" (an album containing 40 paintings, 150 poems and a travel record of this middle-aged Chinese physician's climb to the peak of Mt Hua in 1381), were also left out because they could not be reproduced faithfully in the given space and format. Other texts, especially those dozens of books that mixed travel experiences with biography, history or "political economy" from the thirteenth to the nineteenth century, were left out for reasons of space and problems of selection. Thus, while the travel-based "study" of Al-Burûnî (1030) is represented in short, we had to leave out the "World History" of Rashid al-Din (b. 1247) and Hsu Chi-yü's global geography of 1848; while extracts from Babur's sixteenth-century autobiography are included, we have left out his daughter Gul Badan Begum's first-hand account of the expeditions and vagaries of Babur's successor, Humayun.

Some travel accounts, like 'Abdu'r-Razzâq's Matla'-I Sa'dain (1444), though sounding promising and variously referred to by historians, could not be obtained.[24] One particularly glaring omission in this regard is the famous (at least in Turkish literary circles) seventeenth-century Ottoman travel writer, Evliya Chelebi, whose book was translated into English in the nineteenth century.

Also omitted are memoirs or autobiographies that describe travels of a different sort: for instance, the two extremely interesting and colourful chapters in the samurai Katsu Kokichi's early nineteenth century autobiography describing Kokichi's adventures when he ran away from home as a youth and wandered over much of Japan.[25] A number of shorter travel accounts—such as Chinese accounts of travel in or visits to the USA in the nineteenth century[26]—have also been left out in order to provide space for more extensive extracts whenever possible.

As a rule, we have also left out letters sent back by embassies as well as personal letters—even the (locally) more visible ones such as the letters of Indian reformer, Raja Rammohan Roy. A selection of letters of travel is an enterprise that ought to be undertaken, but it awaits another volume. Many shorter reports by merchants, diplomats, slaves, bureaucrats etc—sometimes running to pamphlet size and sometimes restricted to a couple of pages—also need to be collected. We have included a bare minimum, reports which—such as the description of a Viking funeral by a "merchant of Baghdad"—were considered too important to be left out.

We are also aware that there must be much that we have left out from sheer ignorance.

VI

As in any such collection, what is significant is not only where the extracts take us, but also where they come from. Asia and Africa are large demarcations, and can be seen as informed, if only in the spirit of resistance, by the presence of Europe. But we have not drawn very strict borders between Asia and Africa or, for that matter, between Europe and Asia-Africa. The point of this anthology, apart from the obvious one of providing non-European travel accounts, is to reveal the time-bound and increasingly Eurocentric nature of our contemporary perceptions of space, including that of what we call Europe today. The inclusion of Moorish writers serves to highlight how porous these borders—which are today seen as leading towards an inevitable "clash" by some political analysts—between "civilizations" were in many periods of history.

Just as we do not draw indelible lines between the three continents which are after all one land mass, we refuse to follow the dotted lines of identity imposed by colonialism on Africa or Asia. For example, we describe ibn Battuta or Omar ibn Said as both African and Arab and do not follow in the steps of colonial commentators who somehow assume that "Arabness" automatically cancels out "Africanness"[27]—a common colonial device that used visible lines of difference to rule peoples in Asia and Africa and that ignored as visible lines of connection to the extent of creating the mutual genocide known as the Partition of India, and its equivalents. Similarly, we do not associate Christianity solely or even predominantly with Europe.[28]

Finally, the question that every reader of travel writing asks him/herself before picking up an anthology: where do these texts take us? The selected travel accounts in this anthology take us everywhere, except to Australia (though Australia is "described" in at least one of the accounts[29]) and the Polar regions. While there are pre-1900 travel texts by Asians describing Australia, we could not obtain copies of them. As editors we suspect that there must be Arabic and, probably, Japanese or Chinese accounts, cartographic or textual, of Australia, but none has been brought to our notice yet. As far as the Polar regions are concerned, we were prevented either by our ignorance (especially of East Russian travel writing) or actual lack.[30] But here again, one should recall: "The Eskimos made journeys with sledges and boats which sometimes took a year or even two. They thereby acquired a detailed knowledge not only of their environment but also of far away regions, a knowledge which was later used by Western explorers." (Stagl, 1995, p. 11)

In spite of the gaps that we have acknowledged above, what has been selected and collocated in this anthology remains fascinating, informative and, in some cases, rare. At least three texts have appeared in print for the first time in English: these include a tenth-century Arab report of a Viking burial and the sarcastic, disgruntled travel writings of the thirteenth-century al-Abdari. A number of rare texts have appear in new translations or (in the case of Leo Africanus, 1526) translations in updated, contemporary English for the first time. Among the new, updated and rare translations are the writings of Zhou Daguan (who described the living city of Angkor Wat in Cambodia in 1297) and the travel and navigational epic of a Turkish "pirate" from the sixteenth century. Various other accounts—ranging from texts by Chinese monks travelling to India in the fifth century to early medieval accounts of the Mongols to an Arab (Christian) cleric's account of South America in the seventeenth century to the diary of Queen Emma of Hawaii in the nineteenth century—are also new, if available elsewhere, or out of print and difficult to obtain. The editors of this anthology hope that bringing together selections from all these different and fascinating texts will not only provide, as one of the travel writers included here puts it, "a gratifying banquet for the reader" but also revive interest in and scholarship of many of these texts.

VII

Whether one likes it or not, such has been the impact of the last four centuries of colonization and neo-colonialism, that we cannot discuss non-European travel writing in isolation from European travel writing.

There are some very interesting points of comparison between early "modern" European travel writing and early travel writing from many other parts of the world. In his essay on early European travel writing (1500-1720), William A. Sherman constructs the following typology of travel writers: editors, pilgrims, errant knights, merchants, explorers, colonizers, captives and castaways, ambassadors, pirates, scientists (Hulme and Youngs, 21-29). Of these, some present straight correspondences—there are many pilgrims, merchants and ambassadors (including royal ones) in the non-European typology too, as the reader will find in this anthology. There are also editors; but it appears that the kind of editorial endeavour that provided a major impetus to European travel writing—"some of the greatest names in early modern [European] travel writing are neither travellers nor writers but editors" (Sherman, in Hulme and Youngs, p. 22)—had rather declined in the late medieval period in many parts of the non-European world or has not been foregrounded and recorded. There were editorial efforts—often by travelers—in both early China and in Arab nations, but they are yet to be explored to the extent to which early European travel collections have been explored, retrieved and contextualized. Similarly, while errant knights obviously do not appear in non-European travel traditions, there are close equivalents: warrior princes fighting to defend land and faith against invaders (Abu al-Fidâ in this anthology) and, differently in Japan, the traditions of the samurai. The pirates of European travel writing have their equivalents in corsair-like explorers, such as the Turkish Pirî Reis in this anthology. The captives and castaways of early European travel writing seem to be, significantly, replaced by the slaves of non-European travel writing, though some travel writing by Muslims captured by Europeans who managed to be released also exists in Arab literature.[31]

Scientists as well as conquerors, if not colonizers, are in evidence in non-European travel writing too, though not in the kind of hegemonizing manner that one notices in colonial European travel writing. This is not surprising keeping in mind the relationship of travel writing to European colonization in the eighteenth and nineteenth centuries: as Roy Bridges puts it, in restrained language, "[during this period], travel writing became increasingly identified with the interests and preoccupations of those in European societies who wished to bring the non-European world into a position where it could be influenced, exploited or, in some cases, directly controlled." (Hulme and Youngs, 53). Explorers, in the colonial European sense that equates exploration with discovery, textual capture (in terms of mapping, recording, governing, or all three) and possession, are also rare in non-European traditions, though there are travel writers who travelled (or sailed) in new directions and wrote of it. Perhaps both European "scientists" and "explorers" are best covered by the term "scholar" in the non-European context.

Hence, if one wants to adapt Sherman's typology of travel writers to the evidence of extant non-European texts, one would have to list the following: Compilers and Editors; Pilgrims, particularly Buddhist and Muslim; Warrior Princes; Conquerors; Captives and Slaves; Ambassadors and other Government Functionaries; Royal Visitors; Pirates and Sailors; and Scholars.

If we try and match the above typology with a typology of travel texts, the five major types would be pilgrimages, travel-based studies, autobiographies, literary essays and travel accounts.

1. Pilgrimages. These are of various kinds.[32] Though usually Buddhist or Muslim,[33] these pilgrimage accounts can describe a "national" circuit (as in Lady Nijô's or Sei Shonagon's accounts) or move across vast regions to places of learning and pilgrimage or to a particular centre of religio-cultural significance (the early Chinese travellers to India in the fifth, sixth and seventh centuries,[34] the Haj pilgrimage[35] of ibn Jubayr in the twelfth century, Blyden's Africanist-Christian pilgrimage to the Holy Land in the nineteenth century). These pilgrimage accounts can also taper into other genres: for instance, while ibn Battuta set out to go to Mecca (which he did), he ended up travelling across 50 countries and dictating what is undoubtedly a travel book in a narrow generic sense rather than the account of a pilgrimage. One can argue that not all pilgrimage accounts can be considered travel books, as pilgrims are often uninterested in all but the sacred. In actual fact, pilgrimage texts should be charted on a continuum between the sacred and the profane. Some are closer to the one end and some to the other. All contain accounts of travel.

2. Studies. In the Asian-African context, these should be seen as equivalent to the various scientific treatises that form a major part of European travel writing, particularly in the eighteenth and nineteenth centuries. Perhaps the fact that I am tempted to call the former "studies" and the latter "scientific treatises" is itself a reflection of the extent to which the term "science"—not by any means unknown in pre-colonial Asian and African societies—has been hegemonized by Europe. Anyway, various kinds of studies are represented here. They include accounts that are in the first person and those that are not. They range from early Chinese bids to procure learned manuscripts and artefacts in India to the influential medieval geography of al-Idrisi in the eleventh century; from al-Burûnî's third-person defence of Brahminical India (based on travel and study) in the early eleventh century to the global history—including an autobiographical section—written by a Syrian scholar-prince in the thirteenth. Ibn Majid (1460), confused by many with the "Gujarati-Moor" sailor who revealed the eastward route to Vasco da Gama's pilot, was basically writing a first-hand nautical treatise, and the Turkish corsair Pirî Reis (1470?) was also engaged in a cartographic and at least partly scholarly endeavour. Some accounts have been left out because they were more "scientific" than "travelogue-like"; these include the writings of the Chinese Gu Yanwu (1613-82) who, according to C. A. Bayly, "travelled across the whole of China recording aspects of local technology, mapping the land, and collecting old inscriptions" (2004, p. 78) as part of a Chinese turn towards "practical evidential research" in the seventeenth century. As is obvious, scholarly travel-based studies could and did taper into other genres, particularly that of autobiography: while Babur's autobiography (b. 1482) contains elements of a study of India, Leo Africanus' study of Africa (1526) is also autobiographical and records, among other things, his shifting notion of identity in the face of hostile European discourses.

3. Autobiographies. This anthology includes many autobiographical texts (Arabic, Persian, Chinese, Japanese etc; from a dozen different countries; by princes as well as slaves) and we finally left out some first-person biographies only for lack of space. The autobiographies are of many types: full autobiographies, studies with autobiographical content, memoirs, diaries; autobiographies where the first person is present and autobiographical studies (al-Burûnî) in which the author makes no personal appearance. The mixture of autobiography and travel writing is also at times very intricate. For instance, in Japan, in 1307, Lady Nijô penned the account of her life and travels in a bid to restore the waning prestige of her family and also because, as she put it: "When I attempted to live in lonely seclusion, I felt dissatisfied and set out on pilgrimages modelled after those of Saigyo, whom I have always admired and wanted to emulate. That all my dreams might not prove empty, I have been writing this useless account—though I doubt it will long survive me." However, the predominance of the autobiographical genre and its entanglement with travel writing is not a surprising feature of this book. As Helen Carr puts it, within a European context, "all travel writing is a form of autobiography." (Hulme and Youngs, p. 79) Yes, and I would claim that some autobiographies in the non-European world are forms of travel writing, such as the autobiography of the Mughal emperor, Babur, in the fifteenth century.

4. Travel accounts. The most famous of all non-European travel writers, ibn Battuta (1304), born a generation after Marco Polo, wrote a travel book of the same sort as the more famous Italian. There are also many other travel accounts that set out to record the traveller's experience *per se* rather than write a history, an autobiography etc. These accounts might grow out of various factors—a pilgrimage in ibn Battuta's case or a decision to travel in the case of Abu Taleb—and may be influenced by other genres (as in Dean Mohamed's adaptation of the novel European "novelized" idea of writing his account as a series of letters). But their writing is informed by a clear and direct desire to apprise a certain public of what was experienced during the travels. This type is the direct ancestor of modern travel writing, but by no means the only one. But even this statement, like so many others about the "genre", needs to be qualified and contextualized. In our introduction to the travel diaries of Xu Xiake (1586–1641), included below, this conception of the genre of travel writing is problematized by highlighting that, in the dominant "Western tradition" (which includes Arab travel writers like ibn Battuta), travel writing is an account of the unusual for the home market, while in the Chinese tradition "travel is a meditative immersion into place" (as Martin Leer puts it). In other words, while we have listed travel texts like those by Xu Xiake under "autobiography", they can, with as much legitimacy, be included under "travel accounts" in the Chinese context.

5. Literary essays. The travel writing of Basho in the seventeenth century or Dean Mahomed in the eighteenth can be considered literary essays, in which "essay" has to be understood in its original meaning of an effort rather than a short distinctively Baconian piece of prose. They are also literary because they belong or connect to older or new literary traditions. As the first section of this anthology indicates, this literary heritage—which can cover various genres (including poetry)—remains an important part of travel writing in general. Some of the texts also have a genuine status as literature, either canonical, as is the case of Basho in Japan, or popular. In the eighteenth century, for example, Olaudah Equiano wrote what can be called a moral and socio-literary "bestseller", today the best-known account of a "slave" kidnapped from his African village at the age of eleven, shipped through the arduous "Middle Passage" of the

Atlantic Ocean and sold to a planter in the New World.[36] However, while noting the literary character of such texts, we—as editors—*have not* provided any section in this anthology entitled "literary essays". This is so only partly because of the problem of negotiating literary merit and genres across languages; it is also because all these literary texts can also be fitted into one or more of the above four categories (particularly those of "autobiography/memoir" and "travel account", if both are not defined too narrowly).

Neither the typology of travel writers nor that of travel writing separates African and Asian travel writing in a major way from European travel writing.[37] Similar types are to be found in the history of European travel writing down to the eighteenth and the nineteenth centuries.

However, a difference exists and, to my mind, it comes into being in the eighteenth and nineteenth centuries: the centuries of European capitalist colonization. From the seventeenth century onwards, Asian and African travel texts seem to lose out on editorial attention: they are not compiled and published in the way or numbers in which European travel accounts, *real and fancied*, get compiled and published. By the eighteenth century, Asian and African texts have already started being divested of scientific and philosophical significance: they are soon to be forgotten and ignored or reduced to largely *anthropological* status, a fate shared by Asian and African societies outside the purview of European "modernization". The attitude of African and Asian travellers to Europe had also started changing—from that of an equal cultural commerce to that of cultural defensiveness or, more rarely, abject admiration.

Secondly, and more importantly, in the eighteenth and nineteenth centuries Asian and African travel writing largely comes to lack the two new features that fuel European travel writing: a) mass tourism and b) the consolidation of a genre. It does not take much imagination to understand why mass tourism should have descended—a mixed blessing, by contemporary accounts—on colonizing Europeans rather than colonized Africans and Asians. Africans and Asians continued to travel and write in the eighteenth and nineteenth centuries—as aristocrats, merchants, spouses, servants, sailors, labourers, slaves etc. But their share of leisure market and colonial wealth was seriously limited (and controlled) and they never could claim the sort of wealth that would enable mass tourism to develop—which fuelled travel writing protagonistically (by creating a large readership of potential and actual leisure-travellers) and antagonistically (by forcing many travel writers to define themselves against mass tourism).

Most important of all, the divestment of scientific and philosophical value that earlier African and Asian travel writing was experiencing in most European quarters, and the presence of an impetus towards the colonial centre rather than the colonized margins, affected Asian and African travel writing in one profound manner: it failed to consolidate its earlier versions into a distinct genre and, from the nineteenth century onwards, largely based itself on European models. This, finally, is one of the reasons why contemporary travel writing tends to be traced to the colonial era and no further back by many (otherwise erudite) scholars. It is not that pre-colonial travel writing did not exist in Asia and Africa, as some of these scholars imply; but it is true that modern travel writing in most of Asia and Africa is defined by or against European travel writing.

If the extracts in this anthology had been arranged in rough chronological order, they would have indicated a kind of "pattern" which is obscured by the present arrangement: the tenacity with which Europe, never more than one among many other regions in the early extracts, establishes its discursive singularity and centrality in the texts from the eighteenth and nineteenth centuries. Perhaps this is brought home most poignantly in Section 20 where two African Muslims, enslaved and freshly converted to Christianity, begin to write down their experiences in the USA, one in Arabic and the other in English, by expressing their lack of control of their language of expression—the one because of long disuse and the other because of recent acquisition. It illustrates the fact, noted by recent historians, that while the rise of the modern world was not a European endowment but a process in which all peoples participated interactively, in general after 1780 "the flow of events was now more firmly from Europe and North American outward." (Bayly, 2004, p. 168)

However, these later texts also contest many of the claims of Eurocentricity even as their writers are forced to face the military, economic and "cultural" dominance of Europe in the centuries of colonization. In the nineteenth century, surely, one of the driving forces behind Emily Said-Ruete's account of her life and travels in Zanzibar and Europe must have been her realization that, as she put it, "the East is still considered a place of fairy-tales, about which all kinds of stories may be told with impunity." This also must have influenced the topics chosen by these travellers: for instance, both Said-Ruete and Abu Taleb wrote strong comparative defences of "Oriental" womanhood.[38] Similarly, travelling to London in the 1890 season, the Indian journalist, Malabari, encountered—in Antoinette Burton's words—"challenge after challenge to his presumptions about how to operate as 'the male colonial subject' at the heart of the empire, even while he produced a critical reading of English culture, Western sexual mores, and European modernity itself." (Burton, 156)

The routes these Asian and African writers of the colonial period trace often lead to the "West" but, in their politics, stories and evaluations, they sometimes retain memories of other routes and other directions, those being traced parallel to the hegemonic realities of European colonization and those half-forgotten ones traced before colonization. This anthology aims to offer all these routes to writers and readers today and for the future.[39]

NOTE

The extracts from c. 40 texts (in 33 sections) have been arranged along four of the five broad generic headlines outlined in the introduction: Pilgrimages, Studies, Autobiographies and Memoirs, Travel Accounts, with the fifth (Literary Essays) being left out owing to the problem of going into the matter of literary genres and traditions across more than a dozen languages as well as the overlap that this description has with "autobiographies and memoirs" in particular.

It is important to specify here that the editors have adopted directly from the **translations/editions used** (occasionally editing out very scholarly notes). This means that no completely consistent spelling system has been followed: the spelling of names and places—as well as foreign words—is as close to the original translation as the facilities for copying and computerizing would permit. Except for Sanskrit, Chinese and Arabic (that is, in cases where our knowledge permitted and no copyright clause or historical context cobbled our pens), no attempt has been made to translate older transliterations (especially of Japanese names) into the current forms of spelling them in English.

The different **sections** have been introduced and selected by one or two editor/contributors, with the other editors acting as consultants instead of collaborators. The editors have presented what they find interesting and significant in each of the texts extracted from—though the sections are by no means the only ones that can be considered interesting or particularly significant even by the same editor. In general, an attempt has been made to present coherent sections—and, in that respect, very short extracts have been avoided. It is our hope that many of the sections will provide enough meat for study in class even without recourse to the original manuscript or book. The editors have included relatively short extracts from some of the best-known texts—ibn Battuta and Basho, for instance—in order to save space for texts that are more difficult to obtain.

A selective **bibliography** is to be found at the end of the anthology. Not all the books mentioned in the section introductions are listed, as the editors have decided to list only books that are (more or less) available in English. However, publication details of original sources not available in English have also been provided.

We, the editors, wish to put on record our thanks to Lene Sønderby Bech (Aarhus) for translating the Chinese place and proper names into Pinyin, wherever possible, and Sunanda Bhattacharjea (Delhi) and Ashti Ahmad (USA) for help with the initial copy-editing. We are grateful to Mary Anne of the *American Historical Review* for helping find source material, Professors Adeeb Khalid, Charles Lock and Nabil Matar for advice and encouragement, and to Professor Michael David-Fox and Professor Joshua Fogel for answering our questions. We are also indebted to all the contributors and to the publishers and translators whose prior work enabled this anthology: in every case, this debt has been acknowledged in the relevant sections, and copyright permissions have also been listed on a separate page. If we have left out a reference or an acknowledgment by mistake, we will be happy to have it brought to our attention and we shall hasten to correct it at the first opportunity.

Finally, we lack the words to thank Amitav Ghosh for his invaluable preface.

EDITORS

Justin D. Edwards is associate professor of English at the University of Copenhagen. He is the author of *Exotic Journeys: Exploring the Exotics of U.S. Travel Literature* (University Press of New England, 2001), *Gothic Passages: Racial Ambiguity and the American Gothic* (Iowa UP, 2003) and *Gothic Canada: Reading the Spectre of a National Literature* (University of Alberta Press, 2005). He is also the editor of two collections of essays, *American Modernism Across the Arts* (Peter Lang, 1999) and *Downtown Canada: Writing Canadian Cities* (University of Toronto Press, 2005).

Born and educated mostly in Gaya, India, **Tabish Khair** has a Ph.D. in English from Copenhagen University and teaches as associate professor at the University of Aarhus, Denmark. He is the author of several books, including the study *Babu Fictions* (Oxford UP, 2001), the poetry collection, *Where Parallel Lines Meet* (Penguin, 2000), and the novel, *The Bus Stopped* (Picador, 2004), which was short-listed for the Encore Award. He has also edited an anthology of papers on Amitav Ghosh, published by Permanent Black (Delhi), and contributed to a number of journals and magazines, including New Left Review, Wasafiri, PN Review and the Journal of Commonwealth Literature. Khair reviews occasionally for the *Guardian* (London) and contributes articles to the *Hindu*. Khair won the All India Poetry Prize in 1996 and was made honorary fellow of creative writing of the Baptist University of Hong Kong in 2004.

Martin Leer is a student of Chinese and Arabic and has a Ph.D. in English. After over a decade of teaching postcolonial literatures at the University of Copenhagen he is now *Maître d'enseignements et de recherche* at the University of Geneva. He has published widely on literary geography and as a literary translator.

Hanna Ziadeh is a senior researcher at the Danish-Egyptian Dialogue Institute in Cairo. His book *Sectarianism and Inter-Communal Nation Building in Lebanon* will be published by Hurst & Co. (Publishers), London in 2005.

PILGRIMAGES

Three Chinese Scholars go "West" to India
(Fifth–Seventh century)

Given the relative paucity of cultural and social commerce between India and China in the present, it might strike some readers as astonishing that, in many ways, the Chinese have matched the Arabs and West-Central Asians as the most constant "companions" to Indians across the ages. In the Buddhist phase of Indian history in particular, there was rich commercial and cultural traffic between Chinese regions and Indian kingdoms. This traffic was conducted not only via the land routes across the North-Western frontiers of India but, perhaps for longer, also via the sea-route between India and China. The most visible is obviously the religious traffic—of Buddhist monks and nuns—which stretched across East and South East Asia, reaching Japan, but was particularly heavy in the region between and including Cambodia, China, India and Sri Lanka.

The intensity of this traffic can be gauged from Yijing's account alone. Yijing (?635-713), the third of the travellers represented in this section, preserved records of 60 of his contemporaries who visited India for religious studies.

Moreover, there is also clear evidence that there was heavy commercial traffic between South India and China and that this might well have matched or exceeded the religious traffic. Various embassies were also exchanged and Indian monks such as Vajrabodhi (661-732) worshipped, studied and taught in China as well. Ceylonese (Sri Lankan) monks like Sanghavarmi (fifth century) also travelled to India and China, among other places.

Of the many records left by the Chinese monks who came to India, probably the most famous one is by Shi Faxian, who visited India in 401-410. (The original name of Faxian was Gong: in keeping with tradition, he changed his name and assumed the title of one of the mendicants of Shakya on ordination, before leaving home.) However, as early as the second century we come across evidence of

Chinese scholars travelling to India and writing about it. Faxian's account, the first extensive one, is of considerable interest, but is exceeded by the later Xuanzang's account in both extent and variety. Xuanzang travelled more widely in India and was more interested in matters other than those of faith and scholarship. Of the two, Xuanzang also devoted more time and space to local myths and legends. Finally, Yijing, who followed in their footsteps (like hundreds of other monks), also left behind an important account of his travels in India. The selections below are taken from the accounts of these three priest-pilgrim-scholars.

Shi Faxian (AD 400), had the original name of Gong, which he changed in accordance to custom before leaving home on being ordained into the Buddhist order. He was a native of Wuyang in the province of Shainxi. His early life is recorded in a book called *Gaoseng*, written in 502-507, in the reign of the Liang dynasty. In AD 399, moved by a desire to obtain books not available in China, he set out in the company of other monks from the city of Chang'an. Faxian's work, the *Foguoji*, was first introduced to Europe through a translation by Abel Rémusat (Paris) in 1836.

Xuanzang (AD 629) made a sixteen-year pilgrimage to the India of King Harsha (one of those historical rulers who also achieve legendary fame) and left an interesting account of it—an account that highlights the cultural exchange that has taken place between different regions of Asia and one of the many rich non-European traditions of travel writing. We encounter in his *Da Tang Xi Yu Ji* (*Record of the Western Countries*) not only a record of Mahayana Buddhist beliefs but also a varied description of the people he encountered in China and along the way in Asia and India.

Xuanzang was born in 603 and was the youngest of four brothers. His family name was Chen. At the age of 13, he was ordained as a Buddhist monk, following in the footsteps of an older brother. After some years, he began to travel—a common activity for many monks—in the provinces in search of the best instructors. Finally, at the age of 26, influenced by the recollection of Faxian and Chi-yen (the two great Chinese travellers before him), he resolved to go to the "western regions" to question the sages on points that troubled his mind. A preface, written by Zhang Yue (713-756), has this to say of Xuanzang's journey:

> With a virtue of unequalled character, and at a time favourable in its indications, he took his staff, dusted his clothes, and set off for distant regions. On this he left behind him the dark waters of the Ba river; he bent his gaze forwards; he then advanced right on to the Congling mountains. In following the courses of rivers and crossing the plains, he encountered constant dangers. Compared with him Bowang[40] went but a little way, and the journey of Fa-hien was short indeed. In all the districts through which he journeyed he learnt thoroughly the dialects; he investigated throughout the deep secrets (of religion) and penetrated to the very source of the stream. Thus he was able to correct the books and transcend (the writers of) India. The texts being transcribed on palm leaves, he then returned to China.

Carrying, it needs to be added, holy relics, six golden, silver and sandalwood statues of Buddha, 124 manuscripts (sûtras) and other works (amounting to 520 fasciculi carried on 22 horses).

Yijing (b. 633) was, in his turn, influenced by the accounts of both Faxian and, in particular, Xuanzang. He was 12 when Xuanzang returned to China in AD 645, and his biographer informs us that he made up his mind to follow in Xuanzang's footsteps four years later. However, he actually left on his expedition-pilgrimage in AD 671. He embarked from Canton on a Persian ship and landed at Tamluk in India in 673. Much of his time in India was spent in Bihar—he lived at Nalanda, the famous university-monastery town for ten years—and he also had the experience of being robbed of all his possessions (including clothes) in Bihar. Surely, that is an anecdote that will appeal to many Biharis (like one of the editors of this anthology) in these troubled times. He wrote his memoirs towards the end of his travels. Yijing returned to China in 695 and was received with pomp and honour by the Empress Wu. His biographer reports that he kept himself occupied with literary work until his death in 713.

[The first three extracts have been taken from *Xi Yu Ji* (Chinese Records of the Western World), translated from the Chinese of Xuanzang (AD 629) by Samuel Beal and first published in London in 1884. In these translations, the italicized sections in brackets were added as nuanced interpolations by the translator, Samuel Beal. The extracts from Yijing's writings have been taken from the non-copyright translations included in K.A. Nilakanta Shastri's *Foreign Notices of South India*.]

Faxian on his way to India

I.

Faxian, when formerly residing at Ch'ang-an, regretted the imperfect condition of the *Vinaya pitaka*. Whereupon, afterwards, in the second year of Hongshi…, he agreed with Huijing, Daozheng, Huiying, Huiwei, and others, to go to India for the purpose of seeking the rules and regulations (of the *Vinaya*).

Starting on their way from Ch'ang-an, they crossed the Long (district) and reached the country of K'ien-kwei [Tian Gui?]; here they rested during the rains. The season of the rains being over, going forward, they came to the country of Niutan; crossing the Yanglu hills, they reached Zhang Ye, a military station. Chang-yeh at this time was much disturbed and the roadways were not open. The king of Zhang Yi being anxious, kept them there, himself entertaining them. Thus they met [list of people]… The rainy season being over, they again pressed on…

II.

This land is rugged and barren. The clothing of the common people is coarse, and like that of the Chinese people; only they differ in respect of the serge and felt. The king of the country honours the law (*of Buddha*). There are some 4000 priests, all of the Little Vehicle belief. The laity and the Shramanas of this country wholly practise the religion of India, only some are refined and some coarse (*in their observances*). From this proceeding westward, the countries passed through are all alike in this respect, only the people differ in their language. The professed disciples of Buddha, however, all use Indian books and the Indian language. Remaining here a month or more, again they went north-west for fifteen days and reached the country of the Wu Yi...

...They were on the road a month and five days, and then managed to reach Khotan.

III.
This country is prosperous and rich (*happy*); the people are very wealthy, and all without exception honour the law (*of Buddha*). They use religious music for mutual entertainment. The body of priests number even several myriads, principally belonging to the Great Vehicle. They all have food provided for them; the people live here and there. Before their house doors they raise little towers, the least about twenty feet high. There are priests' houses for the entertainment of foreign priests and for providing them with what they need. The ruler of the country lodged Faxian and the rest in a *sanghârâma*. The name of the *sanghârâma* was Gomati. This is a temple of the Great Vehicle with three thousand priests, who assemble to eat at the sound of the *ghantâ* [gong]. On entering the dining-hall, their carriage is grave and demure, and they take their seats in regular order. All of them keep silence; there is no noise with their eating bowls; when the attendants (*pure men*) give more food, they are not allowed to speak to one another, but only to make signs with the hand...

Xuanzang on the names of India
On examination, we find that the names of India (Tianzhu) are various and perplexing as to their authority. It was anciently called Xindu, also Xiandu; but now, according to the right pronunciation, it is called Yindu. The people of Yindu call their country by different names according to their district. Each country has diverse customs. Aiming at a general name which is best sounding, we will call the country In-tu. In Chinese this name signifies the Moon. The moon has many names, of which this is one. For as it is said that all things ceaselessly revolve in the wheel (*of transmigration*) through the long

night of ignorance, without a guiding star, their case is like the world, the sun gone down;… just so the bright connected light of holy men and sages, guiding the world as the shining of the moon, have made this country eminent, and so it is called Yindu.

Xuanzang on Kashmir

The kingdom of Kashmir is about 7000 li in circuit, and on all sides it is enclosed by mountains. These mountains are very high. Although the mountains have passes through them, these are narrow and contracted. The neighbouring states that have attacked it have never succeeded in subduing it. The capital of the country on the west side is bordered by a great river. The capital is from north to south 12 or 13 li, and from east to west 4 or 5 li. The soil is fit for producing cereals, and abounds with fruits and flowers. Here also are dragon-horses and the fragrant turmeric…and medicinal plants.

The climate is cold and stern. There is much snow and little wind. The people wear leather doublets and clothes of white linen. They are light and frivolous, and of a weak, pusillanimous disposition. As the country is protected by a dragon, it has always assumed superiority among neighbouring people. The people are handsome in appearance, but they are given to cunning. They love learning and are well instructed. There are both heretics and believers among them. There are about 100 *sanghârâmas* and 5000 priests. There are four *stûpas* built by King Ashoka. Each of these has about a pint measure of relics of Tathâgata. The history of the country says: This country was once a dragon lake. In old times the Lord Buddha was returning to the middle kingdom (*India*) after subduing a wicked spirit…, and when in mid-air, just over this country, he addressed Ânanda thus: "After my Nirvâna, the Arhat Madhyântika will found a kingdom in this land, civilise (*pacify*) the people, and by his own effort spread abroad the law of Buddha."…

Yijing on arranging a dinner for Buddhist monks

I shall briefly describe the ceremony of inviting priests, in India as well as in the islands of the Southern Sea. In India the host comes previously to the priests, and after a salutation, invites them to the festival. On the Upavasatha-day he informs them saying, "It is the time."

The preparation of the utensils and seats for the priests is made according to circumstances. Necessaries may be carried [from the monastery] by some of the monastic servants; or provided by the host. Only copper utensils as a rule are used, which are cleansed by being rubbed with fine ashes. Each priest sits on a small chair placed at such a distance that one person may not touch another. The shape of the chair has already been described in chapter iii.[41] It is not wrong, however, to use earthenware utensils once, if they have not been used before. When they have been already used, they should be thrown away into a ditch, for used vessels [lit. "touched vessels"] should not be preserved at all. Consequently in India, at almsgiving places at the side of the road, there are discarded utensils which are never used again. Earthenware of superior quality such as is manufactured at Xiangyang [in China] may be kept after having been employed, and after having been thrown away may be cleansed properly. In India there were not originally porcelain and lacquer works. Porcelain, if enamelled, is, no doubt, clean. Lacquered articles are sometimes brought to India by traders; people of the Southern Sea do not use them as eating utensils, because food placed in them receives an oily smell. But they occasionally make use of them when new, after washing the oily smell away with pure ashes. Wooden articles are scarcely ever employed as eating utensils, yet, if new, they may be used once, but never twice, this being prohibited in the Vinaya.

The ground of the dining hall at the host's house is swept over with cow-dung, and small chairs are placed at regular intervals; and a large quantity of water is prepared in a clean jar. When the priests arrive, they untie the fastenings of their cloaks. All have clean jars placed before them: they examine the water, and if there are no insects in it, they wash their feet with it, then they sit down on the small chairs. When they have rested awhile, the host, having observed the time and finding that the sun is nearly at the zenith, makes this announcement: "It is the time." Then each priest, folding his cloak by its two corners, ties them in front, and taking up the right corner of his skirt, holds it by the girdle at his left side. The priests cleanse their hands with powder made of *peas* or earth-dust; and either the host pours water, or the priests use water out of the jars; this is done according as they find one way or the other more convenient. Then they return to their seats. Next eating-utensils are distributed to the guests, which they wash slightly so that water does not flow over them. It is never customary to say a prayer before meals. The host, having cleansed his hands and feet by this time, makes an offering to saints (images of arhats) at the upper end of the row of seats; then he distributes food to the priests. At the lower end of the row, an offering of food is made to the mother, Hariti.

Yijing on sartorial customs

If we come to India in Chinese garments, they laugh at us; we feel much ashamed in our hearts, and we tear our garments to be used for miscellaneous purposes, for they are all unlawful. If I do not explain this point, no one will know the fact. Although I wish to speak straightforwardly, yet I fear to see my hearer indignant. Hence I refrain from expressing my humble thought, yet I move about reflecting upon these points.

I wish that the wise may pay serious attention and notice the proper rules of clothing. Further, laymen of India, the officers and people of a higher class have a pair of white soft cloth for their garments, while the poor and lower classes of people have only one piece of linen. It is only the homeless member of the Sangha who possesses the three garments and Six Requisites, and a priest who indulges in luxury may use the thirteen Necessaries.[42] In China priests are not allowed to have a garment possessed of two sleeves or having one back, but the fact is that they themselves follow the Chinese customs, and falsely call them Indian.

Now I shall roughly describe the people and their dresses in Jambudvipa and all the remote islands. From the Mahabodhi eastward to Linyi (i.e. Champa), there are twenty countries extending as far as the southern limits of Kwan Chou (in Annam). If we proceed to the south-west, we come to the sea; and in the north Kasmira is its limit. There are more than ten countries (islands) in the Southern Sea, added to these the Simhala island (Ceylon [Sri Lanka]). In all these countries people wear two cloths (Skt. kambala). These are of wide linen eight feet long, which has no girdle and is not cut or sewn, but is simply put around the waist to cover the lower part.

Besides India, there are countries of the Parasas (Persians) and the Tajiks (generally taken to be Arabs) who wear shirt and trousers. In the country of the naked people (Nicobar Isles), they have no dress at all; men and women alike are all naked. From Kasmira to all the Mongolic countries such as Suli, Tibet and the country of the Turkish tribes, the customs resemble one another to a great extent; the people in these countries do not wear the covering cloth (Skt. kambala), but use wool or skin as much as they can, and there is very little karpasa (i.e. cotton), which we see sometimes worn. As these countries are cold, the people always wear shirt and trousers. Among these countries, the Parasas, the Naked People, the Tibetans, and the Turkish tribes have no Buddhist law, but the other countries had and have followed Buddhism; and in the districts where shirts and trousers are used, the people are careless about personal cleanliness. Therefore the people of the five parts of India are proud of their purity and excellence.

Yijing on the Brahmans, the alphabet and memory
The Brahmans are regarded throughout the five parts of India as the most honourable (caste). They do not, when they meet in a place, associate with the other three castes, and the mixed classes of the people have still less intercourse with them. The scriptures they revere are the four Vedas, containing about 1000,000 verses; 'Veda' hitherto was wrongly transcribed by the Chinese characters 'Weituo'; the meaning of the word is 'clear understanding' or 'knowledge'. The Vedas have been handed down from mouth to mouth, not transcribed on paper or leaves. In every generation, there exist some intelligent Brahmans who can recite the 100,000 verses. In India there are two traditional ways by which one can attain to great intellectual power.

Firstly, by repeatedly committing to memory the intellect is developed; secondly, the alphabet fixes one's ideas. By this way, after a practice of ten days or a month, a student feels his thoughts rise like a fountain, and can commit to memory whatever he has once heard (not requiring to be told twice). This is far from being a myth, for I myself have met such men.

The Travels of a Japanese Monk

Contributed by Lene Sønderby Bech
Ennin's Diary: The Record of a Pilgrimage to China
in Search of the Law (838-847)

In the ninth century the Japanese Buddhist monk Ennin (793-864; posthumous title, Jikaku Daishi) travelled to China for the same reasons that the Chinese monks, Faxian, Xuanzang, and Yijing during the preceding centuries travelled to India: to seek the Buddhist law (dharma).

In 838 Ennin travelled to China as a member of an embassy appointed by the Japanese court. He meant to stay in China for a short period of learning but ended up staying for nine years, studying the teachings of different Buddhist schools. He returned to Japan in 847 on a Korean merchantman and brought with him 559 volumes of sutras and sastras, as well as various Buddhist pictures and holy objects. During his travels, Ennin wrote a detailed day-by-day record of his experiences: *Ennin's Diary: The Record of a Pilgrimage to China in Search of the* Law (*Ru Tang qiufa xunli xingji*, Jap. *Nitto guho junrei gyoki*). This is regarded not only as Japan's first real travel diary but also as one of the world's great travel books. The diary covers Ennin's sea fares to and from China and his travels, on foot and by boat, in China. His records of sea fare, shipwrecks, and travels in a foreign country, often without proper permits, tell of danger and hardship, culminating with the Huichang Persecution of Buddhism in the 840s. During the persecution Emperor Wuzong (841-846) ordered the destruction of more than forty-five thousand Buddhist properties, two hundred sixty thousand monks and nuns were forced into laity, while others were killed or injured. In order to get permission to return to Japan Ennin also had to return to lay life.

Ennin was born in the province of Shimotsuke in east Japan. Until the age of nine he was taught classical Chinese literature at home, then he was entrusted to the care of the Buddhist monk Kochi, under whose guidance he studied the Buddhist scriptures. At the age of fifteen he became a student of Saicho (767-822; posthumous title, Dengyo Daishi), founder of the Japanese Tendai (Chinese Tiantai) school of Buddhism. In 804 Saicho had gone to the original Tiantai monastery on Mount Tiantai in south-eastern China to study and had returned to Japan with the teaching. He founded the monastic centre on Mount Hiei, Eryakuji, not far from Kyoto and it was here that Ennin became his disciple. Later Saicho selected Ennin as a transmitter of Mahayana Buddhism and after the master's death Ennin preached on Mount Hiei for several years. A few years after returning from his travels in China, Ennin was appointed chief abbot of the monastic centre and became an influential representative of the Tendao school in Japan.

In China Ennin had wanted to follow in the footsteps of his teacher Saicho and visit Mount Tiantai. Here he meant to collect the texts of the Tiantai school that were still lacking in Japan, to get answers to a list of thirty doctrinal questions from his fellow monks at Mount Hiei, and to master the meditation technique of the Tiantai school. When the embassy with which he had travelled to China left for the capital Chang'an, Ennin and his two disciples stayed behind in Yangzhou to wait for permission to visit the sacred mountain in the south-east. Though he stayed for eight months he never got the permission and was even forced to leave China when the embassy was to return to Japan. However, he conspired with a Korean interpreter living in China and with the Japanese Ambassador to be put ashore on the Shandong coast and hid among the Korean community. Later he learnt that important Tiantai masters had migrated to another centre of Buddhist learning on Mount Wutai in the north and consequently Ennin decided to travel north instead. He stayed for two months on Mount Wutai and continued to Chang'an where he met with leading Chinese and Indian Buddhist scholars.

Ennin's detailed records are an important historical, religious, and linguistic source about life in the latter part of the great Tang dynasty (618-907). Tang marked the epitome of many Buddhist schools in

China and Ennin's diary provides valuable insight information about both daily life and religious festivals in the monasteries, and his recording of the persecution of Buddhism is considered the most authoritative account in existence. Many of the Buddhist schools, including the Tiantai, never recovered from this harsh persecution and afterwards, partly through Ennin's endeavours, Tiantai saw its greatest growth and influence in Japan. Apart from recordings of Buddhist life, Ennin's diary also tells about his dealings with the Chinese bureaucracy, economic conditions, daily life in the cities, the practice of customs and festivals, Korean trade and communities in China etc. The diary is written in Chinese and, apart from the Dunhuang texts, it is one of the most valuable sources for the Chinese vernacular during the late Tang period.

[Extracts from *Ennin's Diary: The Record of a Pilgrimage to China in Search of the Law*. New York: The Ronald Press Company, 1955. Translated from the Chinese and annotated by Edwin O. Reischauer.]

Sea and River Travel

Jowa fifth year, seventh moon:[43] 22nd DAY At dawn the boats were tied to the water buffalo, which pulled them along. At times there were many white ducks and white geese, and there were houses in rows, but from 10 a.m. on we would sometimes go thirty *li* before coming on three or four houses. Sometimes there were some and sometimes not. On into the night we went in the dark and at midnight arrived at a village, the name of which I do not know. The boats stopped there for the night. (p. 20)

Kaicheng fourth year, fourth moon: 24th DAY It was foggy and rainy. Hawsers were holding us in our place of anchorage, but some of them broke. The wind was blowing and the waves were high. The last few days we have lowered eight hawsers (with anchors), but three of the hawsers and anchors have snapped and sunk, and very few remain. If we were to encounter a storm, they could not hold fast. We are extremely worried. (p. 119)

Mountain Travel

Kaicheng fifth year, fourth moon: 28th DAY We entered an open valley and went west for thirty *li*, arriving at the Tingdian Common Cloister at 10 A.M. Before entering the cloister we saw toward the northwest the central terrace,[44] and bowing to the ground we worshipped it. This then is the region of Monjushiri.[45] There are no trees to be seen on the rounded heights of the five summits, and they look like overturned bronze bowls. On looking at them from afar, our tears flowed involuntarily. The trees and strange flowers are unlike those anywhere else, and it is a most unusual region. This then is the gold-colored world of Mt. Qingliang,[46] where Manjusri manifested himself for our benefit.

Since we entered the mountains at 4 P.M. on the twenty-third day up until today we have been going along mountains valleys for a total of six days and, without getting through the mountains, have reached Wutai. Since we left the Mt. Chi Cloister on the nineteenth day of the past second moon right up until now we have gone over 2,300 *li*. Leaving aside rest days, we have been on the road exactly forty-four days and fortunately have been entirely free of illness on the way. (p. 214-215)

The Persecution

Huichang, third year, sixth moon; 27th DAY In the third watch of the night (midnight) fire broke out in the Eastern Market and burned over four thousand houses in twelve alleys westward from the gate of the Controller of the Eastern Market. Public and private money and gold, silver, silks, and drugs were all destroyed.

Huichang, third year, sixth moon; 29th DAY Fire broke out outside the Changle Gate and burned a hayloft. Previously there had been an Imperial edict to burn the Buddhist scriptures in the Palace and also to bury images of the Buddhas, Bodhisattvas, and Heavenly Kings. Later fire broke out in two places and still later, on two nights, fire broke out again in several places in the Eastern Market. (p. 333)

Huichang, fifth year, 28th DAY We reached Yangzhou and saw monks and nuns of the city being sent back to their places of origin with their heads wrapped up. The monasteries are to be destroyed, and their money, estates, and bells are being confiscated by the government. Recently a document came on Imperial command saying that the bronze and iron Buddhas of the land were all to be smashed and weighed and handed over to the Salt and Iron Bureau and a record made of this and reported to the throne.

Jiangduxian dispatched men to take us to Jiangyangxian,[47] but, using bribery, we asked to go to Chuzhou, and the subprefectural government then sent us to Chuzhou. We passed through Gaoyouxian and Baoyingxian. (p. 373)

The Pillow Book of Sei Shonagon (c. 990)

From *Makura no Soshi* (c. 990)

Pilgrimage is one of the main sources of travel writing, and who would be better to give an account of its intimate, subjective detail than Sei Shonagon (born c. 965), the prime witness to Japanese court life in its first heyday of the mid-Heian period. Her voice reaches us across the centuries with an intimacy and studied idiosyncrasy that contradict most "Western" histories of subjectivity. But we know very little about her life: even her literary name consists mainly of the title Shonagon, "minor counselor"; Sei referring to her clan, the Kiyowara. Research suggests that her personal name may have been Nagiko. She served as lady-in-waiting to Empress Sadako during the last decade of the tenth century. Her fate after her years at court remains as shrouded in mystery as her years at court were couched in scandal. The only contemporary reference to her comes from the diary of her greatest contemporary, Murasaki Shikibu, the author of *The Tale of Genji*, which has a fair claim to be described as the world's first psychological novel. Lady Murasaki wrote:

> Sei Shonagon has the most extraordinary air of self-satisfaction. Yet, if we stop to examine those Chinese writings of hers that she so presumptuously scatters about the place, we will find that they are full of imperfections. Someone who makes such an effort to be different from others is bound to fall in people's esteem, and I can only think her future will be a hard one. She is a gifted woman, to be sure. Yet if one gives free rein to one's emotions even under the most inappropriate circumstances, if one has to sample every interesting thing that comes along, people are bound to regard one as frivolous.

Later critics have shared Lady Murasaki's opinions about Sei Shonagon's Chinese poetry. It is her vernacular Japanese prose lists in the *Pillow Book* that come across as exquisite poetry—and indeed in their imagery, rhythm and repetitions seem to have been conceived as such. These are "Elegant Things":

> *A white coat worn over a violet waistcoat.*
> *Duck eggs.*
> *Shaved ice mixed with liana syrup and put in a new silver*
> *bowl.*
> *A rosary of rock crystal.*
> *Wistaria blossoms. Plum blossoms covered with snow.*
> *A pretty child eating strawberries.*

Prose fiction like *The Tale of Genji* and "random notes" (*zuihitsu*) like *The Pillow Book* seem to have been the two major genres of the mid-Heian revival of Japanese literature in the vernacular, largely produced by the women at court, while the men held competitions in Chinese poetry. The court life was one of rigid conventions and divisions, some of which strike a modern reader as exotic to the point of incomprehensibility, while others seem almost "universal", as Sei Shonagon's short list of "Different Ways of Speaking":

> *A priest's language.*
> *The speech of men and women.*
> *The common people always tend to add extra syllables to*
> *their words.*

Of all the narrative parts of *The Pillow Book*, the parts that are not poetically and culturally eloquent lists like the ones quoted, impressionist memories and aesthetic judgements, a surprising amount is concerned with "travel", though of a very restricted sort: court processions, excursions and pilgrimages. It is at these times of movement, it seems, that things may be allowed to happen, people notice each other across genders and classes, and protocol is tested and contested. Sei Shonagon's eyes and ears miss little of this.

[Extracts from *The Pillow Book* (*Makura no Soshi*) (c. 990-1000), from Ivan Morris, Trans. and Ed., *The Pillow Book of Sei Shonagon*. Columbia University Press and Penguin: 1967. Reprinted with permission of the publisher.]

In the First Month When I Go to a Temple

In the First Month when I go to a temple for a retreat I like the weather to be extremely cold; there should be snow on the ground, and everything should be frozen. If it looks like rain, however, I feel most dissatisfied.

Once I went on a pilgrimage to Hase Temple. While our rooms were being prepared, our carriage was pulled up to the foot of the log steps that lead to the temple. Young priests, wearing only their sashes and under-robes, and with those things called high clogs on their feet, were hurrying up and down the steps without the slightest precaution, reciting verses from the Sacred Storehouse or such scraps from the sutras as came into their heads. It was very appropriate to the place, and I found it charming. Later, when we started to climb the steps, we were terrified and kept close to the side, clinging to the banisters. I was amused to see that the priests walked as freely as on an ordinary wooden floor.

Soon, a priest told us that our rooms were ready and asked us to go to them directly; he brought us some overshoes and helped us out of our carriage. Among the pilgrims who had already arrived I saw some who were wearing their clothes inside out, while others were dressed in formal style with trains on their skirts and Chinese jackets. The sight of so many people shuffling along the corridors in lacquered leather shoes and short clogs was delightful and reminded me of the Palace.

Several acolytes and some young men who had the run of the temple grounds and buildings followed us, saying, 'There's a drop now,' 'Here the corridor goes up,' and so on. Close behind us came another group (I have no idea who they were), and they tried to push their way ahead of us. 'Wait a moment,' our guides said. 'These are ladies of quality. You people must keep your distance.' Some bowed and fell back; but others paid no attention at all and hurried ahead, each determined to be the first before the Buddha.

On the way to our rooms we had to pass in front of rows of strangers. I found this very unpleasant; but, when I reached the chapel and got a view past the dog-barrier and right up to the sanctuary, I was overcome with awe and wondered how I could have stayed away for so many months. My old feelings were aroused and they overwhelmed all else.

The lamps that lit the sacred image in the sanctuary were not permanent ones, but had been brought by pilgrims as offerings. They burnt with terrifying brightness, and in their light the Buddha glittered brilliantly. Priest after priest reverently entered the sanctuary, and, kneeling on the platform of worship, held up his petition in both hands and read it aloud. So many people were bustling about that it was hard to make out what any particular priest was saying; but occasionally I could distinguish a strained voice pronouncing some phrase like 'One thousand platforms on behalf of Lord So-and-so'.

I was kneeling down to pray, with the sash of my skirt hanging loosely over my shoulders, when a priest came up to me and said, 'I have brought you this.' He was carrying a bough of anise, and I was delighted by the gesture.

Presently another priest came from the dog-barrier. He told us that he had satisfactorily recited all our petitions and asked how long we expected to remain in retreat; he also gave us the names of some other people who were staying in the temple. When he had gone, the attendants brought us a brazier and some fruit. Our washing-water was poured into a bucket, and I noticed that we had been given a basin without handles. A priest called for our servants and explained where they would be lodged; then, one at a time, the servants went off to their cells.

Now the bell rang for the recitation of the sutras. It was very comforting to think that it rang for me. In the cell next to ours a solitary gentleman was prostrating himself in prayer. At first I thought that he might be doing it because he knew we were listening; but soon I realized that he was absorbed in his devotions, which he continued hour after hour. I was greatly moved. When he rested from his prayers, he started reading the sutras in a voice that was no less impressive for being somewhat inaudible. I was wishing that he would read more loudly so that I might hear every word; but instead he stopped and blew his nose—not in a noisy, unpleasant way, but gently and discreetly. I wondered what he could be praying for so fervently and hoped that his wish might be granted.

Usually when we stayed in temples the days passed rather quietly. The male attendants and boys who accompanied us would spend a good deal of time visiting the priests in their cells, and we were left with very little to do. Then the stillness of the day would be broken by the loud noise of the conch-shell. Or a messenger would arrive with an elegantly folded letter and offerings to pay for a recitation of the sutras; laying everything down, he would call for the acolytes in a voice so powerful that it echoed among the hills. Sometimes the booming of the temple bell became louder and louder until I was overcome with curiosity about who had asked for the readings. Then someone would mention the name of a great family, adding, 'It is a service of instruction and guidance for Her Ladyship's safe delivery.' An anxious period indeed, I thought, and would begin praying for the lady's well-being.

All this happened at an ordinary time, when life in the temple was fairly peaceful. In the First Month things were in an uproar. People were constantly arriving with their requests, and as I watched them I sometimes forgot all about my own devotions.

One day at sunset a large party came to the temple, evidently intending to stay for a retreat. The acolytes bustled about efficiently, installing tall screens (which looked so heavy that I should not have thought they could possibly carry them) and flopping straw mats noisily on the floor. The visitors were taken directly to their quarters, and soon I heard a loud rustling sound as a blind was hung over the dog-barrier to separate their rooms from the sanctuary. All the arrangements were carried out in a most effortless fashion: the acolytes were used to their job.

Presently I heard another rustling sound—this time of silk. It came from a large group of elderly ladies, discreet in manner and distinguished in appearance, who were apparently leaving their quarters and returning home. 'Be careful about fire,' I heard one of them say. 'These rooms are very dangerous.' Among their party was a boy of about seven who called for the attendants and spoke to them in a proud, charming voice that I found very attractive. There was also an adorable child, about two years old, who was coughing drowsily. I wished that the mother or someone else would address its nurse by name so that I might find out who these people were.

The service continued all night, and it was so noisy that I could not get to sleep. After the matins I finally dozed off, only to be woken by a reading of the sutra consecrated to the temple Buddha. The priests were reciting loudly and raucously, without making any effort to sound solemn. From their tone I gathered that they were travelling monks and, as I listened to their voices, which had awakened me so abruptly, I found myself being strangely moved.

I also remember a pleasant-looking young gentleman, evidently from a good family, who did not stay in his cell at night and performed all his devotions during the day. He was attractively dressed in wide, bluish-grey trousers and many layers of white robes. Several pages had accompanied him on his pilgrimage, and I enjoyed watching how respectfully they attended to him. They had provided their master with a special screen, behind which he occasionally prostrated himself in prayer.

When staying at temples, I enjoy wondering who the strangers are; and it is also pleasant to recognize people one knows.

The young men who visited the temple were apt to wander near the women's quarters and spend more time looking in that direction than at the Buddha. Sometimes they would call for one of the sextons and, after a whispered consultation, set off for some other part of the temple. I saw nothing wrong in their behaviour.

At the end of the Second and beginning of the Third Month, when the cherry blossoms were in bloom, I paid another pleasant retreat to the temple. Two or three good-looking gentlemen, apparently travelling incognito, arrived while I was there. They were elegantly dressed in cherry-blossom and willow robes, and they looked very distinguished with the ends of their laced trousers neatly tucked up and fastened. They were accompanied by a very proper-looking attendant, who held an attractively decorated bag of provisions. Their page-boys, who carried flowering branches of cherry blossom, wore hunting costumes of plum red and bright green, with varicoloured under-robes and skirts printed with scattered patches of colour. There was also a slender retainer in their party, who looked extremely attractive as he beat the gong at the entrance to the temple. I recognized one of the gentlemen. Of course he had no way of knowing that I was at the temple, and he did not notice me as he passed near where I stood. Though I had no particular desire to meet him, this rather saddened me. 'If only I could let him know!' I thought, and found my feelings somewhat strange.

Whenever I go to stay in a temple, or indeed in any new place, it seems pointless to be accompanied only by servants. One needs a few companions of one's own class with whom one can chat congenially. There may be some suitable women even among one's maids; the trouble is that one knows all too well what they are going to say. Gentlemen appear to have the same idea; for I notice that whenever they go on a pilgrimage they take along a few agreeable companions.

The Haj and Other Journeys of ibn Jubayr (b. 1145)
From *ar-Rihla*

Ibn Jubayr, whose *Rihla* is the most celebrated of all Arabic accounts of the Pilgrimage to Mecca and Medina, was born in the Emirate of Balansiya (now Valencia, Spain) as the son of an official. He is thus a borderline case for inclusion in this book, but fits its concept well, because the world he travelled in was so different in cultural-conceptual geography from what we know today. "The West" was not Christian or "the East" Muslim, and ibn Jubayr was as much part of Europe geographically as he was part of the Arab world culturally. Actually, the borders of the two were hard to determine in his time. To ibn Jubayr—as the following excerpts show—a Westerner was somebody from "Maghrib" (literally the Occident: "where the sun sets"), which in his day included not only Morocco, but had its great cultural centre in Andalusia, where cities like Córdoba and Granada had good reason to consider themselves the most civilized in the "known", largely Mediterranean, world. Despite the break-up of Muslim unity in the Iberian Peninsula in the previous century and the successes of the Christian *reconquista*, the Andalusia in which ibn Jubayr received a full religious, legal and literary education was a vibrant intellectual centre, where Muslims, Christians and Jews co-habited more or less peacefully under tolerant and often voluptuous courts, where poetry, music, architecture, medicine, science and philosophy flourished. The almost syncretistic theology of ibn Massara, the poetic Sufism of Ghazali, the medical rationalism of ibn Tufail and the neo-Aristotelian logic and metaphysics of ibn Rushd (Averroës) were, however, strongly contested by the book-burning orthodox *fuqaha* (traditional religious scholars).

Ibn Jubayr seems to have followed a middle, though strongly religious course in all these intellectual upheavals and had begun a promising career as a poet and a personal secretary to the Almohad governor of Granada when he developed a strong urge to set out on the pilgrimage at a relatively young age. According to legend this had its origin in an incident where he sat with his employer, who was drinking wine while dictating a letter and offered a goblet to ibn Jubayr. Ibn Jubayr indignantly refused, saying, "I have never drunk alcohol in my life". "By Allah," answered the Prince, "you shall drink seven goblets!" Ibn Jubayr saw no way out of this, but resigned the next day and set off on the pilgrimage as penance. Apocryphal as it no doubt is, this story does show the same curious ambivalence that recurs in the *Rihla*: a joy at the good things in life checked before long by piety, though a piety that is both orthodox and imaginative (note how he varies his invocations in the excerpts that follow, which adds interest both from a theological and a literary point of view: Andalusian Arabic literary style in the period of ibn Jubayr abhorred classical simplicity). It is perhaps hard to separate the person from the Age at this distance, but ibn Jubayr does come across not just as a traveller as opinionated as the average nineteenth-century European travel writer, but as somebody with a keen sense of observation and a critical spirit, with a sense of humour not unlike that of critical Victorians like Sir Richard Burton.

Ibn Jubayr left Granada with his friend Abu-Ja'far al-Qoda'i on 1 February 1183 and returned on 25 April 1185. He visited Alexandria and Cairo, travelled up the Nile, traversed the desert and crossed the Red Sea to Jedda and Mecca, where he stayed for eight months for the Haj of 580 (1184). He left Mecca with a party of Iraqi pilgrims, visited Medina, and then took the classic pilgrim route to Baghdad and Mosul, then turned west to Aleppo and up the Orontes Valley to Damascus, where he stayed for four months (July to September 1184). From here he entered the Crusader-occupied "Holy Land", where we join him below.[48] After his return home he never re-entered public life, but seems to have retired to a modest life as a writer and a religious sage, of a both pessimistic and Sufi bent. He went on two further pilgrimages and finally settled as a sheikh in a Sufi community in Alexandria, where he died.

His *Rihla* set the model for the genre of travel writing in Arabic, and it is obviously a world classic of the genre, which deserves to be better known. With its intimate and personal tone it brings to life a world which is both very different from ours and yet perhaps not so different as fifty or a hundred years ago when the Christian "West" and the Muslim "Middle East" seemed poles apart. Ibn Jubayr was at this point a keen observer of parallels between his own Andalusia threatened by the *reconquista* and political dissolution and the situation in Syria and Palestine before the decisive intervention of Saladin (1187-92), which sent the Crusaders back to the littoral of the Levant. Saladin remains ibn Jubayr's hero, perhaps almost as much for abolishing taxes (Christian rulers are criticized for their imposition of extra taxes, particularly on Muslims) as for defending Islam! Ibn Jubayr, notes one scholar, had "a natural curiosity about Christianity, especially what he perceive[d] to be its 'exotic' elements; but he also seems to sense a seduction, and the potential for a fall from the true faith of Islam."[49] Often travelling on Christian ships, ibn Jubayr also remarked on the parallel between the Muslim kingdoms of Andalusia, which relied on Christian court officials, and the Christian, Norman kings of Sicily, who relied on Muslims. Curiously, he never mentions Jews, so relatively prominent in both places; perhaps they seemed too fully integrated in the Arabic-speaking world. As readers today we may be equally fascinated with the continuities and the reversals between the twelfth and the twenty-first centuries. It is certainly rewarding to see Europeans/Franks portrayed so unselfconsciously by the writer as rude barbarians.

[Note on the translation: Though an English translation from the 1950s exists, this has been unobtainable, and the excerpts below have been translated into English by Martin Leer from Vol. 3 of the French translation by Maurice Gaudefroy-Demombynes, Paris: Librairie Orientaliste Paul Geuthner, 1949-1965, checked against the original Arabic by Hanna Ziadeh. Gaudefroy-Demombynes' Introduction is also the source of most of the information above.]

Description of the City of Tyre

May God destroy it!—This is a city whose defensive strength is proverbial; it never falls obedient and subject into the hands of an aggressor, and the Franks have organised it into a refuge against all vicissitudes for their own kind; they have made it a place of military support for their general security. Its streets and public passages are cleaner than those of 'Akka. Its inhabitants possess, even in their infidelity, a gentler nature. Their inclination and their disposition are more favourable to the well-being of the visiting Muslims; their character is more amiable. Their dwellings are larger and more spacious. The situation of the Muslims here is easier and more peaceful. 'Akka is larger, more tyrannical, more idolatrous. Nothing is stranger than that which one may report on the fortifications and defensive strength of Tyre. The city makes do with two gates; one towards land; the other towards the sea, which surrounds the city except on one side. One may only reach the city gate on the land side by passing through three or four gates, each of which is set in the middle of high flanking buttresses. The gate which gives on the sea is an opening between two elevated towers, which give access to a harbour. No other port has a situation as marvellous as this. The walls of the city surround it on three sides, and it is protected on the fourth side by a wall assembled from a mortar of *jish*. The ships arrive to drop anchor at the foot of this wall. Between the two towers a large chain is suspended which, when raised, stops every ship entering or leaving. The ships only have free passage when this chain is lifted. There are many guards and sentinels in this port, and everything enters and leaves the port under their watchful eyes. This port is admirable due to the beauty of its site. The port of 'Akka, to be sure, has an analogous shape and site, but it does not give access to the great ships, which have to drop anchor in the roads, while smaller craft can enter its protected harbour. The port of Tyre is more perfect, grander, more frequented.

We here made a sojourn of eleven days. We arrived here on a Thursday(?), and we left here on Sunday the 22nd of *jamadi*, corresponding to the last day of September. The craft on which we had hoped to embark seemed to us far too small, and we could not make up our minds to go aboard.

It is appropriate to speak of a spectacle, in which the luxury of this low world revealed itself, and to which we were witness one day, at the port of Tyre: that of a bridal procession. All the Christians, men and women, had assembled on this occasion and distributed themselves in two lines on either side of the door of the bride's house, whom they had arrived to carry away, while trumpets, flutes and other instruments were playing. At length she came out, balanced, with a hesitant gait, between two men who supported her on the right and the left, and who appeared to be close relatives on her maternal side. She had on the most splendid costume and a magnificent gown flowing with trains in gold-brocaded silk, which was the height of the fashion they follow in their dress. She carried a golden diadem on her head, which was enveloped in a hair-net of a golden material, while another similar piece of jewellery, ornamented with pearls, flowed down over the top of her breast. Proud of her ornaments and her costume, she came forward with a languid air, the tip-toeing steps of a pigeon or the floating of a cloud. We sought refuge in God against the troubles of such a sight. In front of her paraded Christian men of high standing, in their most magnificent dress, trailing behind them the trains of their robes; behind them the Christian women, their peers and equals, advanced in a processional manner in their most beautiful garments, posing in the luxury of their costumes. Musicians playing instruments marched in front. Muslims and Christians formed on their route—two lines of spectators, who contemplated them without showing signs of disapproval. They accompanied her in this manner to the house of the groom, where she was allowed entrance and where they spent that whole day in festivities. It was only by chance that we were privileged to witness this pompous spectacle: we ask God that he may preserve us from the danger of being troubled by it!

We returned by sea to 'Akka, where we arrived in the morning of Monday the 23rd of *jamadi*, 1st of October, and we bought passage on a large ship, which was about to set sail for Messina, in the island of Sicily.

We found our peace, during our stay in Tyre, in a mosque which had remained in the hands of the Muslims, who also have other places of prayer here. From one of the Muslim sheikhs of Tyre we learnt that this city had been taken from them in the year 518/1124. 'Akka had been taken twelve years earlier after a long siege, and after having suffered great privations. Because of this they had arrived, as we were told, at a state of mind from which we pray to God that He may spare us. A jealous sense of honour had inspired in them a resolution which God protected them from following: they had decided to gather their women and children in the principal mosque and put them to the sword, so afraid were they of their falling into the hands of the Christians. After this was done, they were to have made their sortie from the city with a fighting spirit irresistible to their enemies and would have thrown themselves upon them with the full force of their souls, to die in one single great sacrifice, where God would decide their fate according to his will. They were dissuaded from this decision by the most pious among them and the doctors of the law. So they decided to surrender the city, on condition that they be allowed to leave alive; and this is what came to pass. They dispersed to Muslim cities. Meanwhile, some of them became so obsessed with love of their native soil that it incited them to return to live among the Christians after concluding a pact of security, which was confirmed for them in writing according to conditions they had set. God is sovereign in his rule of the world. Glory be to Him! His strength is great, and His will imposes itself on all His creation. It is God who dispenses over chance and ease by his strength and power.

Now, there is hardly any excuse before God for a Muslim to stay in a city of unbelievers, except in passing. He finds himself on the soil of Islam protected against the punishments and evil one is prey to among the Christians, against the humiliations and miserable condition of tributaries: for example hearing words to afflict the heart about him whose name God has made holy and whose glory He has exalted [the Prophet Muhammad], particularly from the mouths of the most vulgar and drunken among them; the impossibility of purification; life in the midst of pigs and all manner of unlawful things, and many more things one may hardly mention or enumerate. Guard yourselves, guard yourselves against entering their lands. It is from God one must ask the grace of pardon and mercy against this sin, which makes the steps slippery and which one may not repair except after repentance. It is Him—glory to Him!—who is the Distributor. There is no other master but God.

One of the horrors which afflict the eyes of whoever lives in the lands of the Christians is the sight of Muslim prisoners, who stumble round in leg-irons and are used for the hardest labours and treated like slaves; and also the sight of Muslim captives who have iron chains on their legs. Hearts break at the sight of them, but pity is of no service to them.

A great work of God is done for the Western prisoners[50] taken by the Franks in these Syrian lands: in these lands and elsewhere, every Muslim who upon his death prescribes a legacy on his estate consecrates it specifically to the deliverance of the Western prisoners, in consideration of their exile from their native lands which deprives them of any other mode of deliverance except that which comes from God—for they are foreigners, separated from their country. Among the Muslims, the sovereigns of these lands, and among the women, the princesses, and in general those who have means and fortune make no other legacies on their estate except in this direction. During an illness with which he was afflicted, Nur-ad-Din made a vow to distribute twelve thousand dinars for the ransom of Western prisoners. When he recovered from his illness he sent for them to be ransomed, but among them a certain number were discovered to be not Westerners, but from Hama, a city which formed part of Nur-ad-Din's domain. He ordered that they be sent back into captivity and that Westerners be liberated in their stead, saying, 'Those from Hama have families and neighbours who may buy them free, while the Westerners are strangers without family.' See here the bounty of Divine action towards these people from the West. God has predestined two men of fortune in Damascus in their favour, merchants among the most prominent and among the richest, provided with large fortunes, one named Nasir bin Qawam and the other called Abu-d-Dorr Yaqut, a freedman of al-'Attafi, who do all their business with the coastal regions which have fallen into the hands of the Franks. Their reputation there is without equal and they have confidential bankers everywhere. Caravans come and go transporting their merchandise; their riches are substantial and they exercise considerable influence with Muslim and Christian princes alike. God has put both of them in place for the deliverance of Western captives, from their own proper funds and from those of testators instituting legacies. They are designated to dispose of such funds in this way because of the reputation they have gained by their honesty, their probity and their generosity. There is hardly a Westerner who has been freed from captivity who has not been freed by their hands. Thus constantly on the road they spend their fortune and increase their efforts to deliver the servants of God from the hands of the miscreants, the enemies of Allah—God will never let the reward of benefactors go missing!

By the bad fortune of encounters, of which the evil is only lifted in seeking refuge with God, we had as a travelling companion on the road to 'Akka coming from Damascus, a Westerner from Annaba, a city in the region of Bejaia, who had been taken prisoner and freed by the intercession of Abu-d-Dorr and had remained among his servants. He came with his caravan all the way to 'Akka. Now, he had been in the frequent company of the Christians and had picked up a number of their ways. Satan had possessed him to lose his mind and his way, so much so that he apostatised his faith in Islam, became an unbeliever and a Christian during our stay at Tyre. When we returned to 'Akka we were informed of his story: he had been baptised and sullied himself in apostasy; he had put on the Christian belt and hastily taken the road to hell. May the words of chastisement come real for him, and he will be well equipped for the last and terrible account and the long stay! We implore God that He reaffirm us in the true Word, in this world and the next; that He lets us never deviate from the pure *hanifiyya* religion; and that He allows us to die as Muslims, by His grace and His mercy!

That Pig, the ruler of 'Akka whom they call King,[51] stays in hiding; he hardly ever shows himself. God has smitten him with leprosy and made him taste, in advance, the pains of vengeance. This malady has prevented him, right from his youth, from playing his part in the world, and he is miserable as a result; but the punishment in the other world is more terrible and longer lasting. His Regent, the one who is the master of things in his place, is his maternal uncle, the Count. He is the superintendent of taxes and it is to him that the resources of the Kingdom come as revenue. He it is who dominates all things by his rank, by his prestige and by his elevated position among the damned Franks. It is this damned Count, ruler of Tripoli and Tiberius, who has power and prime place among the Franks. He is considered to be worthy of the kingship and is totally prepared for it. He is portrayed as cunning and devious. He has been, for about eleven years or more, the prisoner of Nur-ad-Din, and was ransomed by paying a considerable sum that he had himself raised in the time of Saladin and at the beginning of his reign. He is tied to Saladin by a link of recognition, servitude and manumission...

Month of *sha'ban* (7.11-5.12 1184)
May God let us participate in His goodness! His crescent remained hidden to us, and we ended the days of *rajab* by counting from the night of Thursday, corresponding to the 8th of November. Since the day of our departure from 'Akka, we had spent twenty-seven entire days at sea, so long that we had lost our sense of being human and were very close to despair and self-abandonment; but one must hope for God's intervention and the omniscient Good who watches over us. The passengers by now had hardly any personal provisions left, but by the grace of God this ship was like a city where all resources were gathered. We found everything we needed to buy, bread and water, all fruits and condiments, pomegranates, quinces, watermelon from India, pears, chestnuts, hazelnuts, dates, walnuts, chickpeas, broad beans fresh and cooked, onions, garlic, figs, cheese, fish; the list is too long; we found all these things for sale.

For all these days we hardly saw sight of land. May God give us a speedy deliverance! Two Muslims who died—may God have mercy on them!—were thrown into the sea and similarly two Christian pilgrims, and a good many died thereafter. One of them jumped living into the sea and was taken by a wave, faster than a glimpse of light. The captain of the ship inherited everything left behind by these Muslim and Christian pilgrims, such is the custom among them in the case of those who die at sea: the heir to the deceased cannot validate his claim to the inheritance. This fact caused us long astonishment...

Month of the holy *ramadan* (6.12.1184-4.1.1185)
May God let us participate in the *baraka* [grace] and the welcome which are His! His crescent appeared on the night of Friday the 7th of December, while we were in front of the Great Continent tossed on the waves. God gave us a wind from the east, of a peaceful force, which took us, little by little at this time, in front of the Great Continent. We there saw farms and numerous fields, and we learned that this was part of Calabria, one of the possessions of the King of Sicily; for his kingdom extends on to the continent for two days' march. In this place many Christian pilgrims disembarked, thus escaping the hardship that the lack and shortages of provisions imposed on the passengers of the ship. Imagine being reduced to a ration of a pound of dried bread to be shared among four, softened with a drop of water, and being content with this. Every one of the pilgrims who disembarked sold that which they retained of provisions, and the Muslims arrived at an amicable understanding with them to buy all that was possible, even though it was very expensive, up to a dirham of good silver for a loaf of bread. But what may one think of a period of two months spent at sea for a voyage that people thought would be accomplished in ten or fifteen days at the utmost. Really provident people had brought provisions for a month, but most only for two or three weeks. This is how, by one of the marvellous encounters of sea voyages, we were able to observe at sea, three crescents of the New Moon, those of the months of rajab, sha'ban and ramadan. On the day when this latter appeared we saw before us the Mountain of Fire [Mt. Etna], the celebrated volcano of Sicily: our joy was great! May God grant us recompense for what we have suffered, point in our favour the sword of His merciful and

generous intervention and prompt us under all circumstances to be faithful to Him and what He decrees!

The favourable wind took us further in our position and on the evening of the Saturday, the second day of ramadan, its force grew and brought the ship on a speedy course. There was but the space between two 'no's for it to push us to the entrance of the Strait, just as night fell. Now, in this strait, the sea narrowed to a distance of six thousand feet, and at the narrowest point even three thousand feet, between the Great Continent and Sicily. In this Strait, the sea runs in a flow similar to the torrent of Arim[52] and boils as if in a cauldron, so much is the water squeezed and compressed. The passage is difficult for ships.

Our vessel continued its course, pushed roughly by the south wind, with the Great Continent on our right and Sicily on our left. In the middle of the night of the Sunday, the 3rd of this blessed month, we were at the longitude of Messina, situated on the island, when the cries of the sailors let us know all of a sudden that the wind was pressing the ship towards one of the two landmasses, and that it would be wrecked there. The captain ordered the sails down immediately; but the sail of the mizzen mast would not come down, and despite their efforts the sailors did not succeed in conquering the force of the wind which filled the sail. After their pointless efforts, the captain began to cut the sail down in pieces with a knife in order thus to stop the progress of the ship. During this difficult manoeuvre the ship scraped its keel against the bottom and touched bottom with its two rudders, the two limbs with which it is steered. A terrible clamour rose up from the ship: this was the advent of the great calamity [Qur'an 79,34]; the breach that could not be repaired, the soundless catastrophe [Qur'an 101,1] which breaks down our resignation. The Christians beat their breasts repeatedly, the Muslims gave themselves up entirely to their Master's will and managed only to hang on to the very last string of hope. The wind and the waves fought so much to wreck the ship that they broke off one of its rudders. The captain threw one of the anchors in with the attention of retrieving it, but without success. He had its cord cut and abandoned it to the sea. When we had thus seen the plight we were in, we remained standing, giving our reins over to death, directing our will towards the purest resignation, awaiting either morning or the predestined hour. Cries went up, lamentations rose among the children and women of Rum [i.e. oriental Christians], a rejected mass outside the hand of obedience to God; the wild ass was still prevented from jumping.[53]

Standing there immobile, we saw the land very close, and we did not know whether to throw ourselves into the sea to swim ashore or wait and see, hoping that God's help would arrive with the morning. We decided to wait. The sailors put the towboat to sea to take what they thought most valuable, men, women and baggage, some of which they succeeded in bringing ashore in one trip, but they did not succeed in bringing the boat back to the ship, it was broken by the waves against the cliffs. Despair then seized the souls still aboard: it was in the middle of this struggle against the elements that the morning broke and brought the aid of God and the Supreme Rescue. We watched avidly: we had before us the city of Messina, less than five hundred feet away, and an insurmountable obstacle was between it and us. We admired God's power in ordaining his decrees and we repeated:

Many are those whose last breath has been drawn at the threshold of their home!

The sun rose: boats arrived from the city to our rescue, for the call had gone out in the city. The King of Sicily, William, came out in person with a group of his courtiers, to oversee the event. We quickly went into the boats, which the violence of the waves barely allowed to reach the ship. Going into the boats was to put the seal to our immense anguish. We finally found safety on terra firma ...

People lost part of their belongings, but 'their return consoled them for the absent haul'.[54] An extraordinary fact was that this *Rumi* King saw the poor Muslims who waited on the ship, since they had no money to pay for disembarkation, for the boat-owners made people pay dearly for their rescue. When he asked about them, he was informed of their situation, and he gave out a hundred quarters of his money, which allowed them to disembark.

The Muslims, all saved, abstained from pronouncing the formal salutation,[55] but they said, 'Praise be to God, the master of men!' The Christians managed to take everything with them that had been theirs on the ship. By the morning of the second day, the waves had made the ship into a wreck and had thrashed it to pieces on the rocks, where it became a warning for whoever saw it, a sign for whoever could understand. It was a miracle that we had been saved from it, and we renewed our commitment to acts of mercy before God, who had accorded us His munificent intervention and the perfection of His predestination, and who had freed us from the fate which had driven us against the Great Continent or one of the islands inhabited by the *Rumis*; for if we had escaped death, we would have remained prisoners there forever. May God help us to pay Him our tribute in the form of acts of mercy, for His munificence and His goodness towards us and for the pity and compassion in which we were regarded, for He commands all of this and is master of regulating merit and goodness. No godliness outside Him!

Among the interventions of God in our favour and the marks of His bounty towards us in these circumstances, we must count the chance that this *Rumi* King was present, for without him all that was in the ship would have been pillaged. It might also have happened that all Muslims who were there would have been reduced to slavery, for this is their custom. Now, the King was in this city because of the fleet he was having built; this was merciful for us. Praise be to God for this proof of a favourable regard and His protection!

Description of the Island of Sicily

…The most beautiful of the cities of Sicily is the residence of its king; the Muslims call the city *al-madina*, and the Christians, Palermo. This is where the Muslim city-dwellers live; there are the mosques, and the souks which are reserved, for the Muslims are numerous in the suburbs. All the other Muslims inhabit farms, villages and other cities like Syracuse, etc. But it is the great city, residence of King William, which is the most important and the most considerable. It was in this city that we were going to reside and from where we hoped to embark towards the place in the Western Lands where God had ordained that we were to go.

The attitude of the King is truly extraordinary. He has a perfect conduct towards the Muslims; he gives them employment; he chooses his officers among them, and all, or almost all, keep their faith secret and remain attached to the beliefs of Islam. The King has full confidence in his Muslim subjects and uses their advice in his affairs and in all of his essential preoccupations, to the extent that the head of his kitchens is a Muslim. He has a troop of black Muslim slaves commanded by a *qai'd* chosen among them. His viziers and his chamberlains are eunuchs, of whom he has a great number, who are members of his government and in whom he confides his private affairs. It is in them that the brilliance of his royal power shows itself, for they wear magnificent clothes, and have superb mounts. They almost have a court each, with attendants and retinue. This King has superb palaces and marvellous gardens, particularly in his capital. In Messina he has a castle, white as a dove, which dominates the sea-coast.

He has numerous pages and slave-girls at his disposal. There is no other king among the Christians who has more royal splendour, more riches, who lives more luxuriously than he. In his use of the power which he commands, in the fine ordinance of his decrees, in the solid assizes of his power, in the just distribution of honours among his men, in the brilliance of his royal pomp, in the display of his finery, he resembles the Muslim kings [of Andalusia]. His royal authority is very notable. He has physicians and astrologers in whom he takes great pride and in whom he believes so much that if he hears that a physician or astrologer is passing through his kingdom, he orders him seized, and he offers him great wealth to make him forget his home country. May God by his grace protect the Muslims from the disorder into which this king may tempt them! He is around thirty years of age. May God protect the Muslims from his iniquity and oppression!

Another extraordinary thing reported about him is that he reads and writes Arabic, and according to what we have heard from one of his personal servants, his motto is 'Praise be to God, as praise is due', and that his father's was: 'Praise be to God, recognition of His godsends' [both sayings of a strongly Muslim tinge].

The women slaves and the favourites in his palace are all Muslims. And I may report an extraordinary thing told to me by this same servant of the King, Yahya ibn Fityan the embroiderer, who does gold embroidery in the royal studio. When a Christian Frankish woman is introduced into the palace, she quickly becomes Muslim, for she is converted by the women just mentioned. These retain all this as a great secret in front of the King. They have wonderful impulses towards the good. Thus we were told how this island was shaken by an earthquake, which made this polytheistic King sorely frightened. He ran through his palace, where he heard nothing but invocations to God and His Prophet spoken by all his women and his eunuchs. If these were troubled by seeing him, he reassured them: 'May each one of you invoke the God he worships and whose faith he follows'.

The officers, who are the eyes of the government and the agents of his royal authority, are Muslims. There are hardly any among them who do not fast in the months prescribed, in the will to be obedient and in the hope of a heavenly recompense; who do not give alms to be closer to God and be received by Him; who do not liberate prisoners; who do not take care of their children and marry them well and are generous to them; who do not do good when they can. All this is the work of God for the Muslims of this island and a secret of secrets of the divine solicitude towards them.

We became acquainted at Messina with one of them, an officer named Abd-al-Masih, one of the most high-ranking and important among them, who had first expressed a desire to meet us; he was magnificent in his generosity towards us. He shared with us the deepest secrets, after having looked carefully round the hall we were in and, for his own safety, after having sent away those of his servants he distrusted. Then he asked us questions about Mecca—may God protect the holy place!—about the venerable tombs there and in the holy city of Medina and those in Syria. We answered his questions, and he awaited our response with a burning desire. He begged us to make him a present of some of the blessed objects which we had brought from Mecca and Medina—may God preserve their holiness! He expressed the desire that we should not be stingy, as much as was in our power. You have had, he said to us, the happiness of being able to manifest your Muslim faith [by going on the pilgrimage]; you have attained the desired goal; you are the winners, if it pleases God, in this pious trade; while we have to hide our faith, fear for ourselves and be forced to worship God and observe the holy rites in secret. We are silenced under the domination of an unbeliever, in the knots of servitude. Our supreme joy is to obtain a benediction by making acquaintance with pilgrims such as yourselves, to ask from them prayers for us, and to cherish gifts that we receive from them and which come from the holy places, in order to make of them objects to assist us in our faith and a treasure to be put with our shroud [i.e. the grave]. In the course of this conversation, our hearts were near breaking, out of sympathy with him. For his benefit we implored of God his ultimate success. We gave him as gifts some of the objects we possessed and which he desired. He generously paid us and thanked us, and he asked us to keep this a shared secret with his friends, the other officers …

Description of Al-Madina (Palermo), capital of Sicily

…In this city the finery of the Christian women is that of Muslim women. With alert tongues, covered and veiled, they are outside on the occasion of the feast we have mentioned; clad in fabrics of silk embroidered with gold, draped in magnificent robes, veiled with veils of many colours; their feet clad in ankle-boots embroidered with gold, they stroll to their churches or to their houses; they wear in other words all the finery of Muslim women, including the jewellery, the powders and the perfumes. By way of literary banter, we remembered this verse of the poet:

'If some day one goes to a church one will meet there both doves and gazelles …'

We ask God to turn us away from this description which is about to take on a futile allure and which is leading us to inane diversions;

we take refuge in Him against the danger of a development that leads to nonsense. For it is towards Him—glory to Him!—that we direct our pious fear and search for pardon ...

The Pilgrimages of Lady Nijô (b. 1271)

From *Towazugatari*

It is difficult to talk of Japan in the same breath as India or Nigeria: not only is Japan one of the few Asian and African countries that were never fully colonized by European powers, it is also a country with a fairly recent history of colonizing other regions. And yet, the imbalance of narrative "power" between the West and all the rest in recent centuries is brought home, to some extent, with reference to *Towazugatari*, which exists in two translations in English but is unlikely to be even as visible as the works of Sappho or Aphra Behn. Written by Lady Yoshimoto Nij_ in 1307, it falls roughly between the two names in terms of chronology and lays fair claim to being considered a text of equivalent literary and historical value as the texts (or fragments) by Sappho and Aphra Behn.

In the introduction to her excellent translation (*The Confessions of Lady Nij_*) of the text, Karen Brazell describes *Towazugatari* as "an autobiographical narrative, a tale of thirty-six years (1271–1306) in the life of Lady Nij_, starting when she became the concubine of a retired emperor in Kyoto at the age of fourteen and ending, several love affairs later, with an account of her new life as a wandering Buddhist nun." She goes on to say that "in my judgement it is one of the finest works in classical Japanese literature."

Lady Nij_'s travel-based memoir was written as part of a Japanese literary genre, and it was partly intended to preserve (or perhaps restore) her family honour. However, for various political and historical reasons, it languished in libraries for nearly seven centuries. It appears that very few copies had been made to begin with and it was only in 1940 that a Japanese scholar, Yamagishi Tokuhei, discovered the last surviving manuscript while going through the extensive Imperial Household Library in Tokyo. Brazell notes that the "war delayed publication of the text until 1950, but it was not until 1966 that complete, annotated— and therefore readable—editions were published."

Lady Nij_ appears to have been sent to Emperor GoFukakusa as the adopted daughter of a prime minister and she was probably treated as a foster daughter by Lady Kitayama, the grand old lady of the period. Such affiliations were a means of social climbing in aristocratic circles, where indicators of status were minutely observed. Obviously descending from an aristocratic background, she appears to have become the Emperor's mistress at the age of fourteen. As her name indicates, she never became the official royal consort, but she was a favoured and high-ranking court lady, who—in keeping with her position—not only participated in the elaborate social rituals of the imperial family but also added to imperial grandeur with her literary and musical training. She took on a number of lovers and finally, partly because she appears to have irritated GoFukakusa's empress, Higashi-Nijô, and lost the eye of GoFukakusa, was forced to leave his palace when she was twenty-six.

Expelled from the palace in 1283, Lady Nijô became a Buddhist nun: the first three books of *Towazugatari* tell of her life as a beautiful and, at times, intriguing lady of court, while the last two describe her travels, thoughts and memories as a Buddhist nun. Throughout her text is distinguished by acuity of perception and a keen observing mind.

The extracts given below in slightly abridged fashion are taken from the beginning of Book IV, when Lady Nijô sets out as a Buddhist nun to visit various holy places and exchanges poems and has conversations not only with famous monks but also with warriors, warlords, officials, prostitutes and travelling commoners. As is the case with many other texts in this anthology, the last two books of *Towazugatari* not only tell us of the travels of the narrator but also provide a vivid glimpse of an entire world of travels and travellers, ranging from princes to beggars.

[For a full translation of *Towazugatari* see K. Brazell's *The Confessions of Lady Nij_* by Anchor Press/Doubleday, New York, reissued by Stanford University Press in 1976.]

Excerpts from BOOK FOUR (1289)

Having left the capital city at moonrise, I knew I had given up my home for good and yet my thoughts lingered on the possibility of return, and I felt that the moon shared the tears that I shed and in which it was itself reflected. How weak I was...

...After a journey of several days I arrived at Red Hill Lodge in Mino province, where I halted for the night, tired and solitary due to unaccustomed travel. Two sisters managed the lodge and their skill as musicians, especially their delicate playing of the *koto* and the *biwa*, reminded me of the past. I could not help noticing that the older sister looked troubled when I ordered some wine and asked the sisters to play for me. She seemed to be on the verge of tears and I felt that we were very much alike. Perhaps she too wondered about the tears that stained the dark cloth of my sleeves and hence, in an act that was unusual for a nun, she wrote this poem and handed it to me on a little sake cup tray:

> *I wonder what passion*
> *Has driven you to this free*
> *Life of drifting like a*
> *Wisp of smoke from Fuji.*

So moved was I by her unexpected empathy that I wrote this poem in reply:

> *The flames of love, orange,*
> *Send forth this smouldering smoke*
> *From Fuji's snowy peak*
> *In the Suruga Range.*

It is difficult to leave this kind of friend and I was reluctant to do so. But of course I could not stay there indefinitely and once again I set forth. I reached the place known as Eight Bridges, and found that the bridges were no longer there and the river had dried up: I felt as if I had lost an old friend...

Continuing on to the Atsuta Shrine in Owari province, I stopped and worshipped there. This shrine used to be in the domain of my father and during its annual festival my father would send it a horse as an offering and request that prayers be said for his wellbeing. In the final year of his illness, my father had added some silk to the usual offering but the horse had died on the way and the surprised local officers had had to substitute another in its place. We had interpreted it as a sign that Gods had not accepted Father's prayers. I now reached the shrine and spent the night there, surrounded by these memories, which evoked feelings of loneliness and sorrow.

I had left the capital late in the second month determined to push hard on my journeys, but I was so unused to travel that my progress was tardy. The third month had already begun now. A luminous moon rose early, filling the night sky as it used to in the city and once again His Majesty's image floated in my memory. Within the holy precincts of the Atsuta Shrine, there were cherry trees blooming in vivid profusion. For whom (I wondered) were they putting on this glorious display?

Blossoms burning against the sky
Near Narumi Lagoon;
How long now before the petals lie
Scattered among the pines?

This I wrote on a slip of paper and I left it tied to the branch of a cryptomeria tree near the shrine.

I remained absorbed in prayer at the shrine before resuming my travels after a week. Approaching the Narumi tidelands I glanced back at the shrine and saw clusters of the scarlet fence that hedged it gleaming through the fog...

... Later that month I reached the island of Eno Shima, a place that is fascinating but not easy to describe. Separated from the mainland by an arm of the sea it has various grottoes. In one grotto, I took shelter with a pious mountain sage who had been practicing austerities for decades. It was a simple yet charming dwelling, fenced with fog and screened by bamboo trees. The sage made me feel at home and presented me with some shells collected in the region. At this, I opened the basket my companion was carrying and offered him a fan made in the capital.

'Living in isolation as I do, I never get any news from the capital', he said. 'For sure, the wind cannot carry things like this to me. I feel as if I have met a friend from the far away past today.' In my heart, I felt so too.

No one was around and no special event was taking place; it was quiet, and yet I failed to sleep that night. I tossed about on my mattress of moss, brooding on the great distance I had travelled. Cloaked with worries I was and I wept mutely into my sleeve. Then I determined to go outside and look about. The horizon faded into a haze that might have been clouds, water, or fog; but the night sky above was so clear, and the brilliant moon stood still and immobile. I felt I had travelled thousands of kilometers. I heard the heart-tearing cries of monkeys from the hills beyond and felt an anguish so intense and sharp that it seemed new to me. This was the journey I had undertaken with only the burden of my thoughts and sorrow in the hope that it would dry my tears. It was distressing to have travelled so far and still not to have escaped the worries of the world...

STUDIES

Al-Burûnî's Defence of Hindu India
From *Kitab al-Hind*

Scientist, traveller and historian, al-Burûnî's (c. 973–1048) reasons for
writing his monumental book are stated at both the beginning and
the end of the text: he wished to present his (Muslim) community
with an accurate and impartial description of India and, in particular,
Indian theological and philosophical doctrines. It is the relationship
this evokes that has induced us to include an extract from al-Burûnî's
book, for al-Burûnî (like many historians and geographers of the age
and unlike some who have been left out) did not travel much in India
and wrote a book that hardly ever refers to his own travels. However,
he did visit India—after years of studying its literature—and not only
learnt Sanskrit but also discoursed widely with Indian scholars and
translated Sanskrit texts.

It is true that al-Burûnî's book qualifies only faintly as a travel
document, and yet it has been included here not only because al-
Burûnî did travel to India or for the breadth of mind that it reveals
and the problems of language, accuracy and representation—so central
to travel writing—that it addresses. It has also been included here as it
is in some ways typical of many early travel accounts—Asian, African
or European—which combined first-hand experience of a limited
nature with either study of the cultures concerned or second-hand
reports (and often both). It is a tradition that is linked to works that
plainly fail to be classified as travel accounts, but which are
nevertheless the fruit of many travels—such monumental works as
Shihâb al-Dîn al-'Umarî's *Masâlik al-absâr fî mamâlik al-amsâr*, the great
fourteenth-century encyclopaedia of the geography, history and
economics of all Muslim countries. As the shortness of the extracts
below indicates, while we want to put this parallel and extensive
tradition of travel (if not explicit travel writing) on record, we prefer
to reserve space for books that depend more on first-hand observation
while travelling.

Al-Burûnî is said to have been the court astrologer of King Mahmud of Ghazna (997-1030), still recalled as a ferocious invader in India. It is more likely that al-Burûnî was a respected (but not politically influential) scholar in a brilliant court, which also included among others, Firdausi (the author of *Shahnama*). That al-Burûnî did not have any special love for King Mahmud is obvious from the clipped nature of his references to the emperor as well as his obvious distaste for religious intolerance. Also, it has to be recalled that al-Burûnî himself entered Mahmud's court as the member of a defeated people and court. Al-Burûnî, or, as his compatriots called him, Abu Raihan, was born in 973 in the territory of Khiva. Distinguishing himself in science and literature, he was politically active in the court of the independent Khiva princes who were finally defeated and deposed by their powerful relative, Mahmud of Ghazna. It was only then—in 1017 AD—that al-Burûnî entered the Ghaznavi court as a captive nobleman and scholar. It is obvious that his reputation as a great astrologer must have played a role in this, though it was common for Mahmud and most kings of the age to incorporate not only scholars but also soldiers of defeated kingdoms into their own forces and courts.

What strikes the reader on reading al-Burûnî is the "modern" mind that his writings, dating from 1030 AD, reveal. For instance, he does not believe in alchemy—clearly distinguishing between such of its practices as are of a scientific nature and such as are used to deceive people. He tries his best to let the "*Hindûs*" (for him, mostly, Vaishnav Brahmins, most likely the dominant school in India at that time) speak for themselves. While painfully aware of the difference of Hindu thought and the fact that religious Muslims would find aspects of it unacceptable, he bridges that difference with the help of Greek philosophy (which formed part of an Islamic education). Al-Burûnî's interest in Hindu thought was by no means exceptional among Muslim intellectuals of the age: among his contemporaries was Kushyar ibn Labban who authored the influential *Principles of Hindu Reckoning* around 1000 AD.

In modern terms, his text is acutely aware of both difference and similarity across cultures. While taking care not to provoke the

"Islamists" of his age, he remains admirably independent and undogmatic in his responses to religion—even reproaching Muslims for having destroyed the ancient civilization of Iran. When critical of some aspect of Hindu society, he nevertheless hastens to remind Arabs that their own ancestors had similar practices. Regarding representation and accuracy, he often appears to be akin to a modern historian or philologist: quoting extensively from original texts and inquiring into the corruption (and the causes of corruption) of the relevant text. It might be best, in this respect, to take a page out of al-Burûnî's book, and quote the author on (explicitly) history and authenticity of representation and (implicitly) reality and language. This is how al-Burûnî's preface to the book begins:

> No one will deny that in questions of historic authenticity hearsay does not equal eye-witness; for in the latter the eye of the observer apprehends the substance of that which is observed, both in the time when and in the place where it exists, whilst hearsay has its peculiar drawbacks. But for these, it would even be preferable to eye-witness; for the object of eye-witness can only be actual momentary existence, whilst hearsay comprehends alike the present, the past, and the future, so as to apply in a certain sense both to that which is and to that which is not (i.e. which either has ceased to exist or has not come into existence). Written tradition is one of the species of hearsay – we might almost say, the most preferable. How could we know the history of nations but for the everlasting monuments of the pen?

Al-Burûnî, who appears to have found Mahmud's hedonistic and far less zealous successor to his liking, died in c. 1050 after a period in royal favour.

[The following extracts are from the original Arabic book—Abu al-Raihân Muhammad ibn Ahmad al-Burûnî's *India: An Accurate Description of All Categories of Hindu Thought, as well as those which are*

Admissible and those which must be Rejected—as translated by Dr Edward C. Sachau and first published in 1910. They have been taken from a reprint entitled *Alberuni's India,* brought out by Low Price Publications, Delhi, in 1996.]

Extracts from Chapter LXVI: On Pilgrimage and the Visiting of Sacred Places

...Pilgrimages are not obligatory to the Hindus, but facultative and meritorious. A man sets off to wander to some holy region, to some venerated idol or to some of the holy rivers. He worships in them, worships the idol, makes presents to it, recites many hymns and prayers, fasts, and gives alms to the Brahmans, the priests, and others. He shaves the hair of his head and beard, and returns home...

...We have already quoted Hindu traditions to the effect that in the Dvîpas there are rivers as holy as the Ganges. In every place to which some particular holiness is ascribed, the Hindus construct ponds intended for the ablutions. In this they have attained to a very high degree of art, so that our people when they see them, wonder at them, and are unable to describe them, much less construct anything like them. They build them of great stones of an enormous bulk, joined to each other by sharp and strong cramp-irons, in the form of steps (or terraces) like so many ledges; and these terraces run all around the pond, reaching to a height of more than a man's stature. On the surface of the stones between two terraces they construct staircases rising like pinnacles. Thus the first steps or terraces are like roads (leading round the pond) and the pinnacles are steps (leading up and down). If ever so many people descend to the pond whilst others ascend, they do not meet each other, and the road is never blocked up, because there are so many terraces, and the ascending person can always turn aside to another terrace than that on which the descending people go. By this arrangement all troublesome thronging is avoided.

In Multan there is a pond in which the Hindus worship by bathing themselves, if they are not prevented.

The Samhitâ of Varâhamihira relates that in Tâneshwar there is a pond which the Hindus visit from afar to bathe in its water.

Regarding the cause of this custom they relate the following – The waters of all the other holy ponds visit this particular pond at the time of an eclipse. Therefore, if a man washes in it, it is as if he had washed in every single one of all of them…

…The Hindus have some places which are venerated for reasons connected with their law and religion, e.g. Benaras [Varanasi]. For their anchorites wander to it and stay there for ever, as the dwellers of the Ka'ba stay for ever in Mekka. They want to live there to the end of their lives, that their reward after death should be the better for it. They say that a murderer is held responsible for his crime and punished with a punishment due to his guilt, except in case he enters the city of Benaras, where he obtains pardon.…

Extracts from Chapter LXVIII: On What is Allowed and Forbidden in Eating and Drinking

…Originally killing in general was forbidden to them [Hindus], as it is to the Christians and Manichæans. People, however, have the desire for meat, and will always fling aside every order to the contrary. Therefore the here-mentioned law applies in particular only to the Brahmans, because they are the guardians of the religion, and because it forbids them to give way to their lusts. The same rule applies to those members of the Christian clergy who are in rank above the bishops…not to the lower grades, such as presbyter and deacon, except in the case that a man who holds one of these degrees is at the same time a monk.

As matters stand thus, it is allowed to kill animals by means of strangulation, but only certain animals, others being excluded…Some Hindus say that in the time of Bharata, it was allowed to eat the meat of cows, and that there then existed sacrifices part of which was the killing of cows. After that time, however, it had been forbidden on account of the weakness of men, who were too weak to fulfil their duties…This theory, however, is very little substantiated, as the prohibition of the meat of cows is not an alleviating and less strict measure, but, on the contrary, one which is more severe and more restrictive than the former law.

Other Hindus told me that the Brahmans used to suffer from the eating of cows' meat. For their country is hot, the inner parts of the bodies are cold, the natural warmth becomes feeble in them, and the power of digestion so weak that they must strengthen it by eating the leaves of betel after dinner...As this is the case, they forbade eating cows' meat, because it is essentially thick and cold.

I, for my part, am uncertain, and hesitate in the question of the origin of this custom between two different views.

(Lacuna in the manuscript)

As for the economical reason, we must keep in mind that the cow is the animal which serves man in travelling by carrying his loads, in agriculture in the works of ploughing and sowing, in the household by the milk and the product made thereof. Further, man makes use of its dung, and in winter-time even of its breath. Therefore it was forbidden to eat cows' meat; as also Al-Hajâj forbade it, when people complained to him that Babylonia became more and more desert...

Extracts from Chapter LXVIX: On Matrimony...

No nation can exist without a regular married life, for it prevents the uproar of passions abhorred by the cultivated mind, and it removes all those causes which excite the animal to a fury always leading to harm...Every nation has particular customs of marriage, and especially those who claim to have a religion and law of divine origin. The Hindus marry at a very young age; therefore the parents arrange the marriage for their sons...No gift is settled between them. The man gives only a present to the wife, as he thinks fit, and a marriage gift in advance, which he has no right to claim back, but the wife may give it back to him of her own will. Husband and wife can only be separated by death, as they have no divorce.

A man may marry one to four wives...Some Hindus think that the number of the wives depends upon the caste; that accordingly, a Brahman may take four, a Kshatriya three, a Vaishya two wives, and a Shudra one...

If a wife loses her husband by death, she cannot marry another man. She has only to choose between two things—either to remain a widow as long as she lives or to burn herself; and the latter eventuality is considered preferable, because as a widow she is ill-treated as long as she lives...

The Horizons of al-Idrisi in the Eleventh Century

From *Kitab nuzhat al-mushtâq fi-khtirâq al-afâq*, also known as *Kitab Roger* (1154)

Abu Abdallah Muhammad ibn Muhammad ibn Abdallah ibn Idriss al-Qurtubi al-Hasani, known as al-Idrisi (probably 1099-1166), was born in Sabtah in the Maghrib (now the Spanish enclave of Ceuta), where his family, descendants of the Hamudid dynasty, had fled in 1057. He studied in Córdoba and seems to have travelled through most of the Mediterranean world as a young man. In 1145, he became court geographer to the Norman King Roger II of Sicily. He disappears from the Arabic annals at this point, perhaps because he was considered a renegade, and the date of his death is much debated. But, as the following extract makes abundantly clear, it was to Roger he dedicated what was undoubtedly the most extensive and scientific work of geography since Ptolemy.

The author of *Kitab nuzhat al-mushtâq fi-ikhtirâq al-âfâq* (*Book of Peregrination of He Who Longs to Penetrate New Horizons*) is close to an incarnation of the Arab ideal of "*al-âlim al-adîb*", the scientist poet, which the universalists of the European Renaissance had to measure themselves against: a Maghriban aristocrat and a descendant of the Prophet; an accomplished courtier and poet; a first class herbalist, who was enough of a polyglot to give the names of plants in his botanical works in six languages (Arabic, Latin, Greek, Persian, Berber, Sanskrit), with a deep knowledge of both ancient Greek and contemporary Arabic philosophy and sciences. Though the major part of his extensive oeuvre is in medicine and botany, he has remained best known for his geography. *The Book of Roger* is more than the summation of the knowledge of his day: Not satisfied with compiling and updating the classic Greek and Arab geographies, al-Idrisi and Roger, as the Preface makes clear, interrogated the men of science of the day and cross-checked their unsatisfactory statements with experienced travellers, who were questioned together and apart; and al-Idrisi took upon himself to check on countries and witness natural geographical phenomena such as the Atlantic tide on the coasts of Portugal and Brittany.

If ibn Khaldun in the fourteenth century was to "pre-invent" the "historical method" of nineteenth century Europe, al-Idrisi replaced the perceptual and measured earth at the centre of geography, where it had been in Ptolemy's day, but was not to reappear in Europe until the cartographic revolution of the sixteenth century. Other medieval maps, geographies and travel accounts centre the world conceptually in the promised Jerusalem or holy Mecca. The dazzling lapis blue mappamundi, which accompanies *The Book of Roger*, is a sectioned, climatic map, not a circle embraced by a crucified Christ as in the OT maps of medieval Europe, nor even the Biblical maps of the itineraries of Abraham and Moses in the first Dutch atlases of Ortelius and Mercator. The humanly shaped, the all too worldly and secular, once Islamic, now Norman Sicily lies at the centre, surrounded by the Mediterranean. The descriptions of neighbouring and exotic lands and cities transcend the purposes of taxation and conquest, their arrogance is rather that of the sceptical scientist fitting together Ptolemaic theory and the wildly differing and often fabulous accounts with which he had to work. Al-Idrisi's descriptions of human wealth and natural resources do not purport to show the extent of the expansion of Islam or the might of his king, except in so far as this king wishes to move beyond what he controls to understand and place human history in its natural context.

Al-Idrisi's theoretical framework was that of Ptolemaic geography, as he sets it out in his "Prolegomena":

> The Earth is round as a sphere, and ... the waters adhere to it and are maintained by means of an equilibrium which does not allow any variation ... The Earth is, like the waters, plunged in space like the yolk in the middle of an egg, that is in a central position. The air surrounds it on all sides, it attracts it towards space or repels it; God knows what the truth is on

this point. The Earth is stable in the middle of space and all created bodies are stable on the surface of the Earth, the air attracting what is light and the Earth attracting what is heavy, like a magnet attracts iron.

The terrestrial globe is divided in two equal parts by the equinoctial line (Equator), which extends from west to east, this is the length of the Earth and the longest line of the terrestrial sphere, just as the zodiac is the longest line of the celestial sphere. The circumference of the Earth is divided into 360 degrees at the Equator: each degree measures 25 parasangs, and each parasang 12,000 coudées [ancient French measurement of 50 centimetres]; every coudée 24 fingers and every finger 6 grains of barley lying back to back. According to this report the circumference of the Earth is 132,000,000 coudées or 11,000 parasangs. This is the calculation of the Indians. But according to Herates [Eratosthenes], who measured this circumference, and divided it in equal parts, each comprising a hundred miles, it is 24,000 miles or 12,000 parasangs. Starting from the Equator and moving towards either pole, one counts 90 degrees and all corresponding latitudes are of the same dimensions. But there are only habitable lands up to the 64th degree, measuring from the Equator; the rest is a complete desert because of the intense cold and the abundant snows.

The whole of the population of the globe inhabits the northern (septentrional) part; the regions to the south are abandoned and deserted because of the heat of the rays of the sun. These regions being situated in the inferior orbit of this star result in the waters drying up and the absence of all living things; for animals, no less than plants, may not live where there is no water or coolness.

The Earth is essentially round, but not of a perfect circularity, since there are elevations and depressions, and the waters run into each other. The Ocean surrounds half the globe without interruption like a circular zone, in such a way that it appears to be halved, as if it were an egg plunged into water contained in a bowl; this is how half the Earth is plunged into the sea. The sea is itself surrounded by air, and the air registers the attractions and repulsion mentioned.

The habitable part of the Earth is divided by scholars into seven climates, each of which extends from the west to the east. This division is not established according to any naturally existing lines, but according to ideal lines imagined by astronomers. In every climate is a large number of cities, of forts, of villages and of peoples who bear no resemblance to each other ... These seven climates are cut through by seven seas ... These seas are also called gulfs. Six of them are contiguous, only one is separate and without communication with the others.

The first of these seas, situated in the inhabited part of the globe, is the sea of China and of the Indies, of Sind and Yemen. It extends from the east and from 13 degrees latitude along all the Equator; it bathes China, then India, then Sind, and then the South of Yemen and ends at the Strait of Bab al Mandeb. This is its length, and according to trustworthy travellers, mariners who have ventured there and persons who have set sail from one country to the next from the Red Sea all the way to Wacwac, this length is 4,500 parasangs...

This is where the following excerpts begin, with the regions least known to al-Idrisi: China, Indochina, Indonesia and Wacwac (New Guinea). It is notable how much real information about the spice islands and the silk harbours comes through, despite the lack of clarity about place-names, political and geographical features, for example about what are islands and what peninsulas (some of it no doubt due to copyists' errors: the copy of the manuscript translated below dates from 1344). Even the New Guineans seem to emerge from fogs of myth and prejudice, maybe even Australia in the tantalizing suggestions that the Chinese sometimes go beyond Wacwac: the fabled Wacwac Tree mentioned, but rejected by al-Idrisi, was indeed putatively placed in Australia by the Australian historian Manning Clark. Al-Idrisi is certainly not free from prejudice: about people with black skin, for instance. But it is remarkable how far his sceptical method went in sifting information from myth, and in trying to place all the wonders of the world in measured space, al-Idrisi is almost as breathtaking as the accuracy of Eratosthenes and the Indians in calculating the circumference of the Earth.

Al-Idrisi is also a challenge for the modern ideal of a man of the world: a "Western" Muslim at the service of a Northern Christian king at a time where the Islamic world is reeling from Christian incursions: the *reconquista* in his beloved Andalusia and the Crusades in the East; his life and work at the Arabic-speaking Norman court in Palermo ridicule our modern superficial concept of multiculturalism as mere toleration of juxtaposed ghettos.

The Book of Roger, of which ten wonderfully illustrated manuscripts survive, divides the world into climates and sections and above all itineraries. It is geography as travel writing, proposing to King Roger and the modern reader a long journey through these horizons, where descriptions of landscape and customs are interleaved with semi-personal narratives, historical summaries, explanations of natural phenomena and application of geographical theories.

[The following translation is by Martin Leer from the French translation by P.Amédée Jaubert, *Géographie d'Édrisi: Recueil de Voyages et de Mémoire publié par la Société de Géographie*, Paris: chez Arthus Bertrand, 1836 (Tome premier) and L'Imprimerie Royale, 1840 (Tome second). No more recent translation has been available, but al-Idrisi's work is visually accessible on the CD-Rom put out by the Bibliothèque Nationale in Paris in connection with its exhibition of the manuscripts in 2001]

Al-Idrisi: Geography
From the Preface
All grace goes back to God [Allah], the essentially great and powerful being; incorporeal; endowed with goodness, beneficence and long-suffering; sovereign judge who can do everything; who is merciful and

compassionate; who governs everything; who possesses an infinite science; who has given to all that he has created perfect forms, knowledge of which is engraved in every heart and resides in all spirits on visible and incontestable proof.

His force and his power are certain and evident indications of his glory. All languages announce his goodness, which is confirmed by faith. Confirmation perfects the beings which emanate from his divine will, the power that enables the recognition of his existence and his eternity. Among the main creations of this will, heaven and earth are, to the man of just spirit and right sense, signs of a high instruction. He admires first of all heaven, its immense height, the beauty of the stars and the regularity of their course, among these stars the sun and the moon which shine in the firmament; the sun, seat of the light that produces the day, the moon which like a torch dissipates the obscurity of the nights. These miraculous signs teach him the march of the seasons and the turning of the centuries. He then remarks the earth of which this same will fixed the cradle, determined the extent, inside of which it made the waters flow, principal sources of vegetation and necessary conditions for the fertility of the fields and the freshness of pastures; the earth which is permitted for the joy and habitation of man, who is the favoured object in the movements imprinted for all the heavenly bodies, of man in whom this divine will has inspired the instinct to separate good from evil and the useful from the dangerous, and given the ability to transport himself wherever he wants, by land or sea, crossing the immensity of spaces. All is proof of the existence of God.

Of all the beings formed by this divine will, the eye may not discern nor the spirit imagine one more accomplished than *Roger, King of Sicily, of Italy, of Lombardy and Calabria, Prince of Rome.* This great King, whom heaven has endowed with glory and power, protector of the religion of Christ, is the most famous and the best of all monarchs. His absolute will is his motive of conduct in all affairs. He makes friends and enemies according to his will; he governs and judges his peoples with equity and impartiality, and listens to their requests with patience and attention. He has established in the administration of his territories the most admirable order and the most perfect elements of happiness; he has carried arms victoriously from the rising to the setting sun, as witness the neighbouring and distant countries he has made obedient to his will; as witness the sovereign of his own cult [the Pope], whose pride he has humiliated. He owes these astonishing successes to the valour of his armies well equipped with all things, to the power of his fleets whose operations are protected by heaven itself. His glory shines in all eyes, his name fills the world, is on all tongues and in all ears. Which desire could he form that was not to be followed by the fastest accomplishment? Which project, however difficult it might be, would he not be able to execute? ...

... As the extent of his possessions has grown, as the respect accorded to his subjects everywhere has risen, and as he has brought under submission lands conquered from other Christian princes, this Prince, following the interest he has in noble and curious studies, has concerned himself with the statistics of his vast estates. He wished not only to know in a positive manner the limits by which they were circumscribed, the routes across land and sea which traversed them, the climates in which they were situated, the seas which bathed their shores, the canals and rivers which watered them; but he even wanted to add to this knowledge the knowledge of other lands that were not under his authority, in all the space that it has been agreed to divide into seven climates, on the authority of those writers who have treated of *geography* and who have attempted to determine the extent, the subdivisions and the dependencies of every climate. To this end he consulted ... [numerous books in Arabic and Greek] ...

Instead of finding in these books clear, precise and detailed information, he encountered nothing but obscurities and motives for doubt, and so called to his presence persons specially conversant with these matters and asked them questions, which he discussed with them, but he obtained no more enlightenment from them. Seeing that this was the case, he determined to seek out educated travellers in all his lands; he called them to his presence and interrogated them through interpreters, sometimes together, sometimes apart. All the times when they agreed, and their reports were unanimous on one point, this point was admitted and considered certain. When it was otherwise, their advice was rejected and put aside.

He concerned himself with this work for fifteen years, without pause, without ceasing to examine for himself all the geographical questions, to seek a solution to them, to verify the exactness of facts, before obtaining the certainty of knowledge that he desired.

Thereafter, he wanted to know in a positive manner the longitudes and latitudes of places and the respective distances between points which the persons mentioned had agreed on. To this purpose he had a large drawing-board prepared, and on this he had traced, one by one, by means of a pair of iron compasses, the points indicated in the diverse books consulted, which had been fixed according to the assertions of their authors, and which in the general examination had been proved perfectly exact. Finally, he ordered that a planisphere be cast in pure silver without alloy, of an enormous size and a weight of 450 Roman pounds ... On this he had engraved, by skilled artisans, the configuration of the seven climates with their regions, countries, near and far coasts, arms of the sea, seas and water-courses; he made them indicate deserts and cultivated land, their respective distances by frequented routes, either in miles or other known measures, and the destinations from ports; he warned his workers to follow scrupulously the model traced on the drawing-boards, without deviating in any way from the measurements they found indicated there.

He ordered the composition of a book, for the interpretation of this planisphere, containing a complete description of the cities and towns of the territories, of the cultures and nature of the inhabitants, of the extent of the seas, of the mountains, of rivers, of plains and shallows. This book was to treat also the species of grains, the fruits and plants produced in the various countries, the properties of these plants, the arts and customs in which the peoples excelled, their articles of export and import, curious objects which had been remarked or were famous in the seven climates, the state of the populations, their exterior appearance, their mores, their customs, their religions, clothing and their speech.

I have given to this work the title: The Peregrinations of the One

Who Longs to Penetrate New Horizons.

This work was finished in the last days of the month of *shiwâl*, in the year 548 of the Hijra (corresponding to mid-January, A.D.1154).

First Climate, Ninth Section

This section contains the description of the part of the Indian Ocean known as the China Sea, and a part of the sea named Darlazoui. In this sea are several islands, which we will mention shortly.

We say that in the middle of this sea is a part of Sofala ... and that one of the inhabited places of this country is the city of Djesta, not very large. One here finds gold in large quantities; its exploitation is the sole industry and principal resource of the inhabitants. They eat sea turtles and shellfish. Dourah is little known among them. This city is situated in a large gulf that ships may enter. 'The inhabitants of Djerbesta, who have no ships or pack animals, are obliged to carry their own goods, and to render each other reciprocal service. The merchants of Comor and of Mehraj go to them and are well received and trade with them.' From the city of Djerbesta to the city of Daghouta is a voyage of 3 days and 3 nights and to Comor 1 day.

The city of Daghouta is the last of Sofala, country of the east; it is situated in a large gulf. Its inhabitants walk about naked, while they hide their sexual parts with their hands when approached by the merchants who come to them from the other islands. Their women have a sense of modesty and never go to the markets or the meeting-places because of their nudity; this is why they stay secluded at their homes. Gold is found in this city and in its hinterland, more than anywhere else in Sofala. This country borders on that of the Wacwac, where two 'miserable towns are to be found, sparsely populated because of the rarity of matters of subsistence and resources of any kind.' One is called Derou and the other Nebhana. In the vicinity is a large market village called Da'rgha. 'The inhabitants are black, hideous of face and deformed of complexion; their language is a form of whistling. They are absolutely naked and little visited by strangers. They live off fish, shellfish and turtles.' They are (as we have said) neighbours of the island of Wacwac, of which we will shall speak later,

God willing. All of these countries and islands are situated in a large gulf. Neither gold, nor ships, nor commerce, nor beasts of burden are found there. As for the island of Djalous, its inhabitants are Zendjes; they live, as we have said, from anything that falls into their hands.

'In the island is a mountain, whose soil is mixed with silver. If one approaches this soil with fire, it dissolves and becomes silver.' From the island of Lankialilious there is a voyage of two days and five from this last to the island of Keleh, 'which is very large, and where there lives a king who is called the Djaba or the Indian Prince. On this island is a mine which produces an abundance of tin. The metal is very pure and brilliant; but the merchants mix it fraudulently after its extraction and transport it everywhere. The clothing of the inhabitants is the tunic; it is of the same form for men and women.' The island produces rattan and excellent camphor. The tree which gives this resin resembles the willow, apart from the fact that it is much larger: more than a hundred people can sit under the shade of one tree. The camphor is obtained by making incisions in the top of the tree, from which runs a large enough quantity to fill several jars. When this opening has stopped running, one makes another lower down towards the middle of the tree where the drops of camphor start running; for it is a gum produced by this tree which thickens in the wood. After this operation the tree becomes useless; it is left behind as one moves on to another. The wood of the camphor tree is white and light. Many tales are told about this island of marvels, the description of which appears excessively fantastic.

In the vicinity of this island are those of Djaba, Selahat and Heridj. They lie at a distance of two parasangs, more or less, one from the other. They all obey the same king. 'This Prince is called Djaba; he wears a mantle and a tiara of gold enriched with pearls and precious stones. His money carries his image. He has much devotion for the *boud*. This word *boud* means temple in the Indian language. That of the king is very beautiful and covered on the outside with marble. In the interior and around the *boud* are idols made of white marble with heads crowned with gold and other coronets. Prayers in these temples are accompanied by chants and take place with much pomp and order. Young and beautiful women here execute dances and other agreeable games, in front of the persons praying and assembled in the temple. A certain number of these young girls are attached to each *boud*; they are fed and clothed by the establishment. This is why, when a woman has given birth to a girl who is remarkable for her body and her beauty, she is presented at the *boud*. When she reaches adolescence, the young girl is dressed in the most beautiful clothes that it is possible to obtain, and accompanied by her family and her parents, she is led by the hand of her mother to the temple to which she has been consecrated. She is confided to the care of the temple servants, and the family retires. From there she passes into the hands of women instructed in the arts of dance, music and other games which it is necessary for her to learn. When she has become sufficiently proficient, she is again dressed in magnificent clothes and rich jewels, and she is attached in an unbreakable manner to service in the temple. She may never again leave, nor cease her functions. Such is the law of the Indians who worship the *boud*…

First Climate, Tenth Section

This section covers the last habitable lands on the Eastern side, beyond which all is unknown; the China Sea, called also Sakha and by some the Senf Sea; this is an arm of the Ocean called *the Obscure Sea*, because it is in effect dark and nearly always agitated by impetuous winds and covered by thick tenebrous mists. This sea reaches the Ocean near the Land of Gog and Magog, and at its lower end reaches the uninhabitable lands to the North. This tenebrous sea extends also to the Western side, as we have said, and to the islands of the Wacwacs in the meridional parts and all around to the Austral Sea. This Ocean is agitated by strong winds and subject to abundant rains. The maritime winds [the monsoon] blow six months in one direction, and the other six months in the opposite direction.

There are here a large number of islands, some of which are frequented by merchants, the others never visited, because of the difficulty of the sea routes, the fear which the sea inspires, variations in the direction of the winds, the ferocity of the islanders and lack of communication and neighbourly relations with the known peoples.

The island called el-Moudja, situated in the Darlaroui Sea, is ruled by various kings who are white in colour, but who do not wear the species of coat known as the *azar*. The inhabitants, in terms of their costume and ornaments, have much in common with the Chinese. They have many horses, which they use to wage war on their neighbouring kings. This island reaches the places where the sun rises. The animals which produce musk and civet are found here. The women are the most beautiful in the world; they always have long hair, and they do not try in any way to hide it. They go bareheaded, decorated only with ribbons from which shells of various colours are suspended and fragments of mother-of-pearl. From this island to that of Suma is two days.

Suma is very large, very fertile in grain and cereals. Various species of birds that are good to eat are found here that are not seen elsewhere in the Indies, and many coconut palms. Suma is surrounded by a large number of small, but inhabited islands. The king is called Camroun. It rains often here and is very windy. The depth of the sea surrounding it is about 40 fathoms. The mountains of this island produce camphor superior to that of all other countries. On some of these islands there is a people called Fondjet, with black, curly hair, who attack the ships with war machines, weapons and poisoned arrows. It is difficult to combat their attacks, and few of those who enter their waters or who fall into their hands are saved. Each of these men wears around his neck a necklace of iron, copper or gold. At the borders of this sea, on the Chinese side, is the island Almaid about four days navigation from China, about the same distance as from the island of Suma to that of Anam. From here one enters the Senf Sea. 'Among all the seas which we have mentioned there is none where the rains are so frequent or the winds more violent; sometimes storms let the rain pound for two days without interruption. The islands of the Senf Sea produce aloe wood and other perfumes. Neither the extremity nor the extent of this sea is known. On its coasts are the lands of a king called Mihradj, who possesses a great number of populous islands, fertile, covered by fields and pastures, and producing ivory, camphor, nutmeg, mace, cloves, aloe wood, cardamom, kababé and other substances, which are indigenous here. The lands of this prince are much frequented, and there is no king in the Indies who possesses anything comparable to these islands, where the commerce is great and well-known.' One of these islands is Almaid. This contains a large number of cities, is larger and more fertile than Moudja, 'and its inhabitants resemble the Chinese more than others, I would say, more than all neighbours of the Chinese. The kings have black and white slaves and beautiful eunuchs.' Their lands and their islands border on China. 'They send Ambassadors and presents to the sovereign of that empire.' This is where the ships coming from the Chinese islands assemble and are stationed. It is towards this island that they sail and from this point that they depart to go elsewhere. From the island of Senf to the islands of Sendi Foulat is a voyage of 10 days. The island of Sendi Foulat is very large; it has fresh water, cultivated fields, rice and coconut palms. The king is called Resed. The inhabitants wear the *fouta* either as a coat or with a belt. The island of Sendi Foulat is surrounded on the Chinese side by mountains difficult of access, where strong winds blow. This island is one of the gateways to China. From there to the city of Khancou is a four days journey.

The gateways to China are twelve in number; these are mountains situated in the sea: between each mountain is an opening by which one arrives at the harbour cities of China towards which one is moving. All the 'scales' of China are placed thus in gulfs, it is through here that the ships enter.

The people possess riches in abundance and large flocks of sheep. As to the water in the gulfs, it is sweet from the moment of the coming and going of the tide; then the flood fills them with the water of the sea, which arrives twice in 24 hours.

At these 'scales' are the markets, the merchants, people who come and go, buildings, merchandise being loaded and unloaded. One is always safe in this country. Justice characterises their monarchs, it is the basis of their laws and of their conduct. This is why the inhabitants can live peaceably together, and the country is rich; there are few people in distress and many reasons for hope; people are not overly concerned with expenses, and much good is done. All the peoples of India and China punish thieves by death, love peace, and render justice to each other; they do not need to run to magistrates and arbitrators all the time. All is done according to their nature, with which they were created and with which they were imprinted. The King Camroun holds two islands in fealty, one of which is called Famousa and the other Lasma. The colour of the inhabitants of these islands is white; the women here are of a ravishing beauty. The men are brave and enterprising; they live off piracy on ships from the better markets, especially when they are at war with the Chinese, and there is neither peace nor truce between them.

From the island of Moudja to that of the Storms, takes four or more days of navigation. This latter is so named because white fogs dangerous for ships sometimes arise from within the island. A tongue thin and long comes out from the island accompanied by a strong wind. When this tongue reaches the surface of the water it results in a kind of boiling, the waves are agitated as if by a terrible whirlwind, and if it reaches the ships it engulfs them. The storm arises after that and it begins to rain, without clear indication of whether this rain comes from the sea or how this thing has come to pass. On this are hills of a kind of sand, which when touched by fire turns into pure silver. In the area of the Wacwac islands, neighbouring this, are many small islands and mountains inaccessible to travellers because of the extreme difficulty of the sea-routes and communications. The inhabitants are infidels, who know of no religion and have not received any law. The women are bareheaded and wear only combs of ivory ornamented with mother-of-pearl. One woman may wear as many as twenty of these combs. The men wear their hair in the kind of hairstyle we call *al-canîs* and the Indians call *al-buhari*. They remain in their fortified villages in the mountains without leaving them or permitting visitors. Still visitors do go up to observe their buildings on the mountainside, and sometimes the inhabitants address them in an incomprehensible language. Such is their constant behaviour. After this is the island of Wacwac, beyond which one ignores what exists. However, the Chinese go there sometimes, though rarely. There are a number of islands, uninhabited except by elephants and a multitude of birds. There a tree here about which Mas'udi reports such unlikely things that it is impossible to recount them here: beyond which He on High is powerful in all things.

From the island of Senf to that of Malai is 12 days, through islands and rocks that rise out of the water. The island of Malai is very large. It is the longest of the islands, the most significant in terms of culture, the most fertile in its mountains, and covers the largest landmass. One may engage in the most advantageous commerce on this island, which has elephants, rhinoceros, and many kinds of perfume and spices, such as cloves, cinnamon, nard and nutmeg. In the mountains are gold mines of excellent quality. It is the best in China. The inhabitants of these islands have houses and castles constructed of wood, which are transported on water to their destination; they also have windmills, where they make rice, wheat and other cereals into flour which they eat.

From the island of Almaid to that of Sanji is three short days. 'This is a fertile island, populous, where fresh water is found. The colour of the inhabitants is between white and tawny. They wear copper ornaments in their ears. The men wear one *fouta* and the women two. They live off rice. There are many sugarcane and coconut palms and goldmines known for both quantity and quality. One sees on this island various statues placed along the coast. They all lift their right arm as if to say to the spectator: Return to where you came from, for behind me there is no land where it is possible to go.' From this island one turns towards the islands of Sila, which are of a great number and very close to one another. There is here a city called Ankouah, whose territory is so fertile and abundant in all things that the foreigners who come here settle down and do not leave. It has gold in such quantity that the inhabitants make it into leashes for their dogs and monkeys. They also make clothes of gold and sell them. There is also an abundance of gold in the islands of Wacwac. The merchants go there with those who search for gold; they smelt the mass of this metal and export it in ingots. They also export gold powder, which they cast in their own country according to a process known to them. The islands of Wacwac also produce ebony of an incomparable beauty.

The China Sea, the part of the Senf Sea which is contiguous with it, and the Darladeri Sea as well as those of Herkend and Oman are subject to ebb and flood. It is reported that in the Sea of Oman and the Gulf of Fars [Persia], this phenomenon takes place twice a year, in such a way that floods are experienced during the six months of summer in the Eastern Sea, while the opposite is the case in the Western Sea; while the ebb is reported in the West during the other six months.

As a great number of opinions have been expressed on this topic of the tide, we feel obliged to report summarily what has been said, to complete the explanation of this phenomenon.

Aristotle and Archimedes claim that it is due to the action of the sun combined with that of the wind and the waves (as it appears in the Atlantic, which is the Ocean), which produces the flood, while the ebb occurs when the winds die down. But Satoios [Poseidonios?] thinks that the cause of the flood resides in the successive waxing of the moon until it is full, and the ebb is thus attributable to the waning phases of his star. This opinion is in need of development and explication ... [Al-Idrisi tends towards a compromise between the two explanations] ...

... All the Chinese ships, great or small, that navigate in the China Sea are solidly constructed of wood. The pieces of timber are disposed geometrically one over the other, protected by palm fibres and caulked with flour and fish oil. In the China Sea and the Indian Ocean there are large animals 100 yards long and 25 wide, on the backs of which grow bumps of rocks and shellfish like vegetation, by which the ships are sometimes damaged. Mariners recount that they attack these animals with arrows and thus force them to move out of their way. They add that they pierce the smallest of these animals and boil them in cauldrons, that their flesh dissolves and turns into liquid fat. This oily substance is renowned in the Yemen, in Aden, on the coasts of Fars and Oman, and in the Indian Ocean and the China Sea. The people of these regions make use of this substance for filling the hulls of the ships.

Of the many marvellous things one may see in the China Sea and the Indies and which are reported by the merchants who sail to these parts are the mountains and straits found in these seas. There are sometimes black birds the size of four-month babies who board the ships without harming anyone and refuse to leave. This is for the mariners a sign of the approach of the wind called *the deceiver*, which is very dangerous. They try to protect themselves and take precautions against its approach, relieving the ship of some of its load, throwing into the sea all that comes from it, especially all fish and salt, of which they keep absolutely nothing, and finally by shortening their masts by two yards or more for fear that the ship may break. In fact, the wind never fails to rise. Finally the mariners meet with the tempest by confiding themselves to divine protection; they are saved or they perish according to how it pleases God. They have another sign of salvation, when God allows it: this is the appearance in one of their masts of a gold-coloured bird which shines like a flame, and which is called *al-bahman*. When they see it, they know they have been delivered; this is something that has been seen so often and repeated so often by travellers that no reasonable doubt is left as to its reality...

Two Chinese Accounts of the Early Mongols
(1221 and 1237)
From *Mengda Beilu* and *Heida Shilüe*

The *Mengda Beilu* (*Thorough Account of the Mongol Tartars*) and the *Heida Shilüe* (*Brief Account of the Black Tartars*) are two of the earliest Chinese written accounts of the Mongol Tartars of the Plains, who from Genghis Khan onwards were to have such profound and devastating effects on the Middle Kingdom. From the fall of the Tang dynasty in 907, the warring Chinese had sought alliances with a succession of Barbarians from the West: first the Kitan, who established the Empire of Liao round present Beijing (Peking); then the Tangut, who established the kingdom of Xi Xia to the West; and the Jurchen or Jin Barbarians, who won most of Northern China (and gave us the name China). All these peoples had adopted Chinese ways relatively quickly. The border people to the West were the Turcoman Uighurs until the sudden rise of the Mongols under Genghis Khan from 1206. By 1279 Genghis' grandson Kublai was Emperor of all China.

The accounts excerpted below were both commissioned by the Southern Emperors of the Song Dynasty (1127-1279) from ambassadors to the court of Genghis and his son Ogodai and form an interesting comparison to the *Relazioni* sent in by Venetian ambassadors to the Doge and Senate of the Serene Republic, though of course they predate the most famous and in its time most controversial Venetian "relation", Marco Polo's account of China under the Mongols. In China the genre of Western Travels became so popular, through these works and others such as *The Secret History of the Mongols* (1227-64), *The Travel Notes of a Journey to the West* (by the Daoist monk Chang Chun, 1228) and *Accounts of the Personal Campaigns of The Emperor Shengwu* (i.e. Genghis Khan, 1260-85) that these accounts lost reliability and merged with the picaresque, as can be seen in the famous novel *Monkey* by Wu Chengen (1500-1580), whose Chinese title is *Xiyouji* (Record of a Journey to the West).

The *Thorough Account* (*Mengda Beilu*) was written in 1221 by Zhao Hong at the instigation of the then governor of Beijing, which was to be rebuilt by the Mongols in its present form under the name Dadu in 1267. Little is known of Zhao Hong except that he was not of Han Chinese extraction, but probably came from one of the peoples of Jin "civilized" by the Chinese. It is a very factual account in 17 encyclopaedic chapters, of which the four excerpted here both confirm the image China and Europe seem to share of the Mongols, at the same time as they possess the wonder of an "exotic" system of classification and comparison so dear to Borges' and Foucault's use of (fictional) Chinese encyclopaedias. Both the *Thorough* and the *Brief Account* are fine examples of the trouble one culture has of accounting for another on first meeting and of the different attitudes adopted by different witnesses.

The Brief Account (*Heide Shilüe*) is interestingly dialogic in its structure, consisting of short and often prejudiced or simply wrong encyclopaedic entries by Peng Daya, supplemented by modest, but far more accurate eye-witness accounts by Xu Ting, who was not only far more sympathetic, but verges on what in European accounts would be called "primitivism". Peng Daya accompanied Ambassador Zou Shen Zhi on his first journey to Ogodai's court in Karakorum in 1234; Xu Ting went on Tsou's second, longer expedition in 1235-6. Peng Daya was later, in the course of his career, promoted to be Governor of Chongjing, where he took it upon himself to rebuild the city walls sacked by the Mongols in 1236. According to critics his attitude to the work was summed up in the characteristic saying, "If one does not see money as money and human beings as human beings, there is no reason why the walls cannot be rebuilt." He was later dismissed, exiled and had his forehead tattooed by the Emperor for cruelty and corruption, but was posthumously rehabilitated. Little is known about the later career of Xu Ting, who came from a family of scholars and philosophers, and who seems to have died young while trying to collect his travel impressions into a book.

[A Note on the Translation: These texts belong to a long range of Chinese "Western travels". They have been translated by Martin Leer from the German scholarly and annotated translation by Erich Haenisch, Yao Zongwu [Yao Ts'ung-wu], Peter Olbricht and Elisabeth Pinks, *Meng-ta Pei-lu und Hei-ta Shih-lüeh: Chinesische Gesandtenberichte über die Frühen Mongolen 1221 und 1237*, Wiesbaden: Otto Harrassowitz, 1980. Notes are based on this edition and René Grousset's monumental *The Empire of the Steppes: A History of Central Asia* (1939), English transl., New Brunswick: Rutgers University Press, 1970. Hard brackets in the excerpts below indicate translator's comments; soft brackets in the *Brief Account* are Xu Ting's interpolations in Peng Daya's text.]

From *Mengda Beilu (Thorough Account of the Mongol Tartars)*

Chapter 1: Foundation of the Empire

When the Tartars first arose, their land lay northeast of the Kitan. Their tribe stems from a branch of the Shatuo. Other than that little has been known of them in the course of time.

There are three kinds of Tartars: black, white and wild. Those that are called White Tartars are of gracious aspect, in behaviour they are polite and responsive, and they treat their elders with filial piety. In grief at the death of their parents they weep and cut their faces with knives. When I once rode out with the Tartars, I asked those among them who did not look so ugly and had scars from knife-wounds on their cheeks, 'Are you a White Tartar?' and every time I got the answer 'Yes'. When they have taken Chinese boys and girls prisoners, they bring them up, but they still despise them. In intercourse with others they are friendly and entertaining. As for the descendants of this tribe, their kingdom is now ruled by the Princess Alaqai Begi, a daughter of the Tartar ruler Genghis. The second Ambassador Jubkhan, who a short while ago has paid our court a return visit, is also a White Tartar. Every time when I rode out with Jubkhan [during my stay with the Tartars] he was always exquisitely polite and took the greatest care of me. He said, 'You have exerted yourself so much for our sake. Please accept many apologies that we haven't taken better care of you!'

Those that are called the Wild Tartars are very poor. They are very obtuse and unpolished, and the only things they understand are to ride and to follow the Horde.

The present Emperor Genghis as well as his generals and ministers and high officials are all Black Tartars. The Tartars are in general not very tall of stature, the tallest not over five foot two. There are none who are corpulent. Their faces are broad and short, with very prominent cheekbones. Their eyes have no double lid. Their hair and beard grow sparsely. Their appearance is quite coarse. But the Tartar ruler Temujin [the personal name of Genghis] has a big and strong body; he has a broad forehead and a long beard. He is a man of giant size, and for this reason he is so different.

Genghis is the son of a group headman, Kieh-lou. A group headman in their country is an officer of ten horsemen. Now he is the ruler of the empire founded by him. In translation his name is Emperor Cheng Jizi. He has conquered the East and subdued the West.[56] Thus his empire has become great and mighty.

Chapter 7: The Military

The Tartars grow up in the saddle on horseback, and for each and every one of them it is a routine matter to practice fighting. From spring to winter they go hunting every day. This is their way of life. This is why they have no foot soldiers, all are cavalry. For mobilisation, even of several hundred thousands, hardly anything in writing is required. Camp is broken by repetition of the order by word of mouth from the General to the Leaders of the Thousands to the Leaders of the Hundreds to the Leaders of the Tens.

When they want to attack a big city, they always storm the smaller towns around it first and capture the inhabitants in order to force them into service. They pass round the order: 'Each horseman has the duty to capture ten men!' When they have gathered enough people, each one of them is ordered to deliver a certain amount of fodder or combustibles or soil or stones; day and night they are forced to do this, and whoever is slow, is killed. They are forced to fill in the moats of the fortifications and so level them in no time. Or they are forced to service on the siege-ladders, catapults and other war material. Tens of thousands are sacrificed mercilessly in this way. No city attacked in this way has remained unconquered. And when a city is conquered, they destroy it all without consideration for whether it is old or young, beautiful or ugly, poor or rich, resistant or obedient. Pardon is almost never given. Those who, from the very beginning of the attack, do not follow orders are executed, no matter their rank.

At every conquest of a city, the loot is set aside and distributed according to a set formula to every man in the army from the highest to the lowest. No matter whether the loot is rich or poor, one tenth is set aside as a gift to the Emperor Genghis. The other loot is distributed according to rank. Ministers and high officials, who have remained in Mongolia and not taken part in the raid, are rewarded with their share.

Plans for the war raids are not confirmed till the third or fourth month and then sent on to the individual countries. Then, in the great assembly on *chungwu* day [the fifth day of the fifth month][57] council is taken on the whole plan of operations for the following autumn. Afterwards they all return to their own country to retire from the heat and take care of their flocks. In the eighth month they all assemble in Yendu [Beijing] and the campaign begins.

Chapter 12: Customs

The Tartars have no regard for age and take pleasure in men in their prime. It is not part of their habit to carry on private feuds. On New Year's Day and on the fifth day of the fifth month they all worship the sky. This belongs to the customs which they took over from the Jin during their long stay in Yanjing.

Their favourite entertainment is their proclivity to drinking bouts. When the Governor Muqali returns from a campaign, the ladies of his household by ancient tradition host feasts in his honour, one after the other, day after day. It is the same with his subordinates.

It is not, for the most part, their custom to wash their hands;

when they grab meat or fish and get their hands greasy, they just dry them on their long outer garments. They wear their clothes until they are worn out, and they never take them off to wash.

The women often powder their forehead with yellow powder. This is an old Chinese cosmetic which they have taken over and not changed till the present.

From Genghis himself to the servants of his people they all shave their head... This resembles the three locks of hair left standing on the heads of Chinese children. The lock of hair over the forehead is cut when it grows longer. The locks of hair on both sides of the head are collected into little horns and allowed to hang over the shoulders.

Chapter 16: The Women

It is the custom, among the highest as well as the lowest ranks, to bring their women and children along on their campaigns—so that, as they themselves explain, the women and children can take care of baggage, clothes, money and goods. The women in particular have the task of setting up their tents made of felt, saddling the horses and distributing the loads among wagons and camels. They are highly skilled riders. Their dress has similarities with that of Chinese Daoists. The wives of the tribal chieftains all wear the *Gugu* head dress. The frame of this head dress is braided from iron thread; it resembles a 'bamboo wife'[58]. It is about three feet long, mounted with red or blue brocade and decorated with pearls and gold. On top is another stick around which red or blue embroidery-thread has been wound for decoration. Further they wear a coat with wide sleeves, which resembles the Chinese crane robe[59]; it is broad and long and trails along the ground. When they walk it is held up by two waiting-women.

Men and women sit together; they are not forbidden to toast each other[60]. When our Ambassador to the North visited the Governor, he was proposed a toast at the very first greeting. The Governor was sitting with his wife, Princess Laiman, and all the ladies-in-waiting, of whom eight were named *fu-jen* [concubines]. They take part in all feasts. Those who were pointed out to me as *fu-jen* were all gleaming white and of beautiful mien. Four of them were obviously noble ladies of the Kin Barbarians, and four were Tartar women. The fourth of these *fu-jen* was an extraordinary beauty and a particular favourite of the Governor. They were all dressed in the clothes and caps of the Hu Barbarians.

From *Heida Shilüe (Brief Account of the Black Tartars)*

Chapter 9: The Dwellings

Peng Daya:

Their dwellings are all domed tents of felt [yurts]; they have no permanent houses with walls or beams. They are always on the move for water or grass and have no permanent abode.[61]

When the Ruler of the Tartars moves the site of his tent, to go felt-patch hunting[62], the whole of the so-called 'court' moves with him; this is called: breaking camp. Their wagons are drawn by oxen, horses and camels. Wagons on which there is a 'hut' in which it is possible to sit and lie down, which are called yurt-wagons. Carts on which there are poles at the four corners or whose four ends are connected with boards and which have a waterproof cover are called eating-wagons. The carts are organised in fives like a train of ants. It winds on for a length of fifteen miles, and from left to right in its breadth it reaches half its length in a straight line. If they find water, they stop. This is called: making camp.

The yurt of the Ruler is turned towards the south. This is followed by the yurts of the concubines, and the so-called 'Guards' and the so-called 'Officials'. Wherever the yurt of the Ruler of the Tartars is erected during the hunt, it is called an *ordo*[63]. His golden yurt is only called a 'great *ordo*' when the so-called imperial concubines and all the hordes move with it. It is erected in a cove among the mountains with its back against a hill in order to be protected from the force of the wind. It is like the movement of the travel camp of the Chinese Emperor. There is no fixed term to the stay: sometimes they move after a month, sometimes not till after a quarter.

Xu Ting:

When I, Ting, came to the Steppes, they had erected the Golden Yurt. I believe they had erected it purposely, in expectation of the arrival of an embassy, which had been sent personally by His Majesty the Emperor of our Dynasty, in order to give the embassy an impressive first sight. When Ambassador Zou arrived with his embassy earlier, they had not erected it. And when Ambassador Cheng arrived with a later embassy or Ambassador Zhou with an even later embassy, they had not erected it on either occasion.

As regards its construction, it is the largest felt tent of the Steppes. From top to bottom it is covered in felt. In the middle in various places windows made of wickerwork have been inserted in order to let in light. Over a thousand strings hold the yurt in place. The threshold and the posts are all covered with gold. Hence the name. Inside there is room for several hundred people.

The giant bed on which the Ruler of the Tartars sits, looks like the teacher's dais of a Buddhist temple. It is similarly ornamented with gold. The Imperial Ladies sit according to rank as if in a gallery.

There are two types of domed tent. In the style of Yanjing a skeleton is made from willow-branches, like the wind-shelters of the South; it can be rolled up and unfolded. In front is a doorway. From above it looks like an umbrella. At the top is an opening. This is called the window on heaven. All of it is covered with felt. This type of yurt can be transported on horseback.

In the style of yurt-building of the Steppes a solid circle is made by intertwining willow-branches, and over that felt is stretched and fastened. These yurts cannot be rolled up. They are transported on waggons. When the supply of water and grass are exhausted, the people move. There have never been fixed dates for this...

Chapter 24: Matters of Administration

Peng Daya:

As regards their matters of administration, they write with wooden twigs. Their writing looks like frightened snakes and writhing earthworms; it looks like the magical writing in the Books of

Heaven; their characters look like the *wu, fan, Gong*[?] and *chi* of musical notation. They are closely related to the characters of the Uighurs.

Xu Ting:

I, Ting, have concerned myself with this. The Tartars originally had no writing. Today, however, they use three different kinds.

For written communication in the Tartar lands proper they always use small pieces of wood, three or four inches in length on which they make incisions in the four corners. If for instance ten horses are to be sent, they make ten notches. As a rule they only cut the required number. Their customs are pure and their thoughts honest. Hence also their language is without ambiguity. According to their laws, liars are punished by death. Thus nobody dares to betray. Even if they had no writing, they would still be capable of founding an independent state. These small pieces of wood are the same as the wooden tablets of antiquity.

For their written correspondence with the Uighurs they utilise the Uighur system of writing. Chinqai[64] is the master of this. The Uighur system of writing has only 21 letters. The others are formed by adding something on one or the other side of the letter.[65]

For written correspondence with the conquered Chinese states, with the Kitan and the Jurchen, they make use exclusively of Chinese writing. Chucai [Ch'u-ts'ai][66] is the master of this. But apart from this, before the date at the end of the letter, Chinqai in his own hand writes in Uighur letters the words: 'To be sent to NN'. This is presumably a security measure that is directed only at Chucai. Hence every piece of writing has to be marked with such a confirmation in Uighur; without it it has no official validity. This is obviously a measure to make sure that all correspondence passes through Chinqai's hands, in order to ensure mutual control.

In the city schools in Yanjing it is mainly the Uighur writing that is taught along with translation into the Tartar language. No sooner have the pupils learnt to translate, than they begin to function as interpreters and then in company with Tartars go on violent rampages, where without inhibitions they begin to act as masters of punishment or favour and extort bribes, goods, services and foodstuffs.

The systems of writing that the Kitan and the Jurchen originally possessed are never used by the Tartars.

Chapter 36: Riding and Shooting Skills

Peng Daya:

As regards their riding and shooting skills, the children from an early age are bound to a board and this is bound to the horse. So they ride all the time with their mother [on the same horse]. At three years of age they are bound with a rope to the saddle in such a way that they have something to hold on to with their hands. Then they gallop along with the others. By four or five they all carry small bows with short arrows, and when they are grown they hunt during all the four seasons. When they ride fast, they always stand up on their toes in the stirrups without sitting down. Thus about eight or nine tenths of their weight lies in the movement of their feet and only one to two tenths in their seat. They are fast as the whirlwind and heavy as a mountain when they turn on the enemy. They turn to the left and the right in the saddle like birds on the wing. Thus they can look to the left and still shoot to the right; and above all, they do not always shoot backwards.

As regards their shooting while on their feet, they stand with their legs spread, broad in the groin, with their hips pointing downwards. Thus they manage to put all their weight into the shot and pierce the plates of the enemy armour.

Xu Ting:

I, Ting, have seen with my own eyes how a Tartar woman, when she gave birth to a child on the Steppes, immediately after the birth dried the child with sheep's wool, wrapped it in a shawl, bound it into a small box four feet long and one foot broad, and how the woman simply took the child under her arm and rode away on her horse…

A Chinese Account of the "Lost City" of Angkor

From *Shuofu* (c. 1298)

When and after Angkor Wat was "discovered" by the French Henri
Mouhot in 1860, European travellers and writers stressed how
unexpected it was to find an entire city—and a truly magnificent
one—covered by forest. Local people—who had lived near many of
the splendid temples and other ruins—reportedly did not know how
old the buildings were and ascribed it to immemorial times.[67] No
historical document seemed to exist about this lost city. However
documents and records and first-hand knowledge of the place did
exist, including an entire account of Angkor as a functioning capital.
This account was written by Zhou Daguan (Chou Ta-Kuan) after a
year-long stay in Cambodia from 1296 to 1297.

Zhou Daguan's account—translated as *Notes on the Customs of
Cambodia* only in 1967 (based on a French translation from 1902)—
depicted a rich and extensive urban world that to some extent,
exceeded the imagination of the nineteenth-century European
"discoverers" of Angkor. It was a world that had extensive trade and
diplomatic relations with faraway kingdoms in India and China:
Daguan was himself part of a Chinese embassy from Timur Khan, the
grandson and successor of the great Kublai Khan. The Angkorean king
to whom Daguan led his embassy probably did not pay homage to
Kublai/Timur Khan, though unlike his predecessor he did not flaunt
the Mongol's authority openly. His name was Indravarman III (1295-
1308), and he ruled over the last days of a once-glorious empire
(founded c. 802) from Angkor Wat, one of the greatest cities known
to humankind.

Angkor Wat had been built by Suryavarman II (1113-1150) and
dedicated to Vishnu (while the Cambodian people were already
predominantly Buddhist). Only eight decades before Daguan's arrival,
the reign of Jayavarman VII (1181-?1219) had marked the peak of the
architectural achievements associated with Angkor Wat and adjoining

cities. In order to appease the people who were increasingly adopting Buddhism, Jayavarman had converted to Buddhism while retaining many aspects of Vaishnav Hinduism. He had also launched a massive building project, including the reconstruction of Angkor Thom with the Bayon as the central temple and the building of Ta Prohm and Preah Khan temples. He had built 102 hospitals and 121 pilgrim hostels along the roads leading to Angkor, raising the kingdom to its pinnacle of glory but also taxing its resources and probably contributing to its subsequent decline. Jayavarman VII had also promulgated the cult of the *deva-raja* (God-king), which Daguan observed. Daguan was suitably impressed by the respect paid to the king by the people, but by the time he arrived the cult of the *deva-raja* had lost in prominence and it was possible for the king to come out among the people.

The city Daguan visited was fed by an intricate network of shallow and brilliantly planned canals and protected by fortifications, which he described in his concise notes about flora, fauna, domestic life, architecture, religion, trade, politics, customs, etc. His book is in many ways an early version of a possible tourist's handbook, providing not only information but also occasional comments about what to do and what to expect. While the accuracy of his depiction cannot be doubted, it should also be borne in mind that Daguan brought to his observations a certain set of cultural, gender-specific and political values, and that his depiction of Cambodian life was largely obtained from an elitist perspective. Historical evidence indicates that, at least in certain matters, Daguan described "what was" rather than what was coming into being. The world he visited was obviously in the process of drastic change from a Hindu-Brahmin elitist culture to a more popular Buddhist ethos. The Angkorean empire was under threat from different sides by the late twelfth century. The Thais had attacked from the West and the Chams from the East. Relationship with the Mongol empire of Kublai Khan and his successor was also tense. All of this would culminate in the sacking of Angkor by the Thais in the thirteenth century, and its subsequent abandonment. This perception of threat and change does not really come through in Daguan's notes, though he does state how ill equipped and ill trained the Angkorean army was.

Who was Zhou Daguan and how were his notes preserved? This is what Paul Pelliot writes in the introduction to the 1902 French translation: Zhou Daguan was a "native of Yung-chia [Yongjia], in the province of Chekiang [Zhejiang]. In 1296–1297, he was assigned to duty with a Chinese embassy which passed nearly a year in Cambodia. Returning to China, he wrote his account—presumably at once, but certainly before 1312. He was still living in 1346. Shortly before the fall of the Mongol dynasty (1368) his *Notes* were incorporated in a lengthy compilation of one hundred chapters (largely composed of excerpts) ascribed to one T'ao Tsung-I [Tao Zongyi] and called the *Shuo fu*." Pelliot's own translation was based on a later transcription in *Guji Shuohai*, even though various other manuscripts based on the *Shuofu* also exist. Pelliot's French version was translated into English by J. Gilman d'Arcy Paul for the Social Science Association Press of Bangkok in 1967, with the help of a grant from Alexander B. Griswold of the Breezewood Foundation. This translation was reprinted by the Siam Society, Bangkok, in 1987 and our translation below, based (with some abridgement) on Pelliot's French translation, has been checked against the English translation wherever possible. The reader is also referred to the English translation for the entire text that runs to about 70 pages in print.

[Translated by the editors from the French translation by Paul Pelliot in *Bulletin de l'Ecole Française d'Extrême Orient*, 1902, and corrected against the authoritative English translation by J. Gilman d'Arcy Paul in *Chou Ta-Kuan: The Customs of Cambodia*, Bangkok: The Siam Society, 1993, to which the reader is referred for a full translation of Zhou Daguan's text.]

First Excerpt: Childbirth

On giving birth to a child, a Cambodian woman immediately makes a poultice of hot rice and salt and applies it to her intimate parts. She takes it off in twenty-four hours, thus preventing any unfortunate after-effects: it results in renewing the young mother's maidenhood. When first informed of this, my credulity was severely taxed. However, I was lodged in a house where a girl gave birth, and I was able to observe that the very next day she was up and around, carrying the baby in her arms and taking him to the river for a bath. This is truly amazing!

Everyone I talked to said that Cambodian women are highly sexed. They are ready for intercourse just a couple of days after giving birth: if the husband does not respond, he may be discarded. When a husband is called away on business, the women endure his absence for a period of time. But if he is absent for more than ten days, the wife may say, 'I am not an (insubstantial) ghost; how can I be expected to sleep all alone?' However, some of them are said to remain faithful in spite of their strong sexual impulses.

The Cambodian women age very rapidly, doubtless because they marry early and become mothers at an early age. Twenty or thirty year old Cambodian women can resemble Chinese women of forty or fifty.

Second Excerpt: The Royal Palace and The King

All official buildings and homes of the aristocracy, including the Royal Palace, face the east. The Royal Palace stands north of the Golden Tower and the Bridge of Gold: it is one and a half miles in circumference. The tiles of the main dwelling are of lead. Other dwellings are covered with yellow-coloured pottery tiles. Carved or painted Buddhas decorate all the immense columns and lintels. The roofs are impressive too. Open corridors and long colonnades, arranged in harmonious patterns, stretch away on all sides.

In the state-room of the King, there is a golden window, framed with mirrors in square columns. Below the window stands a frieze of elephants. I have heard that the palace contains many a marvellous sight, but the inner dwellings and sections are so strictly guarded that I have had no occasion to see them.

A golden tower rises from the palace and the King climbs to a room at the top of this tower to sleep every night. It is commonly rumoured that a power, shaped like a serpent with nine heads, which is the Lord of the entire empire, dwells in this tower. Each night this being appears in the shape of a woman, with whom the King sleeps. Not even the wives of the King may enter this room. At the second watch, the King comes out and can then sleep with his wives and concubines…

Third Excerpt: Clothing

All men and women, including the sovereign, knot their hair and leave their shoulders bare. They wear a thin strip of cloth around the waist, and they draw a larger piece of cloth over this when leaving the house.

Many rules, based on rank, govern the selection of materials. The king wears fabrics that include some that are rich and sleek and valued highly at three or four ounces of gold. Although fabrics are woven in Cambodia, many types of fabrics are imported from Siam and Champa. Indian weaving is preferred for its skill and refinement.

Only the king may wear clothes woven in an all-over pattern. On his head he wears a diadem. At times, he takes off the diadem and weaves a garland of fragrant jasmine-like blossoms into his hair. He wears about three pounds of pearls around his neck. His wrists, ankles and fingers are adorned with numerous bracelets and gold rings, all set with cat's-eyes. His feet are bare. The soles of his feet and his palms are coloured red with henna. He carries a golden sword outside the palace.

Only common women are permitted to colour the soles of their feet and their palms. Men are forbidden to do this. High officers and princes are allowed to wear fabrics decorated with patterns of recurring groups of flowers. Ordinary mandarins can only wear fabric with two groups of flowers, and this is also allowed to the women. However, if a newly-arrived Chinese man wears clothes with two groups of flowers [inappropriate to his position], this cannot be charged against him, for he is 'a man who does not know the rules.'

Fourth Excerpt: Daughters and Maidenhood

On a daughter being born to a Cambodian family, the parents bless her thus: 'May the future bring you a thousand husbands!' If the parents are rich, they hand over their daughter at the age of seven to nine (eleven, if the parents are poor) to a Buddhist or Daoist priest for 'deflowering'. This ceremony is known as *zhentan*. Every year the proper authorities announce a day corresponding to the fourth Chinese moon and cause it to be announced all over the land. Families with daughters ripe for *zhentan* notify the authorities. The authorities send to each family a candle bearing a certain mark. At nightfall on the announced day, the candle is lit: the moment for *zhentan* has come when the candle burns down to the mark made on it.

The family would have chosen a priest—Buddhist or Daoist, according to their place of residence—a fortnight before this date. Such is the demand that the services of the higher class of priests are all engaged well in advance by rich or prestigious families, and the poor have to do with what they can find. Rich families load the priests with presents of wine, rice, silk, fabrics, areca-nuts, silver plates, whose value often exceeds one hundred piculs, or two or three hundred ounces in Chinese money. Presents from poorer families may be worth thirty or forty piculs, depending on the family fortune. If girls of poor families find themselves approaching eleven without the means to pay the priest, generous people may help them with contributions. This they call 'acquiring merit.' A priest is not permitted to perform this ceremony for more than one girl every year. Also, he cannot [change his mind and] pledge himself to initiate another girl once he has accepted his fee.

The night of the ceremony consists of a great feast, with music. A platform is erected in front of the girl's houses and on it are placed figurines, sometimes exceeding ten, sometimes less, of animals and persons. All this is not expected from the poor. In keeping with ancient custom, these figurines stay in place for a week. Next, a procession carrying palanquins and parasols and playing music sets out to fetch the priest. The priest is brought to and seated in one of two pavilions hung with brilliantly coloured silks that have been set up; the other pavilion contains the girl. The two talk together, but their conversation can scarcely be heard because of the music. It is lawful to break the peace of the night on these occasions. I have been told that at a certain moment the priest enters the girl's pavilion and deflowers her with his hand, dropping the first fruits into a vessel of wine. It is said that the parents of this girl, her relations and neighbours stain their foreheads with this wine, or even taste it. Some also claim that the priest has intercourse with the girl; others deny this. It is hard to ascertain the exact truth as the Chinese are not allowed to witness these proceedings.

At the break of day, the priest is escorted back home with palanquins, parasols and music...

Navigating with ibn Majid (*floreat* 1460)

From "The Eleventh fa'ida" of *Kitab al-fawa'id fi usul al-bahr wa al-qawa'id* (*The Book of Profitable Things and Rules of Navigation*)

This is probably one of the strangest texts in the anthology, but may also be the one that has historically had the greatest importance in the world. A persistent story claims that Ahmad ibn Majid was the person to betray the sea route from East Africa to India to Vasco da Gama. Qutb al-Din al-Nahrawali (1511-82) in his *The Ottoman Conquest of Yemen* wrote that the Portuguese, at a loss as to how to cross the Arabian Sea, "continually sought information regarding this sea until a skillful sailor named Ahmad ibn Majid put himself at their disposal. The leader of the Franks called Almilandi [i.e. Almirante] had become friendly with him and he used to become intoxicated with the Portuguese admiral. This sailor being intoxicated showed the route to the admiral, saying to the Portuguese, 'Do not approach the coast on this part [i.e. the east coast of Africa, north of Malindi]; steer straight for the open sea; you will then reach the coast of India and be sheltered from the waves.'"

This story has been repeated by Western scholars, who have collapsed the author of the nautical treatise and Vasco da Gama's pilot, even though the Portuguese sources at the time (but not da Gama himself) identify the pilot as a "Gujerati Moor". But ibn Majid's English translator G. R. Tibbetts thinks the navigator has been unjustly maligned. His treatise was so famous right up until the nineteenth century among Indian Ocean navigators that his name had become a collective name for pilots, and maybe da Gama just laid his hands on the *fa'ida* (profitable thing, good advice) given below.

The author ibn Majid certainly was not a Gujerati, but a Peninsular Arab, born in Julfar into a family of famous navigators, and operating out of Oman. Over forty different literary works are attributed to him, mostly didactic nautical verse. What seems to have been his last work is the long poem *Al-Sufaliya* (dated 1500), which bewails the advent of the Portuguese in the Indian Ocean and the loss of the world of the Arab–Indian trade which had been ibn Majid's family's for generations.

The shipping connections between India and the Arabian Peninsula and Golf go back to Sumerian times, and the first-century *Arya Sura* famously sees the Buddhisattva in the figure of the perfect pilot:

> He possessed every quality desired in such a one. Knowing the course of the celestial luminaries, he was never at a loss with respect to the regions of the ship, being perfectly acquainted with the different prognostics, the permanent, the occasional and the miraculous ones, he was skilled in the establishment of a given time as proper and improper, by means of manifold marks, observing the fishes, the colour of the water, the species of the ground, birds, rocks, etc. He knew how to ascertain rightly the parts of the sea, further he was vigilant, not subject to drowsiness and sleep, capable of enduring the fatigue of cold, heat, rain and the like, careful and patient. So being skilled in the art of taking a ship out and bringing her home, he exercised the profession of one who conducts the merchants by sea to their destination.

Like sailors everywhere until the advent of the Global Positioning System, ibn Majid would certainly have understood all this, and it is reason enough why a pilot in his day was known as a *mu'allim*, a learned man, a scholar. He may not have been a great literary stylist; both his prose and his use of the *qasida* poetic form for long passages dealing with astronomy and calculation may be stilted; but he certainly shows great learning in poetry and history in his *Fawa'id* (plural of *fa'ida*), even if he begins his history of navigation with the Ark, and claims that the sciences of astronomy and calculation and the astrolabe were invented before Noah by Idris. His criticism of previous Arabic treatises on navigation is sounder: they are the products of theorists; he combines theory with practical experience!

The 12 sections of his book deal with 1) the invention of the compass; 2) the qualities of a pilot; 3) the lunar mansions and the zodiac, compass rhumbs; 4) star lore; 5) miscellaneous; 6) three types of routes, the important collation of route, bearing and latitude; 7) *qiyas*, the measurement of latitude; 8) *isharat*, landmarks and signs and *siyasat*, shipboard policy; 9) a short account of the coasts of the world; 10) description of the important islands; 11) the monsoons, seasons for sailing to India; 12) a description of the Red Sea. Section 11 has been chosen as the most readable and possibly the greatest secret.

[The information in the introduction above and the translation below are taken from G. R. Tibbetts in *Arab Navigation in the Indian Ocean before the Coming of the Portuguese*, Oriental Translation Fund New Series vol. XLII, London: Royal Asiatic Society of Great Britain and Northern Ireland, 1971. Extract reprinted with the kind permission of the Royal Asiatic Society, London.]

The Eleventh *Fa'ida*

The seasons around Soqotra [Suqatra]

The beginning of the season when you can travel to Soqotra from the Arab coast is very difficult for the man who is not conversant with it—from Aden, Yemen and Somalia in the beginning of the Kaws and at the end of it[68] and from al-Atwah and Zafar and India from the beginning of the Saba to the end of it is not difficult. Only from Fartak and Hairij [is it difficult] because one travels to it from all these places in a wind of two sails.[69] They do not travel from Fartak and Hairij, unless the wind is light because they are travelling contrary to the Kaws[70] and hence are not able to use it and also contrary to the Azyab and thus are not able to use that, except with difficulty and taking advantage of breezes and lulls.[71] When you set out to it from al-Shihr the sea is impossible from the 310th to the 20th (28th September–12th December) [f. 73r] of the year and the 343rd (?).[72] In the 360th day (17th November), the Azyab wind blows strongly and you are not able to make it from al-Shihr. It reaches as far as Hairij on the 350th day (7th November) sometimes reaching it and sometimes not. The case of Hairij is similar to the 'wind of two sails' also needing a light wind and it comes to an end after the Shihr season when using the Azyab wind. The Shihri season ends after the Fartak and the Hairiji seasons when using the Kaws wind. Fartak is closed for six months and open for six months and when the Azyab is strong Hairij and Shihr are closed until the 80th day (10th February) and open for the interval between the two winds at the beginning of the Airan.

In the beginning of Kaws, the unexpected can happen from al-Shihr and its neighbourhood until the 170th day (11th May), for there is a strong south wind on its (Soqotra's) landward side[73] and it is no good after this, for the current is then very strong and you tend to be dragged towards the deep sea and you cannot prevail against it. This is a gamble for life and limb, because it comes at the time of the well-known *zuhun*[74] in the north of Soqotra, between the two winds, as far as 6_° P.S. From Shihr and Hairij in the Kaws wind is more successful than from Zafar or Fartak, and Zafar is better in the Azyab wind. The Azyab is a greater (?)[75] season than the Kaws, because the ports under it are not closed by it. No ports are open in the Kaws, because the opening of the outer Ocean is in a Kaws direction and facing the Dabur wind and the south wind while the Saba winds blow from the inhabited part of the world.[76] Understand this wonderful and strange fact, the like of which you will not hear in navigational science from anyone other than me.

From Fartak when you start in the 140th or 150th day (11th, 21st April), [the wind] will bring you to Soqotra, but this is no good from Shihr. It is best to set out from Soqotra to Shihr and Hairij in the 100th day (2nd March) and to Fartak in the 110th -160th day (12th March-1st May) it is no good at other times, for then it is a gamble— and from there to Zafar from the 120th-170th day (22nd March-11th May) and to Gujerat and Hormuz at both ends of the Kaws season. This is sufficient [f. 73v] a description for Soqotra.

Only the very skilful navigator knows the whole of this. There is no doubt that some of this is well known and we have mentioned it in summary form. Not every man tells what he knows...

From the East Indies to Africa and back

Know the occurrences of all seasons and winds. [The season for sailing] from Manaqabuh and Fansur and the ocean side of Sumatra to the African coast begins on the 60th day of the year (21st January) and is not good at any other time. The same applies from Sunda bari and Lasem in Java. The journey from Madagascar to the African coast has two seasons, at the beginning of the Kaws which is a weak season and at the end of the Kaws which is also weak. But the people of all the southern climates, when they wish to sail at the end of the Dabur winds have to put up with rains as far as the equator and this is sufficient [on these monsoons].[77] Similarly with people from Sofala and the estuary region (Akhwar) to the Zanj coast and from the land of Timor to Jawa and the neighbouring places, from Maluku, al-Ghur and Jawa and all the islands of the South; they only travel at the end of the Damani wind, every man in accordance with the suitability of his place and his boat.

The seasons of the land of the Turks are not known properly or those of their northern sea, but we can guess them by their winds which are opposite to our [f. 75v] and their sea is closed when our season opens at the beginning of the Saba winds. This statement is based on the fact that their lands are opposite the Saba wind and its waves in the same way as Zafar is opposite the Kaws wind and its waves, and in the Saba, the land shields us whilst in the Dabur, the land shields them. The skilful navigator should not conceal from himself all the winds and all the seasons of the world for they are derived from the winds unless it be a miracle, for the miracle has no law to itself. So beware always of making landfalls close to the limits of the seasons and know the proper season for every landfall. We will now mention special danger spots when making landfalls. [A detailed list of eight special danger spots follows]…

The seasons of the ancients

As for the seasons of old in which our fathers and grandfathers sailed, various things are said. 'Ali al-Hubbi told me, 'I travelled with your father, the well-known pilot versed in this science, the navigator Majid

b. Muhammad b. 'Amr in the 140th day (11th April?) and by the 160th (1st May?) we were over Soqotra and this was before these days in the beginning of the time of the Karimi merchants and during the Turkish dynasty and the rule of the Beni [Bani] Ghassan,[78] they used to leave Soqotra to the north both coming and going, but now they still leave it so coming and going[79] and in coming from India it appears similar to the mountain of Shihr and thereabout.' They used to have written in their old *rahmanj*,[80] 'When you see the mountain sticking halfway above the water, sound the depth and if there is no bottom it is Soqotra and if it strikes the bottom it is the land of Shihr and that neighbourhood.' They used to travel from al-Atwah to Bengal on the 270th day of the year (19th August?) [f. 77r] and from Aden to India on the 250th (30th July?) and in spite of all this they were never free from the *zuhun* of Shihr. They did not have to endure the 'typhoon' storms at sea because of the strength of the sea all the way from Fartak to India with strong unvarying winds. For the typhoon would not mix with these. For when the end of the season comes and the winds begin to full, typhoon storms begin there. But the *zuhun* of Shihr were worse than the typhoon because of the size of the waves which the strong southern wind drives. This is experienced through the straight between Guardafui and Soqotra. When they experience this it is as if they were in a blazing fire.[81] Now this method and these seasons have changed and not one of the merchants who is left knows about it so that he must ask those who know, all of them, when in need, for some help. Time has betrayed them, as the author has stated in a poem:

> Oh night, time has grudged us thy presence,
>> Whenever peace contends with peace.
> Come let us, carefree, do what thou desirest,
>> For what thou hast always wanted, I will be surety.
> Behold, the maiden of beauty, perfect,
>> A maiden of fourteen, completely matured.
> The wine and the stringed instruments are ready,
>> My good fortune is clear; hence my boasting.

> The turtledove sings on its branch, its voice
> > sways with rapture, living yet tender.
> The surface of the plain blossoms as a rose;[82]
> > the flowers of the meadow as the flowers of Paradise.
> The vine makes a bower with its leaves,
> > And the drinking companions say, 'surely this is the
> > place'.
> I arose then to enjoy the pleasure of youth,
> > Mixing the water of the vine with the water of the
> > tongue.
> I plucked the pomegranate of her breast
> > A fruit from a sapling, pleasing and tender.
> I attained what no one can name
> > What no one else had ever yet attained.
> While the candle which was between us appeared,
> > As a silver spear with a jewelled tip.
> While the tops of the trees waved above us,
> > Shaking as the hearts of cowards,[83]
> Until dawn gave to us the morning,
> > And the worshipper had to hearken to the Mu'ezzin's
> > voice.
> Then the arrow struck us, separating us,
> > Is there a thing which time has not pierced?

Perhaps the sailing seasons are also victims of time for some reason that our minds are not aware of. It has been said that the season gets later every year by one degree, but in every law God is the only one who really knows.

We have mentioned in this book the whole gamut of useful things by which knowing and enquiring men of the past and of the present have profited and can still profit, not omitting any. 'Wisdom is the ambition of the believer. So search out your ambition even from among the Unbelievers.'[84] For this art is of the mind and not of narration. It is desirable that a man should know this and should ask questions on it and even more questions and take the good from it and discard the bad and meditate on the divisions of the season. For if a man miscalculates by a *zam* when calculating sailing dates, he will be held up with the ship and all the possessions in it which he has only accumulated after much hard labour, especially near al-Bab and Fartak and al-Hadd. For a ship setting out with an east wind from al-Hadd will reach Yemen, but another in the bay of Qalhat with an east wind will not reach it, although there is only an hour between the two. Also he who sets out from al-Bab with a southern wind for India and Hormuz, will reach it, but he who is a *zam* inside al-Bab will never do it. One may see the sails of the other [but that is all], especially as the stray breezes become more persistent as the monsoon weakens. Every decision is important when dealing with sailing dates...

Piri Reis: The Voyages of a "Corsair"
From *Kitab-i bahriye* (1526)

Muhuddin Piri Reis was born at the naval base of Gelibolu (later known to "Westerners" as Gallipoli during the First World War) as a nephew of Kemal Reis, the most famous Turkish admiral and privateer or "corsair" of the period. He seems to have joined his uncle's ship at the age of 11 or 12, and participated in many battles and the obligatory piracy all over the Mediterranean. The Turkish Navy at the time, like Queen Elizabeth's English Navy later, passed from war to piracy as the situation warranted, and the Reises became popular heroes like Raleigh, Drake and Frobisher. Piri Reis first gained fame as a ship's commander in the Turco-Venetian War (1499-1502) and served as an officer of the Turkish Navy under the reign of Sultans Bayezid II and Selim I and part of the reign of Süleyman I, while he continued his studies of map-making, geography and other navigational matters.

Sometime around 1500 Piri Reis came into possession of a copy of Columbus's portolan of his "discoveries" in the "West Indies", and his main claim to subsequent fame is that he became the first to draw an accurate map of the American coastline in c. 1513, including Cabot's and Cabral's discoveries of the North and South American continents. A Turkish map in Arabic script thus predates the first accurate European maps by a decade, which shows both the top secret nature of maps at the time and the close connections between "West" and "East" in the Mediterranean that our modern conceptual geography often tends to forget. Piri Reis's knowledge of the "New World" was by no means first-hand, however, as is also clear from the excerpts from his *Kitab-i bahriye* given below. In his lifetime the American map was no doubt less important than his map of the Nile Delta, which he presented to Sultan Selim on his visit to the newly conquered Alexandria in 1517.

The other side of European expansion became Piri Reis's fate. In

1547 he was appointed Hind Kaptanligi, Admiral of the Turkish Navy in the Indian Ocean, which had been greatly expanded in 1525 to combat the activities of the Portuguese. In 1548 he conquered the main strategic forts of the Sheikh of Aden, who was an ally of the Portuguese, and in 1552 he recaptured the castle of Muscat from the Portuguese with a fleet of 30 Mediterranean galleys ranged against 70 Portuguese ships, many of them heavy caravels. Having suffered heavy losses he retreated to Basra for help, but was refused by the Ottoman Governor there. When he finally made his way back through the Straits of Hormuz and Bab al-Mandab to Suez with two ships, Pirî Reis, by then well into his eighties, was executed for abandoning his command.

The *Kitab-i bahriye*, presented to Sultan Süleyman I in 1526, contains Pirî Reis's maps and his descriptions of all the parts of the world; in the case of the Mediterranean all of it was based on first-hand knowledge. The first part, concerned with the general shape of the world, the main seas, islands, continents and seaports and the importance of the science of map-making as practised by the Franks, is written in rhyming couplets. The excerpt given below is the end of this first part, before the text shifts to prose for the description of the Mediterranean.

[This transcreation is based on the translation by Robert Bragner from the official Turkish edition of the book, *Kitab-i bahriye*, Historical Research Foundation, Istanbul Research Center, Istanbul: 1988, edited by Ertugrol Zekâi Ökte. The information above comes mainly from the Introduction by Mert Bayat.]

Pirî Reis (1470–1554)

From *Kitab-i bahriye* (*The Book of the Sea*) (1526)

(The Chapter of the Sea known as the Sea of Maghrib)

Having heard of the Sea of Zenc, hear now
Of Maghrib Sea: earlier no one knew how

Vast 'twas or what its watery depths contained.
But now they have discovered all that remained
Hidden from sight, for such was Almighty's grand
Design: its shores are bordered with land.
No small island this, hear the truth I say,
They traced its rim through many nights and days
And looked for limits and its end in vain.
They knew then 'twas no isle but a vast main.
These lands are southwest from where we are,
They lie four thousand miles from Gibraltar.
Those who have been there and have returned file
Their distance at two hundred thirty mile.
Eight hundred and seventy years from the flight
To Medina this land did come to sight,
Or that is what historians write in all:
Antilles is what this land they call.

(The Chapter of the Strange Circumstances of the Sea of Maghrib and its Goods)

Hear now of what those lands reveal or hoard:
What is there man's? All things are from the Lord.
There's gold in mountains of that new country,
And pearls four fathoms deep in the blue sea.
Four parrot species there are: black, red, white
And green, and one that is variously pied.
Some have reported of men whose two eyes
Are least a span across, on each head lies
A cap of parrot wool. Their faces slant
Or flat, their brows apart. They live off plant.
Their headdresses of wool much decorated:
One cap we saw ourselves when we were fated
To board a boat from them captured. Those days
We roamed the Mediterranean's wide ways
And fought relentlessly the faithless foe.

On that captured ship, friend, believe me, know,
We found a blackish stone like a touchstone
With which they struck iron, O God alone
Can tell what it was, for it sliced iron
Like butter, and remained unbroken, one.
I simply narrate what my eyes did see.
Such stones are found in that distant country:
They chop their firewood with such stone. They feed
Off vegetation, grasses, leaves and weed,
And naked like an animal they cross one's track.
Their mouths when open seem to be all black.
What reason for this, well may you ask, friend:
Their gums and teeth are surely blackened
By leaves they eat. No religion, no rite
They have; some live in caves away from light,
Savages all. But now the Spanish are
Amidst them, having come from so far,
The warlike Spanish infidel,
To turn the savages faithless as well.

The Ambivalence of al-Hasan or Leo Africanus

Introduced by Pekka Masonen

From *Cosmographia & Geographia de Affrica* (1526)

The man we know as Leo Africanus was born in Granada in 1494. His background was not particularly important, though he was seemingly proud of his Granadan ancestry. He did not, however, stay for long in Granada, as his parents moved soon to Morocco. Contrary to popular belief, they were not driven to exile by the intolerant Spanish policy towards the Muslim population in Granada but rather followed the example set by the noble families of the city. Boabdil, the last Muslim ruler of Granada, had already emigrated to Morocco in 1493. Leo's family settled in Fez where he studied at the Islamic university of al-Qarawiyyin. After his studies, Leo entered the service of the Wattasid Sultan of Fez. All we know about Leo's early life is based on the few autobiographical remarks in his own work.

According to his own words, Leo began his itinerant career in 1507-8, when he visited the eastern Mediterranean. In the winter of 1509-10, Leo accompanied one of his uncles on a diplomatic mission to Timbuktu. Two years later he allegedly revisited Timbuktu, though this time on personal affairs. From Timbuktu, he claimed to have extended his travels to Jenne, Mali, Hausaland, and Bornu and thence to Egypt, returning to Fez in 1514. From Morocco, Leo extended his wanderings to Algeria and Tunisia, including a visit to Constantinople. In the spring of 1517, he was in Rosetta where he witnessed the Ottoman conquest of Egypt. He then proceeded to Arabia. Leo was returning to Tunis, when he was captured by Spanish corsairs in the Greek waters in June 1518. As there are no independent sources on Leo prior to his capture, we cannot rule out the possibility that some parts of his adventures may represent a literary invention by a cunning captive who wanted to make himself appear as more interesting—and more important—in the eyes of his captors.

At first Leo was taken to Rhodes, the headquarters of the Knights of St. John, but he was soon transferred to Rome where he was presented to the magnificent Medici Pope Leo X (1513-21) who was planning a crusade to North Africa. From this point of view, the appearance of a learned Moroccan who was willing to provide the Pope and his counsellors with accurate information of North Africa was certainly like a gift from heaven. Leo was freed and given a pension. Moreover, he agreed to convert to Christianity and was baptized on 6 January 1520, receiving the name Johannes Leo de Medicis, or Giovanni Leone in Italian—according to his noble patron—or Yuhanna al-Asad al-Gharnati, as he called himself in Arabic ("John Leo of Granada"). It seems that he took the epithet "Affricano" (African). In sixteenth-century European geography, the toponym Africa meant Mediterranean Africa only (or the Barbary Coast, as it was commonly called), whereas sub-Saharan Africa was referred to as Guinea or Ethiopia. We do not know what made Leo accept his fate so easily, but his behaviour was not extraordinary among Muslim captives in Italy or Christian captives in North Africa.

Following the death of his patron, Leo Africanus left Rome. One reason was probably that the new Pope, Adrian VI (1522-23), the former imperial viceroy of Spain, was suspicious about the presence of a converted Morisco at the papal court. Another reason was certainly the outbreak of plague which killed nearly half of Rome's population. Leo settled in Bologna, where he befriended Jacob Mantino, a Jewish physician and refugee from Spain. Leo was always delighted when he met other refugees from Granada during his travels and he certainly sympathized with Mantino who had also lost his native land. With the help of Mantino, Leo prepared an Arabic-Hebrew-Latin medical vocabulary, of which the Arabic part has survived. This manuscript is now preserved at the Escorial Library in Spain (Ms. Arabo 598) and it contains Leo's autograph, which is one of the few existing sources for his original Arabic name: al-Hasan b. Muhammad al-Wazzan.

It is not known if Leo Africanus was travelling elsewhere in Northern Italy or beyond the Alps. He returned to Rome by 1526, living there under the protection of the new Medici Pope Clement VII (1523-34). He must have left Rome again before the sack of the city by the imperial forces in early May 1527. Subsequently, he escaped to Tunis where he is customarily believed to have spent the final years of his life. Considering, however, that Leo had no personal connection to the city and that he had reconverted to Islam, he hardly wanted to witness the Spanish conquest of Tunis in 1535 (though it is suggested that he might have died in this conquest). Against this background, it is probable that Leo Africanus eventually returned to Fez where his relatives were still living.

Leo Africanus completed his magisterial work on African geography, according to his own words, in Rome, on 10 March 1526. It seems that Leo wrote his work directly in Italian, though he may have relied on Arabic notes which he could have composed during his travels. An Italian manuscript version of Leo's work was found in 1931 and it was purchased by the Biblioteca Nazionale in Rome (Ms. VE 953). The style in this manuscript (entitled *Cosmographia & Geographia de Affrica*) differs greatly from that of the Italian printed edition, but the manuscript clearly represents the original text written by Leo himself. The manuscript is still unpublished save some extracts. The importance of the manuscript is that it conveys Leo's own voice better than the printed version which portrays his editor's rendering of him.

Leo's work was printed at Venice in 1550, bearing the title *Descrittione dell'Africa*. It was incorporated in the first volume of the anthology of travels and discoveries, *Delle navigationi et viaggi*, edited by Giovanni Battista Ramusio (1485-1557). This anthology was an immediate success and several reprints followed. Leo's text was also translated into major European languages: French and Latin versions appeared both in 1556; an English one in 1600; a Dutch in 1665; a German in 1805. Modern times have produced more translations in Castilian, Russian, Hausa, and Arabic.

The principal reason for the popularity of Leo's work was that there were not many rival sources for North African geography available. According to a contemporary reader, Leo Africanus discovered a new world for Europeans, just like Columbus had found

America. This especially concerns Leo's description of Sudanic Africa. One of the most exciting elements was Timbuktu which Leo pictured as a centre of the West African gold trade. This image turned in the hands of his later copyists into a vision of an African Zipangu, which had an important impact in the beginning on the European exploration of the West African interior at the end of the eighteenth century. Leo maintained his authoritative position until the British and French explorers, such as Mungo Park and René Caillié, brought more reliable information on the area.

Despite its title, Leo's work is not a comprehensive exposition of Africa. The emphasis is on the Barbary Coast and especially on Morocco. The description of Fez alone takes as much space as the two sections reserved for Tunisia and Libya. As to the rest of the continent, Leo's knowledge was limited to Sudanic Africa. He wrote nothing about the West African coast, the Congo, or Christian Ethiopia, which were already familiar to European readers from the Portuguese reports. As to the approach, Leo's work represents the literary genre of "the routes and realms" which was favoured by medieval Arabic authors. On the other hand, a similar approach was also used by many Renaissance scholars, such as Olaus Magnus in his description of the northern peoples (*Historia de Gentibus Septentrionalibus*, Rome 1555), who considered geography, ethnography, and history inseparable subjects.

The perspective is throughout Islamic and Moroccan, though Leo was clever enough not to jeopardize the benevolence of his patrons by praising his native land and Islam too far. At the same time he was also careful enough not to endanger his reputation among the Muslims by defaming his native land and Islam. Leo clearly understood his delicate position between the worlds, though the antagonism in his work is not necessarily Islamic/Christian or Moroccan/Italian but rather Granadan/North African and urban Arab/rural Other. He drew many parallels between Morocco and Italy—partly to make his description better understandable to European readers, but also because the urban culture of Renaissance Italy was in his eyes equal to the sophisticated urban culture of the great North African cities, which Leo considered the paragon of civilized life. He felt no sympathy towards those who lived outside the civilized world: the black Africans were mere savages, as were the nomadic Berbers. Their negative images in Leo's description reflect the prejudice of an urban Arab rather than the values of contemporary European culture.

Scholarly interest in Leo Africanus was revitalized by Amin Maalouf's acclaimed historical novel which was published first in French in 1986 (*Léon l'Africain*). An English translation appeared in 1988 (*Leo the African*). Following the popularity of this novel, some Moroccan scholars have begun to pay attention to Leo and now, after over four hundred years, they finally accept him as part of their cultural heritage.

[Sources: Pekka Masonen, "Leo Africanus: The Man with Many Names", *Al-Andalus-Magreb. Revista de estudios árabes e islámicos y grupo de investigación al-Andalus–Magreb*, viii–ix, fasc. 1 (2000–2001), pp. 115–143; Dietrich Rauchenberger, *Johannes Leo der Afrikaner. Seine Beschreibung des Raumes zwischen Nil und Niger nach dem Urtext*, Wiesbaden 1999: Orientalia Biblica et Christiana 13; Oumelbanine Zhiri, *L'Afrique au miroir de l'Europe: fortunes de Jean-Léon l'Africain à la Renaissance*, Geneva 1991: Travaux d'Humanisme et Renaissance, no. 247.]

Selected extracts from Leo Africanus's *Cosmographia & Geographia de Affrica*

The commendable actions and virtues of the Africans

Those Arabs who inhabit Barbary or the coast of the Mediterranean Sea are greatly addicted to the study of good arts and sciences, and those things that concern their law and religion are esteemed by them in the first place. Moreover, they have been heretofore most studious of Mathematics, Philosophy and Astrology; but these arts (as it is aforesaid) were four hundred years ago utterly destroyed and taken away by the chief professors of their law. The inhabitants of cities do

most religiously observe and reverence those things that appertain to
their religion: yea, they honour those doctors and priests, of whom
they learn their law, as if they were petty gods. Their Churches they
frequent very diligently, to the end they may repeat certain prescript
and formal prayers; most superstitiously persuading themselves that
the same day wherein they make their prayers, it is not lawful for them
to wash certain of their members, when as at other times they will
wash their whole bodies... Moreover the inhabitants of Barbary are
of great cunning and dexterity for building and for mathematical
inventions, which a man may easily conjecture by their artificial
works. Most honest people they are, and destitute of all fraud and
guile; not only embracing all simplicity and truth, but also practising
the same throughout the whole course of their lives: albeit certain
Latin authors, who have written of the same regions, are far otherwise
of opinion. Likewise they are most strong and valiant people,
especially those who dwell on the mountains. They keep their
covenant most faithfully; insomuch that they would rather die than
break a promise. No nation in the world is so subject to jealousy[85]; for
they would rather lose their lives than put up with any disgrace to
their women. So desirous they are of riches and honour that therein
no other people can go beyond them. They travel in a manner over
the whole world to exercise traffic[86]. For they are continually to be
seen in Egypt, in Ethiopia, in Arabia, Persia, India, and Turkey: and
whithersoever they go, they are most honourably esteemed of: for
none of them will possess any art, unless he has attained unto great
exactness and perfection therein. They have always been much
delighted with all kind of civility and modest behaviour: and it is
accounted heinous among them for any man to utter in company, any
bawdy or unseemly word. They have always in mind this sentence of
a great author: Give place to thy superior. If any youth in presence of
his father, his uncle, or any other of his kindred, does sing or talk of
loud matters, he is deemed to be worthy of grievous punishment.
Whatever lad or youth once chances into any company that
discourses of love, withdraws from them no sooner than he has heard
or understood what their talk tends towards. These are the things

which we thought most worthy of relation as concerning the civility, humanity, and upright dealing of the Barbarians: let us now proceed unto the residue. Those Arabians that dwell in tents, that is to say, that bring up cattle, are of a more liberal and civil disposition: to wit, they are in their kind as devout, valiant, patient, courteous, hospitable, and as honest in life and conversation as any other people. They are most faithful observers of their word and promise; insomuch that the people, which before we said to dwell in the mountains, are greatly stirred up with emulation of their virtues. However the said mountaineers, both for learning, for virtue, and for religion, are thought much inferior to the Numidians, albeit they have little or no knowledge at all in natural philosophy. They are reported likewise to be most skilful warriors, to be valiant, and exceeding lovers and practitioners of all humanity. Also, the Moors and Arabians inhabiting Libya are somewhat civil of behaviour, being plain dealers, void of dissimulation, favourable to strangers, and lovers of simplicity. Those that we earlier named white, or tawny Moors, are steadfast in friendship, as likewise the indifferently and favourably esteem of other nations, and wholly endeavour themselves in this one thing, namely, that they may lead a most pleasant and jocund life. Moreover they maintain most learned professors of liberal arts, and such men are most devout in their religion. Neither is there any people in all Africa that lead a more happy and honourable life.

What vices the foresaid Africans are subject to

Never was there any people or nation so perfectly endowed with virtue, but that they had their contrary faults and blemishes: now therefore let us consider whether the vices of the Africans do surpass their virtues and good parts. Those that we named the inhabitants of the cities of Barbary are somewhat needy and covetous, being also very proud and high-minded, and wonderfully addicted unto wrath; insomuch that (according to the proverb) they will deeply engrave in marble any injury be it never so small, and will in no wise blot it out of remembrance. So rustic they are and void of good manners, that scarcely can any stranger obtain their familiarity and friendship.

Their wits are but mean, and they are so credulous, that they will believe matters impossible, which are told them. So ignorant are they of natural philosophy, that they imagine all the effects and operations of nature to be extraordinary and divine. They observe no certain order of living nor of laws. Abounding exceedingly with choler, they speak always with an angry and loud voice. Neither shall you walk in the day-time in any of their streets, but you shall see commonly two or three of them together by the ears. By nature they are a vile and base people, being no better accounted of by their governors than if they were dogs. They have neither judges nor lawyers, by whose wisdom and counsel they ought to be directed. They are utterly unskilful in trades of merchandise, being destitute of bankers and money-changers: wherefore a merchant can do nothing among them in his absence, but is himself constrained to go in person whithersoever his wares are carried. No people under heaven are more addicted to covetousness than this nation: neither is there (I think) to be found among them one of a hundred, who for courtesy, humanity or devotion's sake will vouchsafe any entertainment to a stranger. Mindful they have always been of injuries, but most forgetful of benefits...The shepherds of that region live a miserable, toilsome, wretched and beggarly life: they are a rude people, and (as a man may say) born and bred to theft, deceit, and brutish manners. Their young men may go a-wooing diverse maids, till such time as they have obtained a wife. Yea, the father of the maid most friendly welcomes her suitor: so that I think scarce any noble or gentleman among them can choose a virgin for his spouse: albeit, so soon as any woman is married, she is quite forsaken of all her suitors; who then seek out other paramours for their liking. Concerning their religion, the greater part of these people are neither Mohammedans [Muslims], Jews, nor Christians; and hardly shall you find so much as a spark of piety in any of them. They have no churches at all, nor any kind of prayers, but being utterly estranged from all godly devotion, they lead a savage and beastly life: and if any man chances to be of a better disposition (because they have no law-givers nor teachers among them) he is constrained to follow the example of other men's lives and manners. All the Numidians being most ignorant of natural, domestic and commonwealth-matters, are principally addicted to treason, treachery, murder, theft, and robbery. This nation, because it is most slavish, will right gladly accept any service among the Barbarians, be it never so vile and contemptible…Likewise the inhabitants of Libya live a brutish kind of life, neglecting all kinds of good arts and sciences. Never as yet had they any religion, any laws, or any good form of living…They spend all their days either in most lewd practices, or in hunting, or else in warfare: neither wear they shoes nor garments. The Negroes likewise lead a beastly kind of life, being utterly destitute of the use of reason, of dexterity of wit, and of all arts. Yea they so behave themselves, as if they had continually lived in a forest among wild beasts. They have great swarms of harlots among them; whereupon a man may easily conjecture their manner of living: except their conversation be somewhat more tolerable, who dwell in the principal towns and cities, for it is like that they are somewhat more addicted to civility.

Neither am I ignorant, how much mine own credit is impeached, when I myself write some homely [negatively] of Africa, to which country I stand indebted both for my birth, and also for the best part of my education: Howbeit in this regard I seek not to excuse myself, but only to appeal to the duty of a historiographer, who is to set down the plain truth in all places, and is blame-worthy for flattering or favouring any person. And this is the cause that has moved me to describe all things so plainly without glossing or dissimulation: wherefore here I am to request the gentle Reader, friendly to accept of this my most true discourse, (albeit not adorned with fine words and artificial eloquence) as of certain unknown strange matters…

…For mine own part, when I hear Africans evil spoken of, I affirm myself to be one of Granada: and when I perceive the nation of Granada to be discommended, then I profess myself to be an African. But herein the Africans shall be the most beholden to me; for that I only record their principal and notorious vices, omitting the smaller and more tolerable faults.

Of the kingdom of Tombuto [Timbuctoo]

This name was in our times (as some think) imposed upon this kingdom from the name of a certain town so called, which (they say) Mense Suleiman founded in the year of the Hegeira 610[87], and it is situated within twelve miles of a certain branch of Niger, all the houses whereof are now changed to cottages built of chalk, and covered with thatch. Howbeit there is a stately temple to be seen, the walls whereof are made of stone and lime; and a princely palace also built by a most excellent workman of Granada. Here are many shops of artificers, and merchants, and especially of such as weave linen and cotton cloth. And hither do the Barbary-merchants bring cloth of Europe. All the women of this region except maid-servants go with their faces covered, and sell all necessary victuals. The inhabitants and specially the strangers there residing are exceedingly rich, insomuch that the [current] King [has] married both his daughters to rich merchants. Here are many wells, containing most sweet water; and so often as the river Niger overflows, they convey its water by certain sluices into the town. Corn, cattle, milk, and butter this region yields in abundance: but salt is very scarce here; for it is brought hither by land from Tegaza, which is five hundred miles distant. When I myself was here, I saw one camel-load of salt sold for 80 ducats. The rich king of Tombuto has many plates and sceptres of gold, whereof some weigh 1300 pounds; and he keeps a magnificent and well-furnished court. When he travels anywhere, he rides upon a camel, which is lead by some of his noblemen; and so does he when he goes to war, while all his soldiers ride on horses. Whosoever will speak to this king must first fall down before his feet, and then taking up earth must sprinkle it upon his own head and shoulders: which custom is ordinarily observed by them that never saluted the king before, or come as Ambassadors from other princes. He has always three thousand horsemen, and a great number of footmen that shoot poisoned arrows, attending upon him. They have often skirmishes with those that refuse to pay tribute, and so many as they take, they sell unto the merchants of Tombuto. Here are very few horses bred, and the merchants and courtiers keep certain nags which they use to travel on:

but their best horses are brought from Barbary. And the king so soon as he hears that any merchants are come to town with horses, he commands a certain number to be brought before him, and choosing the best horse for himself, he pays a most liberal price for it. He so deadly hates all Jews that he will not admit any into his city, and whosoever Barbary merchants he understands have dealings with the Jews, he presently causes their goods to be confiscated. Here are great store of doctors, judges, priests, and other learned men, that are bountifully maintained at the king's cost and charges. And hither are brought diverse manuscripts or written books out of Barbary, which are sold for more money than any other merchandise. The coin of Tombuto is of gold without any stamp or inscription; but in matters of small value they use certain shells brought hither out of the kingdom of Persia, four hundred of which shells are worth a ducat, and six pieces of their golden coins with two third parts weigh an ounce. The inhabitants are people of a gentle and cheerful disposition, and spend a great part of the night in singing and dancing through all the streets of the city; they keep great store of men and women slaves, and their town is much in danger of fire: at my second stay there, half the town almost was burnt in five hours space. Without the suburbs there are no gardens nor orchards at all.

Of the customs, rites, and fashions of the citizens of Cairo

The inhabitants of Cairo are people of a merry, jocund and cheerful disposition, such as will promise much but perform little. They exercise merchandise and mechanical arts, and yet they do not travel out of their own native soil. Many students there are of the laws, but very few of other liberal arts and sciences. And albeit their colleges are continually full of students, yet few attain perfection. The citizens in winter are clad in garments of cloth lined with cotton: in summer they wear fine shirts, over which shirts some put on linen garments curiously wrought with silk and others wear garments of chamblet and upon their heads they carry great turbans covered with cloth of India. The women go costly attired, adorning their foreheads and necks with frontlets and chains of pearls, and on their heads they wear a sharp and slender bonnet of a span high, being very pretty and rich. Gowns they wear of woollen cloth with straight sleeves, being curiously embroidered with needlework, over which they cast certain veils of most excellent fine cloth of India. They cover their heads and faces with a kind of black scarf, through which beholding others they cannot be seen themselves. Upon their feet they wear fine shoes and pantofles, somewhat after the Turkish fashion. These women are so ambitious and proud that all of them disdain either to spin or cook: whereof their husbands are constrained to buy victuals ready made at cook shops: for very few, except such as have a great family, prepare or dress their victuals in their own houses. Also they vouchsafe great liberty to their wives: for the good man being gone to the tavern or victualling-house, his wife tricking up herself in costly apparel, and being perfumed with sweet and pretty odours, walks the city to solace herself and parley with her kinsfolk and friends. They ride upon asses more than horses, which are broken to such gentle pace that they go easier than any ambling horse. These asses they cover with most costly furniture, and let them out unto women to ride upon, together with a boy to lead the ass, and certain footmen to run by. In this city, like in diverse others, great store of people carry about sundry kinds of victuals to be sold. Many there are also that sell water, which they carry up and down in certain leather bags upon the backs of camels: for the city (as I said before) is two miles distant from the Nile. Others carry about a more fine and handsome vessel with a cock or spout of brass on it, having a cup of Myrrhe or crystal in their hands, and these sell water for men to drink, and for every draught they take a farthing. Others sell young chickens and others fowls by measure, which they hatch after a wonderful and strange manner. They put great numbers of eggs into certain ovens built upon sundry lofts, which ovens being moderately heated will within seven days convert all the said eggs into chickens… The cook shops stand open very late, but the shops of other artificers shut up before ten of the clock, who then walk abroad for their solace and recreation from one suburb to another. The citizens in their common talk use ribald and filthy speech: and (that I may pass over the rest in silence) it often falls about that the wife complains of her husband to the judge that he does not do his duty or fails to content her sufficiently at night, whereupon (as is permitted by Mahumetan [Muslim] law) the women are divorced and married unto other husbands. Among the artisans whosoever is the first inventor of any new and ingenious device is clad in a garment of cloth of gold, and carried with a noise of musicians after him, as it were in triumph from shop to shop, having some money given to him at every place. I myself once saw one carried about with solemn music and with great pomp and triumph, because he had bound a flea in a chain, which lay before him on a piece of paper for all men to behold. And if any of them chance to fall out in the streets, they presently go to buffets [come to blows], and then a great number of people come flocking about them to see the conflict, and will not depart thence till they have reconciled them. Their most usual food is buffles [buffalo?] flesh and great store of pulse: when they go to dinner or supper, if their family be little, they lay a short and round tablecloth, but if their household be great, they spread a large cloth, such as is used in the halls of princes...

[The above extracts have been selected from the following book, with the spelling and syntax minimally revised to bring it closer to contemporary usages of English: *The History and Description of Africa and of the Notable Things Therein Contained, Written by Al-Hassan ibn-Mohammed Al-Wezaz Al-Fasi, a Moor, Baptised as Giovanni Leone, but better known as Leo Africanus. Done into English in the Year 1600 by John Pory, and now edited, with an introduction by Dr Robert Brown.* Originally published by the Hakluyt Society and reprinted in three volumes by Burt Franklin, Publisher, New York.]

AUTOBIOGRAPHIES, DIARIES
&
MEMOIRS

Memoirs of a Syrian Prince-Polymath

From *al-Mukhtasar fī akhbâr al-bashar* (*A Short History of Mankind*)

There is a crater on the moon called Abulfeda. It was named in honour of Ismail Abu al-Fidâ (1273-1331), a Syrian prince, warrior, poet and polymath. However, the honour ought not to mislead us regarding Abu al-Fidâ's significance in scientific terms: he was one of the many aristocrat-scholars who lived in the centuries of Muslim dominance, not really a leading scholar, poet or scientist of his place or age. And yet, he left behind a number of books, including a book that is partly a memoir describing his services, battles and travels, as well as important historical events. Two of his works gained significant popularity in the Middle East and, a bit later, in Europe as compendia of the latest knowledge in geography and history.

Abu'l-Fida was born in November-December 1273 in Damascus: his family had fled Syria owing to strong reports of a Mongol invasion. As P. M. Holt puts it in the only available translation of the "memoir" sections of Abu'l-Fida's history compendium, "During the first thirty years of the lifetime of Abu al-Fidâ, the [newly established] Mamluk sultanate was an embattled power... and Muslim Syria, a salient into enemy territory, was always the base for the Holy War, and sometimes its theatre."[88] The Mamluks—basically a centralized military aristocracy of slaves—were faced with two threats, the greater one of Mongol invasions and the lesser one of Frankish crusades. By the end of Abu'l-Fida's lifetime—during the peaceful third reign of al-Nâsir Muhammad, considered by many to be the zenith of the Mamluk sultanate—the Mongols had converted to Islam and the Frankish threat had been significantly reduced. Among the points of human interest in Abu'l-Fida's memoirs are the hidden traces of genuine and deep friendship between the author and his superior, the Sultan al-Nâsir Muhammad.

P. M. Holt points out that "like other educated men of his time, Abu'l-Fida was a polymath and a poet."[89] He took serious interest in the sciences, especially medicine, geography, astronomy and mathematics, and seems to have tried to gain knowledge all through his active career as a warrior, governor and, finally, the ruler of the small but crucially located principality, Hamâ. Abu'l-Fida versified a legal treatise and two of his works were studied well into the seventeenth century in Europe. These were his geography, *Taqwîm al-buldân* (*Survey of the Countries*), in which he used astronomically determined locations and recorded the longitudinal position of places. It should be noted here that, according to some scholars, Europeans were unable to determine the longitude until the eighteenth century and, in any case, Europeans owed their knowledge of longitude to Arabs and the Chinese. Selections from *Taqwîm al-buldân* were translated into Latin by John Greaves, the Oxford astronomer and mathematician, in 1650.

The other book by Abu'l-Fida that gained popularity as a compendium in the Middle East and Europe was *al-Mukhtasar fî akhbâr al-bashar* (*A Short History of Mankind*), again used by European historians as late as the seventeenth and eighteenth centuries. The part of *al-Mukhtasar fî akhbâr al-bashar* that continues to be of interest to us is its fourth and final section, which provides us with both the history of the Mamluk sultanate and an account of the life and times of Abu'l-Fida. The extracts below are taken from that section, translated and published as *The Memoirs of a Syrian Prince*, a book of about 100 pages, by the historian P. M. Holt in 1983. Holt states that his translation is based on the Cairo reprint of the Istanbul edition of Abu'l-Fida's book. A summary French translation by W. MacGuckin de Slane also exists but, according to Holt, it contains "numerous omissions".

The memoir part of *al-Mukhtasar fî akhbâr al-bashar* recounts the principal events of Abu'l-Fida's life from the thirteenth year to three years before his death. Holt states that Abu'l-Fida refers to himself before he turned 13 only once and quotes Abu'l-Fida thus: "In the year there were strong reports that the Mongols would invade Syria, and the people fled in panic. In it, in jumâdâ I [November–December 1273] was born the humble writer of this short story, Ismâ'îl b. Ali b. Mahmûd b. Muhammad b. Umar b. Shahanshah b. Ayyub, in the house of ibn al-Zanjîlî in Damascus the divinely protected, for our family had fled from Hamâ to Damascus because of the reports of the Mongols." Abu'l-Fida and his family, a branch of the princely Ayyubids who had ruled not only Hamâ but also Egypt, Aleppo etc. in the recent past, were to return to Syria soon. Even though the Mamluks had replaced the Ayyubids, in later years, the Ayyubid Abu'l-Fida was to reach a very good understanding with the Mamluk Sultan, al-Nâsir Muhammad. After supporting al-Nâsir's successful bid to regain the sultanate in 1310, Abu'l-Fida was returned to Hamâ as the governor of the principality that his family had ruled in the past. Two years later—and this is further evidence of the trust and affection between the two men—al Nâsir recognized Abu'l-Fida as an autonomous ruler, the Sultan of Hamâ. On Abu'l-Fida's death, al-Nâsir respected his friend's wishes and ensured that Abu'l-Fida's son, Muhammad, who is often mentioned in the memoirs, succeeded Abu'l-Fida as the Sultan of Hamâ. But soon afterwards Sultan al-Nâsir died himself and the position of Abu'l-Fida's son crumbled: he was asked to move to Damascus as a military officer by the new Sultan. With that, the last Ayyubid "sultanate", long effectively powerless and restored only by the generosity of the overlord Mamluk sultan, came to an end.

Abu al-Fidâ's memoirs contain two basic types of travel narratives, reports that he has heard from other travellers (extract 1) and accounts that take us through many of his own marches and travels (the other two extracts). In this, they are not atypical: a similar travel-based memoir by Babur, the first Mughal emperor of India, is also extracted in this anthology. These two selections are meant to stand in for many such accounts well into the eighteenth century: accounts in which travel might not have been aesthetically or discursively privileged, but still accounts of travel of a different type in a different time and place.

[Selections from *Memoirs of a Syrian Prince*, translated with an introduction by P. M. Holt, Wiesbaden: Franz Steiner Verlag Gmbh, 1983. Some of the footnotes have been omitted or simplified for a general readership. Reproduced with the kind permission of the publisher, Franz Steiner Verlag of Stuttgart, Germany.]

[First Extract:]

On 28 *shawwâl* of this year 697 [8 August 1298] died the learned scholar Shaykh Jamâl al-Dîn Muhammad b. Salim b. Wâsil, the chief Shâf'î judge of the divinely guarded Hamâ. He was born in the year 604 [1207-8], and was an eminent master, outstanding in many sciences, such as logic, geometry, theology, jurisprudence, astronomy and history. He was the author of good books including *Mufarrij al-kurûb fî akhbâr banî ayyûb and al-Anbrûriyya fî al-mantiq*, which he wrote for the emperor, the king of the Franks, the lord of Sicily, when he, the judge Jamâl al-Dîn, went as Ambassador to him in the days of al-Malik al-Zâhir Baybars al-Sâlihî. He made a good abridgement of al-Aghânî, and wrote other works. I visited him many a time in Hamâ, and used to show him the problems I had solved in Euclid, and learn from him. I likewise read under his instruction his commentary on the *Manzûma* of ibn al-Hâjib on prosody, for indeed Jamâl al-Dîn wrote a good detailed commentary on this *Manzûma*...

He went to the emperor as Ambassador from al-Malik al-Zâhir Baybars, the lord of Egypt and Syria in the year 659 [1261]. The meaning of the Frankish word "emperor" [*inbaratûr*] is "king of the commanders" [malik al-umarâ]. His kingdom is the island of Sicily and Apulia and Lombardy on the long mainland. Jamâl al-Dîn said, "The father of the emperor whom I saw was called Frederick, and he was on good terms with the sultan al-Malik al-Kâmil. Then that Frederick died in the year 648 [1250-1], and there succeeded to rule over Sicily and the other parts on the mainland his son Conrad. Then Conrad died, and was succeeded by his brother Manfred, son of Frederick. Each of them who reigns is called 'emperor'. Among the kings of the Franks, the emperor was on good terms with the Muslims, and loved the sciences."

He said, "When I reached the Emperor Manfred, he received me honourably, and I stayed with him in one of the towns of the long mainland adjacent to Andalusia, a town of Apulia. I had several meetings with him, and found him a man of distinction, a lover of the rational sciences, who knew by heart ten theorems of Euclid."

He said, "Near the town I was in was a city called Lucera[90], all the inhabitants of which are Muslims of the island of Sicily. They keep up the Friday prayer, and display openly the tokens of Islam."

He said, "I found that the greatest companions of the Emperor Manfred were Muslims. The call of the muezzin and the prayer were openly practised in his camp. From the town where I was, Rome was a five days' journey."

He said, "After my leaving the emperor, the Pope (the caliph of the Franks) and the king of France agreed to seek out the emperor to fight him. The Pope had excommunicated him. All this was because of the emperor's leaning towards the Muslims. His brother, Conrad, and his father, Frederick, were likewise excommunicated by the Pope of Rome because of their leaning towards Islam."

He said, "When I was with him, he told me that the position of emperor was held before Frederick by his father. When Frederick's father died, Frederick was a growing youth; and a group of the kings of the Franks had designs on the Empire, each of them hoping that the Pope would bestow it on him. Frederick was a wily youth from the German nation. He had a meeting with each of the kings who wanted to take the Empire for himself, and said to him, 'I am not competent for this position, nor do I want it. When we meet the Pope, then say, "The spokesman in this matter should be the son of the late emperor, and I am satisfied with whoever he is satisfied to award the Empire to." Then if the Pope passes the choice in that to me, I will choose you and no-one else. My purpose is to be associated with you.' He spoke in this way to everyone of the kings separately; they gave him credence, trusted him and believed in his sincerity. When they met with the Pope in the city of Rome, Frederick being with them, the Pope said to those kings, 'Whom have you in mind in the matter of this position, and who is the most worthy of it?' He placed the crown of the kingdom before them, and everyone of them said, 'I have appointed Frederick as arbitrator in this, for he is the emperor's son, and the most worthy of the company to be heard in the matter.' Then

Frederick arose and said, 'I am the son of the emperor, and I am the most worthy of his crown and his position, and all the company are satisfied with me.' He placed the crown on his head, and they were all stupefied. He went out hastily with the crown on his head, having a company of his courageous German companions mounted and ready. He mounted, and his German companions gathered around him, and they conveyed him to his land under their protection."

The Judge Jamâl al-Dîn said, "The Emperor Manfred, son of Frederick, continued to reign, and the Pope and the King of France sought him out with their hosts. They fought and defeated him, and seized him. The Pope ordered him to be put to death, so Manfred was put to death, and the brother of the king of France ruled his land after him." That was, I am inclined to think, in the year 663 [1264-5]....

[Second Extract:]

In this year I sent to ask leave of our lord the Sultan to go to the Holy Hijâz. He granted me leave, and I made my preparations. I dispatched dromedaries to al-Karak, and sent my boys and the heavy baggage with the Syrian Pilgrimage-caravan. The Sultan graciously sent me 1,000 dinars in cash for my expenses. I received orders from him that I should fetch out the common people from all the country to the Pilgrimage-caravan of Hamâ, and that my camels might go where I pleased, either before or after the Sultan's *mahmal* [party], as I thought best. I received these favours with abundant prayer for him, and left Hamâ on Friday, 14 *shawwâl* of this year, corresponding to 1 *shubât* [Feb. 1314], proceeding by horse to al-Karak. Thence I went on by dromedary, and sent the horses and mules back to Hamâ. I took six led horses with me, and was accompanied by a number of Mamluks with bows and arrows. I went ahead of the caravan to the City of the Prophet (the blessing of God and peace be on him), which I reached on Friday, 20 *thu al-qa'da* [8 March 1314]. I accomplished the pilgrimage to the Prophet's tomb by myself, and stayed until the caravan caught up with me. Then I went ahead of them, and reached Mecca on Saturday, 5 *thu al-hijja* [23 March], where I stayed. Then we went out to Arafât, and performed the *wuqûf* on Wednesday; then we returned to Minnâ, and completed the ritual of the Pilgrimage. I then performed the Lesser Pilgrimage, for I had performed this Greater on its own, as is al-Shafi'I's chosen usage, and in the first Greater Pilgrimage I performed them together. Then we returned home… I reached Hamâ on 11 *muharram* '14 [27 Apr.]. My journey from Mecca to Hamâ took about twenty-five days, including more than three days spent at Medina, al-Ma'allâ, Birkat Zîzâ and Damascus, so that my actual journey-time from Mecca to Hamâ was less than twenty-two days. I travelled by dromedary, taking a horse and a mule with me, and stopped for nothing. This was my second Pilgrimage: I had made my first Pilgrimage in the year 703 [1304].

The sultan sent from Cairo to Mecca an expeditionary force and amirs from the troops of Damascus. With them he sent abu al-Ghayth b. abî Numayy to be installed in Mecca. They were to arrest or drive out his brother, Humayda b. abî Numayy, because he had made himself master of Mecca, and was following evil courses there. The commander of the expeditionary force was Sayf al-Dîn Taqsubâ al-Husâmî. When I met him in Mecca, he gave me a warrant from our lord the Sultan to the intent that I should assist him with men and advice to take Humayda. When we drew near to Mecca (God Most High guard it), Humayda left, and fled to the desert. So we installed abu al-Ghayth in Mecca. He exploited it, taking what the members of caravans from Yemen and elsewhere bring to its lord. He likewise extorted taxes from the merchants, and established himself there. We shall relate what ensued, God Most High willing…

A company of Banû Lâm joined forces with the nomad Arabs of the Hijâz with the intention of intercepting the rabble of the Pilgrimage-caravan whom they might come upon between Tabûk and home as the pilgrims returned. They went to Dhât Hajj, where they fell in with the rabble, and killed about twenty or more of them. They then got the victory over Banû Lâm, routed them, and took about eighty dromedaries from them, while Banû Lâm returned secretly to Hunayn.

[Third Extract:]

I had left Hamâ without taking a mount of my own or any travelling equipment. He [the Sultan] provided for me, and lodged me with the judge Karîm al-Dîn. He was most generous to me in various ways—clothing, riding animals and food. He had tents pitched for my personal use with everything I needed in the way of bedding, food and menials for me personally. In addition there was no end to the robes of honour of various kinds which I might confer on whom I wished. Throughout the journey, both going and returning, the Sultan would hunt gazelle with falcons, while I by his favour would look on, and he would send me some of his bag of gazelles.

While we were on the way, his decree came to me: "When I reach Egypt, I will make you sultan, and you shall go home as sultan." I asked to be excused from that, deprecated it, and complained of it, deeming myself too small and his august name too great for it to be shared. So the matter remained in suspense until he reached his capital as mentioned. I lodged with the judge Karîm al-Dîn at his house inside the Zuwayla Gate near Bayn al-Qasrayn where I stayed. The Sultan's decree for the sending of the insignia of the sultanate came to me. The lords and the amirs presented themselves: they were Sayf al-Din Ulmâs the Chamberlain[91], Sayf al-Dîn Qijlis, the Amir 'Alâ' al-Dîn Aydughmush the Constable[92], the Amir Rukn al-Dîn Baybars al-Ahmadî[93], and the Amir Sayf al-Dîn Taynâl[94], also a chamberlain. About twenty of the amirs of the Bodyguard presented themselves with a complete livery of satin brocade, the august dagger of the sultanate, the saddle-cover woven with Egyptian gold and above it the parasol, three standards and flags, a diploma conferring the sultanate, the pages of the Royal Wardrobe, a sword-bearer with two swords hanging from his shoulder, and the heralds.

All this came to the Mansurîyya college in Bayn al-Qasrayn. A fully harnessed horse was brought me. I mounted it in the early morning of Thursday, 17 *muharram*, corresponding to 28 *shubât* [28 Feb. 1320] with the insignia listed. The amirs walked part of the way and mounted. When I was near the Citadel, they all dismounted, and I kept on until I approached the Citadel. I dismounted and kissed the ground to the Sultan facing the Citadel, and I kissed the august diploma. Then accompanied by the vice-regent, His Excellency Sayf al-Dîn Arghûn al-Dawâdâr, I went up to the Citadel and had an audience of the Sultan that morning. I kissed the ground, and he showed me favours such as a father never showed his child. Thereupon he commanded me to proceed to Hamâ saying, "You've been away some time, so go home." So I kissed the ground and bade him farewell.

I took the post-horses by mid-afternoon of that Thursday, having the insignia of the sultanate with me on a post-horse, and proceeded until I was near Hamâ. The amirs and judges there came out to meet me. I rode with the insignia, and entered Hamâ in the morning of Saturday, 26 *muharram* of this year, corresponding to 8 *âthâr* [March], after the reading of the diploma of the sultanate at Naqîrîn in a tent which had been pitched there. Were it not for fear of prolixity, I would transcribe it...

The Accidental Travels of a Korean Official

Contributed by Lene Sønderby Bech

From *P'yohae-rok* (1488)

The Korean official Ch'oe Pu's (1454–1504) diary of his nine months of travel in China tells of a travel never meant to take place. Ch'oe had just gone to the Korean island Cheju, of which he was appointed in 1487 Commissioner of Registers, when he heard of his father's death. He set sail to return to his hometown Naju, a prefectural town on the southwest tip of the Korean peninsula, but got caught in a storm and drifted across the Yellow Sea to the coast of China. Under Chinese escort he travelled north to Beijing, where he joined an embassy from Korea and finally made his way back to mourn his father's death. Ch'oe's diary of his travels to and in China, *A Record of Drifting across the Sea (P'yohae-rok)*, was completed after his return to Korea in 1488. The diary was compiled in obedience to a royal edict and presented to the Korean king the same year. It is written as a day-by-day account and records topographical, cultural, and historical observations about the landscape, villages and towns Ch'oe passed, as well as a record of his encounters and conversations with people he met en route. These are a varied crowd of officials, bandits, scholars, angry villagers, and students.

The first part of the diary tells of Ch'oe's near fatal shipwreck and records the days adrift in the sea. On the fifth day Ch'oe records, "This day a dense fog obscured everything. Things a foot away could not be made out. Towards evening, rain streamed down heavily, abating somewhat with night. The frightening waves were like mountains. They would lift the ship up into the blue sky and then drop it as if down an abyss. They billowed and crashed, the noise splitting heaven from earth. We might all be drowned and left to rot at any moment." (p. 34) With tears in their eyes Ch'oe's staff told him: "Conditions are critical; there is no hope. Please change your clothes and wait for your fate to come." (p. 34) In despair Ch'oe prepared to die, asking heaven what sin he had committed and praying for his staff and the ship crew to be spared. The next day the sea was a little calmer and six days later the boat came to the first of several islands. Before the boat reached the Chinese coast, however, they encountered Chinese pirates who robbed them of all their spare clothes and food rations, threw away their oars and anchor, tortured Ch'oe and sent their boat adrift towards the limitless sea again. After a few days of starvation and utter hopelessness, because they no longer were able to steer the boat, they rode on an east wind and finally reached the shores of China.

Ch'oe and his party arrived on the Chinese coast without permit or any official business, the coast guards therefore suspected them of being Japanese pirates and they were escorted north to Beijing. The main part of the diary tells about the northbound journey through the eastern parts of China. Ch'oe travelled on foot, by riverboat, or riding in a sedan-chair, and visited, among other places, Hangzhou and Suzhou. Ch'oe has left some of the most beautiful descriptions of Ming dynasty (1368-1644) China, though he often encountered such beautiful scenery or examples of architectural grandeur that defied his attempts to describe them. His accounts of the southern parts tell of a prosperous region with many villages and well-guarded cities with impressive houses, well dressed people, and plenty of food and drink. The north is depicted as poorer and more desolate; food supplies at the stations they stop at are often limited and the fear of bandits more apparent.

As a Korean official Ch'oe had received a Confucian education and passed the civil service examinations modelled on the Chinese examination system. Confucianism had not yet achieved the same kind of dominance it had in China and was later to have in Korea as well. But Ch'oe was a strong believer in Confucian ethics and his knowledge of and strict adherence to Confucian rituals seem to have impressed the Chinese officials and literati he met, and it probably saved him and his party from danger and trouble during their travels in China.

After surviving a dramatic shipwreck, meetings with pirates and bandits, and the hardships of his travels in China, Ch'oe was to meet with new perils a decade after his return to Korea, but this time there was no happy end for him. In 1498 rivalries within the Korean government led to the first of four "Literati Purges" (the others were in 1504, 1519, and 1545). Some Confucian ministers were killed, others lost their positions and were deprived of their goods, while still others, Ch'oe included, were whipped and exiled. At the time of the second purge in 1504 Ch'oe, who was still in exile, was executed.

[Extracts from *Ch'oe Pu's Diary: A Record of Drifting across the Sea*. Translated with introduction and notes by John Meskill. Tucson: The University of Arizona Press 1965. Reprinted with the kind permission of the Association for Asian Studies, Inc., USA.]

Eighteenth Day, Intercalary First Month. An Encounter with Chiliarch Xu Qing on the Road. This day it rained hard.

By midnight, then, as we were driven on by villagers, the road passed over a high hill, where pines and bamboo grew thickly. We met a man, named Wang Yiyuan, who described himself as a recluse scholar. He pitied us for braving the night and the rain and being driven on painfully. He stopped the villagers briefly and asked me what had happened, and I informed him, too, of the circumstances of our being blown adrift by the wind. Yiyuan grieved for me; he called for wine and urged it on me. I said, 'When we Koreans observe mourning for parents, we do not drink wine or eat meat, garlic, oniony plants, or sweet things for fully three years. I am deeply grateful for your kindness in offering me wine, but I am in mourning now, and I venture to decline.'

Yiyuan then served me tea and my staff wine. He asked, 'Does your country have the Buddha, too?'

I answered, 'My country does not revere the Buddhist law, it honors only the Confucian system. All its families make filial piety, fraternal duty, loyalty, and sincerity their concern.' Yiyuan took my hands and looked at me compassionately, and we parted.

The villagers drove us on, and we came to a large mountain range. My feet were swollen like cocoons, and I could not go forward.

The villagers seized my arms, pulled me in front, pushed me from behind, and over we went. We were passed on for over twenty *li* (and came to another village, where) there was a big bridge. The villagers, who struck us indiscriminately with crooked sticks, were recklessly cruel and plundered greedily. O San was carrying my horse saddle, but a man beat him off, seized it, and took it away. Beaten forward with sticks, we fell down and wept.

We crossed two ranges and were turned over to another village. It was approaching dawn. When I asked what the village with the big bridge had been, a man said, 'Xianyan village.'

Ever since we had landed, all the onlookers by the road had sawed their arms across their throats, making gestures at us as if to cut off their heads, and we did not know what they meant.

We reached Pufeng Village. The rain let up a little. An official came with military officers and asked me, 'What is your nationality? How did you come here?'

I said, 'I am a Korean. I have placed in the examinations twice and am a minister close to the King of the country. I had been given the state duty of touring an island, but hurrying into mourning, I put out from land, encountered a wind, and drifted here. Through hunger and thirst enough for dying many times, I have barely clung to life. I have been repeatedly driven on by villagers. In this extremity of suffering, I am fortunate enough to meet an official here, making it the moment of my rescue.'

The official first served me congee and then solid food. He also ordered my staff to prepare food and eat. When I asked the official's name and position, one Wang Gua said, 'He is Xu Qing, Chiliarch (*qianhu*) of Haimen Garrison (*wei*).[95] He defends Tangtou Stockade; having heard that Japanese were raiding the coast, he came specifically to take them prisoner. Take care.'

I lay down exhausted at the side of the road; my four limbs would not move. Xu Qing said to me, 'The laws of China are strict. You strangers may not stay here long upsetting the law-abiding people.' He ordered military officers to drive us on quickly. When we had gone about five *li*, there was a public office, which was Tangtou Stockade.

We passed a long embankment, somewhat over ten *li* long. Rain fell heavily again... (pp.50-51)

29th Day, Ninth Month. Passing Ningbo Precture (Fu). This day it rained.

Zhai Yong and we rode in sedan-chairs and crossed a large river. On the bank of the river was an extremely beautiful Buddhist temple, in front of which were five small pagodas and two big ones. Then we passed (from Xubaiguan to Beidu River).

From Niutou Waiyang northwest to Lianshan Station, mountain peaks rose everywhere in clusters and ranges, some crossing others. Rushing streams and steep cliffs were scattered through them thickly. When we reached that river, flat, open lands and broad fields were apparent at a glance. We saw the distant mountains only as eyebrows. On the north shore of the river an embankment had been built, which was a place up over which boats were pulled. North of the embankment a levee had been built to canalize the river. Tenders were moored to the bank in a row.

Zhai Yong led us into the boats, and we passed thirteen stone bridges and went more than twenty *li*. On the east levee of the river, village gates were everywhere. To the southwest we saw the Siming Mountains, adjoined to Mt. Tiantai in the southwest and to the Kuaiji, Qinwang, and other mountains in the northeast. It was where He Zhizhang[96] had been when he was young.

We rowed up to the wall of Ningbo Prefecture. The wall was built across the stream, and all the gates of it were double and of two stories. Outside the gates was a second wall, and the moat, too, was double. All the gates of the wall were arched and had iron doors that would admit a single boat. We rowed inside the wall and came to Shangshu Bridge. Beyond the bridge the width of the river was about five hundred feet. We passed Huizheng Bridge and Shejitan. Altogether we passed more than ten big bridges in the town. I cannot record adequately the wonderfully beautiful sights. We rowed out the north gate, which was the same as the south gate. I do not know the circumference of the wall, but the prefectural capital, Ningbo

Garrison, the seat of Yin County, and Siming Station were inside it.

We reached and passed Dade Bridge, which had three arches. It was raining extremely hard, and we moored for the night in the river. (pp. 67–68)

17th Day, Third Month. Fair.
(We went from Zhengjiakou to Liangjiazhuang Station and beyond.) In the evening we arrived in front of Gucheng County and stopped. I said to Fu Rong, 'The moon is bright tonight and the wind favorable. Why do we not leave?'

Fu Rong said, 'Did you see the three corpses floating in this river?'

I said, 'I saw them.'

Fu Rong said, 'They were all killed by bandits. This region has suffered successive famines, and many people have been driven into banditry. They do not know that you were set adrift and all your baggage lost. On the contrary, they will take it that as foreigners, you must have valuable things. All of them have greedy hearts. Then, too, on the road ahead settlements are few and scattered, and the bandits are many and reckless. That is why we do not leave.'

I said, 'On this journey, I have already met bandits from Ningbo Prefecture. The last person I want to meet in my life is a bandit.'

Fu Rong said, 'In general, the temperament of the Chinese in the north is forceful and violent. In the south it is mild and docile. The Ningbo bandits were men from south of the Yangtze; even though they were of the outlaw type, therefore, they plundered without killing people. That is what saved you. When these northerners plunder, they invariably kill the people. Either they put them in ditches or float them on rivers or the sea. That accounts for the floating corpses we saw today.' (p. 112)

8th Day, Fourth Month. Cloudy.
Yang Rulin, Wang Yan, and Chen Dao, students of the National University, wearing black hats and blue collars round their throats, came and said, 'Do the students in your country also wear these?'

I said, 'All young students, even though they are in remote villages or secluded lanes, wear them.'

They said, 'In your country is there also "specialization in Classics"?'

I said, 'In the examinations in my country, those versed in the Classics and Books are passed. The students, therefore, study the Four Books and Five Classics thoroughly. Those who have mastered only one Classic do not attain the rank of full-fledged Confucian scholars.' (p.125)

The Travel Memoirs of Babur (b. 1482)

From *Babur-nama*

The *Babur-Nama* tells the tale of Zahiruddin Muhammad Babur's struggle first to assert and defend his claim to the throne of Samarkand and the region of the Fergana Valley. After being driven out of Samarkand in 1501 by the Uzbek Shaibanids, he ultimately sought greener pastures, first in Kabul and then in northern India, where his descendants were the Moghul (Mughal) dynasty who ruled in Delhi until 1858. The memoirs of his travels offer a highly educated Central Asian Muslim's observations of the world in which he moved. There is much on the political and military struggles of his time but also extensive descriptive sections on the physical and human geography, the flora and fauna, nomads in their pastures and urban environments enriched by the architecture, music and Persian and Turkic literature patronized by the Timurids. The selections here have been chosen to provide a range of his travel writings from the material he recorded at the end of the 1490s and in the first years of the sixteenth century.

In 1494, at age 12, Babur acceded to an uncertain position as a minor ruler in Fergana, in Central Asia; at his death in 1530 he controlled much of northern India, having founded what would become the "Mughal" empire. As well as covering key historical events, his life story, the *Babur-Nama*, offers a fascinating picture of ordinary (aristocratic) life in Islamic Central and South Asia around 1500. It may not be a good starting point for the newcomer to the period, but it should not be restricted to academia, either.

Babur begins his travel writing by describing the geography of Fergana and some background history. He then recounts his part in the internecine conflicts between the Timurids (descendants of Temür/Tamerlane) over Khurasan, Transoxiana, and Fergana and their loss to the Uzbeks under Shaybani. Initially a puppet of others, used for Timurid legitimacy, Babur gradually became a real leader. His fluctuating fortunes saw him take and lose Samarkand twice;

eventually he was forced into a kind of "guerrilla" existence in the mountains. In 1504 he left Transoxiana with a few hundred companions, acquired the discontented followers of a regional leader in Badakhshan, and took Kabul. From there he began carving out a domain for himself, in a process combining pillage and state-building.

The story breaks in 1508, with a large lacuna in our manuscripts; it resumes in 1519, when we find Babur solidly established in Kabul and campaigning in and around what is now Pakistan. Matchlocks (not mentioned at all previously) are now in regular use, though restricted to the elite. A more personal change is Babur's fondness for riotous parties and use of both alcohol and the narcotic *ma'jun*, contrasting with his teetotal youth. After another lacuna the work finishes with the years 1525 to 1529, covering the battle of Panipat, the conquest of Delhi, and the defeat of a Rajput coalition at the battle of Khanua (in which battle artillery played a key role). India was only a consolation prize for Babur, however, as he always compares it unfavourably with Kabul and his beloved Samarkand.

Though Thackston claims it is "the first real autobiography in Islamic literature", the *Babur-Nama* contains little personal reflection. Babur is frank and open, but tends to describe actions rather than motivations. The *Babur-Nama* does, however, extend far beyond the military and political history summarized above. Babur includes descriptions of many of the places he visits and is interested in flora and fauna and techniques of hunting, fishing, and agriculture; there are also set-piece geographical overviews of Fergana, Transoxiana, and the area around Kabul, as well as a twenty-page description of Hindustan. And on a few occasions he describes events at a distance, outside his own direct experience (for example battles between the Persians and the Uzbeks).

The extracts from the *Babur-Nama* are meant to stand in not only for a complex and fascinating book but also for other texts, for the Mughal era was rich in biographies and histories containing first-hand travel descriptions. Babur's daughter, Gul-Badan Begum's (1523-1603) *Humayun Nama* is merely one such text left out from this anthology. In the *Humayun Nama*, Gul-Badan Begum wrote a first-hand biography of her brother and Babur's son and successor, Humayun.

[Extracts from *Babur-nama*, as translated from the original Turki text of Zahirud-din Muhammad Babur Badshah Ghaznvi by Annette S. Beveridge in New York by AMS Press and London by Sang-E-Meel Publications in 1922. Original footnotes retained with some editing.]

Description of Samarkand

Few towns in the whole habitable world are so pleasant as Samarkand. It is of the Fifth Climate and situated in lat. 40° 6′ and long 99°. The name of the town is Samarkand; its country people used to call Ma wara'u'n-nahr (Transoxania). They used to call it *Baldat-i-mahfuza* because no foe laid hands on it with storm and sack.[97] It must have become[98] Musalman in the time of the Commander of the Faithful, his Highness 'Usman. Qusam ibn 'Abbas, one of the Companions[99] must have gone there; his burial-place, known as the Tomb of Shah-i-zinda (The Living Shah, *i.e.*, Faqir) is outside the Iron Gate. Iskandar must have founded Samarkand. The Turk and Mughul hordes call it Simiz-kint.[100] Timur-Beg made it his capital; no ruler so great will ever have made it a capital before (*qilghan aimas dur*). I ordered people to pace round the ramparts of the walled-town; it came out at 10,000 steps. Samarkandis are all orthodox (*sunni*), pure-in-the Faith, law-abiding and religious. The number of Leaders of Islam said to have arisen in Ma wara'u'n-nahr, since the days of his Highness the Prophet, are not known to have arisen in any other country.[101] From the Matarid suburb of Samarkand came Shaikh Abu'l-mansur, one of the Expositors of the Word. Of the two sects of Expositors, the Mataridiyah and the Ash'ariay, the first is named from this Shaikh Abu'l-mansur. Of Ma wara'u'n-nahr also was Khwaja Ismai'il *Khartank*, the author of the *Sahih-i-bukhari*.[102] From the Farghana district, Marghinan—Farghana, though at the limit of settled habitation, is included in Ma wara'u'n-nahr,—came the author of the *Hidayat*, a book than which few on Jurisprudence are more honoured in the sect of Abu Hanifa.

On the east of Samarkand are Farghana and Kashghar; on the west, Bukhara and Khwarizm; on the north, Tashkint and Shahrukhiya,—in books written Shash and Banakat; and on the south, Balkh and Tirmiz.

The Kohik Water flows along the north of Samarkand, at the distance of some 4 miles (2 *kuroh*); it is so-called because it comes out from under the upland of the Little Hill (*Kohik*)[103] lying between it and the town. The Dar-i-gham Water (canal) flows along the south, at the distance of some two miles (I *shari'*). This is a large and swift torrent,[104] indeed it is like a large river, cut off from the Kohik Water. All the gardens and suburbs and some of the *tumans* of Samarkand are cultivated by it. By the Kohik Water a stretch of from 30 to 40 *yighach*,[105] by road, is made habitable and cultivated, as far as Bukhara and Qara-kul. Large as the river is, it is not too large for its dwellings and its culture; during three or four months of the year, indeed, its waters do not reach Bukhara. Grapes, melons, apples and pomegranates, all fruits indeed, are good in Samarkand; two are famous, its apple and its *sahibi* (grape).[106] Its winter is mightily cold; snow falls but not so much as in Kabul; in the heats its climate is good but not so good as Kabul's.

In the town and suburbs of Samarkand are many fine buildings and gardens of Timur Beg and Aulugh Beg Mirza.[107]

In the citadel, Timur Beg erected a very fine building, the great four-storeyed kiosque, known as the Guk Sarai.[108] In the walled-town, again, near the Iron Gate, he built a Friday Mosque[109] of stone (*sangin*); on this worked many stone-cutters, brought from Hindustan. Round its frontal arch is inscribed in letters large enough to be read two miles away, the Qu'ran verse, *wa iz yarfâ' ibrahim al-qawa'id min al-bayt*.[110] This also is a very fine building. Again, he laid out two gardens, on the east of the town, one, the more distant, the Bagh-I-bulandi,[111] the other and nearer, the Bagh-I-dilkusha.[112] From Dilkusha to the Turquoise Gate, he planted an Avenue of White Poplar, and in the garden itself erected a great kiosque, painted inside with pictures of his battles in Hindustan. He made another garden, known as the Naqsh-i-jahan (World's Picture), on the skirt of Kohik, above the Qara-su or, as people also call it, the Ab-i-rahmat (Water-of-mercy) of Kan-i-gil. It had gone to ruin when I saw it, nothing remaining of it except its name. His also are the Bagh-i-chanar,[113] near the walls and below the town on the south,[114] also the Bagh-i-shamal (North Garden) and the Bagh-i-bihisht (Garden of Paradise). His own tomb and those of his descendants who have ruled in Samarkand, are in a College, built at the exit (*Chaqar*) of the walled-town, by Muhammad Sultan Mirza, the son of Timur Beg's son, Jahangir Mirza.[115]

Among Aulugh Beg Mirza's buildings inside the town are a College and a monastery (*khanqa*). The dome of the monastery is very large, few so large are known in the world. Near these two buildings, he constructed an excellent Hot Bath (*hammam*) known as the Mirza's Bath; he had the pavements in this made of all sorts of stone (? Mosaic); such another bath is not known in Khurasan or in Samarkand.[116] Again,—to the south of the College is his mosque, known as the Masjid-i-maqata' (Carved Mosque) because its ceiling and its walls are all covered with *islimi*[117] and Chinese pictures formed of segments of wood.[118] There is great discrepancy between the *qibla* of this mosque and that of the College; that of the mosque seems to have been fixed by astronomical observation.

Another of Aulugh Beg Mirza's fine buildings is an observatory, that is, an instrument for writing Astronomical Tables.[119] This stands three storeys high, on the skirt of the Kohik upland. By its means the Mirza worked out the Kurkani Tables, now used all over the world. Less work is done with any others. Before these were made, people used the Ail-khani Tables, put together at Maragha, by Khwaja Nasir Tusi,[120] in the time of Hulaku Khan. Hulaku Khan it is, people call *Ail-khani*.[121]

(*Author's note.*) Not more than seven or eight observatories seem to have been constructed in the world. Mamum Khalifa[122] (Caliph) made one with which the *Mamumi* Tables were written. Batelmus (Ptolemy) constructed another. Another was made in Hindūstan, in the time of Raja Vikramaditya Hindu, in Ujjain and Dhar, that is, the Malwa country, now known as Nandu. The Hindus of Hindūstan use the Tables of this Observatory. They were put together 1,584 years ago.[123] Compared with others, they are somewhat defective.

Aulugh Beg Mirza again, made the garden known as the Bagh-i-maidan (Garden of the Plain), on the skirt of the Kohik upland. In the middle of it he erected a fine building they call Chihil Situn (Forty Pillars). On both storeys are pillars, all of stone (*tashdin*). Four turrets, like minarets, stand on its four corner-towers, the way up into them being through the towers. Everywhere there are stone pillars, some fluted, some twisted, some many-sided. On the four sides of the upper storey are open galleries enclosing a four-doored hall (*char-dara*); their pillars also are all of stone. The raised floor of the building is all paved with stone.

He made a smaller garden, out beyond Chihil Situn and towards Kohik, also having a building in it. In the open gallery of this building he placed a great stone throne, some 14 or 15 yards (*qari*) long, some 8 yards wide and perhaps 1 yard high. They brought a stone so large by a very long road.[124] There is a crack in the middle of it which people say must have come after it was brought here. In the same garden he also built a four-doored hall, know as the Chini-khana (Porcelain House) because its *izara*[125] are all of porcelain; he sent to China for the porcelain used in it. Inside the walls again, is an old building of his, known as the Masjid-i-laqlaqa (Mosque of the Echo). If anyone stamps on the ground under the middle of the dome of this mosque, the sound echoes back from the whole dome; it is a curious matter of which none know the secret.

In the time also of Ahmad Mirza the great and lesser Begs laid out many gardens, large and small.[126] For beauty, and air, and view, few will have equalled Darwish Muhammad Tarkhan's Char-bagh (Four Gardens).[127] It lies overlooking the whole of Qulba Meadow, on the slope below the Bagh-i-maidan. Moreover it is arranged symmetrically, terrace above terrace, and is planted with beautiful *narwan*[128] and cypresses and white poplar. A most agreeable sojourning place, its one defect is the want of a large stream.

Samarkand is a wonderfully beautified town. One of its specialities, perhaps found in few other places,[129] is that the different trades are not mixed up together in it but each has its own *bazar*, a good sort of plan. Its bakers and its cooks are good. The best paper in the world is made there; the water for the paper-mortars[130] all comes from Kan-i-gil,[131] a meadow on the banks of the Qara-su (Blackwater) or Ab-i-rahmat (Water of Mercy). Another article of Samarkand trade, carried to all sides and quarters, is cramoisy velvet.

Excellent meadows lie round Samarkand. One is the famous Kan-i-gil, some 2 miles east and a little north of the town. The Qara-su or Ab-i-rahmat flows through it, a stream (with driving power) for perhaps seven or eight mills. Some say the original name of the meadow must have been Kan-i-abgir (Mine of Quagmire) because the river is bordered by quagmire, but the histories all write Kan-i-gil (Mine of clay). It is an excellent meadow. The Samarkand sultans always made it their reserve,[132] going out to camp in it each year for a month or two.

Higher up (on the river) than Kan-i-gil and to the south-east of it is a meadow some four miles east of the town, known as Khan Yurti (Khan's Camping-ground). The Qara-su flows through this meadow before entering Kan-i-gil. When it comes to Khan Yurti it curves back so far that it encloses, with a very narrow outlet, enough ground for a camp. Having noticed these advantages, we camped there for a time during the siege of Samarkand.[133]

Another meadow is the Budana Qurugh (Quail Reserve), lying between Dil-kusha and the town. Another is the Kul-i-maghak (Meadow of the deep pool) at some four miles from the town. This also is a round[134] meadow. People call it Kul-i-maghak meadow because there is a large pool on one side of it. Sl. 'Ali Mirza lay here during the siege, when I was in Khan Yurti. Another and smaller meadow is Qulba (Plough); it has Qulba Village and the Kohik Water on the north, the Bagh-i-maidan and Darwesh Muhammad Tarkhan's Char-bagh on the south, and the Kohik upland on the west.

Samarkand has good districts and *tumans*. Its largest district, and one that is its equal, is Bukhara, 25 *yighach*[135] to the west. Bukhara in its turn, has several *tumans*; it is a fine town; its fruits are many and good, its melons excellent; none in Ma wara'u'n-nahr matching them for quality and quantity. Although the Mir Timuri melon of Akhsl is sweeter and more delicate than any Bukhara melon, still in Bukhara many kinds of melon are good and plentiful. The Bukhara plum is famous; no other equals it. They skin it, dry it and carry it from land to land with rarities (*tabarruklar bila*); it is an excellent laxative medicine. Fowls and geese are much looked after (*parwari*) in Bukhara. Bukhara wine is the strongest made in Ma wara'u'n-nahr; it was what I drank when drinking in those countries at Samarkand[136]...

(Babur's rule in Samarkand)

When I was seated on the throne, I shewed the Samarkand Begs precisely the same favour and kindness they had had before. I bestowed rank and favour also on the Begs with me, to each according to his circumstances, the largest share falling to Sl. Ahmad *Tambal*; he had been in the household Begs[137] circle; I now raised him to that of the great Begs.

We had taken the town after a seven months' hard siege. Things of one sort or other fell to our men when we got in. The whole country, with exception of Samarkand itself, had come in earlier either to me or to 'Ali Mirza and consequently had not been over-run. In any case, what could have been taken from districts so long subjected to raid and rapine? The booty our men had taken, such as it was, came to an end. When we entered the town, it was in such distress that it needed seed-corn and money-advances; what place was this to take anything from? On these accounts our men suffered great privation. We ourselves could give them nothing. Moreover they yearned for their homes and, by ones and twos, set their faces for flight...

(A personal episode and some verses by Babur)

In those leisurely days I discovered in myself a strange inclination, nay! as the verse says, 'I maddened and afflicted myself' for a boy in the camp-bazar, his very name, Baburi, fitting in. Up till then I had had no inclination for any-one, indeed of love and desire, either by hear-say or experience, I had not heard, I had not talked. At that time

I composed Persian couplets, one or two at a time; this is one of them:

> *May none be as I, humbled and wretched and love-sick;*
> *No beloved as thou art to me, cruel and careless.*

From time to time Baburi used to come to my presence but out of modesty and bashfulness, I could never look straight at him; how then could I make conversation (*ikhtilat*) and recital (*hikayat*)? In my joy and agitation I could not thank him (for coming); how was it possible for me to reproach him with going away? What power had I command the duty of service to myself? One day, during that time of desire and passion when I was going with companions along a lane and suddenly met him face to face, I got into such a state of confusion that I almost went right off. To look straight at him or to put words together was impossible. With a hundred torments and shames, I went on. A (Persian) couplet of Muhammad Salih's[138] came into my mind:

> *I am abashed with shame when I see my friend;*
> *My companions look at me, I look the other way.*

That couplet suited the case wonderfully well. In that frothing-up of desire and passion, and under that stress of youthful folly, I used to wander, bare-head, bare-foot, through street and lane, orchard and vineyard. I shewed civility neither to friend not stranger, took no care for myself or others.

> *[Turki]*
> *Out of myself desire rushed me, unknowing*
> *That this is so with the lover of a fairy-face.*

Sometimes like the madmen, I used to wander alone over hill and plain; sometimes I betook myself to gardens and the suburbs, lane by lane. My wandering was not of my choice, not I decided whether to go or stay.

[Turki]
Nor power to go was mine, nor power to stay;
I was just what you made me, O thief of my heart.

(Irrigation)

The greater part of the Hindustan country is situated on arable land. Many though its towns and cultivated lands are, it now has running waters.[139] Rivers and, in some places, standing are its 'running-waters.' (*aqar-sular*). Even where, as for a town, it is practicable to convey water by digging channels this is not done. For not doing it there may be several reasons, one being that water is not at all a necessity in cultivating and orchards. Autumn crops grow by the downpour themselves; and strange it is that spring crops grow even when no rain falls. To young trees water is made to flow by buckets or a wheel. They are given water constantly during the first three years; after which they need no more. Some vegetables are watered constantly.

In Lahor, Dibalpur and those parts, people water by means of a wheel. They make two circles of ropes long enough to suit the depth of the well, fix strips of wood between them and on these fasten pitchers. The ropes with the wood and the pitchers are put over the well-wheel. At one end of the axle a second wheel is fixed, and close (*qash*) to it another wheel with an upright axle. This last wheel the bullock turns; its teeth catch in the teeth of the second, and thus the wheel with the pitchers is turned. A trough is set where the water empties from the pitchers and from this the water is conveyed everywhere.

In Agra, Chandwar, Biana and those parts, again, people irrigate with a bucket; this is a laborious and filthy way. At the water's edge they set up a fork of wood, having a roller adjusted between the forks, tie a rope to a large bucket, put the rope around the roller, and tie its other end to the bullock. One person can drive the bullock, another empty the bucket. Every time the bullock turns after having drawn the bucket out of the well, the rope lies on the bullock-track, in pollution of urine and dung, before it descends again into the well...

In Hindustan hamlets and villages, towns indeed, are populated and set up in a moment! If the people of a large town, one inhabited for years even, flee from it they do it in such a way that not a sign or trace of them remains in a day or a day and a half. On the other hand, if they fix their eyes on a place in which to settle, they need not dig water-courses or construct dams because their crops are all rain-grown,[140] and as the population of Hindustan is unlimited, it swarms in. They make a tank or dig a well; they need not build houses or set up walls—*khas*-grass (*Andropogon muricatum*) abounds, wood is unlimited, huts are made, and straightway there is a village or a town!...

Don Juan of Persia: Diaries of Uruch Beg (b. 1560)

Contributed by Prem Poddar

From *Relaciones de Juan de Persia* (1604)

Uruch Beg[141] was born in 1560 to Sultan Ali Beg, a prominent noble in the Persian court of Muhammad Khudah Bandah. On the death of Sultan Ali Beg in 1585 during the unsuccessful siege of Tabriz, Uruch Beg assumed command of his father's regiment, and enjoyed a successful diplomatic and military career under Shah Abbas the Great, who ascended to the Persian throne in 1588. Abbas' achievement during his reign was to secure peace and stability for Persia after the series of calamitous wars with the Ottoman Empire that had dominated the sixteenth century. Abbas' great grandfather, Shah Isma'il, the founder of the Safavi monarchy in Persia, had fuelled the conflict with the Turks by proclaiming the Shi'ism practised in Persia as the true and orthodox version of Islam, and renouncing the Sunni branch [a large majority of Muslims in the world are Sunni] of the Ottoman Empire as heretical and infidel. These uncompromising religious differences continued to define Turkish-Persian relations at the close of the sixteenth century, so that when the English adventurer Sir Anthony Sherley arrived in Isfahan in 1599, Abbas was strongly motivated to seek potential allies in the Christian West to oppose the Ottoman Empire. As a consequence, he approved Sherley's proposal of sending a Persian embassy to Western rulers, and promptly assembled a distinguished group to be led by the Ambassador Husayn 'Ali Beg, and including Uruch Beg. The embassy set out in July 1599 and followed a route that can be easily traced today, enjoying successful diplomatic meetings with potentates in Russia, Germany, Rome, Spain and Portugal. Despite failing to visit five of the sovereigns on his initial list—those of England, France, Scotland and Poland, and the Doge of Venice—Husayn 'Ali Beg decided in early 1602 to return home, and left Lisbon for Persia via the sea route round the Cape of Good Hope. Uruch Beg, however, had converted to Christianity and remained in Spain, adopting the name of Don Juan of Persia and enjoying the sponsorship of Margaret of Austria, the Queen of Spain. In May 1605, he was killed in a scuffle in Valladolid, and to avoid embarrassing questions, his assailants abandoned his corpse to the town dogs.

Uruch Beg kept a detailed diary of his travels in Persian, and after his conversion in 1601, collaborated with his Spanish mentor, the Licentiate Alfonso Remon, to rewrite them in Castilian Spanish. The completed work appeared in 1604 as *Relaciones de Juan de Persia* (a year before the first chapter of *Don Quixote* appeared), and in a letter prefixed to the text, Remon explains the extent to which he helped and guided Don Juan, not only with his Spanish, but also with historical, geographical and ecclesiastical details. Remon had access to an excellent library in Valladolid, and drew extensively on a number of authors in different languages to flesh out Don Juan's tale, most notably Giovanni Botero, Giovanni Thomaso Minadoi, Agathias and J. J. Boissard. The resulting text makes for a demanding read, as the particularities and finer details of the journey recounted by Don Juan alternate with both the more general descriptions gleaned by Remon from scholarly sources, and the conversion narrative celebrating Don Juan's embrace of the Catholic God. The tangibility of the described objects is sometimes also reminiscent of Spanish accounts of encounters in the New World; Cortés' sketch of Aztec royals in the early sixteenth century is just one instance. The complexity of the text is compounded by the change in audience: originally written in Persian to inform the court of Abbas the Great about the West, the final Castilian version is intended for Spanish readers, and combines extensive detail about the East with a powerful narrative of pro-Catholic propaganda. Indeed, it is important to register that the extracts reprinted below describing Don Juan's experiences in Southern Europe constitute a relatively small part of Don Juan's *Relaciones* as a whole; two-thirds of the work describe Persian history and Persia's wars in the sixteenth century with the Turks, and only the final third the travels of the embassy to the West.

[Extracts from G. Le Strange (ed. and trans.), *Don Juan of Persia, a Shi'ah Catholic, 1560-1604*. London: George Routledge, 1926, pp. 282-7, 291-4, 296-9.[142]]

When we had come to Florence, the Duke,[143] who was not in residence, being abroad on a hunting expedition, sent orders for them to give us rooms in his own palace, and many of his nobles came half a league outside the city gate to receive us, they brought us in riding in three magnificent coaches. Thus we came to the palace surrounded by a multitude of persons, where the Grand Duke's own servants waited on us. Then when we had been in Florence a fortnight, well entertained and seeing all the sights of this most famous city, which is notable for the richness of its many magnificent buildings, the Duke sent for us to come to him in Pisa, where he was residing with the Grand Duchess. On arrival we were received by his brother the prince Giovanni de' Medici, who next brought us to the palace, where the Duke and Duchess gave us a very affable reception. Here they kept us ten days, with princely entertainment, showing us the rich and curious treasures that are the property of the Duke. Afterwards they took us to see a new city that was being built there, and which will be a very magnificent place. There is also a fortress in the building, and a safe entrance to be made to the harbour, which will then become one of the finest ports in all the Mediterranean Sea. To do these works they have here more than five thousand slaves at work. The Grand Duke now presented our Ambassador with a fine gold chain to go round his neck sixteen times, supporting a medallion with his portrait, set in precious stones; and he gave another of like value to Sir Anthony Sherley.[144] The gentleman of the suite he honoured and gave presents to likewise. Then appointing one of his chamberlains to accompany us, he instructed him to pay all our travelling expenses as far as Rome, and so dismissed us.

Thus we took our leave of him, and proceeded on to Siena, where we remained while a gentleman was sent forward to Rome, riding post, to inform the Pope[145] that we were stopping in Siena awaiting permission to come and kiss the foot of his Holiness. After three days that we were waiting in Siena his Holiness sent a Cardinal to us, who welcomed us in his name, and gave orders in all matters that were necessary for our entertainment. Now here in the city of Siena our Ambassador had a quarrel with Sir Anthony Sherley, and matters would have come to a bad pass, had not the Cardinal, whom his Holiness had sent to us, been present to compose the dispute, though indeed he could not prevail on our Ambassador to allow Sir Anthony to enter Rome in his company, as originally it had been intended. The cause of this quarrel of our Ambassador with Sir Anthony was in the matter of thirty-two chests of presents, which, as already explained, had been given in charge of the English shipmaster [at Archangel] to be brought direct to Rome. The Ambassador was now demanding of Sir Anthony the due delivery of these chests, in order that he might make his Holiness a suitable present of what was in them, which, indeed, would have been a gift of much magnificence. It now appeared that the whole affair had been a cheat, for no chests had ever been brought to Rome, Sir Anthony having sold or bartered away their contents, namely those seven gifts of price [for the Pope and the Princes], to that English merchant captain, while we were travelling by sea in the Baltic Gulf or Northern Ocean. This in truth was the fact of what had happened, for we had notice of how our pieces of brocade and cloths had afterwards been publicly sold by the English merchants in Muscovy.

At length, however, this quarrel between us was accommodated by the kind offices of the Cardinal, and we went to Rome, where a nephew of the Pope came out to receive us a league beyond the city gate in company with a following of Roman gentlemen. Many coaches too had been sent out for our convenience and honour, but it was thought more seemly that we should ride, and so we entered Rome, each of us Persians, on horseback, accompanied by two Roman gentleman riding on either hand, while the nephew of his Holiness had the Ambassador on the one hand, with another great nobleman on the further side. The whole country outside the gate appeared on this occasion so thronged with coaches that I reckon there were more than one thousand of them, and more than four thousand gentleman on horseback or riding mules, while the number of those on foot who had come out to meet us was quite incalculable. As we entered into the city more than a hundred pieces of artillery were fired in a salute from the Castle of Saint Angelo from neighbouring towers, also a volley from the Papal matchlockmen, who were thus charged to do us honour at our coming. On entering the city they conducted us to a house, or palace, not very far from the Vatican Palace, where the Pope was in residence, and thitherto came to us a chamberlain of his Holiness, who offered to all of us much hospitality, and he lodged with us afterwards, providing till we departed whatever we required, and ordering everything for our convenience. Then, after we had been taking our rest for three days in Rome, his Holiness sent ordering us to come to him. And it was then again that our Ambassador had trouble on account of the doings of Sir Anthony, for he had to send to the Pope saying how impossible it was for him to go that day to kiss the foot of his Holiness, because he lacked the needful present, which Sir Anthony had cheated him of, and prevented his bringing—as has already been explained. But the Pope sent answer that the matter of presents was of no importance, that he himself would see to the affair later and make some arrangement to remedy the evil.

Our Ambassador thereupon consented to present himself, and accompanied by many gentlemen we set out for the Sacred Palace, and as we entered all the Cardinals came out to meet us, conducting us to the hall where we found his Holiness seated on the Pontifical Throne. At his feet, before it, was spread a carpet, on which cushions, on one of which the Ambassador took his seat, after having duly kissed the Pope's foot. His Holiness then gave us his blessing, saying, 'May God make you Christians'; and on this the Ambassador, with due respect, gave him the letter from the King of Persia. This the Pope received honourably, and then conversed, through the interpreter, for some time with our Ambassador, who among other matters acquainted him with the fraud and craft of Sir Anthony in the matter of presents. To which his Holiness replied: 'I do not chastise those who come to me, and still less those who are sent to me by the King of Persia. Let them carry him to the King of Spain, and let his Majesty chastise him.' Soon after this the Ambassador asked leave to retire, when his Holiness, on rising, again gave us his blessing and then went out. The Cardinals afterwards conducted us as far as the palace gate, whence the Papal chamberlain had charge of us to our lodging. Each day after this his Holiness would send to enquire how we fared, and then would give command that we should go out and see the sights of Rome. And daily the Cardinals or Princes would call on the Ambassador, and then we would go out to see those great churches and holy relics; and on the banks of the Tiber we would visit the various gardens and many orchards thereabout.

After we had passed two months thus in Rome, his Holiness sent our Ambassador a gold chain and 2,000 ducats; and to each of us, Secretaries of the Embassy, the Pope gave a chain and also his portrait. On this we went to take our leave of his Holiness, and to crave his benediction, asking permission to depart into Spain. The Pope granted us this most graciously, and appointed further a Canon of Barcelona, called Francisco Guasque, who should accompany us thither, the Canon being given charge of the funds of money necessary for our journey expenses as far as Spain. Now when we were just ready to leave Rome, and looked to see Sir Anthony to go with us, he did not appear, nor indeed could we come by news of any of the other Englishmen, for all of them had taken their departure, whither none knew. Thus we left Rome without the Englishmen, and next, when we had gone forth we perceived that three of our fellow Persians too were wanting. We therefore went back to find them, and discovered that already God had begun the work of His divine Grace. For these three Persians who had now left us we found in the palace of his Holiness in Rome, and they were studying to become Christian converts. The Ambassador was thereby much perturbed, and seeking audience of the Pope, his Holiness answered him that the Divine Law was indeed one kindness, that none by force was brought to believe, that all were free to act as they would, and that what he, the Pope, was doing was done in accordance with God's will. On this the

Ambassador spoke to the three men apart, and finding them steadfast and firm of purpose to become Christians, left them. He with the rest of us then departed from Rome.

❋   ❋   ❋

They now conducted us on to the presence chamber where the King [of Spain] was standing. The Ambassador came forward bearing the Letter, and this, after the Persian fashion, was written in letters of gold and coloured ink on a sheet of paper more than a yard in length and curiously folded, for the length in Persian style was doubled up, as for example is done in Spain with a folio sheet, and the paper was three finger-lengths in breadth. The Ambassador had brought the Letter enclosed in a bag of cloth of gold, and he carried this in his turban close upon his head, from whence he had now taken it, and first kissing it, then presented it to the King. His Majesty raising his bonnet, received the Letter, and through the interpreter informed himself of what the King of Persia had written, and now learnt what was the object of our embassy. This becoming known to him, he replied that he greatly esteemed the friendship which the King of Persia was offering him, that most gladly would he do all that the Shah had written desiring to be done, and that he would later send a reply to this Letter. Meanwhile we were to divert ourselves and take our ease. After all this had been said and done, on either side, the Ambassador begged permission to take leave of his Majesty, and we thereupon withdrew and returned to our lodgings accompanied by the escort, as we had come. We remained for the following two months nobly complimented at Court, being taken out in his Majesty's coaches, or on horseback, going to see the most notable sights of the city, and further were entertained by dancing at balls, and more particularly we saw bullfights and tilting in the ring. Now all these public festivals seemed to us to be better done in Spain than in any of the kingdoms we had previously visited, for the Spaniards, even in matter of sport, possess a grandeur and composure which is lacking in all other nations.

In the midst of these festivities a matter was happening which was to cause much disquietude to our Ambassador. Among his Secretaries of Embassy who had accompanied him from Persia, being of his suite, was his nephew, whose name was 'Ali Quli Beg, and he, because the subject pleased and interested him was now wont to attend the rites and services of the Christian Church. He had further come to appreciate the Spanish mode of life, and for convenience was accustomed to wear the Spanish dress. This at first apparently was done as a matter of mere curiosity and amusement, but in truth it was soon patent that, as we may opine and believe, the hour had struck in which God Almighty—who in past times had opened a path, with His right hand, through the waters of the Red Sea, whereby dry-shod the Children of Israel had gone over, and with His other hand had closed again the waters to cover and drown the satraps and all the Princes of Egypt—was now intent that in Spain He should be proclaimed again as God Almighty. For from the remotest parts of Asia He would bring, to the opposite limits of Europe, men with hard rebellious hearts, these to become softened anon, and like wax to melt in the enjoyment of the warm glow of Evangelical doctrine. Blessed, therefore, be His loving-kindness, and happy eternally this Persian gentleman to have accepted and profited by the mercies which God had vouchsafed him in causing him to become a Christian. I therefore return to my narrative and say that 'Ali Quli Beg, having now resolved to become a Christian and be baptised, forthwith acquainted us with his intention, and next retiring from among us put himself in the hands of certain Fathers of the Society of Jesus, that they might instruct him in the Faith and proceed to become a catechumen.

It appears to me also a matter of conscience that I should declare my belief, here in this place, that the true faith has been revealed by God, for His greater glory, solely and wholly to the Church [Apostolic of Rome], this indeed for the greater good and advantage of all true Christians, who thereby may through her teaching learn to walk in the way of truth and orthodoxy.

❋ ❋ ❋

Next we visited the palace known as the Casa del Campo of Madrid, where the fountains, gardens and tanks would need a special volume for their description, and then we entered Madrid, which is one of the greatest and most beautiful cities in all Spain. But its grandeur and many curious sights are so well known that it were better to be silent and not attempt to describe what others have already sufficiently portrayed. Leaving Madrid we journeyed on to Aranjuez, which is the summer-palace of the Kings of Spain, built likewise by his late Majesty King Philip II on the banks of the mighty river Tagus. The gardens of Aranjuez with their adjacent shrubberies, tanks, lakes, pleasure grounds, with thickets for game, great and small, are so extensive and of so many different kinds, with such fine trees and fruit orchards, also diverse beasts and birds brought from remotest India, that it were impossible to describe them all even in many volumes, and thus when we state that Aranjuez has been given the name of the Ninth Wonder of the World we have said all that here is needful. We visited also, as our journey lay through it, the Imperial city of Toledo, the capital of the gothic Kings. There is here the Alcazar, and we saw too the Machine[146] by which water is brought up from the depth of the gorge of the Tagus to the level of the city which lies above its bed; also we were brought to the Cathedral, which is the metropolitan church of Spain, whereby the city of Toledo is known as the Spanish Rome.

From this city we made our way travelling through the province of Estremadura to the town of Truxillo, where as many noble families have their origin, and next came to the city of Merida, which in ancient days was a second Rome, as to-day may be seen from the great extent of its ruins. The Ambassador wished to rest for a day in Merida, and here an immense number of people had collected in a vast crowd to gaze at us.

Now there was in our company, as ever had been since leaving home, our Alfaqui [al-faquih: religious scholar], he being, as one might say, the Ambassador's travelling Chaplain, and the [Arabic] name by which he was known was Amyr, for though he was Persian by birth, in point of fact he was a lineal descendant of the family of the prophet Mahomed. Now he on this occasion was standing at the door of our lodgings and there came to be much pushing in our doorway, when suddenly a man of insolent temper in the crowd, and lacking bowels of compassion, for there was no apparent provocation, struck out at the Alfaqui Amyr with a dagger, and killed him on the spot. As it was almost night-time when this happened it proved impossible to ascertain who had done the deed, although the magistrate used every means in his power, putting in prison an immense number of persons to satisfy the loud demand of the Ambassador, who seemed at first of opinion that he himself must return immediately to Valladolid to lay his complaint before the King. We learnt, however, on enquiry that his Majesty was at this moment no longer resident in the capital, being away on a hunting excursion, and it was therefore agreed that we should proceed straight to Lisbon, and while preparations there went forward for our embarkation, that I should travel back to Valladolid and give an account to his Majesty of how our poor Alfaqui had for no just cause been killed, and make demand that the assailant should be punished. We therefore proceeded to bury our Alfaqui Amyr according to Persian rites, with the ceremonies usual in our creed, in some ground outside Merida, and all the city came out to see the sight, which caused them much entertainment. From Merida then we went on to Badajoz, which is a city standing on the frontier between Spain and Portugal, and the civil-governor here, who is a gentleman of noble birth, and named Don Juan de Avalos, lodged us in his own house, giving us all we required, and paying every attention to our comfort. From Badajoz we finally set out for Lisbon, the great city celebrated throughout Spain for its noble situation, the name recalling that of him who was its founder, Ulysses [for ancients had named Lisbon Olisipp]. It is the capital and the largest town in Portugal, and has a population of more than 80,000 householders [or 360,000 souls]. Further, here is a great harbour, at the mouth of the Tagus, where the river comes out to the Ocean, which same is the chief port whence all ships start that sail for India the Greater, and the New World.

Now as soon as we, after leaving Badajoz, had come to Aldea Gallega we sent across to let the Viceroy of Portugal, Don Cristobal de Mora, know that we were there, he forthwith dispatched to us four galleys with many gentlemen in attendance, who now brought us into Lisbon. Here they gave us a grand reception, making festival, and hospitably lodged us in a magnificent palace. After we had taken our repose during some days, being sumptuously entertained by the Viceroy, and further by many of the Portuguese noblemen and private persons of Lisbon, for certainly they are the most hospitable of hosts, our Ambassador ordered me to return with the Canon to Valladolid, to give his Majesty a true account of the death of our Alfaqui. I forthwith proceeded to carry out his command, and herein is made evident the truth of that which King David the man of God hath spoken—namely, that the hand of God doth guide the hearts of men in accordance with His divine will. For as soon as I had got to Valladolid I went to see 'Ali Quli Beg at the Jesuit House, and no sooner had I begun to talk with him, and to hold converse with the Fathers of the House of Jesus—religious men as discrète as they are learned—when it became manifest how God Almighty willed that a miracle should be worked in me. For I began immediately to feel an inordinate longing in my heart to seek and find His holy name—and while I was yet a prey to this confusion of mind, and unable to declare clearly my desire, the Divine Will loosed my slow tongue—even as with Moses of old—and just as I was returned to my lodging house I urgently called upon the Fathers to grant me baptism, though no master had yet given me any sufficient instruction in religion.

In the Persian script and language, even as before had been the case with my Diary, I now constrained my hand to write down the prayers, the articles of belief, the Commandments, and other Christian ordinances that were necessary for instructing one like me, an infidel, who was about to become a catechumen. That due praise may be paid to the Divine Grace, I have here given this very particular account of my experiences and conversion, for it is His marvellous providence which thus works in those whom he calls to His Church, and to union with the faithful.

The Travel Diaries of Xu Xiake (1623)

From *Xu Xiake youji*

Xu Xiake (1586-1641), previously spelled Hsü Hsia-K'o, is widely regarded in China as the greatest Chinese traveller of all time, but despite the efforts of his modern translator Li ji [Li Chi] he is still not as known to the world as Basho or ibn Battuta, let alone their Western counterparts. The difficulty of recognition may lie in the way he and classical Chinese literature see the genre of travel writing. The "Western tradition", which in fact includes Arab travel writers like ibn Jubair and ibn Battuta, is primarily concerned with the way in which an individual mind, at best an eccentric one, responds to the places he or she is travelling through. Travel writing is an account of the exotic for the home market, written with more or less immersion in or sympathy with the cultures and landscapes described. Travel is the textual trace of places passed in time on the individual mind, even if the travel is a pilgrimage. To Xu travel is a meditative immersion into place, where the distinction between text, mind and place is erased in keeping with the classical Chinese tradition which sees landscape painting and poetry as one integrated genre. This is the case also with Basho, of course, but in Basho text, mind and place are integrated in a *haiku*-like antimetaphysics, which is still distinctly the product of an individual sensibility. With Xu what seems remarkable is the modest disappearance of the self into a religious–aesthetic contemplation, which is perhaps only possible in a culture with a widely shared landscape aesthetics such as the Chinese cult of mountains. Thus writing and landscape, observer and observed, do not stand in opposition to each other: rather the writing is to be seen as an inscription like the poem on a scroll, but also on the landscape itself, adding to the many inscriptions that have made the landscape into a "view" and a "state of mind" in the first place. Partly ideographic writing like the Chinese adds to this reflexivity: thus Xu gave all his sons names which contained the mountain radical.

Xu was born in a village near Jiangyin on the Huang River into a family of officials, landowners and men of letters. Unusually for their class, neither Xu nor his father ever took any official examinations, preferring the life of free intellectuals. Xu lived during the breakdown of the Ming Dynasty, in a period of intense political upheaval and anti-intellectualism; he associated with the oppositional intellectuals of the Hanlin Academy, whose leader, Huang Dao Zhou (1585-1646) was one of his closest friends, but Xu never seems to have been involved in politics himself. Rather, he was admired by his friends for his freedom and detachment, which is partly why one of them named him Xiake (which was not his official name): the character *Xiá* referring to the rosy clouds of dawn which in Daoism are associated with the essence of the sun and attaining immortality, and *ke* meaning a visitor, a brief sojourner in this world. Early in his boyhood, Xu had developed a taste for unusual books not part of the official curriculum, books on history, geography and topography, and it was partly as an effort to improve Chinese geographical literature that he conceived of his great project (supported by his widowed mother, who accompanied him on an extended trip as late as her eightieth year) of visiting everywhere in China where it was possible.

From 1609 to 1636 Xu travelled, indeed largely walked, almost every year to various parts of China, keeping his travel diaries as an essential part of the experience. Having visited all known sights in his native Southern and Northern China, including the then little explored Huang Shan mountains, which Xu's writings were partly responsible for making into one of China's major tourist attractions, in 1636 he set out on a long journey to the unexplored regions of the Southwest: Guangxi, Hunan and Yunnan. Xu set out with two servants and a monk, who wished to take a copy of the Fahua Sutra he had written in his own blood to Jizi Mountain (Mt. Kukkutapada) in Yunnan. It fell to Xu to take his ashes and the sutra there, and he returned alone in 1640, worn out with foot and skin disease, having to be carried home in a sedan chair to die. But he had travelled throughout the Southwest, testing his geographical hypotheses about mountain ranges and the flow of rivers; on this last journey scientific inquiry seems, according to the translator Li ji, to have outweighed landscape aesthetics as a motive for travelling.

The extant travel diaries cover 150 days prior to 1636 in 40,000 words, an average of 270 words a day; but the last journey into the Southwest resulted in entries for 700 days, totalling 450,000 words or an average of 640 words. Very little of this has been translated into English: even the book from which the following passage has been taken, Li ji's *The Travel Diaries of Hsü Hsia-k'o* (Hong Kong: The Chinese University of Hong Kong, 1974) is as much résumé as translation, learned and informative though it is.

Songshan, the prime of the five sacred mountains venerated by the Chinese since antiquity, had fallen somewhat into disrepute when Xu visited it. For the first time since the Han Dynasty and the foundation of the nearby city of Luo by the Duke of Zhou at the beginning of the Zhou Dynasty, the region around Songshan had not been politically central to the Ming, out of a memory of how the Jurchen invasion swept away the entire imperial family from their capital at Luoyang at the end of the Northern Song Dynasty. But the mountain preserved many stories, which were as central a part of Xu's appreciation of mountains as "natural beauty": not least the story of the mountain's major "publicity stunt" during the visit of the Han Emperor Wu in 110 BC, when on ascending the mountain the Emperor and his retinue clearly heard the mountain call out, "Long live the Emperor!"

[Extracts from Li ji [Li Chi], *The Travel Diaries of Hsü Hsia-k'o*. Hong Kong: The Chinese University of Hong Kong, 1974. Published with acknowledgement to the translator and the publisher.]

The Travel Diary of Xu Xiake (1568-1641)

Diary

Ever since my childhood, I have cherished a desire to see all five sacred mountains. The Prime Sacred Mountain being rated above the five sacred ones, my longing to see this one has been even greater. I also have long wished to travel to Xiang and Yun, to pass my hands over the mountain Taihua, and to set off from Jianke (Sword Pavilion) through the whole length of Lianyun (Covered Plank Way) to Emei Shan. But the increasing age of my mother limits my ambitions, and my tours have to be made according to pre-arranged plans. It would take an inordinate amount of time to travel by boat. It would be faster if I went by land and returned by boat, but if I travelled both ways by land, I could include both Song Shan and Taihua in one pilgrimage.

Accordingly, I set out on my journey on March 1, 1623, in the year of Guihai (1623), and made Song my first objective. After nineteen days I reached Huangzong Tien, a small village of Zhengzhou in Henan. Here I went up the stone slope on the right of the village, and viewed Shengseng Chi (Holy Monk's Pool), which is a pool from a spring, collecting its clear green water halfway up the hill. Under it is a maze of deep gorges, all so dried that there was not a drop of water in them. I went down and walked on its floor, following the winding turns of Xianglu Shan (Incense Burner Mountain) southward. This mountain is shaped like an inverted incense burner with its three legs sticking up in the sky. Surrounding it are other mountains, charming the visitor with their gently beautiful colours. The bottom of the gorge is filled with masses of stones with the colour of purple jade, rocky cliffs rising on both sides. As I walked through the gorge, I imagined how beautiful it must look when filled with a clear torrent spurting pearls and jets of water.

Ten *li*, and I mounted the Shifo Ling (Stone Buddha Hill), another five *li* and I entered the boundary of Mi Xian, where the Song could be viewed from a distance of sixty *li*. Taking a by-path southeast for twenty five *li*, we passed Mi Xian and reached Tianxian Yuan (Heavenly Goddesses' Temple), which is sacred to the three heavenly goddesses, the three daughters of the Yellow Emperor. The celebrated white pine is in the court at the rear of the temple. Legend has it that the three maidens shed their mortal bodies here. It takes four people with outstretched arms to surround the mighty trunk of this pine, from which three huge branching trunks shoot clear up out of a circle of stone railings into the clouds. The bark is as smooth as congealed lard and its whiteness is like face powder. What an extremely impressive sight this great tree makes with its white jade-like trunks towering to the sky, its entangled boughs coiling and uncoiling, and its jade-green sprays dancing in the wind! To the north is a pavilion with poems of appreciation written all over it, and there I lingered a long while. Looking down where the gorge makes an abrupt drop, I saw water dripping from an overhanging crag...

...*March 23*. All traces of clouds have vanished. Went to the central hall to worship before starting out for Nan Zhai (South Castle) which is the highest summit of Lesser Room, equal in height to Great Room and noted for the steep and erect hills that bear the name Jiuding Lianhua (Nine Lotus Tripot Cauldrons). The lower hills embracing its back, called Jiu Yu Feng (Nine Breast Hills), crawl east to join Great Room, with the Shaolin Monastery on its northern side. This monastery is a compact and beautiful piece of architecture. In its courts, new and old inscriptions stand in rows, all in perfect condition. The two pines bordering the walk inside are tall and elegant, as if measured to order. The peak Lesser Room reclines horizontally in front of it, giving the tourist who is unable to see its summit from below the feeling that he is facing an enormous wall. That is why it is said that Lesser Room is seen best when viewed from a distance. The night before, when I had asked for directions to it, I was told that the road had been closed by snow, making it impossible to go there. Although I find that a bright day is the finest for mountain climbing, I mounted Great Room in an enveloping fog, which some people take as a sign of rejection from the mountain spirits. They do not know that the colossal proportions of that peak are best seen when only half of its profile is revealed, unlike Lesser Room whose beauty lies in overlappings and intricate turnings that can be spoiled by even a few fleecy clouds. I was lucky enough to have chanced upon such a perfect day. How could I miss it? I set off, crossed the gorge to Erzi An (Second Patriarch Monastery), another six or seven *li*, and was surprised to find an end to the earthen hills and the beginning of rocky ones. Rocky crags dropped vertically to form a ravine, from which a torrent crashed down, breaking itself upon a jutting rock below. This was the Zhulian (Pearl Curtain).

Staff in hand, I made for it, but the lower I went the more I lost my way. After a long while, however, I found it. The crag was not so open and grand as Lu crag, but it was deep and more pointed. Under it was a deep tarn of clear water, banked all round with firm snow. Farther up, I found Liandan Tai (Alchemist's Terrace), overhanging on three sides with its fourth side leaning on a green cliff, and a pavilion called Xiao You Tian which had hardly ever before felt the clogs of a mountain climber. After this it was a straight toil up to a rocky ridge which hung entirely by itself between two perpendicular cliffs of immeasurable height. There was not one inch of earth clinging to it, so I had to use both my hands and feet to scramble up. There were seven *li* like this before I reached a big hill which was wide and easy; here, suddenly, the perilous rocks give way to earth again.

I then ascended southward through the brushwoods about five *li* and came to the summit of South Castle. Here again, the screening earth came to an end. The South Castle was actually the northern peak of Lesser Room, but viewed from Shao-lin Monastery it appeared on the south side. The summit was riven in the middle into two parts. The northern side spread like a screen while the southern side stood like a row of spears only ten feet away. Rising between the deep ravine was a hill which towered above all the other peaks, called the Zhexiang Tai (Terrace of Plucking Stars). This was the center of Songshan. Its highest pinnacle was entirely cleft from the northern side, so there was absolutely no way to cross. Peeping down, however, I espied a connecting trail, so I took off my gown and followed it till I reached the top. There I viewed the nine hills of the southern peak standing erectly in front of me. Half of the crags back of the northern peak turned round from behind, appearing bottomless. As I stood there taking in the view, a sudden blast of wind nearly swept me off. Turning northeast from the South Castle, I descended the earthen hill and saw big impressions of tiger's paws. Walking another five or six li in the tall brushwood, I reached a thatched house where I made a fire in the stones and cooked some rice gruel. After several bowls of it, both hunger and thirst were gone.

Asking the monk in the thatched temple to show me the way to Dragon Tarn I descended a hill whose ridge became increasingly narrow as the earth on it began again to be mixed with rocks and covered with vines and brambles. I advanced by pulling upon those till I suddenly found myself confronted by a steep rock of immense height blocking the path. I turned up and as I descended from there, the hill seemed to slope more windingly. I soon came upon another steep rock, making it necessary to go backwards and forwards for several *li* in a circuit round a valley. After that I found the way out to a place called Longtan Gou (Dragon Tarn Gutter). When I looked up toward the place where I had got lost, I saw only precipitous cliffs and rocks balanced above cliffs of immense height. Numerous springs dashed and flowed among the gloomy and deep clefts of the crags, reflecting the gorgeous colors of shinning silk. I followed the stream and when I turned with the gorge. I found cells of monks as thick as beehives and swallows' nests on both sides. After five *li*, I came to the First Dragon Tarn, and then the Second Dragon Tarn, and so out of the gorge. The night was spent at Shaolin Monastery.

Olaudah Equiano's Voyage to Slavery and Freedom (1789)

From *The Interesting Narrative of the Life of Olaudah Equiano, Or Gustavus Vassa, The African. Written by Himself*

Olaudah Equiano (Gustavus Vassa), b. 1745, was kidnapped from his African village at the age of eleven, shipped through the arduous "Middle Passage" of the Atlantic Ocean, "seasoned" in the West Indies and sold to a planter in the American colony of Virginia. He was later bought by a British naval officer, Captain Pascal, as a present for his cousins in London. After ten years of enslavement throughout the North American continent, where he assisted his merchant slave master and worked as a seaman, Equiano bought his freedom. At the age of forty-four he wrote and published his autobiography, *The Interesting Narrative of the Life of Olaudah Equiano, Or Gustavus Vassa, The African. Written by Himself*, which he registered at Stationer's Hall, London, in 1789. More than two centuries later, this work is recognized not only as one of the first works written in English by a former slave, but perhaps more important as the paradigm of the slave narrative, a new literary genre.

Born in 1745, Equiano recalls his childhood in Essaka (an Igbo village now in southeast Nigeria), where he was adorned in the tradition of the "greatest warriors". He is unique in his recollection of traditional African life before the advent of the European slave trade. Equally significant is Equiano's life on the high seas, which included not only travels throughout the Americas, Turkey and the Mediterranean but also participation in major naval battles during the French and Indian War (Seven Years' War), as well as in the search for a Northwest Passage led by the Phipps expedition of 1772-73. Equiano also records his central role, along with Granville Sharpe, in the British Abolitionist Movement. As a major voice in this movement, Equiano petitioned the Queen of England in 1788. He was appointed to the expedition to settle London's poor Blacks in

Sierra Leone, a British colony on the west coast of Africa. Sadly, he did not complete the journey back to his native land.

Despite these attractive accomplishments, however, Equiano's most important work is his autobiography, which became a bestseller, rivalled in popularity by Defoe's *Robinson Crusoe*. He published nine different editions of his autobiography before his death in 1797, including an American edition (1791), and German and Dutch editions, 1790 and 1791 respectively. By 1837, nine more editions had been published. Along with its firsthand testimony against slavery, the extracts reprinted here include his richly detailed seagoing adventures that take him throughout Europe and the Americas. In 1767 the self-emancipated Equiano returned to England to work as a hairdresser for wealthy clients and study music and mathematics. In 1773 he returned to sea to participate in an expedition to the North Pole. And after travelling through Central America, Equiano settled in England in 1777.

[Extracts from *The Interesting Narrative of the Life of Olaudah Equiano, Or Gustavus Vassa, The African. Written by Himself* (1789), written by Olaudah Equiano in English, Leeds: James Nichols, 1814]

Voyage to England

I now totally lost the small remains of comfort I had enjoyed in conversing with my countrymen; the women too who used to wash and take care of me were all gone different ways, and I never saw one of them afterwards.

I stayed in this island for a few days, I believe it could not be above a fortnight, when I and some few more slaves that were not saleable amongst the rest, from very much fretting, were shipped off in a sloop for North America. On the passage we were better treated than when we were coming from Africa and we had plenty of rice and fat pork. We were landed up a river a good way from the sea, about Virginia county, where we saw few or none of our native Africans and not one soul who could talk to me. I was a few weeks weeding grass and gathering stones in a plantation, and at last all my companions were distributed different ways and only myself was left. I was now exceedingly miserable and thought myself worse off than any of the rest of my companions, for they could talk to each other, but I had no person to speak to that I could understand. In this state I was constantly grieving and pining and wishing for death rather than anything else. While I was in this plantation the gentleman, to whom I suppose the estates belonged, being unwell, I was one day sent for to his dwelling house to fan him; when I came into the room where he was I was very much affrighted at something I saw, and the more so as I had seen a black woman slave as I came through the house, who was cooking the dinner, and the poor creature was cruelly loaded with various kinds of iron machines; she had one particularly on her head which locked her mouth so fast that she could scarcely speak, and could not eat nor drink. I was much astonished and shocked at this contrivance, which I afterwards learned was called the iron muzzle. Soon after I had a fan put into my hand to fan the gentleman while he slept, and so I did indeed with great fear. While he was fast asleep I indulged myself a great deal in looking about the room, which to me appeared very fine and curious. The first object that engaged my attention was a watch which hung on the chimney and was going. I was quite surprised at the noise it made and was afraid it would tell the gentleman anything I might do amiss: and when I immediately after observed a picture hanging in the room, which appeared constantly to look at me, I was still more affrighted, having never seen such things as these before. At one time I thought it was something relative to magic; and not seeing it move I thought it might be some way the whites had to keep their great men when they died and offer them libations as we used to do to our friendly spirits. In this state of anxiety I remained till my master awoke, when I was dismissed out of the room to my no small satisfaction and relief, for I thought that these people were all made up of wonders. In this place I was called Jacob, but on board the *African Snow* I was called Michael. I had been some time in this miserable, forlorn, and much dejected state without having anyone to talk to, which made my life a burden, when the kind and unknown hand of the Creator (who in every deed leads the blind in a way they know not) now began to appear, to my comfort; for one day the captain of a merchant ship called *Industrious Bee* came on some business to my master's house. This gentleman, whose name was Michael Henry Pascal, was a lieutenant in the Royal Navy, but now commanded this trading ship which was somewhere in the confines of the country many miles off While he was at my master's house it happened that he saw me and liked me so well that he made a purchase of me. I think I have often heard him say he gave thirty or forty pounds sterling for me, but I do not now remember which. However, he meant me for a present to some friends in England, and I was sent accordingly from the house of my then master, one Mr. Campbell, to the place where the ship lay; I was conducted on horseback by an elderly black man (a mode of travelling which appeared very odd to me). When I arrived I was carried on board a fine large ship, loaded with tobacco, etc. and just ready to sail for England. I now thought my condition much mended; I had sails to lie on and plenty of good victuals to eat, and everybody on board used me very kindly, quite contrary to what I had seen of any white people before; I therefore began to think that they were not all of the same disposition. A few days after I was on board we sailed for England. I was still at a loss to conjecture my destiny. By this time however I could smatter a little imperfect English, and I wanted to know as well as I could where we were going. Some of the people of the ship used to tell me they were going to carry me back to my own country and this made me very happy. I was quite rejoiced at the sound of going back, and thought if I should get home what wonders I should have to tell. But I was reserved for another fate and was soon undeceived when we came within sight of the English coast. While I was on board this ship, my captain and master named me *Gustavus Vasa*. I at that time began to understand him a little, and refused to be called so, and told him as well as I could that I would be called Jacob: but he said I should not, and still called me Gustavus; and when I refused to answer to my new name, which at first I did, it gained me many a cuff; so at length I submitted and was obliged to bear the present name, by which I have been known ever since. The ship had a very long passage, and on that account we had very short allowance of provisions. Towards the last we had only one pound and a half of bread per week, and about the same quantity of meat, and one quart of water a day. We spoke with only one vessel the whole time we were at sea, and but once we caught a few fishes. In our extremities the captain and people told me in jest they would kill and eat me, but I thought them in earnest and was depressed beyond measure, expecting every moment to be my last. While I was in this situation, one evening they caught, with a good deal of trouble, a large shark, and got it on board. This gladdened my poor heart exceedingly, as I thought it would serve the people to eat instead of their eating me; but very soon, to my astonishment, they cut off a small part of the tail and tossed the rest over the side. This renewed my consternation, and I did not know what to think of these white people, though I very much feared they would kill and eat me. There was on board the ship a young lad who had never been at sea before, about four or five years older than myself: his name was Richard Baker. He was a native of America, had received an excellent education, and was of a most amiable temper. Soon after I went on board he showed me a great deal of partiality and attention and in return I grew extremely fond of him. We at length became inseparable, and for the space of two years, he was of very great use to me, and was my constant companion and instructor. Although this dear youth had many slaves of his own, yet he and I have gone through many sufferings together on shipboard, and we have many nights lain in each other's bosoms when we were in great distress. Thus such a friendship was cemented between us as we cherished till his death, which to my very great sorrow happened in the year 1759, when he was up the Archipelago on board his Majesty's ship the *Preston*, an event which I have never ceased to regret as I lost at once a kind interpreter, and agreeable companion, and a faithful friend; who, at the age of fifteen, discovered a mind superior to prejudice, and who was not ashamed to notice, to associate with, and to be the friend and instructor of one who was ignorant, a stranger, of a different complexion, and a slave! My master had lodged in his mother's house in America: he respected him very much and made him always eat with him in the cabin. He used often to tell him jocularly that he would kill me to eat. Sometimes he would say to me the black people were not good to eat, and would ask me if we did not eat people in my country. I said, No: then he said he would kill Dick (as he always called him) first, and afterwards me. Though this hearing relieved my mind a little as to myself, I was alarmed for Dick and whenever he was called I used to be very much afraid he was to be killed, and I would peep and watch to see if they were going to kill him: nor was I free from this consternation till we made the land. One night we lost a man overboard, and the cries and noise were so great and confused in stopping the ship, that I, who did not know what was the matter, began as usual to be very much afraid and to think they were going to make an offering with me and perform some magic, which I still believed they dealt in. As the waves were very high I thought the Ruler of the seas was angry, and I expected to be offered up to appease him. This filled my mind with agony, and I could not any more that night close my eyes to rest. However when daylight appeared I was a little eased in my mind, but still every time I was called I used to think it was to be killed. Some time after this we saw some very large fish, which I afterwards found were called grampuses. They looked to me extremely terrible and made their appearance just at dusk, and were so near as to blow the water on the ship's deck. I believed them to be the rulers of the sea, and as the white people did not make any offerings at any time I thought they were angry with them: and at last, what confirmed my belief was, the wind just then died away and a calm ensued, and in consequence the ship stopped going. I supposed that fish had performed this, and I hid myself in the fore part of the ship through fear of being offered up to appease them, every minute peeping and quaking: but my good friend Dick came shortly towards me, and I took an opportunity to ask him, as well as I could, what these fish were. Not being able to talk much English, I could but just make him understand my question, and not at all when I asked him if any offerings were to be made to them: however, he told me these fish would swallow anybody, which sufficiently alarmed me. Here he was called away by the captain, who was leaning over the quarter-deck railing and looking at the fish, and most of the people were busied in getting a barrel of pitch to light for them to play with. The captain now called me to him, having learned some of my apprehensions from Dick, and having diverted himself and others for some time with my fears, which appeared ludicrous enough in my crying and trembling, he dismissed me. The barrel of pitch was now lighted and put over the side into the water: by this time it was just dark, and the fish went after it, and to my great joy I saw them no more.

However, all my alarms began to subside when we got sight of land, and at last the ship arrived at Falmouth after a passage of thirteen weeks. Every heart on board seemed gladdened on our reaching the shore, and none more then mine. The captain immediately went on shore and sent on board some fresh provisions, which we wanted very much: we made good use of them and our famine was soon turned into feasting almost without ending. It was about the beginning of 1757 when I arrived in England, and I was near twelve years of age at that time. I was very much struck with the buildings and the pavement of the streets in Falmouth, and indeed any object I saw filled me with new surprise. One morning when I got up on deck, I saw it covered all over with the snow that fell overnight: as I had never seen anything of the kind before I thought it was salt, so I immediately ran down to the mate and desired him, as well as I could, to come and see how somebody in the night had thrown salt all over the deck. He, knowing what it was, desired me to bring some of it down to him: accordingly I took up a handful of it, which I found very cold indeed, and when I brought it to him he desired me to taste it. I did so, and I was surprised beyond measure. I then asked him what it was; he told me it was snow, but I could not in anywise understand him. He asked me if we had no such thing in my country, and I told him, No. I then asked him the use of it and who made it; he told me a great man in the heavens, called God: but here again I was to all intents and purposes at a loss to understanding him, and the more so when a little after I saw the air filled with it in a heavy shower which fell down on the same day. After this I went to church, and having never been at such a place before I was again amazed at seeing and hearing the service. I asked all I could about it, and they gave me to understand it was worshipping God, who made us and all things. I was still at a great loss, and soon got into an endless field of inquiries, as well as I was able to speak and ask about things. However, my little friend Dick used to be my best interpreter, for I could make free with him and he always instructed me with pleasure: and from what I could understand by him of this God, and in seeing these white people did not sell one another as we did, I was much pleased; and in this I thought they were much happier than we Africans. I was astonished at the wisdom of the white people in all things I saw, but was amazed at their not sacrificing or making any offerings, and eating with unwashed hands and touching the dead. I likewise could not help remarking the particular slenderness of their women, which I did not at first like, and I thought they were not so modest and shamefaced as the African women.

I had often seen my master and Dick employed in reading, and I had a great curiosity to talk to the books as I thought they did, and so to learn how all things had a beginning: for that purpose I have often taken up a book and have talked to it and then put my ears to it, when alone, in hopes it would answer me; and I have been very much concerned when I found it remained silent.

My master lodged at the house of a gentleman in Falmouth who had a fine little daughter about six or seven years of age, and she grew prodigiously fond of me, insomuch that we used to eat together and had servants to wait on us. I was so much caressed by this family that it often reminded me of the treatment I had received from my little noble African master. After I had been here a few days I was sent on board of the ship, but the child cried so much after me that nothing could pacify her till I was sent for again. It is ludicrous enough, that I began to fear I should be betrothed to this young lady, and when my master asked me if I would stay there with her behind him, as he was going away with the ship which had taken in the tobacco again, I cried immediately and said I would not leave him. At last by stealth one night I was sent on board the ship again, and in a little time we sailed for Guernsey where she was in part owned by a merchant, one Nicholas Doberry. As I was now amongst a people who had not their faces scarred like some of the African nations where I had been, I was very glad I did not let them ornament me in that manner when I was with them. When we arrived at Guernsey, my master placed me to board and lodge with one of his mates who had a wife and family there; and some months afterwards he went to England and left me in care of this mate, together with my friend Dick. This mate had a little daughter, aged about five or six years, with whom I used to be much delighted. I had often observed that when her mother washed her face it looked very rosy, but when she washed mine it did not look so: I therefore tried often times myself if I could not by washing make my face of the same colour as my little playmate (Mary), but it was all in vain, and I now began to be mortified at the difference in our complexions. This woman behaved to me with great kindness and attention, and taught me everything in the same manner as she did her own child, and indeed in every respect treated me as such. I remained here till the summer of the year 1757, when my master, being appointed first lieutenant of His Majesty's ship the *Roebuck* sent for Dick and me and his old mate: on this we all left Guernsey and set out for England in a sloop bound for London. As we were coming up towards the Nore where the *Roebuck* lay, a man-of-war's boat came alongside to press our people, on which each man ran to hide himself. I was very much frightened at this, though I did not know what it meant or what to think or do. However, I went and hid myself also under a hencoop. Immediately afterwards the press-gang came on board with their swords drawn, and searching all about, pulled the people out by force, and put them into the boat. At last I was found out also: the man that found me held me up by the heels while they all made their sport of me, I roaring and crying out all the time most lustily: but at last the mate, who was my conductor, seeing this, came to my assistance and did all he could to pacify me, but all to very little purpose till I had seen the boat go off. Soon afterwards we came to the Nore where the Roebuck lay, and to our great joy my master came on board to us and brought us to the ship. When I went on board this large ship I was amazed indeed to see the quantity of men and guns. However my surprise began to diminish as my knowledge increased, and I ceased to feel those apprehensions and alarms which had taken such strong possession of me when I first came among the Europeans, and for some time after. I began now to pass to an opposite extreme; I was so far from being afraid of anything new which I saw that, after I had been some time in this ship, I even began to long for a battle. My griefs too, which in young minds are not perpetual, were now wearing away, and I soon enjoyed myself pretty well and felt tolerably easy in my present situation...

Dean Mahomed Writes from the Centre
From the *Travels of Dean Mahomet* (1794)

Dean Mahomed's career marks, in its very choice of profession and allegiance (as well as, finally, land of residence), a crucial change in the political and socio-economic structuring of India. It was a change related to the consolidation of colonization in the mid-eighteenth century. As the second son of a (deceased) officer with aristocratic relations but not much land, Dean Mahomed would have probably chosen an administrative or military career with the family's traditional patron, the Nawabs of Bengal. Dean Mahomed did choose a military career, but with the Bengal Army of the British East India company at a time when the Bengal army, like the British Raj, was still assuming its final colonial colours and dimensions.

Born in Patna in 1759, Dean Mahomed chose to attach himself to Godfrey Evan Baker, a newly-arrived Cadet from Cork, in spite of the objections of his mother:

> ...Nothing could exceed my ambition of leading a soldier's life: the notion of carrying arms, and living in a camp, could not be easily removed: my fond mother's entreaties were of no avail...I told her I would stay in the camp: her disappointment smote my soul—she stood silent—yet I could perceive some tears succeed each other, stealing down her cheeks—my heart was wrung— at length, seeing my resolution fixed as fate, she dragged herself away and returned home in a state of mind beyond my power to describe...

Dean Mahomed was 10 years old (by one account) when he took this decision, and Baker probably in his mid-teens. However, the decision was to keep the men together for the rest of their lives, until Baker's death on his return to Ireland, and it was to take Dean Mahomed across much of India and finally to Ireland in 1784.

In 1793, a series of advertisements proposed to publish "by

SUBSCRIPTION, in TWO VOLUMES DUODECIMO, Adorned with Plates, the Travels of DEAN MAHOMET, Through Several Parts of the Eastern Territory (Being a Native of India), in which is circumstantially related the Manners, Religion, Manufactures, Productions, etc. of the different Countries through which he passed..." The advertisements went on to promise not only "a particular account of the Solemn Procession of the Grand Nabobs and Rajahs from their Palaces to their Places of Worship", but also "an accurate Account of the Wars in India." Dean Mahomed was 34 at the time and, as the advertisement indicates, sensitive to the image that Europe harboured of both Indians and Eastern religions (Islam or Hinduism). Perhaps writing in English, he could not simply offer a "banquet" of European marvels to Indians, as Abu Taleb writing in Indo-Persian could; he had to face the English-knowing world and defend Indians and India against the "boasting philosophers" of Europe. The line he took—that Indians were more natural and "innocent" than Europeans—was neither new nor surprising (keeping in view eighteenth-century discourses), but the attempt remains significant. Often in the book, he appears to be implicitly or explicitly correcting dominant English views—of India as an exotic land or a land of seductive depravity, of Muslims as blind followers of a depraved and oppressive religion.

At the time the advertisement appeared, Dean Mahomed was married and settled in Cork. He had become a member of the protestant Church some years back. He had married one Jane Daly (a Catholic), whose parents—as Michael H. Fisher argues in an excellent study of the *Travels* [147]—appear to have dissociated themselves from the couple, even though the couple did have their supporters in polite society. What is interesting is also the fact, as Fisher points out, that the way the marriage took place—by the posting of a substantial bond—indicates not only the doubts that the concerned Church harboured over the legality of the marriage but also the fact that Dean Mahomed was reasonably affluent.

At least some of the riches—not to mention much of the rising fortunes of the Bakers—must have been accumulated in the years in which Dean Mahomed accompanied Godfrey Evan Baker across the length and breadth of North India: from Patna to the Bihar frontiers, down the Ganges to Calcutta and Awadh. In 1784, having visited Madras, Dean Mahomed accompanied Baker back to Ireland. As Fisher notes, when Dean Mahomed disembarked at Cork late in 1784, he must have been assailed with impressions both familiar and strange. Cork and Calcutta were colonial port cities of a similar architectural style and mercantile nature. However, not only would the breweries (six million gallons of porter annually) and abattoirs (100,000 barrels of pork annually) of Cork have created a distinct impression, Dean Mahomed must also have had to get used to sight of poor *white* men, women and children.

Financially, Dean Mahomed appears to have done well in Britain, though not always. Moving from Cork to London and then to Brighton, Dean Mahomed made influential friends in polite British society and finally turned his "Indianness" to economic advantage. However, his first major business venture, the Hindoostanee Coffee House (1810-12) in London—probably the first such to promise authentic Indian cuisine (including ornate hookahs), served on bamboo cane furniture and in rooms adorned with Indian paintings— ended in bankruptcy. In his 50s, and with a family to support, Dean Mahomed had to move to humbler lodgings and seek service. However, he was back soon. He moved to Brighton with his family and set up his famous "Baths" in that city. The baths were immensely successful and received the patronage of the British royalty. As Fisher puts it, "his therapeutic skills and self-promotion as expert in the 'Indian Medicated Vapour Bath' and 'shampooing Surgeon' would quickly lead to his most illustrious career."

Dean Mahomed claimed to have introduced shampooing in the West, and it appears that his *Travels* (completed on 15 January 1794) was the first book in English by an Indian. The book was dedicated to Colonel William A. Bailie and written in the form of a series of letters to an imaginary friend. In writing it, Dean Mahomed might have had social prestige in mind—as the language of the text shows, he was a man of literary interests. He definitely wanted to put on record a defence of the "manners of my countrymen", perhaps also for his descendants. He might also have been influenced by the fact that certain Black authors (Africans and people of African descent) had already written about their cultures or their experiences in Europe— Fisher claims that "Dean Mahomed almost certainly knew, and may have met, one of the most influential of such early Black authors." This Black author would have been Olaudah Equiano, who toured Ireland in 1791, and extracts from whose book are also included in this anthology.

In 1822, Dean Mahomed wrote and published another book, *Shampooing, or, Benefits Resulting From the Use of the Indian Medicated Bath, As Introduced Into This Country, by S. D. Mahomed (A Native of India)*. He was also the founder of a family that contributed in many ways to British history in spite of racial discrimination at times: two of his sons followed in his footsteps while one established a successful fencing academy and gymnasium. His grandsons were to become doctors, vicars, architects and scientists: one of his grandsons, Frederick Akbar Mahomed (1849-84), was a pioneer of clinical research. Two of Dean Mahomed's great-grandsons died fighting for the British in the First World War, one as an engineer in the Scots Guards and the other in the Royal Flying Corps. Less is known about Dean Mahomed's daughters and granddaughters, who seem to have married and adopted British surnames.

Dean Mahomed died in February 1851, his wife, Jane, preceding him in December 1850.

[Extracts from *The Travels of Dean Mahomet*, written originally in English.]

Letter I

Dear Sir,

Since my arrival in this country, I found you have been very anxious to be made acquainted with the early part of my Life, and the History of my Travels: I shall be happy to gratify you; and must ingenuously confess, when I first came to Ireland, I found the face of every thing about me so contrasted to those *striking scenes* in India, which we are wont to survey with a kind of sublime delight, that I felt some timid inclination, even in the consciousness of incapacity, to describe the manners of my countrymen, who, I am proud to think, have still more of the innocence of our ancestors, than some of the boasting philosophers of Europe.

Though I acknowledge myself incapable of doing justice of the merits of men, whose happy manners are worthy the imitation of civilized nations, yet, you will do me the justice to believe, that the gratification of your wishes, is the *principal* incitement that engages me to undertake a work of this nature: the earnest entreaties of some friends, and the liberal encouragement of others, to whom I express my acknowledgements, I allow, are secondary motives.

The people of India, in general, are peculiarly favoured by Providence in the possession of all that can cheer the mind and allure the eye, and tho' the situation of Eden is only traced in the Poet's creative fancy, the traveller beholds with admiration the face of this delightful country, on which he discovers tracts that resemble those so finely drawn by the animated pencil of Milton. You will here behold the generous soil crowned with various plenty; the garden beautifully diversified with the gayest flowers diffusing their fragrance on the bosom of the air; and the very bowels of the earth enriched with inestimable mines of gold and diamonds.

Possessed of all that is enviable in life, we are still more happy in the exercise of benevolence and goodwill to each other, devoid of every species of fraud or low cunning. In our convivial enjoyments, we are never without our neighbours; as it is usual for an individual, when he gives an entertainment, to invite all those of his own profession to partake of it. That profligacy of manners too conspicuous in other parts of the world, meets here with public indignation, and our women, thought not so accomplished as those of Europe, are still very engaging for many virtues that exalt the sex…

Letter VI

Dear Sir,

We had scarcely been one night at Fulwherea [Phulwari], when some straggling villagers of the neighbouring country, stole unperceived into our camp, and plundered our tents and marquees, which they stripped of every thing valuable belonging to officers and privates. It happened, at the same time, that they entered a store tent, next to Mr. Baker's marquee, where I lay on a palankeen, a kind of travelling canopy-bed, resembling a camp bed, the upper part was arched over with curved bamboo, and embellished with rich furniture, the top was hung with beautiful tassels and adorned with gay trappings; and the sides, head, and foot were decorated with valuable silver ornaments. In short, it was elegant finished, and worth, at least six hundred rupees; for which reason, such vehicles are seldom kept but by people of condition. Every palankeen is attended by eight servants, four of whom, alternately, carry it, much in the same manner as our sedan chairs are carried in this country [Ireland]. But to return—the villagers having entered the store-tent above mentioned, bore me suddenly away to a field about a half a mile from the camp, on the conveyance I have just described to you, which they soon disrobed of its decorations, and rifled me of what money I had in my pocket, and every garment on my body, except a thin pair of trousers. So cruel were the merciless savages, that some were forming the barbarous resolution of taking away my life, lest my escape would lead to a discovery of them; while others less inhuman, opposed the measure, by observing I was too young to injure them, and prevailed on their companions to let me go. I reached the camp with winged feet, and went directly to Mr. Baker, who was much alarmed when he heard of my dangerous situation, but more astonished at my arrival; and when I related by what means my life was spared, and liberty obtained, he admired such humanity in a savage breast.

A few of those ravagers, who loitered behind the rest, were first detected by the guard, pursued, and taken: the track of others was, by this clew, discovered: many of whom were apprehended, and received the punishment due to their crimes, for such wanton depredations. They were flogged through the camp, and their ears and noses cut off, as a shameful example to their lawless confederates. Their rapacity occasioned us to delay longer at Fulwherea, than we intended. We had scarcely suppressed those licentious barbarians, when our quiet was again disturbed by the nocturnal invasion of the jackals that infest this country, ferocious animals not unlike the European fox; they flocked into our camp in the silent midnight hour, carried off a great part of the poultry, and such young children as they could come at. It was in vain to pursue them; we were obliged to endure our losses with patience.

Having dispatched the proper people to supply the markets, we left Fulwherea early on the eight morning after our arrival, and proceeded in our march towards Chrimnasa, which lay about ninety miles farther off. We reached Turwherea, on the first day's march, where we had a river to cross, which retarded us three days, on account of our numbers. As the weather was very warm, we advanced slowly, and found it exceedingly pleasant to travel along the roads shaded with the spreading branches of fruit-bearing trees, bending under their luscious burthens of bananas, mangoes, and tamarinds. Beneath the trees, were many cool springs and wells of the finest water in the universe, with which the whole country of Indostan abounds: a striking instance of the wisdom of Providence, that tempers 'the bleak wind to the shorn lamb,' and scorching heat of the torrid zone on the way-worn traveller.

The former natives of this part of the world, whose purity of manners is still perpetuated by several tribes of their posterity, having foreseen the absolute necessity of such refreshment, and that in the region they inhabited, none could be more seasonable than founts of water for the use of succeeding generation, contrived those inexhaustible sources of relief in situations most frequented; and to prevent any thoughtless vagrant from polluting them, took care to inspire the people with a sacred piety in favour of their wells, and a religious dread of disturbing them. For this reason, they remain pure and undefiled, through every age, and are held in the most profound veneration. Wherever we found them, on the march, our Besties stopped to afford the men some time to recover themselves, and take in a fresh supply of water, which was carried by bullocks, in leathern *hanpacallies* or bags made of dried hides, some of which were borne by the Besties on their shoulders.

Letter XI

Dear Sir,

Our stay in Calcutta was so short, that I have been only able to give you some account of the town, forts, and environs; and am concerned that I could not contribute more to your entertainment, by a description of the manners of the people, as we received too sudden orders to march to Barahampore, where we arrived in the year 1773, having met with no extraordinary occurrence on the way. The cantonments here are situate on the banks of the river Bohogritee [Bhagirathi], and consist of twenty-two barracks, besides a magazine, stores, and offices. There are two barracks on the south near the river, in which the Colonels and Majors reside: six on the east, and six on the west, occupied by the other Officers: in the northern direction, the privates of the Artillery and Infantry Corps dwell: the Commander in chief has a superb building, about a mile from the barrack of the privates; and the intermediate space between the different barracks, which form a square, is a spacious plain where the men exercise. Barahampore is very populous, and connects with Muxadabad [Maurshidabad] by a irregular chain of building, comprehending Calcapore [Kalapur] and Casambuzar [Cossimbazar], two famous manufactories of silk and cotton, where merchants can be supplied on better terms than in any other part of India. The city of Muxadabad, to which I had been led by curiosity, is the mart of an extensive trade among the natives, such as the Moguls, Parsees, Mussulmen, and Hindoos; the houses are neat, but not uniform, as every dwelling in constructed according to the peculiar fancy of the proprietor: those of the merchants are, in general, on a good plan, and built of fine brick made in the country; and such as have been erected by the servants of the Company, near the town, are very handsome structures. The city, including the suburbs, is about nine miles in length, reaching as far as Barahampore; and the neighbouring country is interspersed with elegant seats belonging to the governors, and other Officers; among which, was the Nabob Mamarah Dowlah's [Mubarak al-Daula's] palace, finished in a superior style to the rest, and surrounded with arched pillars of marble, decorated with variegated purdoes—over the arches, native bands of music played on their different instruments, every morning and evening—on the side of the palace flowed the river Bohogritee in winding mazes: on the other, stood the Chouk, where people assembled to sell horses, wild and tame fowl, singing birds, and almost every product and manufacture of India.

Soon after my arrival here, I was dazzled with the glittering appearance of the Nabob, and all his train, amounting to about three thousand attendants, proceeding in solemn state from his palace to the temple. They formed in the splendour and richness of their attire one of the most brilliant processions I ever beheld. The Nabob was carried on a beautiful pavilion, or meanah, by sixteen men, alternately, called by the natives, Baharas, who wore a red uniform; the refulgent canopy covered with tissue, and lined with embroidered scarlet velvet, trimmed with silver fringe, was supported by four pillars of massy silver, and resembled the form of a beautiful elbow chair, constructed in oval elegance; in which he sat cross-legged, leaning his back against a fine cushion, and his elbows on two more covered with scarlet velvet, wrought with flowers of gold. At each side of his magnificent conveyance, two men attended with large whisks in their hands, made of some curious animal's tail, to beat off the flies. The very handles of those whisks were of silver. As to the ornaments of this person—he wore a very small turban of white muslin, containing forty-four yards, which quantity, from its exceeding fineness, would not weigh more than a pound and half; a band of the same encompassed his turban, from which hung silver tassels over his right eye: on the front was a star in diamond of the first water: a thin robe of fine muslin covered his body, over which he wore another of cream-coloured satin, and trousers of the same, trimmed with silver edging, and small silver buttons: a valuable shawl of camel's hair, was thrown negligently about his shoulders; and another wrapped round his waist: inside the latter, he placed his dagger, that was in itself a piece of curious workmanship, the hilt being of pure gold, studded with diamonds, and embellished with small chains of gold.

His shoes were of bright crimson velvet, embroidered with silver, and set round the soals and binding with pearls. Two Aid-du-Camps, one at each side, attended him on horseback; from whom he was *little* more distinguished in splendour of habiliment, than by the diamond star in his turban. Their saddles were ornamented with tassels, fringe, and various kinds of embroidery. Before and behind him, moved in the pomp of ceremony, a great number of pages and near his person slowly advanced his life guard, mounted on horses: all were clad in a stile of unrivalled elegance: the very earth with expanding bosom, poured out her treasures to deck them; and the artisan essayed his utmost skill to furnish their trappings.

His pipe was of a serpentine form, nine cubits in length, and termed hooka: it reached from his lips, though elevated his situation above the gay throng, to the hands of a person who only walked as an attendant in the train, for the purpose of filling the silver bowl with a nice compound of musk, sugar, rose-water, a little tobacco finely chopped, and worked up together into a kind of dough, which was dissolved into an odoriferous liquid by the heat of a little fire made of burnt rice, and kept in a silver vessel with a cover, called Chilm, from which was conveyed a fragrant cool smoke, through a small tube connecting with another that ascended to his mouth.

The part which the attendant held in his hand, contained at least a quart of water: it was made of glass, ornamented with a number of little golden chains admirably contrived: the snake which comprehends both tubes was tipped with gold at each end, and the intermediate space was made of wire inside a close quilting of satin, silk, and muslin, wrought in a very ingenious manner: the mouth piece was also of gold, and the part next to his lips set with diamonds.

A band of native music played before him, accompanied with a big drum, conveyed on a camel, the sound of which, could be heard at a great distance: and a halcorah or herald advanced onward in the front of the whole company, to proclaim his arrival, and clear the way before him. Crowds of people from every neighbouring quarter, thronged to see him. I waited for some time, to see him enter into the temple with all his retinue, who left their shoes at the door as a mark of veneration for the sacred fane into which they were entering. The view of this grand procession, gave me infinite pleasure, and induced me to continue a little longer in Muxadabad.

Letter XII

Dear Sir,

Shortly after the procession, I met with a relation of mine, a Mahometan, who requested my attendance at the circumcision of one of his children. Previous of this ceremony, which I shall describe in the order of succession, it may be necessary to premise, that a child is baptized three times according to the rites of this religion. The first baptism is performed at time of the birth, by a Brahmin who, though of different religious principles, is held in the utmost veneration by the Mahometans, for his supposed knowledge in astrology, by which he is said to foretell the future destiny of the child; when he discharges the duties of his sacred function on such an occasion, which consists in nothing more than this prophecy, and calling the child by the most favourable name, the mysteries of his science will permit, he receives some presents from the parents and kindred, and retires.

The second baptism, which takes place when the child is four days old, is performed by the Codgi, or Mulna, the Mahometan Clergyman, in the presence of number of women, who visit the mother after her delivery; he first reads some prayers in the alcoran, sprinkles the child with consecrated water, and anoints the navel and ears with a kind of oil extracted water from mustard seed, which concludes the ceremony. The Priest then quits the women's apartment, and joins the men in another room. When he has withdrawn, the Hajams' wives enter the chamber, and attend the mother of the child with every apparatus necessary in her situation: one assists to pare her nails, and supplies her with a basin of water to wash her hands in: and others are employed in dressing her in a becoming manner. Several Ladies of distinction come to visit her, presenting her their congratulatory compliments on her happy recovery, and filling her lap, at the same time, with a quantity of fresh fruit, as the emblem of plenty. When this ceremony is over they sit down to an entertainment served up by the Hajams' wives, and prepared by women in more menial offices. Their usual fare is a variety of cakes and sweetmeats. The men, who also congratulate the father, wishing every happiness to his offspring, are regaled much in the same manner. Thus is the second baptism celebrated: from which the third, which is solemnized on the twentieth day after the birth, differs only in point of time.

The Mahometans do not perform the circumcision, or fourth baptism until the child is seven years old, and carefully initiated in such principles of their religion as can be well conceived at such a tender age. For some time before it, the poorer kind of people use much economy in their manner of living, to enable them to defray the expenses of a splendid entertainment, as they are very ambitious of displaying the greatest elegance and hospitality on such occasions. When the period of entering on this sacred business is arrived, they dispatch Hajams or Barbers, who from the nature of their occupation are well acquainted with the city, to all the inhabitants of the Mahometan profession, residing within the walls of Muxadabad, to whom they present nutmegs, which imply the same formality as compliment cards in this country. The guests thus invited assembled in a great square, large enough to contain two thousand persons, under a *semiana* of muslin supported by handsome poles erected at a certain distance from each other; its sides were also made of muslin, and none would be suffered to enter but Mahometans. The arrival of the Mulna was announced by the Music, who had a kind of orchestra within the semiana: attended by one of the Hajams, he approached the child who was decked with jewels and arrayed in scarlet muslin, and sat under a beautiful canopy richly ornamented with silk hangings, on an elegant elbow chair with velvet cushions to the back and sides, from which he was taken and mounted on a horse, accompanied by four men, his nearest relations, each holding a drawn sword in his hand, who also wore a dress of scarlet muslin. People of condition, among the Mahometans, contribute largely to the magnificence of this ceremony; and appear on horseback in the midst of the gay assembly, with their finest camels in rich furniture led after them.

But to return—the child was conducted in this manner to a chapel, at the door of which he alit, assisted by his four relations, who entered with them into the sacred building, where he bowed in adoration to one of the Prophets, repeating with his kindred, some prayers he had been before taught by his parents; after his pious duty is over, he is again mounted on his horse, and led to another chapel, where he goes through the same forms, and so on to them all, praying with the rest of the company, and fervently imploring in the attitude of prostrate humility, the great Alla to protect him from every harm in the act of circumcision.

After they had taken their rounds to the different places of worship, they returned to the square in which the semiana was erected, and placed him under the glittering canopy, upon his accustomed chair. The music that played before him suddenly ceased, when the Mulna appeared in his sacerdotal robes, holding a silver basin of consecrated water, with which he sprinkled him; while the Hajam slowly advancing in order to circumcise him, instantly performed the operation. In this critical moment, every individual in the numerous crowd, stood on one foot, and joined his father and mother in heartfelt petitions to Heaven for his safety. The Music again struck up, and played some cheerful airs: after which, the child was taken home by his parents and put to bed. The company being served with water and napkins by the Hajams, washed their hands and sat down barefooted on a rich carpet, to partake of a favourite dish called by the natives *pelou*, composed of stewed rice and meat highly seasoned, which they are in general fond of. The entire scene was illuminated with torches, which, by a strong reflexion of artificial lustre, seemed to heighten the splendour of their ornaments.

African Muslim Slave Narratives of the Nineteenth Century
From Umar ibn Said's untitled Arabic autobiography (1820s) and
Nicholas Said's "A Native of Bornoo" (1867)

Both the texts included in this section enjoy some visibility as slave narratives. The fact that they have been included here suggests that the term "slave narrative" is a justified but limiting designation. It obscures the perception that the authors of these texts had identities that exceeded the meanings of the English word "slave", imposed on them at the intersection of their histories with the history of the West. It also obscures the fact that their texts were not just "slave narratives" but also autobiographies, social documents, travel accounts etc. The latter applies particularly to the second narrative, that by Nicholas Said, whose account includes travels after becoming a free man. The fact that this account peters out at exactly the moment when Said, a freed man, sets out to travel to America on his own agency indicates that "slave narratives" exist because textual and discursive space, however contested, was provided for their existence while various other accounts, including travel ones (and sometimes even by the same person), do not exist because no such space was made available for their inscription, publication and/or preservation.

The 'Western' intersection was momentous but not definitive for many 'slaves'. Allan D. Austin, whose books—and the texts cited in them—have provided the basis for this section, has done pioneering and foundational work in the field of early Black American history and writing, in particular records of and by approximately 40,000 African Muslims who were brought to the Americas as slaves. The emphasis of his research has been, as he puts it in one of his books, "on stories by African Muslims—a proud people, influential beyond their numbers on both sides of the Atlantic Ocean—who until very recently had been almost completely neglected by modern America's eagle-eyed historians and storytellers."[148]

These stories are varied—they include the story of the African-born Lamine Kebe who declared, in 1835, that "there are good men in America, but all are very ignorant of Africa"; Job Ben Solomon (author of an extant memoir) who was brought to the British colony of Maryland in 1750 and returned to Africa as a sort of agent; the six-foot-tall and otherwise-imposing Ibrahim Abd ar-Rahman Jallo who not only managed to be freed and returned to Africa but also bought the freedom of much of his family, and many others. All these men—and, at times, the women with them—undertook arduous journeys, often under taxing circumstances. In this they were not any different from thousands of other African slaves. What, however, made them conspicuous was, at times, their knowledge of writing and always their knowledge of Biblical stories (through the Qur'an). Both these "assets", Austin suggests, enabled some of these African Muslims to weather the assaults of servitude and, what is more interesting, leave behind written accounts. Many of these accounts—in Arabic or in a native African language written in the Arabic script—are yet to be translated or made available to a wider readership, though Austin has tried to do so in two of his books and other scholars have recently started publishing in this area. However, some of the accounts are available and we have included two in this section that describe, in concise form, both journeys and experiences of substantial interest. Though one of them was written in Arabic and the other in English, both texts, among other things, seem to be acutely aware of the issue of language.

Umar ibn Said

The first extract is taken from the only extant autobiography by an American slave in Arabic on the continent (another such autobiography exists, written by a slave in Jamaica). It was written—along with many other extant manuscripts, including a "Bible in Arabic"—by Umar ibn Said. These manuscripts were published or written between 1819 and 1864. Umar ibn Said was taken up by Christian evangelists as one of the "saved": this probably accounts for the fact that so many of his writings were also saved, though it has also resulted in a number of myths around this distinguished "prince" who converted to Christianity. Like many such conversions, it appears to have been a matter of convenience or the result of a more syncretic sense of religion than that available to the evangelists. Umar ibn Said, as is evident from the extracts below, probably did not see acceptance of the Christian God as severing him from his Muslim Allah[149], and in this he was not altogether unique. A number of Muslim slaves accepted Christianity while continuing to retain a Muslim identity: some of them probably saw no contradiction in calling a recognizably similar God by another of his many Qur'anic names, others probably did so as a political necessity. Records and memoirs show that at least eight such converted slaves "reverted" to Islam as soon as they returned to Africa or gained freedom. It is also interesting to note that the author of the second extract, who was converted in Russia, explicitly complains about the conversion while displaying a deep and abiding affection for the master who induced him to convert.

Much has been written and said about Umar ibn Said—and it is difficult to extricate the strands of fiction from those of fact. What we do know is that he was a Fula African and had been a Qur'anic scholar before enslavement. His ultimate purchaser in America was James Owen and the Owen family, who appear to have treated him kindly and for whom he retained a deep affection. Early evangelist accounts liked to portray him as an Arab prince and comment on his light colour, but the only existing daguerreotype and his autobiography prove that he was an African, a Tukolor Fula, with colour, hair and physiognomy of "distinctly African character" (in the words of one contemporary commentator). He was probably born around 1765 in present-day Senegal and he never forgot his family even after years of enslavement and removal. His father died young and he was raised by an uncle largely as a future Qur'anic scholar. He was captured in a war around 1807 and sent to America as a slave the same year. The rest of Umar ibn Said's life in America was marked by his conversion in 1821 as well as a tendency to provide progressively darker pictures of his years in Africa, In this, says Austin, he differs from some other African slaves (like Abd ar-Rahman and Lamine Kebe), and might have been influenced by discourses of the "dark continent" in Christian circles. In 1811, he was bought by Jesse Owen in North Carolina, where he had been arrested as a vagrant (having run away from a cruel master), and he lived with the Owen family until his death.

Umar ibn Said's autobiography first appeared in English translation in 1864, translated by Theodore Dwight Jr. The authoritative translation, from which the extracts below have been taken, appeared in the *American Historical Review* in 1925. The first few pages of the manuscript contain quotations from the Qur'an, recalled from memory, and the rest contains a short autobiography, addressed to someone called Sheikh Hunter (who has not yet been identified). The manuscript is shorter and focuses less on travel than some other comparable slave documents of eighteenth- and nineteenth-century America, but it has been included here as it is to some extent a good example of the shorter (often generically-mixed) texts left behind by slaves like Umar ibn Said. The main text of the original 1925 translation has been extracted and reproduced faithfully down to the punctuation marks. This has been done in order to convey the covert ambiguity of Said's statements—especially those relating to religious belief—though a comparison with the Arabic original (not available to us) would have been of great interest in this regard.

[Sources: "Umar ibn Said's Legends, Life, and Letters", chapter 7 of *African Muslims in Antebellum America* by Allan D. Austin, 1997, New York: Routledge; "An Autobiography of Omar ibn Said, Slave in North Carolina, 1831", *American Historical Review*, XXX, No. 4, July 1925, pp. 787-95; and "Omar ibn Said, A Slave who Wrote an Autobiography in Arabic" by George H. Calcott, *Journal of Negro History*, No. 39, 1954, pp. 58-63.]

Mohammed Ali ben Said or Nicholas Said

Nicholas Said's much longer autobiography (written in English), as extracted below, provides many of the details that the reader requires—as does the introduction (carried in full below) that accompanied the autobiography when it first appeared in *The Atlantic*

Monthly. Said was born in 1833 in present-day Nigeria and came from a prosperous military-merchant family. He was captured by Tuareg raiders in 1849, marched across the Sahara Desert and sold as a slave in Tripoli. His experience as a slave was different from those of most ordinary slaves, as he had the luck of finding good and rich masters in Africa as well as Europe and America. He was released by his master, a Russian aristocrat, in 1859, after traversing much of Europe, and travelled of his own volition to South and North America. Fluent in six or seven languages, he became a teacher in Detroit, Michigan, in 1862, and joined the 55th Regiment of Coloured Volunteers in 1863. He was mustered out in 1865 and disappeared from sight after that, though we know that he died in 1882. Before he dropped out of sight, he appears to have been admired by fellow soldiers as "a pleasant person, a sophisticated storyteller and a competent soldier." A photograph of Said from 1863 (?) depicts a dark and handsome African man, in a buttoned up regimental coat, with very short hair and a particularly self-reliant and determined look.

The extracts (2) below are taken from Mohammed Ali ben Said alias Nicholas Said's autobiography as it appeared in *The Atlantic Monthly* in October 1867, with an introduction by a commanding officer, probably one Norwood P. Hallowell. It is only in the 1990s that interest in Said was re-triggered with the discovery of a portrait and a newspaper article.

[Sources: "A Native of Bornoo", *The Atlantic Monthly*, October 1867, pp 485-95, accessed from Cornell University Library's "Making of America" section; and "Mohammed Ali ben Said, or Nicholas Said: His Travels on Five Continents", chapter 9 of *African Muslims in Antebellum America* by Allan D. Austin, New York: Routledge, 1997.]

1. Extracts from Umar ibn Said's Arabic Autobiography:

In the name of God, the merciful the gracious.—God grant his blessing upon our Prophet Mohammed. Blessed be He in whose hands is the kingdom and who is Almighty; who created death and life that he might test you; for he is exalted; he is the forgiver (of sins), who created seven heavens one above the other. Do you discern anything trifling in creation? Bring back your thoughts. Do you see anything worthless? Recall your vision in earnest. Turn your eye inward for it is diseased...

From Omar to Sheikh Hunter.

You asked me to write my life. I am not able to do this because I have much forgotten my own, as well as the Arabic language. Neither can I write very grammatically or according to the true idiom. And so, my brother, I beg you, in God's name, not to blame me, for I am a man of weak eyes, and of a weak body.

My name is Omar ibn Said. My birthplace was Fut Tûr[150], between the two rivers. I sought knowledge under the instruction of a Sheikh called Mohammed Seid, my own brother, and Sheikh Soleiman Kembeh, and Sheikh Gabriel Abadl. I continued my studies twenty-five years, and then returned to my home where I remained six years. Then there came to our place a large army, who killed many men, and took me, and brought me to the great sea, and sold me into the hands of the Christians, who bound me and sent me on board a great ship and we sailed upon the great sea a month and a half, when we came to a place called Charleston in the Christian language. There they sold me to a small, weak and wicked man, called Johnson, a complete infidel, who had no fear of God at all. Now I am a small man, and unable to do hard work so I fled from the hand of Johnson and after a month came to a place called Fayd-il[151]. There I saw some great houses. On the new moon I went into a church to pray. A lad saw me and rode off to the place of his father and informed him that he had seen a black man in the church. A man named Handah [Hunter?] and another man with him on horseback, came attended by a troop of dogs. They took me and made me go with them twelve miles to a place called Fayd-il, where they put me into a great house from which I could not go out. I continued in the great house (which, in the Christian language, they called jail) sixteen days and nights. One Friday the jailor came and opened the door of the house and I saw a great many men, all Christians, some of whom called out to me, 'What is your name? Is it Omar or Seid?' I did not understand their Christian language. A man called Bob Mumford[152] took me and led me out of the jail, and I was very well pleased to go with them to their place. I stayed at Mumford's four days and nights, and then a man named Jim Owen[153], son-in-law of Mumford, having married his daughter Betsey, asked me if I was willing to go to a place called Bladen[154.] I said, Yes, I was willing. I went with them and have remained in the place of Jim Owen until now.

After I came into the hand of Gen. Owen a man by the name of Mitchell came to buy me. He asked me if I were willing to go to Charleston City. I said, 'No, no, no, no, no, no, no[155], I not willing to go to Charleston. I stay in the hand of Jim Owen.'

O ye people of North Carolina, O ye people of S. Carolina, O ye people of America all of you; have you among you any two such men as Jim Owen and John Owen[156]? These men are good men. What food they eat they give to me to eat. As they clothe themselves they clothe me. They permit me to read the gospel of God, our Lord, and Saviour, and King; who regulates all our circumstances, our health and wealth, and who bestows his mercies willingly, not by constraint. According to power I open my heart, as to a great light, to receive the true way, the way of Lord Jesus the Messiah.

Before I came to the Christian country, my religion was the religion of 'Mohammed, the Apostle of God—may God have mercy upon him and give him peace.'[157] I walked to the mosque before daybreak, washed my face and head and hands and feet. I prayed at noon, prayed in the afternoon, prayed at sunset, prayed in the evening. I gave alms every year, gold, silver, seeds, cattle, sheep, goats, rice, wheat, and barley. I gave tithes of all the above-mentioned things. I went every year to the holy war against the infidels. I went on pilgrimage to Mecca, as all did who were able.—My father had six sons and five daughters, and my mother had three sons and one daughter. When I left my country I was thirty-seven years old; I have been in the country of the Christians twenty-four years…

[Here follow lines providing details of and praising the Owen family.]

...Formerly I, Omar, loved to read the book of the Koran the famous. General Jim Owen and his wife used to read the gospel, and they read it to me very much,—the gospel of God, our Lord, our Creator, our King, He that orders all our circumstances, health and wealth, willingly, not constrainedly, according to his power.—Open thou my heart to the gospel, to the way of uprightness.—Thanks to the Lord of all worlds, thanks in abundance. He is plenteous in mercy and abundant in goodness.

For the law was given by Moses but grace and truth were by Jesus the Messiah.

When I was a Mohammedan[158] I prayed thus:'Thanks be to God, Lord of all worlds, the merciful the gracious, Lord of the day of Judgment, thee we serve, on thee we call for help. Direct us in the right way, the way of those on whom thou hast had mercy, with whom thou hast not been angry and who walk not in error. Amen.'— But now I pray 'Our Father', etc., in the words of our Lord Jesus the Messiah.

I reside in this our country by reason of great necessity. Wicked men took me by violence and sold me to the Christians...

[The rest of the account repeats events from his life that have already been narrated and praises the Owens.]

2. Extracts from Mohammed Ali ben Said or Nicholas Said's "A Native of Bornoo":

The introduction, probably written by one of Said's commanding officers, prefaced the extracts from Said's lost autobiography published in *The Atlantic Monthly* in October 1867, pp. 485-495:

Nicholas Said, at the time of his enlistment in the army of the Union, during the third year of the great Rebellion, was about twenty-eight years of age, of medium height, somewhat slenderly built, with pleasing features, not of the extreme negro type, complexion perfectly black, and quiet and unassuming address.

He became known to the writer while serving in one of our colored regiments; and attention was first directed to his case by the tattooing on his face, and by the entry in the company descriptive book, which gave "Africa" as his birthplace.

Inquiry showed that he was more or less acquainted with seven different languages, in addition to his native tongue; that he had travelled extensively in Africa and Europe, and that his life had been one of such varied experience as to render it interesting both on that account and also on account of the mystery which surrounds, notwithstanding recent explorations, the country of his birth. At the request of those who had been from time to time entertained by the recital of portions of his history, he was induced to put it in writing. The narrative which follows is condensed from his manuscript, and his own language has been retained as far as possible.

Extracts from Nicholas Said's Autobiography:

Reader, you must excuse me for the mistakes which this article will contain, as you will bear in mind that this language in which I am now trying to write is not my mother tongue; on the other hand, I never had a teacher, nor ever was at school for the purpose of acquiring the English. The only way I learned what little of the language I know was through French books.

I was born in the kingdom of Bornoo, in Soodan, in the problematic central part of Africa, so imperfectly known to the civilized nations of Europe and America.

Soodan has several kingdoms, the country of the Fellatahs and Bornoo being the most powerful,—the territorial extent of the latter being some 810,000 square miles.

These nations are strict Mohammedans, having been converted some two or three centuries ago by the Bedouin Arabs and those from Morocco, who, pushed by want of riches, came to Soodan to acquire them. Different languages are found in each nation, some written and some not; but the Arabic is very much in use among the higher class of people, as the Latin is used by the Catholic priests. Especially the Koran is written in Arabic, and in my country no one is allowed to handle the Sacred Book unless he can read it and explain its contents.

Bornoo, my native country, is the most civilized part of Soodan, on account of the great commerce carried on between it and the Barbary States of Fezzan, Tunis, and Tripoli. They export all kinds of European articles to central Africa, and take gold-dust, ivory, &c., in return.

Bornoo has had a romantic history for the last one hundred years. The whole of Soodan, more than two thousand miles in extent, was once under the Maïs of Bornoo; but by dissensions and civil wars nearly all the tributaries north of Lake Tchad were lost. In 1809 a shepherd arose from the country of the Fellatahs and assumed the title of Prophet. He said to the ignorant portion of his countrymen, that Allah had given him orders to make war with the whole of Soodan, and had promised him victory. They believed his story, and the legitimate king was dethroned and the false prophet, Otman Danfodio, was proclaimed Emperor of the Fellatahs. The impostor went at once to work, and in less than two years conquered almost the whole of Soodan, excepting Kanem, a tributary to my country. Bornoo, after a manly effort, was compelled by force of arms to submit to the yoke of the Fellatahs.

In 1815 Bornoo arose from its humiliating position, to shake off the yoke of Danfodio. Mohammed el Anim el Kanemy, the Washington of Bornoo, was the man who undertook to liberate his country and restore her former prestige... [There follows a description of the wars and negotiations leading to the triumph of el Kanemy.—Ed]

My father was the descendant of a very illustrious family. He was the first man who had a commission under El Kanemy when he went to Kanem to recruit his forces. He was made a Bagafuby, or captain of one hundred cavalry, and was in every engagement which El Kanemy went through. The name by which my father was known was Barca

Gana[159]. My great-grandfather was from Molgoi. He established himself in Bornoo many years ago, and was greatly favored by the monarchs of that country. My mother was a Mandara woman, the daughter of a chief. I was born in Kooka, a few years after the Waday war of 1831. We were in all nineteen children, twelve boys and seven girls. I was the ninth child of my mother. All my brothers were well educated in Arabic and Turkish. Two of them, Mustafa and Abderahman, were very rich, having acquired their wealth by trading in ivory and gold-dust. Both had been to Mecca as pilgrims. My father himself was rich, but when he was killed, our elder brother seized the greater part, and those who were not eighteen years of age had to leave their share in their mother's hands. Five cleared farms and a considerable amount of gold fell to my share. I do not know how much the gold amounted to, but my mother used to tell me, that I would have as much as either of my elder brothers.

After my father's death I was given to a teacher to be instructed in my native tongue, and also in Arabic. In the space of three years I could read and write both languages. I was tried in my native tongue, and passed; but I could not pass in Arabic, and my mother and uncle returned me to the teacher for eighteen months. I stayed the required time, and then was tried and passed.

I was then old enough to be circumcised. Three hundred boys went through the ceremony at once, and were then dressed in white clothes, and received according to custom a great many presents. Fifteen days we ate the best that Kooka had, the king himself giving us the best he had in his palace. This generally happens only to the sons of those who have distinguished themselves in the army, or, to explain myself better, to those of the military aristocracy. At the end of this time all of us went home. For my part, this was the first time I had slept in my father's house for four years and seven months. I was very much welcomed by my mother, sisters, and brothers, and was a pet for some time.

After returning from school to my father's house, I judged about four or five years afterwards, I was invited, in company with three of my brothers, by the eldest son of the governor of the province of

Yaoori and Laree, who lived in the town of the latter name, to visit him. This part of the province is very charming. The forests are full of delicious game, and the lake of fish and beautiful aquatic birds; while in the dry seasons the woods and uncultivated plains are worthy to be called the garden of Eden. In my childhood I had quite a passion for hunting, one of my father's great passions also. In spite of the efforts of my elder brothers to check me in it, I would persuade other boys to follow me into the thick woods, to the danger of their lives and mine. My worthy mother declared several times that I would be captured by the Kindils, a wandering tribe of the desert. Her prophecy was fulfilled after all, unhappily for myself, and perhaps more so for those I had persuaded with me. While on the visit just spoken of, one day,—it was a Ramadan day, anniversary of the Prophet's day,—I persuaded a great number of boys, and we went into the woods a great way from any village. We came across nests of Guinea fowl, and, gathered plenty of eggs, and killed several of the fowl. We made a fire by rubbing two pieces of dry stick together, and broiled the chickens and eggs. Then we proceeded farther, and came across a tree called Agoua, bearing a delicious kind of fruit. We all went up the tree, eating fruit and making a great deal of noise. We frolicked on that tree for many hours. Presently several of the boys told me they heard the neighing of horses. We then all agreed not to make so much noise, but we were just too late. In about a quarter of an hour we were startled by the cry, 'Kindil! Kindil!' The boys who were nearest to the ground contrived to hide themselves in the thicket. It happened that I was higher than any one, and while coming down with haste, I missed my hold and fell, and lay senseless. When I opened my eyes, I found myself on horseback behind a man, and tied to him with a rope. Out of forty boys, eighteen of us were taken captive. I wished then that it was a dream rather than a reality, and the warnings of my mother passed through my mind. Tears began to flow down my cheeks; I not only lamented for myself, but for those also whom I persuaded into those wild woods. Meanwhile our inhuman captors were laughing and talking merrily, but I could not understand them. About six hours' ride, as I suppose, brought us to their camp. The tents were then immediately taken down, the camels loaded, and we started again travelling night and day for three long days, until we came to a temporary village where the chief was. After we got there we were all chained together, except four, who were taken pity upon, on account of their age and birth. It was then night, and nearly all the camp was under the influence of hashish, an intoxicating mixture of hemp-seed and other ingredients, which when too much is eaten will intoxicate worse than whiskey, or even spirits of wine. While the robbers were drunk, we boys were consulting and plotting to run away. We succeeded in breaking the chains, and four of the oldest boys took their captors' arms, cut their throats, jumped on their horses, and succeeded in making their escape. When it was found out, they gave each of us fifteen strokes in the hollows of our feet, because we did not inform them.

A little while after our comrades' escape we started on again. This time we had to go on foot for five days, until we reached a town called Kashna, belonging to the Emperor of the Fellatahs, but situated in the country of Houssa, where we were all dispersed to see each other no more. Fortunately, none of my brothers were with me in the woods.

My lot was that of an Arab slave, for I was bought by a man named Abd-el-Kader, a merchant of Tripoli and Fezzan. He was not an Arabian, however, but a brown-skinned man, and undoubtedly had African blood in his veins. He had at this time a large load of ivory and other goods waiting for the caravan from Kano and Saccatoo. This caravan soon came, and with it we started for Moorzook, capital of the pachalic of Fezzan. Although we numbered about five hundred, all armed except slaves who could not be trusted, a lion whom we met after starting, lying in our path, would not derange himself on our account, and we had to attack him. Twelve men he killed, and wounded five or six, and then escaped. He was hit somewhere, as they found blood where he lay, but it was not known where. When he roared, he scared all the horses and camels composing the caravan. Abd-el-Kader was one of those who attacked the lion, but he was not hurt.

Five days after we left Kashna, we came to the first oasis. Here the plains were all barren and sandy, but full of gazelles, antelopes, and ostriches. The principal tree growing here was the date-palm, and the water was very bad, tasting salty.

As the caravan travelled toward the east, the ground rose by degrees. If I am not mistaken, we passed five oases before we came into the country of Tibboo, a mountainous region between Bornoo and Fezzan, the inhabitants of which suffer considerably from the Kindils, though they are also robbers themselves. The capital of Tibboo is Boolma, built on a high mountain. I was disappointed when I saw the city, for I had heard that it was quite a large place. Laree, the smallest town in Bornoo, is a place of more importance. The people of Tibboo are of dark-brown complexion, and are noted in Soodan for their shrewdness. The day that the caravan happened to be at Boolma, two parties were in a warlike attitude about a fair maid whom each wished their chief to have for a wife. We did not stay long enough to see the issue of the fight, and two days' journey took us out of the kingdom of Tibboo.

As soon as the oasis of Tibboo was left, the country became very rocky,—the rock being a kind of black granite; and the Arabs had to make shoes for both their camels and slaves, for the rocks were very sharp, and if this precaution had not been taken, in a few hours their feet would have been so cut that they could not have proceeded farther. Some Arabs would rather lose four or five slaves than a single camel. They rode very seldom. In a journey of ten or twelve weeks, I saw Abd-el-Kader ride but once, and the majority never rode at all.

[Said's journey continues—the narrative includes descriptions of towns and regions passed—until he reaches Abd-el-Kader's house.— Ed.]

After reaching Abd-el-Kader's house, I found that he was a poor man. The reader can form some idea from his living in the capital, and having but one wife, all his property consisting of a piece of land about two and a half miles from the city, a few donkeys, ten camels, old and young, an Arab slave, and myself. While I was yet with him he bought also a young Fellatah girl. As soon as we arrived, he sent me with Hassan, his slave, to the farm, where I worked some fifteen days. I told him then that I was not used to such work, and prayed him to sell me to some Turk or Egyptian. He asked me what my father used to do, and I told him that he was a warrior and also traded in gold-dust and ivory. On hearing my father's name he opened his eyes wide, and asked me why I did not tell him that in Soodan. He had known my father well, but had not seen him for fifteen rainy seasons. From that day Abd-el-Kader was very kind to me, and said he had a great notion to take me back. He, however, sold me after all to a young Turkish officer named Abdy Agra, an excellent young man, full of life and fun. This officer was always with the Pacha, and I believe was one of his aides. His wife was a Kanowry woman. He used to bring home money every night and often gave me some. After he had dressed me up, I accompanied him to the Pacha's every day. He spoke my language very correctly, only with an accent, like all strangers trying to speak Kanowry, and he began to teach me Turkish. Strange to say, in Fezzan the Bornoo tongue is in great vogue, rich and poor speaking Kanowry. I stayed with Abdy Agra more than three months; but one day he told me that he had to send me to his father in Tripoli. So long as I had to be a slave, I hated to leave so excellent a man, but I had to go. Accordingly, when the caravan was to start, he sent me in charge of Abd-el-Kader, the man from whom he bought me. Before leaving the city we went to a house that I had never seen before, and had our names registered in a book by a very benevolent-looking man, who wore spectacles on his eyes, something I had never seen before, and which made me afraid of him. As we passed out of the city gate we were counted one by one by an officer.

On our arrival at Tripoli, Abd-el-Kader took me to an old house in a street narrow and dirty beyond description, where we passed the night. The next morning he went with me to my new master, Hadji Daoud, the father of Abdy Agra. When we found him he was sitting on a divan of velvet smoking a narghile. He looked at that time to be about forty-five years old, and was of very fine appearance, having a long beard, white as snow. Abd-el-Kader seemed well acquainted with him, for they shook hands and drank coffee together. After this we proceeded to the Turkish Bazaar, where I found that he was a merchant of tobacco, and had an extensive shop, his own property. Hadji Daoud had three wives; the principal one was an Arabian, one was a native of my country, and one, and to do her justice, the best looking of them all, was a Houssa girl. He believed in keeping a comfortable table, and we had mutton almost daily, and sometimes fowl. He had but one son, and he was far away. He told me that he intended to treat me as a son, and every day I went to the shop with him. He treated me always kindly, but madam was a cross and overbearing woman.

About this time my master started on his third pilgrimage to Mecca, leaving a friend in charge of his store, and taking me with him. We went by sail from Tripoli to Alexandria, touching at Bengazi. From Alexandria we went by cars to Ben Hadad, thence to Saida and Cairo, the capital of Egypt. From Cairo we travelled to Kartoom, at the forks of the Nile, and thence to Gondar, the capital of Abyssinia, where we stayed only twenty-four hours, my master being in continual fear of his life from the natives, who differed from him in belief, and then started for Zela, a port on the Red Sea. From Zela we sailed to Muscat, and thence proceeded to Mecca. I had not come of my own free will and for the express purpose of a pilgrimage, and therefore I was not permitted to go with Daoud to the grave of the Prophet, and was obliged to content myself without the title of Hadji, which is one much respected among the Mohammedans. We had returned as far as Alexandria on our way home, when my master was informed that his store and a great deal of property, in fact, all his goods and money, had been destroyed by fire. This made the good man almost crazy. He did not hesitate to tell me that he should have to sell me; but said that he would take care that I should have a rich and good master, a promise which he kept. The next day, with the present of a good suit of clothes, I was put on board a vessel bound for Smyrna and Constantinople. I was to be landed at the former city. On this vessel was a young man of eighteen, one of the crew, who spoke my own language. I have heard it only twice, I think, since that time.

At Smyrna I was sold to a Turkish officer, Yousouf Effendi, a very wealthy man, and brother-in-law to the celebrated Reschid Pacha, the Minister of Foreign Affairs. He had a great many houses in Smyrna, as well as Constantinople. We sailed the next day for the latter city in a man-of-war steamer, the Abdul Medjid. My duty was that of a Tchidboudji, which consists in filling and cleaning their pipes and narghiles. This was all that I had to do, while I was well dressed in cloths and silks, and had plenty of leisure time. After a service of eighteen months with Yousouf Effendi, he gave me to his younger brother, Yousouf Kavass, less wealthy than himself. This brother was, however, a very kind-hearted man, and treated his slaves, a Nubian, a native of Sennar, and myself, very kindly. While in this service I became known to Prince Mentchikoff, the Envoy Extraordinary of Russia at Constantinople, and was finally sold to him by my master. At the declaration of the Crimean war, after sending his things on board the Russian steamer Vladimir, the Prince started with despatches for his August master, via Corfu, Athens, Zara, Trieste, Vienna, Cracow, and Warsaw, to St. Petersburg. I accompanied him on the journey, and as the despatches were of the utmost importance, we travelled with the greatest speed.

The house of my master, to which we went, in St. Petersburg, was situated on the Nevskoi Prospekt, the Broadway of the city, and was built of granite, in the Doric style, and very spacious. His family consisted of his wife, one son, and three daughters, while his servants numbered about thirty. The Prince, however, was not so immensely rich as some Russian aristocrats of his standing. Shortly after his arrival at St. Petersburg, Prince Mentchikoff was assigned to command in the army of the Crimea, and he hastened there, leaving me in St. Petersburg. After his departure, not being satisfied with the way in which the head servant treated me, I engaged service with Prince Nicholas Troubetzkoy.

This family, better known as Le Grand Troubetzkoy, are descendants of the Grand Duke of Lithuania. The Prince's father was noted for skill and bravery in the war of 1828. The Troubetzkoys claim relationship with the Emperor of France, the Duc de Morny, the half-brother of the Emperor, having married the daughter of Prince Serges Troubetzkoy. Prince Nicholas was the youngest of five sons, and lived with his brother André, not far from the Italian theatre, both of them being single.

While in this service, I was baptized in St. Petersburg, November 12, 1855, into the Greek Church, my name being changed from Mohammed-Ali-Ben-Said to Nicholas Said. Prince Nicholas was my godfather. I shall always feel grateful, so long as I live, for Prince Nicholas's kindness to me; but I cannot help thinking that the way I was baptized was not right, for I think that I ought to have known perfectly well the nature of the thing beforehand. Still, it was a good intention the Prince had toward my moral welfare. After I was baptized he was very kind to me, and he bought me a solid gold cross to wear on my breast, after the Russian fashion. I was the Prince's personal servant, going always in the carriage with him.

As the Czar Nicholas was godfather to the Prince, he had free access to the palace. Though he had several chances to become minister at some European court, he always refused, preferring to live a life of inaction. His health, however, was not very good, and he was very nervous. I have seen him faint scores of times in Russia; but when he left Russia, his health began to improve very much.

Everybody acquainted with Russia knows that Czar Nicholas used to make all the aristocracy tremble at his feet. No nobleman, to whatever rank he might belong, could leave the country without his consent, and paying a certain sum of money for the privilege. This measure of the Czar was not very well liked by the nobility, but his will was law, and had to be executed without grumbling.

Prince Troubetzkoy had several times made application for permission to travel, but without success, so long as Czar Nicholas lived; for he hated liberal ideas, and feared some of his subjects might, in the course of time, introduce those ideas from foreign countries into Russia.

The Prince passed the summer season outside of the city, a distance of about twenty-five versts, at a splendid residence of his own, a marble house about the size of the Fifth Avenue Hotel of New York City. Adjoining it was a small theatre, or glass house, containing tropical fruits, and a menagerie, where I first saw a llama, and the interior of the palace was lined with pictures and statues. It was a magnificent building, but was getting to be quite old, and the Prince used to talk of repairing it, though he remarked it would cost many thousand roubles. This estate contained many thousand acres, and four good-sized villages, and was about eight miles square. I had here some of the happiest days of my life.

About this time I went with the Prince to Georgia,—his brother-in-law, a general in that department, having been wounded by the Circassians under Schamyl. We reached Tiflis, the capital of Georgia, in January, and remained there until after the capture of Kars by the English and Turks. While in the Caucasus, the Prince visited some of the neighboring parts of Persia, including Teheran and some smaller towns, and he returned to Russia by way of Novgorod.

After the death of Czar Nicholas, Alexander, his successor, gave the Prince permission to travel where he chose, without limit of time, and on the 24th of February he started, going first to Warsaw, and thence, via Cracow, to Vienna. Here I remained for two months, in charge of his effects, while he visited a sister in Pesth, in Hungary. On his return we went to Prague, and thence to Dresden. At this place, I was greatly bothered by the children. They said that they had never seen a black man before. But the thing which most attracted them was my Turkish dress, which I wore all the time in Europe. Every day, for the three weeks we remained in Dresden, whenever I went to take my walk I was surrounded by them to the number of several hundred. To keep myself from them, I used to ride in a carriage or on horseback, but this was too expensive. I thought the way I could do best was to be friendly with them. So I used to sit in the garden and speak with them,—that is, those who could understand French. They took a great liking to me, for I used sometimes to buy them fruits, candies, and other things, spending in this way a large amount. Prince Troubetzkoy had a brother, Prince Vladimir, living in Dresden, a very handsome and a very excellent man, but suffering from consumption. He treated me very kindly, and when we left gave me several very interesting books, both religious and secular.

[Said's "travels" continue: Dresden, Munich, Wiesbaden, Coblenz, Cologne, Aix-la-Chapelle, Brussels, the fields of Waterloo, Berne, Zurich.—Ed]

…From Zurich we went to Como in Lombardy, where the Prince's eldest brother, Alexander, had a villa on the borders of the lake. After a short stay here, we went on to Verona, and then to Milan, where I was left while the Prince made a short visit to Venice. Here, while left alone, I did not behave as well as I might have done, sometimes drinking too much, and spending my money foolishly. Here also I saw, for the first time since leaving Africa, a countryman. He was named Mirza, and was born about thirty-five miles from Kooka, my native place. He was considerably older than I, and had been away from Africa some fifteen years. He was waiting on a Venetian Marquis whose name I have forgotten.

After a stay of four weeks in Milan, we started, via Genoa, Leghorn, and Pisa, for Florence. Here I attended my master at two levees,—one at the palace of the Grand Duke of Tuscany, where I believe I had a better time than the Prince, and the other at Prince Demidoff's. This latter gentleman is a very wealthy Russian, and is very widely known. He is not a nobleman in Russia, however, but has his title from the Grand Duke. He is well known for the disagreeable propensity he has for beating his servants. While he was in Vienna he was worsted in an attempt to chastise a Hungarian footman, but he would not quit the practice, and has paid several fines imposed by law in consequence.

Our next stopping place was Rome, where the Prince remained for the winter, making meanwhile a short visit to Naples, and leaving in the spring for Paris. We were in Paris when the Prince Imperial was born, and stayed until his christening, which was a very important day there. I remember well the wonder of a young Russian servant-girl, that France should have still so many soldiers as appeared in the procession,—a fraction only, of course, of her army,—after losing so many in the Crimea. The Prince always took a great pride in dress, both for himself and his servants, and particularly here. I was always dressed in Turkish costume, embroidered with gold, and never costing less than two or three hundred dollars.

After a three months' stay in Paris we went to London, where the Prince took rooms at a first-class boarding-house; but he was invited almost all the time to different country seats, where I had very gay times, for the English servants live better than any in Europe.

At the conclusion of his English visit, the Prince returned to Baden-Baden, this time renting a house. While there Napoleon III passed through the place on his way to meet the Czar Alexander; and Prince Troubetzkoy was summoned to Frankfort-on-the-Main to attend on the latter. Here I was one day told by the Prince to dress myself in my best, and go to the Russian Ambassador's to wait on the Emperor at dinner. There were present beside the two Emperors, the King of Wurtemberg, the Grand Dukes of Baden, Hesse Darmstadt, and Nassau, the Ministers of France and Belgium, the Burgomaster of Frankfort, Messrs. Rothschild, and many others. A splendid dinner was served at six o'clock, the usual Russian dinner-hour, and was followed by a ball, which continued until two in the morning. A day previous to the monarch's departure Prince Gortchakoff handed my master thirty thalers as a present for me.

About this time I began to think of the condition of Africa, my native country, how European encroachments might be stopped, and her nationalities united. I thought how powerful the United States had become since 1776, and I wondered if I were capable of persuading the kings of Soodan to send several hundred boys to learn the arts and sciences existing in the civilized countries. I thought that I would willingly sacrifice my life, if need be, in realizing my dreams. I cried many times at the ignorance of my people, exposed to foreign ambition, who, however good warriors they might be, could not contend against superior weapons and tactics in the field. I prayed earnestly to be enabled to do some good to my race. The Prince could not but see that I was very sober, but I never told him my thoughts.

We stayed at Baden-Baden all summer and part of the fall, and then left for Paris. The Prince made this journey to visit his niece, who had just been married to the Duc de Morny, formerly the French Ambassador to Russia. She was a most beautiful person, only seventeen years of age. I was taken to see her, and kiss her hand, according to custom. She at first hesitated to give me her hand, undoubtedly being afraid. I had never seen her in Russia, as she was at the Imperial University, studying. After two weeks we again left Paris for Rome, via Switzerland, again passed the summer at Baden-Baden, again visited Paris, and various other points, until the year 1859 found the Prince again in London.

My desire to return to my native country had now become so strong, that I here told the Prince I must go home to my people. He tried to persuade me to the contrary, but I was inflexible in my determination. After he found that I was not to be persuaded, he got up with tears in his eyes, and said: 'Said, I wish you good luck; you have served me honestly and faithfully, and if ever misfortune happens to you, remember I shall always be, as I have always been, interested in you.' I, with many tears, replied that I was exceedingly thankful for all he had bestowed on me and done in my behalf, and that I should pray for him while I lived. I felt truly sorry to leave this most excellent Prince. As I was leaving, he gave me as a present two fifty-pound bills. It was many days before I overcame my regret. Often I could hardly eat for grief.

I now went to board at the Strangers' Home, at the West India Dock, five miles from where the Prince stopped. Here I waited for a steamer for Africa. Hardly had I been there for two weeks, when a gentleman from Holland proposed to me a situation to travel with him in the United States and West India Islands. I had read much about these countries, and my desire to see them caused me to consent, and we left Liverpool soon after New Year's, 1860.

With this gentleman I went via Boston and New York to New Providence, Long Keys, Inagua, Kingston, Les Gonaives, St. Marc,

Demerara, Martinique, Guadeloupe, and then back to New Providence, and from there by steamer to New York. We remained in New York two months, and then visited Niagara, Hamilton, Toronto, Kingston, Montreal, Quebec, and Ottawa, until, finally, at a small village called Elmer, my employer's funds gave out, and I lent him five hundred dollars of my own money. Of this five hundred I received back only three hundred and eighty, and this failure compelled me to remain in this country and earn my living by work to which I was unaccustomed.

The concluding part of the "introduction" from *The Atlantic Monthly*:

At this point the written narrative of Nicholas ends, at some date during the year 1861. He afterward went to Detroit, and taught a school for those of his own color, meeting there, I believe, a clergyman whom he had seen years before in Constantinople, while a servant to Prince Mentchikoff. At Detroit he enlisted in a colored regiment in the summer of 1863. He served faithfully and bravely with his regiment as corporal and sergeant in the Department of the South, and near the close of the war was attached, at his own request, to the hospital department, to acquire some knowledge of medicine. He was mustered out with the company in which he served, in the fall of 1865. But, alas for his plans of service to his countrymen in his native land! like many a warrior before him, he fell captive to woman, married at the South, and for some time past the writer, amidst the changes of business, has entirely lost sight of him.

The Dairy of Kaleleonalani, Queen Emma of Hawaii (b. 1836)

From *Diary Entries from a Visit to Britain and France* (1865-66)

Queen Emma of Hawaii was born in 1836 either in Honolulu or in Kawaihae on the island of Hawaii, the daughter of George Naea and Fanny Kekelaokalani Young, high-ranking alii (chiefs and "chiefesses"). Emma was the great-granddaughter of Keliimaikai, a half brother of Kamehameha the Great. She was the granddaughter of John Young, an Englishman who counselled Kamehameha, and his second wife, Kaonaeha, a niece of Kamehameha. Emma was offered, as was the custom, to her mother's sister, Grace Kamaikui Rooke and her husband, Dr. T.C.B. Rooke. Unable to have children of their own, the Rookes adopted Emma.

Dr. Rooke was a young English surgeon who had arrived in Hawaii in 1830 and was serving as the court physician. He doted on the baby girl, and while Dr. Rooke raised Emma to be very British, her aunt Grace raised her to be proud of her Hawaiian heritage. She learned about the world from her scholarly father, with the help of many letters from her paternal grandmother in England who instructed Dr. Rooke on how to raise Emma "properly". Emma was educated in Honolulu at the Royal School, established by American Congregational missionaries, and was privately tutored by Sarah Rhodes von Pfister, an Englishwoman of the Anglican faith. In 1856 Emma married young Kamehameha IV, who had become king the year before and to whom she had been long betrothed. Becoming the centre of Honolulu's social circle and busying herself with the affairs of the palace, Queen Emma enlarged its scholarly library, later donated to the Honolulu Library (part of the Library of Hawaii).

Queen Emma's joy at her son's birth turned to sorrow in 1859 when her husband, after several days of drinking, committed what he later called "the great false act of my life". He shot and severely wounded his American secretary, Henry A. Neilson, whom he groundlessly suspected of having an affair with Emma. Although the king threatened to abdicate, he remained on the throne, and Emma helped him refocus his energies towards philanthropy.

Their only son died in 1863, and the king died, apparently of grief, on 30 November 1864. During her mourning, Queen Emma took a new name, Kaleleonalani, which means "flight of the heavenly chiefs". To ease her pain, Emma dedicated herself to many worthy causes, among which was organizing a hospital auxiliary of women to help with the ill. She also helped found two schools, St. Andrews Priory in Honolulu and St. Cross on Maui. Her work included the development of St. Andrew's Cathedral. She journeyed to England where she and her friend, Queen Victoria, raised $30,000 for the construction of the cathedral. Emma also gained the admiration and respect of Queen Victoria, who wrote: "Nothing could be nicer or more dignified than her manner." While she was in England, Emma persuaded Priscilla Lydia Sellon, who headed the Society of the Most Holy Trinity, to journey to Hawaii in 1867 in order to establish more schools.

When King Lunalilo died in 1874, Emma became a candidate for the throne (the Kingdom had become a constitutional democracy). Lunalilo had wanted her to succeed him, but he failed to make the legal pronouncement before he died. Had he done so, she would have reigned as sovereign queen. Instead, an election for a new sovereign was held. Although she campaigned actively, she lost the throne to David Kalakaua. Politics was not her strong suit—humanitarianism was. Her humanitarian efforts set an example for Hawaii's royal legacy of charitable bequests. After her death on 25 April 1885 at the age of 49, she was given a royal funeral and laid to rest in Mauna 'Ala beside her husband and son. Emma Kaleleonalani left the bulk of her estate, some 13,000 acres of land on the Big Island and in Waikiki on Oahu, in trust for the hospital that honours her.

During her life, Queen Emma earned an international reputation while fundraising abroad. In Paris she dined with Emperor Napoleon III and Empress Eugénie *en famille* in the Tuileries Palace, and during a visit to the United States, she met President Andrew Johnson at the

White House. In 1874 Queen Emma returned to private life and philanthropy. Her chief monuments are Queen's Hospital (later called Queen's Medical Center), St. Andrew's Priory, and St. Andrew's Cathedral. When she died in Honolulu, after suffering several cerebral haemorrhages, her financial estate was largely given to Queen's Hospital and her Hawaiian artifacts were donated to the newly created Bishop Museum.

Extracts from Queen Emma's *Diary Entries from a Visit to Britain and France*:

[Her View from a Balcony: Paris]

. . . When we woke the next morning from our short night's rest in Paris, we threw open the long windows and shutters, and slipping out into the little balcony whiled away 15 minutes before breakfast was announced, in looking down upon the rue Marenge [Marengo] at the pretty variegated sights in the street, of the bright dresses of both men and women, market vans, light phaetons, bright shops opposite the road, young demoiselles that trip along with blooming cheeks, and a bundle of sewing for the day's work under their arm, Zsouaves who jostle along with all their medals on their breasts, old women in sabots, white caps, short petticotes and a rainbowie handkerchief folded over their chest and shoulders—now all this was an early morning sight at the end of the street... We sat down to a light breakfast of sweet toast, beautiful coffee sweetened with square lumps of white sugar in large light green cups. . .

[The Cathedral of St. John: Lyon]

. . . When we entered, the voices of priests & boy choristers came sweetly to the ear as they chanted hymns behind the center Alter, where that is always done. This church had nothing prepossessing in it, but rather looked like a bazar of cheap daubs of penny pictures & children's toys—the walls & pillars were well covered with these trumpery trashes of plated eyes, tears, dolls legs, arms, pictures depicting all sorts of accidents, as offerings to the Virgin, who is represented in them as interfering in sickness & other adversities—a woman falling from a window yet saved by her interposition—horse running away & dragging a poor man by one leg on the ground—the good mother is represented under the horse's belly as coming to his rescue on a blue cloud in the dust—houses trumbling down on one & she depicted as appearing among the falling buildings—this & all sorts of subjects. Dirty crutches innumerable were suspended all about the home of 'Mary the Blessed Virgin', as offerings from many poor creatures who have recovered from lameness—in fact the church was tapestried with these cheap Ex voto. In the interieur, here again we saw in one of the dark confessionals some few old & young making many genuflections to a wretched daub of a picture. . .

[A Roman Confessional: Lyon]

. . . At Lyon, I saw the first actual confession, such as one reads about, in the Cathedral du Lyon, a building as large as the Roman Catholic Church in Honolulu, & one which I wished our new Cathedral would be like, it is just the size, & I rather liked the style of architecture, ornamental Gothic. . .

On both sides of the nave are a series of chapels formed underneath the arches (eight in number) in one of which I saw the confessional act, as performed in the Church of Rome. . .

One of the penitents was a beautiful girl, kneeling in the repentant's open recess, where is a crucifix of picture of our Lord hung before her in the queer arrangement of the Confessional box, which is like a low wardrobe with the two ends not enclosed & the center only so, the door of which when the priest enters is shut upon him, & he listens & absolves all the sinner's faults which is made known to him through a finely grated opening in one side—it is precisely like the sentry boxes at the Palace gates at home, just put three of them together side by side & you have it, only a little more elaborate—there were many of them in the Church. Various services were being performed at the same moment, thus we saw confessionals, christenings, private devotions, mass &c in this one Cathedral.

From thence we drove up through long & crowded streets walled in on both sides by high bare wall of old houses, monasteries, gardens, portions of ancient ramparts, barrack walls or wretched dirty apartments. There were frequent niches in them all along containing a figure of the blessed Virgin with arms folded looking down pitifully on you, or outstretched in the attitude of blessing...

[Her View from a Balcony: Marseille]

. . . In the afternoon we saw the Mediterranean over a long flat country like the flat lands of Puuloa, lured into pretty lonely looking bays in the shore. . . [and by] 4 o'clock we were in the 'Grand Hotel du Louvre et de la Paix.' & out on our balcony looking at the live street of Le Cannebiere [Canebière], the great street of Marselles & the hotel the grandest place on it—crowned heads & illustrious visitors go there. I never thought that the colored prints & pictures of street scenes could be so true. Why! it is to the reality! It was a most animated scene all day long. & the variety of costumes is something very gay—the bright dress of Zouave soldiers, each regiment differing in brightness—the sedate looking French proprietaire in plane clothes with overcoats buttoned at the throat, & sleeves not used but dangling about, both hands being buried in the trowsers pockets—the narrow waggons or carts drawn by a tandem team of animals, foremost is the small donkey then a large mule, & a poor horse all with the queer head gear that looks like [a] yoke on their necks with a horn in the top of it covered with tiny globular bells on them that jingle through the streets—the Arabs in their white burnoose enveloping head & all, thrown over one shoulder—the young girls that swarm the streets passing up & down, their hairs so prettily & stylishly made, & who dress in the most becoming of latest Mode de Paris—Americans in their usual quick businesslike walk—Priests in long robes & shovel hats shuffling through the crowd—the women of the lower orders dotting the mass with white by their white caps—the English discernable through that mottled crowd by their tall black hats, excessive simplicity of dress & dignified ladylike & gentlemanlike bearing—Turks with red fezzes & full trowsers, gay broad sashes wound round the waists—sisters of Mercy of many orders & old dresses, sailors, shabby cabs & drivers run about them, & once in a while a fast looking young gentleman dashes through this crowd in his phaeton managing two beautiful bays with his footman in livery & folded arms as stiff as you please behind him.

. . . This was at our feet. The tall house whose ornimental fronts & windows draped with bright sunshades, shop windows glittering with all kinds of purse temptations was opposite to us, piano music coming from our next door neighbors in the adjoining rooms. Now with all this live scene utterly new to me you must not be surprised that I sat out on that balcony a very long time, taking advantage of our being unknown in that place—sat exposed without being known. . .

['We Never Found It So In England']

. . . We were besett by beggars of all sorts (blind, sick, lame, young & old who had gathered round our carriage when we were up at the church) when we came to the foot of the steps again. Our courier however soon dispersed them, aided by a few loud cracks from the driver's whip twirled above his head. At the Marselles railway station I saw a real live Monk who traveled with us part way this morning in the same train. Oh, I watched him with great interest as he passed carrying his bag in one hand—his tonsured bare head, stockingless feet in sandles & the brown coarse robe that was girded at the waist by a cord & crucifix . . . & the hood on his neck had a particular charm for me. . .

Hotel du Louvre

Paris June 9

I sit down immediately to write you of my reception at the Tuileries (which took place at 9 this evening) for fear I may not have long enough time tomorrow for so doing, although I am very tired.

This morning, in returning from a visit with Mr. M [Martin, the Hawaiian Consul] to that part of the Louvre where are shewn the 1st

Napoleon's dresses & traveling things he used to use in his campagnes, Mr. Martin found a note to him from the 1st Grand Master of Ceremonies of the Emperor, conveying the Majesty's wish to receive me at 9 at the Tuilleries this evening. I was little surprised at the shortness of the time given, as we were not quite ready for an evening reception. Mrs. Hasslocher & I started off instantly with Mrs. Martin to hurry up our dressmakers,—at the same time ordered an evening dress, in case of another such short notice. We got home at 5, very much tired from the shopping bother & heat (intense), Mrs. Hasslocher & I in full evening toilets, Mr. Martin & Mr. Hopkins in black evening dress, knee breeches & silk stockings & pumps—all black.

Mr. Martin's carriage drove off at 9 precisely entering the small court of the Tuilleries, adjoining the Place du Carusal. On alighting at the foot of the grand stair case, we were met & shewn up by two Chamberlains, between two rows of liveried footmen that stood on each step, as far as the second flight of stairs, where the Countess de [Lancy?], Dame d'Honour to the Empress, awaited us,—passing through 2 beautiful large rooms, splendidly illuminated & lined on either side of our way with Cent guards [Cent Gardes] in armour & lace, as motionless as statues. For a moment all seemed like the old days of the French court in my imagination.

At the door of the reception room were their Majesties the Prince Imperial & Court. The Emperor came out & met me & then the Empress greeted me kissing & the emperor presented his son Louis. The Empress shewed me into a small room that led from the large reception room, where the Emperor, Empress & the little Prince remained with me—the court & my suite remained in the large room.

Their Majesties were full of inquiries about the Islands, the exports, the climate, food, character & capabilities of the people & soil. The emperor was so surprised when I told him Your Majesty had been to Paris once. He asked what year that was. [and I] told him in the beginning of 1850 & that the late King & yourself were presented to him at one of his soirees when president, at the Elesee Palace. He had forgotten the circumstance but was much pleased about it when I brought it to his recollection. The emperor asked if Your Majesty was married. I said no but we all hope you will soon & he asked what your age is & what relation I am to you & if you had brothers & sisters. The Empress asked whether you spoke French. Of course, said I, & learnt it in Paris.

She laughed very much when I told her that her hot house plant which she was rearing with care in the room we were sitting in on a beautiful little table in a vause of Severe was a forest nuisance. It was nothing less than our Ki plant, from which okolehao [distilled liquor] is made. I told her we fed our cattle on it, thatched houses with it, used it instead of paper for cooking fish & cutlets, & never for one instant would we think of putting a valuable Serve vause on our table for such a plant than they would to put a cabbage plant. . .

After a pleasant conversation of an hour, we went into the other room and mixed with the court, the empress presenting her ladies, & the Emperor all the gentlemen present. He went to one of the windows & brought a stereoscopic instrument for looking at views & carried it himself to the centre of the room for me to look at. He brought me a chair & turned the views himself, while I looked at it. Then he insisted upon giving it to me, & asked me to keep it as a little souvenir of this visit to him & the Empress. I thanked his Majesty very much. I must finish my letter in the morning because I am so sleepy now. . .

The Shah of Iran in European Corridors (1873)

From *Safar nâmeh-e Nâser-ed-Din Shâh be Farang* (Travel Book of
Shah Naser ed-Din in the Countries of the Franks)

Nâser-ed-Din Shâh Qâjâr (b. 1831) was the first Iranian Shah ever to
visit Europe. He also became, rather reluctantly, the great modernizer
of his country and through his travel diaries an important figure in
Farsi literature as a modernizer and simplifier of prose style.

Nâser-ed-Din came to the throne in 1848 as a timid young boy,
who had been brought up as titular Governor of Tabriz, far from the
court in Teheran, in the Azeri-speaking homelands of the Qâjâr
dynasty. Azeri remained his first language, even though he came to
command Farsi perfectly and even some Arabic and French. The Iran
over which the 17-year-old became absolute ruler had been reunited
only in 1796 by his great-uncle Âqâ Muhammad Qâjâr, bringing
stability after the rule of warlords, of whom Âqâ Muhammad had
been one, since the Afghan sack of Teheran and the fall of the Sefevid
dynasty in 1722. To maintain their upstart dynasty, the Qâjârs were
ruthless, even brutal rulers, who often had to seek the assistance of
European powers (first France, later Britain, but always also Russia) to
control rebellions among rivals. During Nâser-ed-Din's reign this
brought the benefits and unsettling effects of "modernization" to Iran.
At first a staunch traditionalist, he later embraced the example of the
Ottoman Empire, against much opposition from within his court and
other members of the ruling tribe, of introducing the technical sides
of modernization, while remaining strongly opposed to any political
reform of the absolute monarchy. The sending of young Iranians to be
educated in Europe and the foundation of the Dar al-Fonûn,
Polytechnical School, in Teheran in 1851 were followed by the
introduction of printing and the telegraph, by means of which the
Shah ruled his subordinates on his frequent long journeys through the
empire and after 1873 his three long visits to Europe. His European
visits resulted in many other new introductions, most interestingly

perhaps the first photographic camera in Iran (which made Nâser-ed-Din the subject of one of the new waves of Iranian films in the 1990s).

The journey of 1873, from which we have excerpted below, came just after the signing of the (in)famous "Reuter Concession", which gave a British subject virtual monopoly on the Iranian economy (as it turned out, most importantly, oil) for 65 years. This explains the Shah's cool reception in Russia and warm reception in Britain, where he received the Order of the Garter from Queen Victoria at Windsor. But more importantly, with the introduction of the modern system of concessions Iran under Nâser-ed-Din becomes a star example of how "modernization" and the expropriation of national wealth have come to go hand in hand and seem synonymous for most "Orientals" in the last two centuries, which explains the emergence and congruence of "anti-imperialist" and "anti-modern" popular mass movements (a classic "modern" phenomenon!) in the affected countries. Nâser-ed-Din's reign fermented an influential movement for constitutional reform, but he was assassinated in a mosque by so-called "anti-European" elements, and a reformed constitution was signed by his successor on the latter's death-bed in 1906. Ironically, too, Nâser-ed-Din's travel diaries became the model for one of the main indictments of the incompetence and corruption of the Qâjârs: the novel *The Travel Diaries of Ebrahim Beg*, published anonymously in Cairo, Calcutta and Istanbul, 1907-9.

Nâser-ed-Din's *Safar Nâmeh* of 1873, which he himself had published, is almost childish and yet also wonderful in its lack of artifice and its straightforwardness. It is both a very curious child's, a no-nonsense officer's and a shrewd court politician's account of "Europe as spectacle", as it had begun to present itself to tourists at that time of the Great Exhibitions. But the journey was also a spectacle in itself: it took its route arduously through the mountains of Northern Iraq, then by ship across the Caspian Sea (the Shah hated ships!) and by train (which he loved) across Russia and Europe. But the relative comfort of modern ways of travel was confounded by the way the Shah travelled. In the ancient manner of royal travels he had a large part of his court travelling with him: advisers like the newly appointed reformist Grand Vizier, Mirza Husayn Khan Moshir od-Dowle, formerly Ambassador to Turkey and negotiator of the Reuter Concession; twelve princes of his dynasty, many hostile to Europeanization; a large part of his harem, including the favourite Anis od-Dowle, who left in a huff when the Shah was persuaded by the Vizier that his travelling with a harem was causing a stir in Europe in the age of Victoria, but he was not persuaded to present her as his European-style queen. In the same manner he also brought a huge mass of food supplies, both live and slaughtered, and gifts and objects to impress the countries and rulers visited. So after two days of travelling in the Tsar's personal railway carriages they "were so dirty that their stench was overall", according to the Russians.

The itinerary took the Shah through the south-eastern expanses of Russia to Moscow and St.Petersburg, where he met with the Tsar for political discussions, to the newly-created German (Hohenzollern) Empire, where he visited and ordered weapons from the Krupp factories, to Belgium, where he was insulted by the "fearless" journalists who called him "a dirty type". In Europe the visit was treated by the emerging popular media as the great spectacle of the "Oriental Despot": no less a figure than Victor Hugo was part of this, denouncing Nâser-ed-Din in person for his great-uncle's ferocious massacres in the 1810s and 1820s. In Britain he was received with pomp and circumstance as confirmation of "the friendship between the two nations" after the Reuter concession, and in France, which was most familiar to him, encountered the strange and tense atmosphere of the Third Republic having just emerged from the Commune, which he describes and analyses in interesting ways, from which a certain identification with the Napoleons (both I and III) seems to linger. On his return journey he travelled through Switzerland and Italy, where he went hunting with King Victor Emmanuel, but did not meet the Pope as he had wished, and on to Austria at the personal invitation of Emperor Franz Joseph to attend the Universal Exposition of 1873 in Vienna. The long journey ended with what we would now call a summit in Istanbul with the other leader of the Islamic world, the Ottoman Sultan. Before regaining his empire by the Caspian Sea, he travelled through the lost Iranian territories of the Caucasus, again entertained by his Russian hosts, and was caught in a storm at sea within sight of the Iranian coast.

The lucidity of Nâser-ed-Din's prose is equalled by the lack of prejudice in his otherwise extensive travel luggage. It is one of those rare texts from the colonial period almost devoid of ethnic and national self-assertion, and of "Oriental" reproduction of an "Orientalism in reverse" on behalf of those on the receiving end of the immeasurable arrogance of Europe. The eye (which is often a royal we) of the Shah is a relatively unfiltered witness to the amazement, appreciation and bedazzlement resulting from the real "cultural encounter" of an instinctive curiosity with "the new" and yet also "common human" world of Europe—from the ballet in Moscow to the Panorama de Paris through the tunnel, for which there was no word in Farsi, so that it had to be translated as a "hole in the mountain". For a text that was intended to be read by the Shah's subjects there is strikingly little self-aggrandizement and a touching immediacy in the interest in mundane and everyday things like zoos and botanical gardens and parks and the way even ordinary Europeans live their lives, which also comes out from the descriptions of people high and low met on the Shah's Grand Tour.

[The following excerpts are translated by Martin Leer from the French translation by Bernadette Salesse, *Journal de voyage en Europe du shah de Perse Nâser ed-Din Qâjâr*, Paris: Sindbad/Actes Sud, 2000, based on the Iranian edition of 1983. Most of the information above comes from the excellent introduction to this translation.]

From Naser ed-Din Shah Qajar's *Travel Diary of a Journey to Europe* (1873)

[Tsaritsin (Volgograd) to Moscow], Friday 18 rabi' I 1290 [16 May 1873]

Three hours and a quarter before the sun set we arrived at Zaritsin, which is the point of departure for the railway, and which is situated on a headland on the Volga. The city is built all along the river. An arm of the river traverses the city and divides it in two. A bridge has been constructed over the river.

A numerous mob was lined up along the streets. As the ship anchored, the 'steam-carriages' appeared, which were to transport us. I left my cabin on the ship after having said my prayers. The Governor of Saratov, to which Tsaritsin belongs, had come to salute us. We made our way to the railway an hour after the sun had set. There the Governor of Astrakhan took leave of us.

The two sides of the railway had been illuminated until a certain distance after the pier. These 'steam-carriages' are the personal carriages of the Tsar. They are magnificent, vast and very well decorated, and contain numerous rooms: dining-rooms, bedrooms, salons, all equipped with lamps, seats, tables and wall seats. The carriages are all connected to each other in such a way that one may pass from one end of the train to the other. The persons who were with me on the *Constantine* were in the same carriages as me, while the princes and the other persons of my retinue are in a train after ours.

This was the first time that we took our seat in a train. It is really good and very comfortable. One may travel five parasangs an hour in this way.

We passed a large bridge on a river, which carries much water and throws itself into the Don. On our way we saw many smaller bridges and, every two or three miles, guardhouses overlooking the railway. At a distance of some parasangs from each other, stations have been built. A station is a place where the train stops in order for the wheels to be oiled, and in order that passengers may drink some coffee or take some food. In fact, it is a relay on the journey. These stations are very well-constructed buildings, with some carriages always present to transport travellers and goods.

Today the railway took us mainly through forests of firs and pines. The carriages moved so fast that we first followed a crow on the wing, then came alongside it and overtook it.

No half-hour passed without our seeing a large village. We spent the night on the train. Early in the morning we passed a long bridge over a river, which runs into the Volga.

Our train stopped to await the one bringing our princes. There we ourselves and our suite re-dressed ourselves in ceremonial clothes to make our entry into Moscow.

Prince Dolgorouki, Governor of Moscow, who is an elderly, respected and highly decorated gentleman, came to receive us. He came to greet us in our carriage. We also received Mr. Kamasov, interpreter for His Majesty the Tsar, and sent by him. He is a very old man who has lived in Iran.

We continued like this, and the city of Moscow appeared. We could see the domes of churches, which are all gold, superb mansions with gardens and flowerbeds, summer residences and manufacturing industries. Then we arrived at the terminal, which is the place where the trains stop.

There is a great affluence. We stepped down from the train. The Governor of the city, generals, high officials were all there. The crowd was beyond counting. A carriage with four horses with escort, and footmen of the Tsar's in superb livery, awaited us. The Grand Vizier, our princes and the officers of our party took seats in carriages behind ours, and this is how we passed through the streets.

Everywhere an extraordinary crowd jostled each other, right until we arrived at the gate of the fort of the Kremlin, which is one of the most famous palaces of Russia, even in the whole of Europe. It is surrounded by a high brick wall of ancient construction, and it is situated on a kind of hill, which dominates Moscow. The arsenal is within this fort, and we passed beside it. Close to the arsenal is the bell of a church in Moscow, which has fallen and is broken. One may not see one larger anywhere. Cannon taken from Napoleon I during his Russian campaign are preserved in the arsenal.

We arrived at the stairs of the palace, and Count Lensdorf, Marshal of the Palace and Master of the domains and parks of Moscow, was there to receive us. He is a young man of pleasant countenance, who speaks perfect French. He was our guide for the visit to the palace. One cannot really describe the Kremlin. We climbed up innumerable steps, which could be mounted without effort. The galleries have columns of porphyry and different stones, and the staircases and corridors have rugs in the middle. On the staircase, to the right going up, hangs a painting showing a battle between the Russians and the Mongols. After this, we entered a large hall, then in an even vaster one, called the Hall of the Knights of St. George, that is to say, the hall of the officers who have received this chivalric order, in the past or recently. Their names are inscribed in this vast and lofty hall, lit by great chandeliers and floor lamps. From there one passes into the throne room, that is to say, the place where the throne is. This is also a vast hall, very long and very high. The throne of the Tsar is at one end, under a dais embroidered with the imperial coat of arms. This is where the imperial crown is put on the head of the Russian Tsars.

In this palace all the stairs are marble. The living quarters are so numerous, from the top to the bottom of the palace that someone who does not know his way around here is lost. A single day is not enough to see them all. A small winter garden similar to the orangeries in Teheran is next to the palace, and strange and rare flowers are on display here: it is very beautiful.

There is also a gallery of paintings, that is to say a very long corridor in which paintings are hung. They have here installed a collection of old paintings in oil. They are beautiful paintings and big vases of porcelain are placed all along the gallery.

After dinner it was still light. We went to see a spectacle. There were many people in the streets, right up to the entrance to the theatre. This is a great hall constructed under Tsar Nicholas [I]. All the levels were full of spectators, men and women. An enormous chandelier is suspended in the middle. Prince Dolgorouki, Governor of Moscow, took place in our box.

The curtain went up, and a strange world appeared. A large number of female dancers began to dance. This type of presentation is called a ballet, that is to say a spectacle of dance without words. In this spectacle the dancers danced and made all sorts of gestures, impossible to describe. In front of the spectators, under the stage, a great number of musicians played without stopping. From a corner of the hall, electric lights of different colours were constantly directed towards the place where the dancing was going on, and visibility was very good. Dancers arrived at every minute with new costumes, and when they had danced well, people in the hall clapped their hands and cried 'bis!', which is to say 'encore!'

For my own part, after a scene, which is called an act, I went into another box, from which I could see the stage from behind. At the end of a scene the curtain fell, and after a quarter of an hour, where people relaxed, the curtain rose again and another scene was played …

[Berlin], Monday *rabi'* II 1290 [2 June 1873]

After lunch we received the foreign Ambassadors in audience. The Ambassador of France did not come, because after M. Thiers [the first President of the French Third Republic] has stepped down, he is no longer accredited. Afterwards we went into another salon, where I said some words to each of the Ambassadors, one after the other.

Then we went in a carriage to the Zoological Gardens. Today is a holiday of the Europeans [Monday after Pentecost], and all the people of the city are out on promenade. Great numbers of carriages circulate in the streets, and musicians play in the parks.

The Zoo possesses several lakes, where all sorts of aquatic birds live. Afterwards we saw a number of large cages where several species of animals are installed separately. One here finds many birds of prey like the eagle and the condor: this is a large and famous bird from America. There is a pair here. They are strange animals, dark brown in colour, very impressive. But their talons are not as sharp as those of the eagle, for they are carrion-eaters.

All species of birds in the world are gathered here. They are too many to enumerate. I was able to see in the live birds that I had only ever seen depicted in books. Afterwards we went into the corridors where the animal predators have their cages. Here they keep the most extraordinary beasts: the enormous lions of Africa with manes, which I have seen in books [the lions of Iran, ancient royal symbols which still survived in 1873, were smaller and had no mane], with thick hanging black manes and heads as large as those of elephants, perhaps larger, with very impressive eyes full of menace, and a magnificent body with velvety fur. The keeper lifted a piece of meat high in the air. The lion stood up to lay its claws on it. It certainly measured three or four *zar'*. The pieces of meat were put on a wagon, which was drawn from cage to cage to distribute the food among the animals. This place, which resembles a corridor, is divided into compartments for the wild beasts and has a door of thick planks, which is lifted by means of chains. At the other side of the door the animals go back and forth. When the door is lifted, the animals go to the other side and their compartment can be cleaned. The floor of the compartments is made of planks and kept very clean. Nobody is allowed to be with the animals. Their meat is fed to them through openings in the front of the cages.

I wanted to stay a little longer to look at this lion, but it was impossible because of the crowd. Then I saw some enormous tigers. Among the tigers of Africa [leopards] and India were two black panthers from Africa. These are very rare animals, and dangerous. One may also see a lioness, who has given birth in this very place. By now, her cubs are large. There are many panthers, cheetahs, hyenas from Africa, which have a disquieting gait and bizarre cries. One also sees different species of monkeys and two elephants: one very fat, which has come from India, the other from Africa. The elephant from Africa is very different from the Indian: it has much larger and wider ears. There are also three giraffes and a zebra, which resembles a wild ass [then very common in the Iranian mountains]. It is a very graceful animal, with striped fur. One may also see bisons, which are the wild buffaloes of Africa and America. There are many very large of these, and some small ones from Tibet [yaks], whose wool hangs down their sides and drags along the ground. They have a very menacing air.

Llamas, animals in between the camel, the cow and the *arqali*, and other fast-running species are parked in vast enclosures surrounded by fences, along with various kinds of mountain goats, *arqali* and gazelles, originating from India and Africa. One may see for instance an *arqali* as large as a horse with pointed, menacing horns, which in no way resembles the *arqali* of Iran, and several species of pigs and wild boar. There are so many animals here that they cannot be counted. All the animals kept here are fed with great care and in the greatest cleanliness.

Different parrots, peacocks, golden pheasants from Australia, which are marvellous birds, and other multicoloured birds fly and play in immense cages.

Afterwards we went by carriage to make a promenade in the city. We entered a place, which looked like a garden, but turned out to be a cemetery. Nevertheless, it was a lovely place. Many governesses were here with little children, who gathered round me, after which we left by carriage and I came home…

Tuesday 5 *jumâdâ* I 1290 [1st of July 1873]

Today we make visits to the Bank of England, the Tower of London, the churches of St. Paul and Westminster and the Houses of Parliament.

This morning after breakfast we went in an open carriage to the City and entered the Tower. We there gave audience to the authorities, and then climbed a very ancient tower. In the centre is a large chest covered in glass and surrounded by a metal grille. Inside are shown several crowns belonging to old kings of England, ornamented with very beautiful stones. In particular one of the crowns has a truly superb enormous ruby. I also saw sceptres and gold vases. A copy in crystal has been made of the diamond *Kûh-e Nûr*, which has been placed there. But the real diamond has been set in brilliants in London and mounted on a brooch, and the Queen wears it on her corsage. She wore it on the day when I went to Windsor. It is a magnificent stone. As we were short of time, we did not see the armory which is also in this fortress…

After this we went to the Bank of England. At our arrival the Governor received us at the gate with all his employees and the members of his board. We saw the offices, the meeting chambers, we visited everything. They have excellent machines and steam engines to print bills and banknotes, to verify the weight of pieces of gold and silver, to discover coins that are too light. We saw everything. Then we inscribed our names in their register and we descended into the caves: we there saw huge quantities of gold and silver ingots. Each ingot weighed two thousand Iranian *tomân*. There were enough there for three of four *korûr*. In the end we returned home.

We saw three curious things there: first, that every machine which prints banknotes has three dials, each with hands like a watch. These dials count every bill printed by means of these hands. For every impulse given by the machine a bill comes out printed and the hand advances by a gradation to the next. All this so that people cannot steal printed bills.

Secondly, they have machines for evaluating coins according to the gold standard and controlling their weight. A large quantity of gold pieces run down an orifice, which resembles a drainpipe; on one side is a kind of box into which the machine drops all the coins which are too light, and on the other side another box which receives the coins which are heavy enough.

Thirdly they have a machine similar to a pair of scissors, which cuts the light pieces into two and puts them out of use so that they may be resmelted.

Returning to our apartments, we took a brief rest. Then we set out in a carriage to meet with Gladstone, the Prime Minister. We sat with him for a little while and then made our way to the Houses of Parliament.

To describe this monument, enumerate its halls, its galleries and corridors, is beyond human capacity. It is said that enormous sums were used for its construction. It was founded 800 years ago, but ten years ago it was greatly enlarged. The official known as 'the Usher of the Black Rod' of the House of Lords, an old man named Clifford, went in front of us and showed us the halls one after the other. Truly, such a grandiose monument is worthy of the Parliament of Britain. We passed through the grand hall called 'the Hall of Waterloo'. This holds two magnificent pictures, one shows the Battle of Trafalgar… and the other the meeting of Wellington and Marshal Blücher, the Prussian Commander who participated in the Battle of Waterloo.

After the defeat of Napoleon, they shake each other's hand on the Waterloo plain and congratulate each other.

We entered the House of Lords. They were all there. This assembly counts around a hundred members[160]. After sitting there for a few minutes, we made our way through halls and corridors to the House of Commons. This has about 350 members. Lord Gladstone, Disraeli and the other Whig and Tory ministers were present. The Whigs sat on one side of the hall and the Tories on the other, and we sat above, in a narrow gallery overlooking the hall. A problem was being debated, on which opinions diverged. The President [Speaker] of the Chamber decided in favour of the larger number, which were called *Majority*. The smaller number were called *Minority*. All the Members rose to be counted outside. The hall was emptied, except for the President. They reentered after a minute. The Whigs were the greater number, they hold the ministries. Then Lord Gladstone, the Prime Minister, came to us and we had a conversation.

After this I rose and went to visit Westminster Abbey, which is next to the Parliament. This is a magnificent monument, all in stone, of ancient and very harmonious construction, with an immense high vaulted ceiling. King Henry VII of England has constructed a very beautiful chapel connected with the Abbey, the vault and the walls are decorated with numerous sculptures, and the tomb of Henry VII is in the centre surrounded by a metal grille.

Many other sovereigns are buried here, as are famous military commanders and poets. The total length of the Abbey is 530 English feet and its height 225 feet...

A very ancient throne may be seen here, on which the English Kings have to be crowned. The stone of the Patriarch Jacob—may peace be upon him—is framed within this throne. This is a large stone on which Jacob has slept. It has passed from hand to hand, from Egypt to Farangestân, before ending with the English Kings. Finally we returned to our residence.

In Parliament is a very important library, in which separate volumes on the Parliamentary Debates are kept along with the English Laws and other writings.

[Cherbourg–Paris], Sunday 10 *jumâdâ* I 1290 [6 July 1873]

Today we are going to Paris. We rose early and we went into a boat which took us ashore. It was very cold. We docked. The stairs were very finely decorated: a magnificent triumphal arch had been constructed, decorated with flowers and branches, hung with wreaths of flowers, lamps, etc. and decorated with all sorts of motifs with weapons, pistols, rifles and lances. Truly, it was made with much skill. So we ascended. A group of officers of the land forces and the navy, officials and others were lined up. The Governor [Préfet] of the Channel presented all of them to us, and I addressed a few amiable words to them while we made our way towards the railway. We entered the carriage and had to wait a short while.

In France, most of the men and women are slim and short. They are not like the Russians, the Germans and the English. Rather they resemble the Orientals....

...The journey by railway from Cherbourg to Paris lasts eight hours, and the distance is 90 parasangs. We reached the suburbs of Paris about an hour before sunset. After having passed a bridge over the Seine outside the city, we entered Paris. We followed the railway, which makes a tour round the inside of the city fortifications, and we arrived in a *quartier* called Passy, where all the important persons in the French government had assembled along with ordinary spectators... [List of dignitaries assembled]... They [the dignitaries] also made speeches, and we replied to them. Then we reascended into our carriages and we began the drive up the Avenue des Champs-Elysées. It is vast and a very pleasant sight. All the avenues we passed were bordered with beautiful trees and superb mansions. We then arrived at the Place de la Concorde, on which is placed a large column brought from Egypt. It is a very animated square. It has two large pools with fountains that are not always working. They are turned on when this is wished. After passing a bridge over the Seine, we entered the Palace made ready for us. M. Buffet, who is at present President of the *Assemblée Nationale*, was standing with several Deputies at the foot of the stairs. He delivered a speech of welcome. I replied. Then I mounted the stairs: the salons and other rooms are vast and very beautiful. The bed I have been given is that of Napoleon at the time of his marriage to Marie-Louise, the daughter of the Emperor of Austria.

I have noticed today a curious state of mind among the French: first of all they are still in mourning over this recent war with Germany and all of them, young and old, are sad and melancholy. The women of the people, ladies and gentlemen still wear mourning dress, with few ornaments and of a great simplicity. Some of them cried occasionally 'Long live the Marshal! Long live the Shah of Persia!' I heard one cry while I went for a promenade in the evening: 'May his reign be firm and long-lasting!'

It seems that in France several parties want a return of the monarchy. Among them there are three tendencies: one wishes for the return of the son of Napoleon III; another that of a descendant of Louis-Philippe; another that of Henri V, who belongs to the Bourbon dynasty, and who is descended from the family of Louis-Philippe, but by another branch. The advocates of a republic are equally numerous, but they too are divided in opinion: some want a red republic, that is a radical one; others want a moderate republic which would have the institutions of a monarchy, but no king; others want something else again. At the moment, governing in the middle of all these parties is very difficult and this situation may have detrimental consequences, unless all these tendencies come to an agreement, and a real monarchy or a real republic is established. Once the French state was the strongest of all, and everybody had to take it into account. Now with all these numerous divergent opinions it is difficult to preserve order within the country...

The Palace in which we reside was previously that of the Parliament, that is, the assembly of deputies of the nation. After the fall of Napoleon III and the installation of a Republic, the deputies and all the figures of State have left for Versailles and have left the city of Paris completely deprived of government administration. The city of Paris, in fact, belongs to the plebeians and the peasants. They may do as they like, the government does not have the means to oppose them. The Palace of the Tuileries, which was the most beautiful palace in the world, is now totally destroyed: the Communards set fire to it. Only the walls remain. I was very sad about it. But thank God, the Palace of Louvre, which was next to that of the Tuileries, has been preserved and has not suffered damage. The City Hall, which was a beautiful monument, and the Palace of the Legion of Honour have both been burnt to the ground. The Communards have broken down and removed the column of Vendôme, which Napoleon I had built from cannon conquered from the enemy, on top of which his statue had been erected and on which scenes from all his battles had been engraved. Now nothing remains except the plinth of the column.

Paris is a very beautiful city, pretty, pleasant, generally sunny; its climate is very similar to that of Iran.

In the evening I went for a drive in a open carriage with Mo'tamad ol-Molk and General Arture. We passed by the Rue de Rivoli and the Boulevard Sébastopol, which are famous streets, by Place Vendôme and the Palace of the Tuileries and we saw several bazars and other shops. Paris is completely lit by gas... A large number of people were out driving or enjoying themselves in the cafés. The Seine does not resemble the Thames: it is narrower and shallower. Great ships may not come here.

In front of our Palace they keep a pretty little garden. It has a pool with a fountain in porphyry of three levels. Also a tent has been erected here. From there one may pass into the Palace of Foreign Affairs [Palais d'Orsay], where our princes are lodged. It is a very beautiful palace. It used to be the Ministry of Foreign Affairs. It has beautiful flowerbeds and a small fountain. The top floor of the palace where we reside has a magnificent bathroom, which I have admired greatly, with hot and cold water, as one wants.

Monday 11 *jumâdâ* I 1290 [7 July 1873]
Among a long list of people received:
I also received the famous Rothschild [Baron Gustave de Rothschild (1829-1911)] in audience: he is another famous Jew, and he possesses a great fortune. We had a conversation. He is a great supporter of his co-religionists and spoke in the name of the Jews in Iran, demanding

that we assure their peace. I told him, 'I have been told that you and your brothers possess a fortune of a thousand *korûr*. I think the best thing for you would be to donate fifty *korûr* to a nation, large or small, in order to buy from it a territory where you can assemble all the Jews of the world, of whom you would be chiefs. You would thus lead them to peace and you would no longer be wanderers or dispersed.'[161]

We laughed a long time, and he did not reply. I assured him that I would protect all foreigners who lived in Iran...

An African-Arab Princess in Europe (1881)
From *Leben im Sultanspalast* (1881)

Emily Said-Ruete was the Princess Salme bint Said ibn Sultan al-Bu Saidi, but was born to a Circassian slave in the royal harem of Oman and Zanzibar. She lived in the palace harem until she eloped with her German fiancé.[162] After her marriage, Said-Ruete travelled throughout Europe, spending long periods in Germany, France and England. The majority of her memoir presents these journeys from the perspective of a woman who converted to Christianity, but who remains sympathetic to Islamic society.

As a traveller in Europe, Said-Ruete comments on the hypocrisy of Western Orientalism, and her travel text offers the voice of the "Oriental other" answering back. Throughout her Memoirs she is forced to contend with European assumptions regarding Islamic life, and she often defends Islamic institutions in an attempt to educate Western subjects. She thus challenges European stereotypes by painting Muslim life in answer to European prejudices. In taking up the racist discourse of the "laziness of harem life" she describes the "devotion to child-care" and other "feminine responsibilities" that consume a woman's day. She also paints a portrait of harem life that is similar to the European drawing room: both, she says, are spaces governed by analogous social and legal regulations which do not make one more circumspect than the other. But, having said this, Said-Ruete's comparisons often privilege the harem system by arguing that harem life provides more flexibility for women than the freedoms enjoyed by European women.   Reprinting Said-Ruete's travel writing is important because it brings a unique voice into the canon of nineteenth-century travel writing. That is, her subject position as a European traveller who has an intimate knowledge and understanding of Islamic society complicates many Western travel narratives of the same period. Her perspectives on harem life and women in Muslim culture are very different from those presented in Emmeline Lott's

The English Governess in Egypt: Harem Life in Egypt and Constantinople
or Edith Wharton's *In Morocco*. Said-Ruete's text forces us to read and
think about these European travel writers in new ways.[163]

[Extracts from Emily Said-Ruete's *Memoiren einer arabischen Prinzessin*
(1886), translated from the German by the editors and checked against
the full English translation published as *Memoirs of an Arabian Princess*.
Translator unknown. Princeton: Markus Wiener Publishers, 2000.]

Woman's Position in the East

...I desire to include some chapters describing various phases of
Eastern life. I do not intend to list all our habits and traditions, as I am
not writing to instruct. I merely wish to enable the European reader
to gain a correct notion of the eminent features of Eastern life in
general...

...I turn immediately to the most momentous of these issues:
the description of the position of women in the East. I find it hard
to speak of this matter for I am convinced that, as a woman born in
the East, I will be considered partial and thus, I fear, I shall not
succeed in eradicating the incorrect and preposterous views existing
in Europe, and especially in Germany, on the position of the Arab
wife. In spite of the ease of communication in these times, the East
is still far too often considered the land of fairy-tales, about which
all kinds of stories may be told with impunity. A [European] traveller
having completed a few weeks tour of Syria, Egypt, Tunisia or
Morocco, sits down to write a thick book on the life and customs
of the East. He has had only superficial experience of the East, and
seen absolutely nothing of domestic life. He sets down the distorted
stories and second-hand accounts of the French or German waiters
at his hotel, or of sailors and donkey boys, and considers these
sources to be most reliable and accurate. But even from these not
much can be learnt, and so the writer pulls on the reins of his
imagination and gallops away into the land of fables. The only
necessary merits of his book, he is convinced, are amusement and
entertainment...

I had a similar experience in Europe, for—to begin with—I judged things in Europe only by their outward appearances. Coming across faces beaming with smiles in European society, I assumed that the condition of husband and wife must be better organised, and that connubial happiness was more present here than in the Muslim East. However, once my children outgrew the age when a mother's continual presence is more desirable than her occasional absence, I was able to experience more of society, and I soon realised that I had entirely misjudged [European] men as well as the general state of affairs. Often have I watched cases in which 'wedded life' meant partners chained together as if expressly to make each other suffer. I have seen too many of such sad cases to be convinced that Christian wedlock is superior or renders people happier than the Muslim marriage...

...First of all, it is quite a fallacy to think that a woman in the East is placed socially on a lower level than a man. The legitimate wife... stands in all respects on a par with her husband: she always retains her rank and the rights and titles accruing from it.

The mere circumstance of her retired lifestyle makes the Arab woman appear to have less rights and be more helpless. But this is a custom existing in all Muslim (and many non-Muslim) nations of the East. Moreover, it is a custom that is exercised more strictly if one belongs to a higher rank... Poor people, who have no or few slaves, are obliged [by economic necessity] to move about more in the daylight, and consequently [their women] enjoy more liberty. Question a woman of this class whether she has qualms about exposing herself so freely, and she will retort: 'such laws are only for rich women!'....

...I have already indicated that the lady of rank may walk out in daylight as well. For example, she might visit a sick relative wearing a veil; she may also appear before a judge to plead her cause in person, for luckily we know nothing of lawyers. But tradition requires that this right be put to use only in urgent cases, and vanity plays a role in upholding this custom for the veil disfigures women to a degree and makes them resemble walking mummies.

I fully admit that this swaddling up of women in the East is often carried too far, though I cannot say that I find the European customs any better. In my opinion, the want of clothes in a ballroom costume of a fashionable [European] lady is carried to another extreme…

Pity is lavished upon the Muslim wife because she has to share her husband's love with one or more. The laws of Islam permit men to have four legitimate wives… But I have never met any many who really had four wives at once. Of course, the poor man can only afford one wife; the rich man too restricts himself to two wives at most, who maintain separate houses.

In the East, obviously, there are also women who know how to take care of themselves—who find out about their suitors and who stipulate a clause in the marriage contract ensuring that their husband would not marry again or purchase a Surie.

In practice and fact, monogamy predominates [in the East]. Whenever a man avails himself of the liberty to have two or more wives, the relations between the wives become rather uncomfortable. Envy leads to raging jealousy with hot-tempered Southern women. Apathy or indifference is never the cause of jealousy, which only arises when we have reason to doubt our power over the object of love and possession. Don't these outbursts of passion prove that the woman in the East can love more intensely than her cooler Northern sisters?

Jealousy turns polygamy into a source of irritation and torment—and that is well. Many men of wealth have such a horror of daily scenes that they prefer monogamy, thus keeping a check on a bad custom. No sensible man, and surely no woman, can either defend or excuse polygamy. But how is it with the Christians in this respect? How is married life in civilised Europe? I do not wish to comment on the fact that in a Christian state the Mormons, who call themselves Christian, are openly and publicly polygamists. Is wedlock considered a sacred institution in Europe? Is it not ironical and delusive to talk of only 'one' wife [in Europe]? The Christian man may marry only one woman, and that is the great superiority of Christianity: the Christian law demands the just and the good, and Muslim law makes allowances for the evil. But custom and practice reduce this evil to a great extent in the East, while sin is rampant in Europe in spite of the law. I should say that the only difference in the position of the wife in the East and in Europe is that the former knows the number and characters of her rivals, while the latter is kept considerately ignorant of them…

…It is a complete myth that the Arab husband treats his wife with less regard than here. This is already safeguarded by religion, which, though neglecting the wife in some regards, recommends her, like a helpless child, to the protection of her husband. The believing Muslim has as much humane feeling as any highly-civilised and moral European. He might be even more strict and rigorous with himself than the European, for he (the Muslim man) believes in the omniscience of the Lord and in just retribution after death.

To be sure, domestic tyrants do exist in both Zanzibar and in Europe. But I may state on my conscience that in Europe I have heard more of loving husbands who think it fit to win their arguments by physical manipulation. Any decent Arab would feel ashamed and dishonoured by such an action…

Great Changes

I was then met with the affection of a young German, who lived in Zanzibar as a representative of a Hamburg mercantile firm. A good many untrue reports have been published with regard to these, to me, important events, and I feel it incumbent on me to briefly mention them here. During the reign of my brother Madjid the Europeans enjoyed a very respected position; they were often gladly received as guests at his house and on his estates, and were always treated with great respect on such occasions. My step-sister Khole and myself were very friendly with all of the foreigners in Zanzibar, which led to various courtesies, such as the custom of the country admitted. The European ladies of Zanzibar for the most part often called upon Khole and myself.

Soon after my removal from Bububu I made the acquaintance of my future husband. My house was next to his; the flat roof of his house was a little lower then my own. He held his dinner parties in a room opposite to where I could watch them; for he knew that this display of a European festivity must be very interesting to me. Our friendship, which in time developed into love, was soon known in the town, and my brother Madjid also was well aware of it, but he never showed any displeasure or made me suffer imprisonment, as the gossips had it.

I was, quite naturally, desirous of secretly leaving my home, where our union was out of the question. The first attempt failed, but a more favourable opportunity soon presented itself. My friend Mrs. D., the wife of Dr. D., the British Vice-Consul at the time, helped me to flee by night aboard the British man-of-war, Highflyer; and everything having been in waiting and preparation for me, we started at once and steered to the north.

We reached Aden safe and sound, where I was received by a Spanish couple, whom I had known in Zanzibar; and there I was to wait for my beloved husband; for he was detained at Zanzibar in winding up his affairs. In the meantime I was instructed in the Christian religion, and I was baptized in the English Church at Aden with the name of Emily. I was then married immediately after according to the English rite. Once married, we left for Hamburg, via Marseilles, where I was received in the kindest manner by my husband's parents and other relations. I soon accustomed myself to the strange surroundings and I worked hard to learn all that was necessary for me. My dearest husband helped me through this stage with the deepest interest. He was especially fond of hearing my first impressions of European life and customs.

Our quiet, happy and contented life was only to last a short while. Only three years after our removal to Hamburg, my dear husband had the misfortune of falling while jumping for a tram-car, and was run over. He died three days later, leaving me alone in the world with three children, of which the youngest was only a few months old. I thought of returning to my native home, but fate decreed that two months after this unspeakable grief my dear brother Madjid also died, he who had always been so kind to me. He had done nothing to harm my fiancé after my departure, but allowed him to settle his affairs in Zanzibar without hindrance, nor did he ever manifest the slightest resentment at my secret flight. Like a true Moslem, he believed in fate and predestination, and was convinced that it was this that carried me off to Germany. He left me with a touching proof of his brotherly love shortly before he died by dispatching a steamer with a full cargo of all kinds of things to Hamburg for presents.

The generous donor suddenly departed this life while the ship was in transit. I have never seen or received any of the goods intended for me, nor had I received any intelligence at the time of Madjid's generous intention. I only learned afterwards that his kind purpose was intercepted, and that the appearance of the ship in Hamburg at the time was reported to be for the purpose of repairs. Nine years later I heard from a friend, who had been aboard the vessel at Gibraltar, and who had then seen the captain, that the cargo was intended for me.

Two years more I lived in Hamburg, but never free from misfortunes. I lost a considerable amount of property through the fault of others, and learnt now that the management of my affairs must be undertaken by myself. The deepest aversion to the place where I had formerly been so happy now completely overwhelmed me—in addition to which my life among the people of that city was not made as pleasant as I could have wished or expected. I removed to Dresden, where I met the kindest advances from all sides. From that place I went to London, of which I will speak in the next chapter. Wishing to lead a quiet life for a time, I lived for some years in pretty Rudalstadt, and there also I made many dear friends, foremost among whom I must mention with gratitude their Royal Highnesses. I soon recovered from my previous poor health, and decided to remove to Berlin for the benefit of my children's education. There, too, my social life was very pleasant. I shall always be deeply grateful for the welcome I received from the most exalted persons there.

Sejid Bargash in London

I had always kept up a correspondence with my native country, and had never given up hoping to see it again, but the callousness of my brother [Bargash] had rendered any reconciliation hitherto impossible. His implacability was not, however, on account of my desertion of the faith, but what he chose to see as a personal affront to him: my renewed friendship with his old adversary Madjid! But I continued to yearn for all of my dear ones at home, and secretly I never relinquished the hope of being once more reconciled to them.

Suddenly a report was spread through the press—in the spring of 1875—a report that moved me greatly. My brother Bargash, the sovereign of Zanzibar since Madjid's death, was to visit London. I took no steps at first to verify the news, nor did I betray the uneasiness it caused me. I had experienced too many disappointments in my life to hold up false hopes, and it required all of the power of persuasion on the part of my friends to convince me to visit London myself. The Secretary of State, Herr von Bülow, held out hopes to me of the diplomatic aid of the Ambassador, Count Münster, which I regret to say, however, proved of little assistance to me.

Before my departure I employed myself by learning English, so as to render myself a little less helpless. For over eight weeks I studied my books, learning English words and reciting dialogues. The thought of having to leave my three children behind dampened my ardour not a little all the time.

After an exhausting journey, I finally arrived in the giant city, where rooms at a hotel had been prepared for me by my dear friends. I had only seen them once before, when they had paid us, or rather my husband, a brief visit during their wedding journey, yet they were extremely kind and devoted to me.

My brother's arrival was only expected a week later, and in the meantime I made myself acquainted with all that was new and quite strange to me. Count Münster, on whom I had called upon my arrival, kindly promised to assist me to the best of his ability.   A few days after my arrival, while I was sitting in the drawing-room of my hotel, buried in sad thoughts, the card of Dr. P., M.P., the brother of a dear friend of mine, was handed to me. I was a stranger to him and to his wife, since deceased, but in both I found two of the most kind-hearted persons, ever ready to pluck the thorns from under my feet. They had come to offer me their services, and to propose that I visit them in their home. I dined with them on the same day, and removed on the following day to their house. Things had thus acquired a more pleasant aspect, so I took fresh courage and hoped that the end of my mission would also take a favourable turn.

My friends in Germany strongly advised me before starting to proceed as cautiously as possible, and in the first instance to try and procure the aid of the British Government on my behalf. I gave way to their advice, even though I had first put my trust in myself and God alone. But in Europe it is often more expedient for a stranger to negotiate matters before entering into delicate personal transactions. Pictures thus rose up in my mind of vague, empty shufflings and, of diplomatic dismissals, of slight coughs given to gain a little time before speaking; these and many more such signs I was soon to be brought face to face with. I was to learn that my fate lay in the hands of those who study and practice, and finally excel in the art of prevarication.

It was not long after my removal to the residence of my kind friends, that the visit of Sir Bartle Frere, afterwards Governor-General of South Africa was announced to me. I only knew him by name, but if ever I received the truth of certain presentiments, it was on this day, on which the hopes dear to me and the future of my children were buried forever. A most unpleasant feeling took possession of me the very moment I beheld the great diplomat, who governed my native country as he chose, and who held my brother Bargash altogether in his power.

After an exchange of civilities, Sir Bartle began to make inquiries about my affairs, and appeared particularly anxious to learn the reason of my visit to London. I told him—although he seemed fully informed on these points already—all about my wishes. There was not much to say after all, as I had only the one thought of being reconciled with my relations. My surprise may be more easily guessed than described, when Sir Bartle, after I had done, put the plain question to me: 'What did I consider of greater value to me—a reconciliation with my relations, or the securing of my children's future prospects?' Even now I am unable to say what I felt on hearing those words; I had been prepared for anything but for this question. I trust I shall not be accused of inconsistency or want of courage, if I wavered and hesitated for a moment. What were my personal hopes and wishes when the welfare of my children was at stake?

After I recovered from the surprise and embarrassment of this unexpected diplomatic move, I asked for an explanation as to the meaning of the question. Sir Bartle coolly stated that the British Government was by no means disposed to mediate between myself and my brother; and that, as its guest, it would be highly unbecoming of me to cause him any annoyance. It is to this day a matter of grave doubt which annoyance he would have considered the greater had he been consulted in either matter; signing the slavery treaty, and therewith giving a formal countenance to the English protectorate, or holding out a reconciling hand to his sister. On the other hand—and this was Sir Bartle's positive proposal—if I would promise not to approach my brother during his stay in London, either personally or in writing, the British Government would undertake to secure the future of my children.

I was as sad as a person can be, who, pining for a fresh drink from a cool spring after a long and dreary journey, finds the longed-for well closed up by some magical power. I had to choose between two alternatives: to act either for myself, and without any help from the British Government, or to accept the proffered aid of the Government in the interest of my children. Mindful of the promise I had given to my motherly friend, Baroness D., at Dresden, not to go alone and unprotected to my brother—though I never doubted that he would accept British law while he was in England—I finally accepted the proposal put forward by Sir Bartle.

The proposal, however, was very vague, and my friend was induced to inquire of Sir Bartle why the Government had so suddenly taken an interest in my affairs. To which the astute diplomat gave three reasons: First, we do the Sultan a favour therewith; second, we keep the princess quiet for a time; and third, we deprive the chancellor, Prince Bismarck, of all pretext of ever taking up the matter himself.

All of these reasons seemed on the surface to be very plausible and reassuring.

In order to avoid even the appearance of a premeditated meeting with my brother, either in public buildings to which everyone has access, or in the park and in the streets, I studied the programme of my brother's daily excursions in the papers; I even requested my kind hostess not to take me on any drives. But to this she would not agree, saying that my health would suffer, and proposed that we should take quite opposite routes, and thus we went West when the Sultan had gone East. Such a precaution was important as far as I was concerned, for I could not have trusted myself to remain mistress of my feelings if a meeting had taken place. On the other hand, there was no little danger of recognition on his part—my own dear mother would not have known me again in my present attire, much less anyone of my brothers, who had hardly ever had an opportunity of seeing me without a mask.

I should have preferred to leave London at once, where I had seen all my hopes destroyed, and to return home. But even this I was not allowed to do. I had to stay many weeks longer, far away from my children, full of anxiety and worry. Sir Bartle had so willed it. Before taking my departure, I was requested to send in a detailed memorial. Not only was I completely inexperienced in this branch of business, but my sorrows had reduced my mental energies. I, therefore, with what remaining hope I had of eventual success, accepted the offer of my kind friends to draw up the memorial for me. And so after a protracted stay in England of over seven weeks I was to leave the country and return to my children; but with what a heavy heart I quitted its shores can easily be imagined!

Zanzibar was already considered at that time a future British colony, so my memorial was first to be submitted to the Indian Government. Several months had passed in nursing my hopes, when they were suddenly broken in upon me one morning when I received a letter from London. This letter included the copy of a document, forwarded to me by the British Government, declining to enter upon any of the terms of my petition that Sir Bartle had so warmly urged upon me. The reason for this refusal was the fact that I had married a German and I was residing in Germany, so this case was within the German, not British, jurisdiction. This flimsy prevarication was the more contemptible, as I had asked no alms of either of the two Governments, but, in the name of justice, the moral support of both. Sir Bartle had himself incited the memorial—the same diplomat who had shortly before destroyed the object of my mission in London with the bribe of securing the future of my children! I had been given to understand that the memorial was intended to be a formal compliance on my part with the compact the British Government had entered into with me, and the former would now carry out theirs as I had carried out mine. But oh! how dearly I was to pay for my credulity!

My husband was German, and I, therefore, was to be regarded as a German subject. Oh! now I perceive! I could lay, of course, no claims to English chivalry or generosity. And yet why, I asked myself, had the truth of my nationality never been realized until my concordance had been extorted? Why did I receive strict injunctions to conform to the compact as though it had been entered into by a British woman? I can only explain it thus: that until my brother had signed the treaty, and so long as he was within reach of any hints I might feel inclined to give him, and be able to give him, from my better knowledge of European tactics, I was bound over on my honour, as any other British citizen, 'to keep the peace', thereby acknowledging my power, as the Sultan's sister, of possibly 'disturbing it'.

But no sooner had my brother regained his shores and I mine, than the last card was played, and I suddenly became once more a German subject. All this I concluded slowly and painfully, and learnt subsequently, as the course of events correctly showed, that I was, in a word, the victim of the 'Humane Policy' adopted by Zanzibar. Let me here, however, distinctly impress my readers with the fact that though I may trace the source of all of my miseries to the wily machinations of the British Government, I feel in my heart not only gratitude, but the deepest affectionate remembrance of kindness and sympathy received at the hands of English society.

TRAVEL ACCOUNTS

Ahmad ibn Fadhlân, Merchant of Baghdad, Reports on a Viking Funeral (AD 922)

From *Risala* (*Letter*): "Account of a (Viking?) Burial in Russia" (922)

Ahmad ibn Fadhlân's account of a burial in Russia in 922 was previously well-known only in Scandinavia and Russia/Ukraine, but is now gaining world-fame owing to the novel by Martin Crichton (*Eaters of the Dead*) which has been made into—as they say—"a major motion picture starring Antonio Banderas" as ibn Fadhlân (*The Thirteenth Warrior*).[164]

But little is known of ibn Fadhlân other than this account. He was a member of a delegation sent by the Khalif of Baghdad al-Muqtadir to the Khagan of the Volga Bulgars, partly to convert the Bulgars to Islam, but also for trading purposes. They left Baghdad in June 921 and arrived at Bulgar on the Volga on 13 May 922. After his return ibn Fadhlân wrote his *Risâlah* (*Letter* or *Little Book*) telling of his journey and the visit to the Bulgars. This was included in part by the geographer Yâqût (died 1229) in his great geographical dictionary, and an original manuscript recovered by A. Zeki Validi in Meshed in Iran in 1923. (The ninth and tenth centuries appear to have been rich in such accounts by Muslim travellers, often merchants: the first extant Arab account of India, a similar text, also dates from the ninth century.)

It is thus a strangely unique and a precise time-shell that we unlock here: a very early piece of "Oriental travel writing" to (what is now) Europe, and a historical document claimed as almost a national myth of origin by Scandinavians, Russians and Ukrainians, but not by Arabs. For much of the nineteenth and twentieth century Scandinavian scholars on the one hand and Russian/Soviet scholars on the other, without much dialogue between the two, have been claiming that the *al-Rusiyyah* in the following account are their ancestors: Viking colonists at one of the outposts of their eastern Norse expansion; or the people just emerging at this time, who will become the founders of Russia. The most convincing evidence (predictably, perhaps) to this editor comes from the Scandinavian side: we know that the Viking (largely Eastern Swedish) colonists along the great Russian rivers called themselves or were called *rûs* (in Arabic and Byzantine sources), and the funerary ceremonies, especially "the Angel of Death" here, correspond to what we know of rites associated with Freja/Frigg, the Norse goddess of fertility, death and the family, and Odin, the shaman-God—interpreter of life and death. A reasonable suggestion as to "national origin" may be that given by James E. Montgomery in his recent close examination of the Arabic source: that the Rusiyyah described here are a group of Vikings becoming creolized or hybridized with various Slavonic groups and Khazars into the new ethnic mix of Russians.

But why should they want to claim these barbarous peoples as ancestors? This has to do with the paucity of written sources about this period in Scandinavian and Russian history, well outside the "civilized world" of a thousand years ago, centred in Baghdad and Byzantium. Without names, descriptions or living traditions, how otherwise attribute the many archaeological remains? But it also has to do with the special qualities of this text, its immediacy, its "eyewitness" mode, its details described in such almost anthropological terms, its apparent lack of bias and moralizing. The moralizing, as in the best "enlightened" ethnographic descriptions, comes interestingly from the subjects of observation: the Rus ironically pitying the Muslim custom of full body burial. All this, along with the slave-woman being sacrificed, gives the text its haunting quality, which has made many writers question ibn Fadhlân's "veracity", partly because what he gives us sounds like "a truth", and not the obvious fabrications and *sauvageries moralisées* of other writers. In general, one might say that of the two production lines of written sources on pre-Christian northern Europe—monastic chroniclers in North/Central Europe and Arabic Muslim merchants involved in what it is still a taboo to call the Northern slave trade in Scandinavia, though that, and not furs and amber, must be the source of those enormous amounts of Arabic coins in the archaeological remains from this time—the monks tend to have their accounts second-hand, based on a certain familiarity with the general culture and first-hand oral accounts by others but mixing insight with tall tales, interpretation and ideological propaganda; the Arab merchant-missionaries on the other hand write eyewitness accounts of cultures so strange to them that they hardly know where to start theorizing and moralizing. This goes for the self-embellishing Spanish-Arabic poet so sensitive to the beauty of Northern women and his own dignity that instead of bending down when going through the low door to a Danish chieftain's wife, he sits down and slides through on his behind; it is of course a kind of "reverse" positive testimony, when you read it "right": the doors were low to prevent armed intruders, not as studied affronts to Spanish-Arabic male pride, and the women enjoyed a status and freedom unknown in Spain at the time. But so many more possibilities of reading go into the self-effacement of a writer like ibn Fadhlân. If this sounds much like European travellers later describing Orientals or Africans or other non-Europeans, the historical precedence at least goes to these Arabs in the North.

[Ahmad ibn Fadhlân, Merchant of Baghdad: "A Viking Burial in Russia, 942 AD." Translated by Martin Leer from Harris Birkeland, *Nordens historie i middelalderen etter arabiske kilder*, Oslo, 1954]

One day I was told that one of their prominent men had died. They then put him in the grave and covered him for ten days, until they had finished cutting and sewing his clothes. This is done in the following way: For the poor among them they make a small skiff and put the dead man in it and burn it. But where a rich man is concerned, they collect his fortune and divide it into three parts. One third goes to his family. One third is used to make clothes for him. And for one third they make *nabîdh* (a liquor), which they drink on the day his slave-woman lets herself be killed and is burned with her master. For they are completely addicted to *nabîdh* and drink it night and day. It often comes to pass that one among them dies with the beaker in his hand. When a chief among them has died, his family ask his slave-women and servants, 'Which among you will die with him?' And then one answers, 'I!' And when that person has agreed, he will have to go through with it, and cannot recant. Even if he wanted to, it would not be allowed. Most of those who agree are slave-women.

When the man I mentioned above died, they said to his slave-women, 'Who will die with him?', and one of them answered, 'I will!' Two other slave-women were entrusted with looking after her and be with her no matter where she went and to serve her; they even washed her feet with their hands. They then began to take care of the dead man, tailoring his clothes and making everything ready, while the slave-woman drank and sang every day as if she was looking forward to a future happiness.

When the day arrived on which he and his slave-woman were to be burnt, I went down to the river where his ship lay. It had been dragged on to the shore, and four supporting poles had been cut for it from birch and other wood. Moreover, something that looked like their big wooden sheds had been placed around it. Then the ship was placed on the wooden scaffolding, and people began to walk up and down speaking to each other in a language I did not understand. The dead man was still in his grave as they had not removed him from it. Thereupon they brought a bench, put it in the ship and covered it with silk rugs and cushions with painted patterns from Byzantium. An old woman, whom they call 'the Angel of Death', spread the rugs on the bench. She was in charge of the sewing of the clothes for the dead man and in charge of the preparation of his body. She is also the one who kills the slave-women. I saw that she was an old giant of a woman, thickset and sombre of aspect.

When the people came to his grave, they first removed the soil from the wooden palisades and then the palisades. Then they dragged him out in the clothes he had died in. I noticed that he had turned black because of the great cold in that country. Together with him in the grave they had put silk, fruit and a stringed instrument. All of this was removed as well. Oddly, the man did not smell, and nothing had changed about him, except the colour of his skin. So they dressed him in trousers, top trousers, a kind of coat and mantle of painted silk with gold buttons, and on his head they put a cap of silk with sable fur. They carried him into the tent they had put up on the ship, where they placed him on the rug and supported him with the cushions.

Then they brought *nabîdh*, fruit and fragrant herbs, which they placed next to him. Further they brought meat, bread and onions and placed it in front of him. Then they brought a dog, cut it into two pieces and put it into the ship. Thereupon they brought all his weapons and put them next to him. Next they brought out two horses and made them run until they broke into a sweat. After which they cut them into pieces with their swords and threw the meat into the ship. They also brought two cows. They likewise cut them into pieces and threw them into the ship. Then they brought a rooster and a hen, killed them and threw them in.

Meanwhile, the slave-woman who wished to be killed was walking up and down, and she went into one after another of their tents, and the master of the tent had intercourse with her, saying, 'Tell your master that I only do this out of love for him.' When Friday afternoon came, they brought the slave-woman to something they had built which looked like a doorframe. She put her hands in the palms of the men's hands and was lifted up so high that she rose above the doorframe, whereupon she said something in the language she spoke. They put her down, but then lifted her up a second time, and she did what she had done the first time. Thereupon they let her down and lifted her up for the third time, and she did what she had done the first two times. Then they handed her a hen and she cut its head off and threw it away, they took the body of the hen and threw it into the ship.

I asked the interpreter what she was doing. He said, 'The first time they lifted her up, she said, "Look, I see my father and my mother." The second time she said, "Look, I see all my dead relatives." The third time she said, "Look, I see my master sitting in Paradise, and Paradise is beautiful and green, and with him are men and servants. He is calling for me, let me go to him now."'

So they took her to the ship. There she took off the two armbands she was wearing and gave them to the old woman they call the Angel of Death, who was the one who was going to kill her. Then she took off her two ankle rings and gave them to the Angel of Death and her daughters. Thereupon they led her into the ship, but did not let her into the tent. Then the men came and they were carrying shields and wooden batons, and they handed her a beaker of *nabîdh*. She sang over it and drank it out. The interpreter said to me, 'She is now taking leave of her friends with it.' Thereupon another beaker was handed her. She took it and lingered somewhat longer over the song, but the old woman hurried her to make her drink it and enter the tent where her master was.

When I looked at her, she looked utterly confused. She wanted to go into the tent, but put her head between it and the ship. Then the old woman took hold of her head and got her into the tent, and the woman followed her. The men now began to beat the batons against the shields to drown the sound of her screams, so that the other girls should not get frightened and refuse to seek death with their masters. Then six men entered the tent, and they all had intercourse with her. Thereupon they put her next to her dead master. Two of them held her legs and two of them her hands. And the woman called the Angel of Death put a rope around her neck and gave it to two men for them to pull. Then she stepped forward with a dagger with a broad blade and thrust it between the ribs of the girl several times, while the two men strangled her with the rope so that she died.

The one who was next of kin to the dead man thereupon stepped forward. He picked up a piece of wood and set it alight. Then he walked backwards, with his back to the ship and his face to the audience, carrying the torch in one hand, while he held the other behind his back; he was naked. In this way they torched the wood they had placed under the ship, after they had put the slave-woman they had killed to rest next to her master. Then people arrived with wood and kindling. Everyone carried a piece of wood on fire at one end. This they threw on to the pyre, so that the fire caught first in the wood, then the ship, then the tent and the man and the slave-woman and everything in the ship. Thereupon a strong and terrible wind rose, so that the flames grew in strength and the fire blazed even more strongly.

Next to me was a man of *al-rûs* [the Viking settlers in Russia], and I heard him speaking to the interpreter who was with me. I asked the latter what he had said to him. The interpreter answered, 'He said you Arabs are stupid.' I asked why. He answered, 'Because you throw the one you love and honour the most into the ground, and the soil and worms and bugs consume him. We on the other hand burn him in a moment, so that he goes to Paradise immediately.' Then he roared with laughter. When I asked him why he laughed, he said, 'The master of the dead man has sent the wind out of love for him to carry him away immediately.'

And really an hour had not passed before the ship, the wood, the slave-woman and the master had turned to ashes and dust of ashes. Thereupon they built in the place where the ship had stood something that resembled a round mound. In the centre of it they erected a large pole of birch. On it they wrote the name of the dead man and the King of *al-rûs*, and then they left.

Al-Abdari: The Disgruntled Traveller
Contributed by Sadik Rddad
From *Rihlat al-Abdari* (1289)

Most of the little biographical information we have about al-Abdari is drawn mainly from his travel narrative, *The Moroccan Journey*, in which he records his travels to Mecca and Medina. He was Abu Abdallah Mohammed ibn Mohammed ibn Ali ibn Ahmed ibn Masoud al-Abdari al-Hihi. He was born and brought up in Haha, an Amzigh (Berber) village in the south of Morocco. His name indicates that he was a descendent of a well-known Arab tribe, Abduddar Qusay ibn Kilab in the Arabian peninsula. Many researchers and Orientalists, including Pons Boigues, Brockleman, Georgy Zaidan, Mohammed ibn Abi Cheneb to name but a few, amazingly claimed that he was from Valencia.[165] This is amazing since he makes it clear in his account that he was from Morocco. Others wrongly attributed to him a book entitled *Madkhal al-shar' al-sharíf'ala al-madhâhib* (*Introduction to Islamic Jurisprudence according to Schools of Thought*). The *Madkhal* was, in fact, written by al-Abdari al-Fassi. It is unknown when al-Fassi was born and when he died. It is conjectured that he died at a young age soon after he came back from Mecca.

As his invaluable narrative shows, al-Abdari was a highly educated, knowledgeable religious scholar and poet, combining the benefit and instruction of ethics and the pleasure of aesthetics. His account is replete with accurate linguistic, geographical and topographic information, and allusions to the Holy Koran and Prophetic traditions. It is embellished by a narrative style common to Arab travel literature known as saj'a (ornamental rhyming prose), together with the insertion of a considerable number of his own poems and those of well-established poets.

Important as it is, *The Moroccan Journey* is weakened by a quasi-absence of historical consciousness. For it seems that his preoccupation with the status of Islamic thought and faith in the countries he visited blinded him to the historical events in the Arab world. It is inconceivable, for example, that the Crusades and their impact on the "Middle East", which should have normally constituted the basic background of his journey, are not even mentioned. Mohammed al-Fassi argues that the unprecedented bitter criticism al-Abdari launched against the people of Alexandria, especially because of their inhuman and immoral treatment of both male and female pilgrims from foreign countries, should be seen within a historical context. Because of the Crusades, draconian measures are imposed by the customs officers in Alexandria on all the pilgrims to make sure that spies and Christian enemies disguised as Muslims are not journeying in the "Lands of Allah". Describing the people of Alexandria, al-Abdari writes: "It is amazing that they intercept the way of the pilgrims both male and female and treat them in a disgraceful humiliating way... they steal their money and everything they have."[166] He then alludes to ibn Jubayr's description of his encounter with the people of Alexandria: "Upon ibn Jubayr's arrival at Alexandria with a big group of Moroccan pilgrims, the 'governor' ordered his men to check both men and women; so they violated the privacy of the Harem." (p. 94)

Al-Abdari set off to Hijaz to perform the fifth pillar of Islam, pilgrimage, on 10 December 1289. He started writing about his journey when he reached Tlemcen. Although al-Abdari entitled his journey *The Moroccan Journey*, he devoted the least space (four pages in the opening of the book and less than two at the end) to the description of the places he visited in Morocco. He travelled through Algeria, Tunisia, Libya, Egypt and their deserts and reached Mecca precisely during the Hajj season. He recorded his visits to the Holy places and mainly his fruitful meetings with various Ulema. Al-Abdari filled his narrative with caustic observations and comments on almost all the countries he visited[167] except for Tunis, which he praised because he considered it a centre of learning and knowledge, where religious scholars occupied a privileged position and people were righteous, virtuous and sociable. "Never have I seen," he wrote, "any such virtuous people as Tunisians anywhere in the West or the East." (p. 41)

It is useful to note that al-Abdari went to the Orient with a sense of Moroccan religious, intellectual and moral superiority as the quest of knowledge in other Islamic countries, which is one of the chief motivations for his journey, proved to fall far short of his expectations. Therefore, his representation of non-Moroccan Muslims is informed by what Johannes Fabian calls "the denial of coevalence". As such his work, I would argue, is discursively, though not ideologically, close to the spirit of the Orientalist tradition. I showed a colleague of mine my translation of an excerpt of al-Abdari's narrative without telling him who the author was. He said that this was the worst Orientalist he has ever read. In fact, *The Moroccan Journey* distinctly marks itself off from the conventions of the Arab travel tradition. Unlike ibn Jubayr who would resort to indirect and rather polite expressions to show his disagreement and opposition to certain beliefs and traditions in the "land of Muslims", al-Abdari does not hesitate to give way to overtly critical statements. As he puts it in the Preface to his account: "I am intending to record as accurately as possible my journey to the Orient. I shall describe some aspects of the places I visit and the status of the people I encounter without equivocation or hinting. I shall neither tend to beautify what is bad, or uglify what is good... I shall record what my eyes see in clear unequivocal expressions." (p. 1) He would later state: "I wished I had encountered only positive things, and I wouldn't have hesitated to praise them." It is undoubtedly al-Abdari's objectivity and authenticity that make his *Moroccan Journey* a popular and indispensable source of information about the religious and intellectual scene in the Arabic world in the thirteenth century.

[This translation is based on the Arabic text of Al-Abdari's travel account, edited and introduced by Mohammed al-Fassi. The full title of the narrative is unconventionally short: *Rihlat al-Abdarî* (*al-Abdari's Journey*) known as *Al-Rihlah al-maghribiyyah* (*The Moroccan Journey*) (AH 688; 1289.) It was published by the Ministry of Education, Rabat, in 1968 and ran to 352 pages. Al-Fassi's fine edition was based on eight manuscripts of al-Abdari's Journey. The manuscripts are available in some Moroccan public and private libraries, including the

Library of al-Qarawiyin in Fez, the Public Library in Rabat, the Royal Library in Rabat, the private library of al-Mukhtar al-Soussi.]

Extracts from Al-Abdari's Travels, or *The Moroccan Journey*
(*Translated by Sadik Rddad*)

We reached Cairo, the city of the kingdom in the oriental country. It was worse than [anything] we had ever seen or heard before. It is a big and overpopulated city, but it is too small to deserve writing even one line about. It transforms an intelligent person into a stupid one, a sane mind into a deranged one, and a good person into an evil one.

Cairo is the site of the lowest, most corrupt, vile and evil people. It is the receptacle of the country's waste [litter] and home to all those who spread corruption and slander in the earth. Invidiousness reigns in their hearts, cheating dwells in their pockets; their cheating is [like] arrows covered in honeyed advice. It is a market where the devil raised his flag and a place where he shows his followers his revelations. They are unanimous about performing evil deeds; they all agree to oppose any kind of agreement (they agree to disagree). The most generous among them is more mean than a firefly; the bravest among them more cowardly than a grasshopper; the most intelligent more ignorant and stupid than a butterfly [the butterfly is a symbol of stupidity], the noblest lower than (more ignoble than) rubbish, the most handsome uglier than a monster, the healthiest paler than the sick, the most eloquent more inarticulate than Baqil [Baqil was known in the pre-Islamic period for his inability to express himself, whereas Quss bin Saida al-Ayadi was a famous eloquent orator. So it was said that someone is as inarticulate as Baqil, or as eloquent as Quss], the most respectable baser than a beggar. Generosity is shyly disguised and hidden and wickedness is a common currency among them. Whoever shows any sign of piety among them is thought to be laying a trap for people, and whoever seeks knowledge is said to be designing to deceive and ensnare people. The scholar, *faqih* and ascetic would do all they could to look so honest and trustworthy that they could easily lay hand on the orphan's property or benefit from the Sultan's generosity. Such is the nature of both young and old people. They prefer the life of the world, which they think is the essence to the Hereafter, which they consider to be accidental. Their expectations and hopes are great and wholesome, and their religion is sickly. Hypocrisy reigns over all their transactions.

Walking among them, I was amazed by their impoliteness and obscenity. When they need to eat or answer the call of nature, they do it in front of people. Their xenophobia has no limits. On my way to Hijaz, I realised that whenever anyone of them started fighting against a stranger, they all came running from different parts of the city towards them [the fighters] just like dogs when they see a strange dog. I had never ever met so querulous and bad-tempered a people in Morocco and Andalusia as the Egyptians. Neither had I seen in Tunisia, Barqa, Hijaz or Shem any group of people as low, envious, vile, spiteful, callous, xenophobic, pernicious, hideous and unfaithful as the inhabitants of Cairo. It is no wonder that a city founded by the slave of infidels, Ghulam bani Ubaid, may Allah curse them all, should combine the nature of slaves and that of infidels. Isn't obscenity their motto and destructive invidiousness their garment? Old people are seen everywhere quarrelling and spend most of their time cursing their ancestors. Children, however, are not influenced by old people; for you would rarely come across any of them committing the same follies and vices. It is said that wisest among them are children and the foolish are old people. This is how Abu Ubaid al- Bakri described them in his book *al-Masalik*. He said that when Abu Dulama returned from Egypt, he was asked about it and stated that one third of it [Egypt] consists of dogs, one third of earth and one third of animals. 'What about people then?' they asked. 'In the first third', he retorted.

What is amazing is the Egyptians' gross negligence of mosques, so that they look like cesspits; the rugs and walls are black and dirty. I went to observe my Friday prayer in one of their congregate mosques and was startled by the heaps of garbage… No Muslim could ever settle in Egypt weren't God so gracious as to send the Turks to rule over them. Their kings are true believers, pious and good-hearted; they help the needy and hold the Ulema in high esteem. They are the pillars of Islam, may God help them...

Visit to Libya

We left Surt like someone running from an enemy or fearing to be devoured by predatory animals. We travelled through the dangerous and unsafe deserts of Sinanah and Menhousha. They are a site of calamities and disasters. There is no shelter and no place for alighting there for travellers and their camels; there are only highwaymen and raiders. Thieves are invincible, unbearable heroes. The little water one finds there is bitter and salty. After a long and tedious journey, where we went through all kinds of hardships and sufferings, we arrived at Barqa. It is the biggest and most extended desert we had ever crossed. There was much rejoicing among the exhausted pilgrims as they reached this place; they were just like a thirsty person who rejoices at seeing water. Barqa is inhabited by Bedouins who are rude and disgusting to the soul. Yet, they entertain visitors and are grateful people in general. They don't intercept the way of the pilgrims (or very rarely if ever).

Their commercial transaction is based on exchange and barter. There is no place for money in their dealings. It's hard to understand the way they buy and sell things. One of the pilgrims tried to haggle with a man over a camel. He offered to exchange it for a young camel and two Dinars. Surprised, the man said he could never ever accept to go home with money in his hands: [']for I have never seen my parents or grandparents bringing it home.['] They therefore have not the slightest idea about the price of things. They use women in their transactions. The pilgrims find it hard to buy food given the repulsive act of dealing with their repugnant women. It is surprising that every woman has to wear a covering over her face; they call it burqu'ah. They walk barefoot among men without covering their arms and heads. They are only keen on covering their faces as though they have no other private parts other than the face. They never suffer to wear the veil properly or to take it off and wash it. It gathers layers upon layers of dirt so much so the women look uglier than the outcast Satan. They become thus subject to caustic tongues and denigrating eyes.

Visit to the Pyramids of Egypt

The pyramids are miraculous constructions inside of which can be found mysterious sciences. They are the wonder of time. There is an unremitting debate about the founder of the pyramids and the purpose behind building them. I don't think it is necessary to linger on this issue here. Judge al-Sa'id author of *Tabaqât* relates that a group of scholars claimed that all the sciences that appeared before the Deluge originated from... Prophet Idriss, May Peace Be Upon Him. He is the first person to have ever talked about star motions and first to have built a temple to worship and praise Almighty Allah therein. They also said that it was he who had warned of an eminent Deluge and seen in a dream that a heavenly disaster (water or fire) shall befall the earth. He was therefore afraid lest Science and books on different crafts should disappear, so he had the pyramids constructed so as to preserve and immortalise them by engraving them.

The aforementioned judge Abu Qasim al-Sa'id pointed out that Manaf was the centre of science and reign in ancient Egypt. But when Alexander founded his city, Alexandria, people longed to move to it, so it became the house of sciences and wisdom. When the Muslims conquered Alexandria [literally: when the Muslims defeated Alexandria], Amr ibn al-As founded his city on the Nile. People moved to it and it became thenceforward the basis of Egypt...

The pyramids were built high in the sky with hewn rocks, arranged so skilfully that they looked like one immense rock. They are circular; their base is wide and they narrow down toward the top to take a conic shape. They have no doors or entrance. It is completely unknown how they were ever built. Al-Bakri mentioned in his book *Al-Mamâlik wa al-masâlik* that Ahmed ibn Toulun of Egypt summoned a 130-year-old wise and knowledgeable man and asked him about the pyramids. The old man said they were constructed to protect the corpses of the kings... Al-Bakri also related that Shunid ibn Sehlun, king of Egypt saw a dream before the Deluge. He was so scared that he ordered the construction of pyramids with rocks and pillars made of iron and lead upon the advice of the fortune-tellers. He meant them to protect his and his relatives' corpses and to safeguard the sciences from an eminent Deluge.

Ibn Battuta, World Traveller (b. 1304)

From ibn Battuta's *Tuhfat al-nazzâr fî ghara'ib al-amsâr wa aja'ib al-asfâr*, also known as the *Rihlah* (*Travels*)

It is difficult to describe ibn Battuta in a nutshell: even the length of his full reported name, Muhammad ibn Abdullah ibn Muhammad ibn Ibrahim ibn Muhammad ibn Ibrahim ibn Yusuf ibn Battuta, indicates less than a fraction of the extent of his travels. Not only did ibn Battuta cover unimaginable stretches of the world in his travels, he also lived in an age whose complex network of economic and cultural links has largely been forgotten in recent times. As Albert Hourani puts it, "The life of the famous traveller ibn Battuta (1304–c. 1377) illustrates the links between the cities and lands of Islam. His pilgrimage [Haj], undertaken when he was twenty-one years old, was only the beginning of a life of wandering. It took him from his native city of Tangier in Morocco to Mecca by way of Syria; then to Baghdad and south-western Iran; to Yemen, east Africa, Oman and the Gulf; to Asia Minor, the Caucasus, and southern Russia; to India, the Maldive Islands and [by way of Malaysia and Indonesia to] China; then back to his native Maghrib, and from there to Andalus and the Sahara."[168] If he had been living today, ibn Battuta would have wandered through the equivalent of approximately 45 modern nations. He travelled three times the distance covered by Marco Polo.

However, what is most remarkable about his extensive travels is the regularity with which he bumped into people he had met earlier. Ibn Battuta was unable to travel incognito in the Maldive Islands because he was recognized by travellers who had met him in India, more than 2,000 kilometres away. In China, he met a man who came from a town neighbouring ibn Battuta's home town in Morocco. In Turkey his caravan was saved from perishing in a snowstorm by an old acquaintance. These and other meetings indicate the rich connections—and the substantial travel for trade, scholarship and career—that existed between the parts of Asia, Africa and Eastern Europe traversed by ibn Battuta.

"Wandered" is probably not the right word to apply to ibn Battuta's travels. Though occasionally motivated by wanderlust, he mostly travelled for specific reasons: either to visit a famous place or shrine, or to carve out a better career. Ibn Battuta belonged to the class of Muslim scholars who were highly cosmopolitan; they moved from one Muslim country to another, seeking knowledge, influence, patronage, posts. These scholars came from all over the "lands of Islam". One of the most accomplished, ibn Marzuk, was not only a contemporary of ibn Battuta but also came from the same region (Western Algeria). Ibn Marzuk, the author of several books on history, religion, ethics and the law, sought education in various places in the Maghrib, the Middle East and Moorish Spain, and also taught or served in other capacities in Granada, Tunis, Castile and Cairo.

Ibn Battuta, it appears, did not share the intellectual accomplishments of ibn Marzuk. Of the two contemporary references to him, one (in *Hidden Pearls* by ibn Hajar) describes him as "not having much of what it takes"—meaning that he was not an eminent scholar. This might account for the fact that ibn Battuta often sought—and obtained—prestigious positions on the outskirts of the Islamic world, where his learning would have carried him further than in Cairo, Granada or Mecca. However, it has to be noted that ibn Hajar also remarked on ibn Battuta's pre-eminence as a traveller and a cultured person in the social sense.

The other contemporary reference to ibn Battuta occurs in ibn Khaldun's famous *Muqaddimah*. This reference is of interest to us because it confirms that ibn Battuta, like Marco Polo, was suspected of telling tall tales in his book (dictated at the end of his travels). There are, no doubt, a couple of exaggerated stories in ibn Battuta's *Rihlah*, though much of it is not only historically accurate but also, at times, a source of much historical information. In this respect, ibn Khaldun's narrative, as paraphrased by Said Hamdun, is worth quoting: "It was suspected that he [ibn Battuta] was a liar, but ibn Khaldun consulted one of the court officials who told him of a man who was put in prison with his son and the boy grew up therein. The lad asked his father about the animals whose flesh was served to them—mutton, beef, camel-meat. However well his father described them, for the boy, sheep, cows and camels were only types of rat, for rats were the only animals he had seen."[169]

On his return to Morocco, ibn Battuta dictated his travels—by royal command—to ibn Juzayy, his editor, and the earliest of the more than 25 extant manuscripts might well have been written by ibn Juzayy. The text, anointed by ibn Juzayy, was called *Tuhfat al-nazzâr fî ghara'ib al-amsâr wa ajâ'ib al-asfâr*, which Tim Mackintosh–Smith translates literally as *The Precious Gift of Lookers into the Marvels of Cities and Wonders of Travel*, and with greater poetic empathy with the original language, as *An Armchair Traveller's Treasure: the Mirabilia of Metropolises and the Wonders of Wandering*.[170] He later worked as a judge in a small town, whose identity has been debated, where he died and was buried.

The extracts chosen from ibn Battuta's *Rihlah* represent the last phase of his travels when, having returned home to Tangier, he visited Spain and then performed an arduous last journey—from Morocco, walking across the Sahara, to the Kingdom of Mali and back. This selection from his travels is important not only as providing an African account of "inner" Africa, but also as being probably the only extant contemporary account of the glorious state of Mali under Mansa Suleyman. In these sections, ibn Battuta comes across as the man he was: at times petty, capable of dropping names and adopting airs, and often incapable of understanding extreme cultural differences, but in general a man of considerable charm, openness, curiosity, courage and felicity of expression.

As ibn Battuta's text is largely available in various languages, we have—in spite of its importance and excellence—extracted only a very small section from it. The extract below has been translated and abridged by the editors with reference to various English editions and, in particular, the translation of H. A. R. Gibb.

[H. A. R. Gibb's *The Travels of ibn Battuta AD 1325-1354* is probably the most extensive and authentic translation in English. Many of the footnotes in our translation below draw upon Gibb. Gibb's translations, which exist in five volumes as well as a condensed version, are the most scholarly version of ibn Battuta's *Travels* in English, though important works of ibn Battuta scholarship also exist in Arabic and other languages. A very useful account of ibn Battuta's African travels (along with a translation) is provided in Said Hamdun and Noël King's *Ibn Battuta in Black Africa*. Another excellent recent and abridged translation (based on the Hakluyt Society translation by Gibb and Beckingham) of the entire *Travels*, and one that this editor recommends as an introduction to the *Rihlah*, is Tim Mackintosh-Smith's *The Travels of ibn Battuta*. All these, and other, translations have been consulted in preparing the translations and notes below.]

The Travels of Ibn Battuta

The Land of the Blacks

After leaving Marrakush, we reached the city of Sala [Sallee], then the city of Minasa [Meknes], the wonderful and the green. The city has orchards and gardens and plantations of olives surrounding it. After this, we reached the capital, Fâs [Fez], God guard it. There I said goodbye to our master and set out on a journey to the country of the Blacks. I reached the beautiful city, Sijilmasa[171], which has abundant dates of very high quality. The city of al-Basra also abounds in dates, but those of Sijilmasa are superior. The irar kind cannot be matched anywhere. I stayed with the jurist abu Muhammad al-Bushrî, whose brother I had met in China. How different they are! He treated me with great generosity. Here I purchased camels and four months' fodder for them.

On the first day of *muharram* in the year fifty-three [14 February 1354[172]], I travelled in a caravan under the leadership of abu Muhammad Yandakân al-Massûfî, God be kind to him. There were many merchants from Sijilmasa and other places in the caravan. After twenty-five days, we reached Taghaza. It is a village devoid of attractions. The strange thing about it is that its houses and mosque are built of blocks of salt and covered with camel skins. There are no trees, only sand under which there lies a salt mine. The thick [salt] slabs are gained by digging: they lie on each other as if they had already been cut and stacked under the ground. One camel can carry two slabs. The only inhabitants of the place are the slaves of the Massûfa, who dig the salt and live on dates brought to them from Dar'a and Sijilmasa, camel meat, and a millet imported from the country of the Blacks. The Blacks come from their country to Taghaza and carry away the salt. A load of it is sold at Iwalatan [Walata] for eight to ten mithqâls, and in the city of Malli for twenty to thirty, sometimes forty mithqals. The Blacks trade with salt as other peoples trade with gold and silver. They hack it in pieces and buy and sell with these pieces…

We spent ten days there, unhappily, for the water is brackish and the place is infested with flies. But it is here that water is collected for the journey into the desert, which lies beyond. It is ten days' travel with no water, or almost none. But we did find enough water in pools left by the rain during our journey. One day we discovered a pool between two hills of rock: it contained sweet water. We quenched our thirst and washed our clothes. Desert truffles are plentiful in that desert. There are so many lice that people wear string necklaces containing mercury around their necks, which kills them.[173]

To begin with, we preceded the caravan and when we found a suitable place we pastured the animals there. We did this till a man called ibn Zîrî was lost in the desert. After that I did not go ahead or fall behind the caravan. There had been a quarrel between ibn Zîrî and the son of his uncle called ibn 'Âdî and they had exchanged insults, so ibn Zîrî had fallen behind the caravan and lost his way. When the caravan halted there was no news of him. I advised his cousin to pay one of the Massûfa to follow his tracks and find him, but he refused. Next day a man of the Massûfa offered to look for him, without any payment. He located his tracks—sometimes they followed the route and sometimes not—but he came upon no other sign of him. We met a caravan on the way. The caravan people told us that some men had been separated from them; they had found one of them dead under the bushes that grow in the sand. He had his clothes on. He had a whip in his hand. There was water only a mile away.

We then reached Tasarahla, where there is underground water.[174] Caravans halt there for three days. They rest, repair and replenish their waterskins, and sew into them coarse bags to protect them against the wind. The *takshîfî* is sent forward from here.

A Rendition of the *takshîf*

Takshîf is the name given to any member of the Massûfa whom the people of the caravan hire to precede them to Iwalatan with written requests to their friends to let houses to them and to meet them with water at four days' journey out of the city. Anyone who has no friend in Iwalatan writes to some merchant there who is known for his benevolent character. This merchant enters into the same relationship and understanding with him. Sometimes the *takshîf* perishes in the harsh desert and the people of Iwalatan know nothing of the caravan, and its people or most of them perish in the desert too. There are many demons in that desert. If the *takshîf* is alone they play tricks on him and delude him till he loses his way and perishes. There is no road to be seen in the desert and no path, only sand thrown about by the wind. You see mountains of sand in a place, and then they have moved to another.

Only he who has frequented the place and has sharp intelligence can be a guide there. Strangely, our guide was blind in one eye and diseased in the other, but he knew the route better than anybody else.[175] The *takshîf* we hired for this journey received a sum of one hundred *mithqâls* of gold. He was a man of the Massûfa. On the seventh night, we saw the lights of those who had come out into the desert to meet us, and we rejoiced.

This desert is bright, luminous. Traversing it, one breathes deeply; one is in good spirits, and safe from robbers. The desert here contains many wild cattle. A flock of them might come so near to a caravan that people can hunt them with dogs and arrows. However, eating their meat creates thirst and, as such, many people avoid it as a consequence. If killed, water is found in their stomachs and I have seen the Massûfa squeezing the stomach and drinking the water. There are also many snakes.

An Anecdote

A merchant of Tilimsan known as al-Hajj Zaiyân was in our caravan. He had the habit of catching these snakes and playing with them. I had asked him not to do this but he would not desist. He put his hand into a lizard's hole one day and found a snake there instead. He grasped it and was about to mount his horse. But the snake bit the finger of his right hand, inflicting severe pain on him. The wound was cauterized, but in the evening the pain worsened. He cut the throat of a camel and kept his hand in its stomach all night. The flesh of his finger loosened and then he sliced off his finger at the base. The Massûfa told me that the snake must have drunk water before biting him, or the bite would have killed him.

When the people coming to meet us with water had reached us, our mounts were given water. We entered an extremely hot desert. It was not like the one we had just experienced. We would leave after the afternoon prayer, travel all night and stop in the morning. Men from the Massûfa and Badama and other tribes brought us loads of water for sale. We reached the city of Iwalatan at the beginning of the month of *rabi' I*[17 April 1352] after a journey of two months from Sijilmasa. It is the first district in the country of the Blacks. The Sultan's deputy here is Farba Husain; farba means 'deputy'.[176]

On arriving, the merchants deposited their goods in a clearing and the Blacks assumed responsibility for them. The merchants went to the Farba who was sitting on a mat in a shelter. His officials were standing in front of him holding spears and bows, and the Massûfa notables were behind him. The merchants stood in front of him, and he spoke to them through an interpreter as a sign of his contempt for them even though they were close to him.[177] On observing their bad manners and contempt for white people, I was sorry I had come to their land. I retired to the house of ibn Badda', a kind man of Sala from whom I had let a house by request.

The inspector of Iwalatan, named Mansha Ju [lit. Royal Slave], invited those who had come in the caravan to a reception. I refused to attend. My companions urged me very strongly to accept, and finally I accompanied the rest. At the reception coarsely ground anli was served mixed with honey and curdled milk. This was put in a half gourd shaped like a large bowl. Those present drank and then left. I asked them: 'Is it for this that the Blacks invited us?' They replied: 'Yes. For them it is the greatest hospitality.' I became convinced that no good could be expected from these people, and I wished to join the pilgrims travelling out of Iwalatan. But I decided to go and see the capital of their king before leaving. I stayed in Iwalatan for about fifty days in all. Its people treated me with respect and were hospitable... The town of Iwalatan is very hot. There were some small palms and they had sowed melons in their shade. Water came from underground sources. Mutton was plentiful. Their clothes were of fine quality and of Egyptian origin. Most of the inhabitants belong to the Massûfa. The women are of exceptional beauty and are more highly respected than the men.

A Rendition of the Massûfa inhabitants of Iwalatan

Their life style is strange and their conditions remarkable. Jealousy is unknown to the men. No one takes his name from his father, but from his maternal uncle. Sons do not inherit, only sisters' sons do. This I have seen nowhere else in the world except among the unbelieving Indians of al-Mulaibar [Malabar]. Nevertheless, these people are faithful Muslims. They are strict in observing the prayers, studying the religious law, and learning the Qur'an. Their women show no shame before men and do not veil themselves, yet they are regular and careful about their prayers. Anyone who wants to take a wife among them does so, but the wives refuse to travel with their husbands. Even if one of them wished to accompany her husband, her family would prevent her. The women have friends and companions among men outside the prohibited degrees for marriage, and the men have women friends. A man enters his own house, finds his wife with her male friend, and shows no disapproval...

...I hired a Massûfa guide to travel to Malli, which is twenty-four days' journey from Iwalatan at a brisk pace. There is no need to travel in a caravan for the road is safe. I set out with three companions. The road has many [baobab] trees of great antiquity and size; an entire caravan can shelter under one of the trees. Some of them have no branches or leaves but the trunk provides enough shade to shelter many people. Some of these trees are hollowed inside and rainwater collects in the hollows, as if it were a well. People drink this water. In some of these trees are bees and honey, which people collect. I passed by one of these trees and found a man inside weaving. He had set up his loom in the tree and was weaving. I was amazed at him.

Ibn Juzayy writes: 'In Andalus there are two chestnut trees and in the hollow trunk of each of them is a weaver making cloth; one of them is on the slope of Wadi Ash [Guadix], the other in Bushshara [Alpujarras] in Granada.'

In the jungle between Iwalatan and Malli, there are trees whose fruits resemble plums, apples and apricots, but they are not quite the same. There are [baobab] trees whose fruits resemble big cucumbers. When it ripens, the fruit splits open: people cook and eat and sell this in the markets. They dig out from the land grains like beans, which they fry and eat. The grains taste like fried chickpeas. Sometimes they grind the grains to make something like a fritter, which is fried with *gharti*, which is a fruit like a very sweet plum, but it disagrees with white people. They crush the kernels and extract an oil for which they have many uses: they cook with it, burn lamps with it, fry their fritters with it, anoint themselves with it, and mix it with a kind of earth and plaster their houses with it, in the way lime is used. It is plentiful and easy to obtain. It is transported from one town to another in big calabashes; one of these calabashes contains what a jar holds in our country. In the country of the Blacks the calabashes are huge, and from them they make bowls, cutting a calabash into two parts and making two bowls out of it. They decorate the bowls beautifully...

A Description of the humility of the Blacks before their King, and how they pour dust on themselves

The Blacks are the most humble of people to their King and they abase themselves thoroughly before him. They swear by him, saying

Mansa Sulaiman ki [King Sulaiman has commanded]. If he summons one of them at his court in the cupola, the man summoned removes his robe and puts on a shabby old one, takes off his turbans and puts on a dirty skull-cap, and enters with his robe and his trousers lifted half way to his knees. He comes forward abjectly, and strikes the ground hard with his elbows. He stands as if he were about to prostrate himself in prayer, and hears what the Sultan says. If he speaks and the Sultan answers him, the man takes his robe off and throws dust on his [own] head. I was astonished that they did not blind themselves [with dust]…

A Description of the funny way poetry is recited to the Sultan
On Feast Day… the poets come in. They are called *jula*, each being a *jail* [bard]. Each of them wears a costume of feathers resembling the *shaqshaq* [woodpecker], replete with a wooden head and a red beak like the head of the *shaqshaq*. They stand before the Sultan in this laughable get-up and recite their poems. I have been told their poetry is a kind of admonition. They say to the Sultan: 'Formerly such and such a king sat on the *banbi* ["throne platform"] and performed such and such noble actions. Do you do noble acts which will be recounted after you?'

Finally, the chief poet ascends the steps of the *banbi* and puts his head in the Sultan's lap; then he climbs to the top of the *banbi* and puts his head on the Sultan's right shoulder, then on his left shoulder, talking all the time in their language. Then he descends. I have been informed that this custom has continued among them since ancient times before Islam, and they have persisted in it…

Al-Mawsuli: An Arab Cleric in South America

Contributed by Nabil Matar[178]

From *Kitab Siyahat al-Khoury Ilyas bin al-Qissees Hanna al-Mawsuli*
(*The Book of Travels of the Priest Ilyas, Son of the Cleric Hanna al-Mawsuli*)

Nothing is known about the Iraqi writer Ilyas Hanna al-Mawsuli except the very little that appears in his account. He was Ilyas, son of the cleric Hanna al-Mawsuli from the Ammoun al-Kildani family. The name indicates that his family originally came from Musil [Mosul]; but in the text, there is a reference suggesting that he was born in Baghdad. He belonged to the Chaldean Church, which was uniate with Rome.

Al-Mawsuli started his journey in 1668 from Baghdad and ended it in 1683. In 1680, he was in Peru when he wrote the first part of his work. He never stated what the purpose of his travel to Europe was, but there was possibly a clandestine element pertaining to diplomatic activity. Many allusions in the account suggest that he was on a mission to European potentates and ecclesiastics: al-Mawsuli was a "lowly" priest but he had, as he wrote, an official Turkish escort at the beginning of his journey; he offered a sword to the Spanish king, carried letters to European church officials, and interacted with nobility, royalty and the Pope. On the galleon that took him to South America, he had his own cabin, which was quite a luxury, and while travelling around in Peru, he had a litter, sometimes a coach; always slaves and servants, dogs and rifles. Only rich travellers could afford such amenities and advantages.

What is intriguing is why the Spanish king gave al-Mawsuli a permit to go to America. The story that al-Mawsuli tells is plausible—that he was rewarded for celebrating mass in the king's chapel—but the Spaniards were very jealous of their possessions in the New World and guarded information carefully lest it fall into heretical adversarial hands (those of the English in particular). That a priest who was an

Ottoman subject and had worked for the Ottoman administration was not viewed as a threat is perplexing: either he was seen to be too Catholic to pose any danger, or the Spaniards may not have thought of the Ottomans as rivals in America. Al-Mawsuli travelled widely and always noted details and distances, suggesting that he was intent on writing an account of his journey, in Arabic, once he finished with his *siyahat* (travels).

In his *exordium*, al-Mawsuli explained that the purpose of writing the account was to show how God had vindicated His church after the secession of the Protestant "heretics": a new world had been discovered whose large populations were Christianized by Catholics and won over to the *sayyid* (master), the Pope. The journey was therefore an affirmation of Christian victory, an account of Jesuit, Dominican, Mercedarian, and Franciscan missions in a land that had become the patrimony of Catholicism.

Al-Mawsuli did not reveal much about his background or legacy in the text. Still, it is possible to form an image of this adventurous priest. He was a strong-willed man, handy with guns, which he used both to defend himself against robbers and to hunt. He was, of course, always conscious of himself as coming from the East—both geographically and ecclesiastically. He recalled the Tigris and the coffee of his homeland, proclaimed his pride in celebrating mass in Syriac, and luxuriated in his bushy beard, which fascinated the Indians. He was very alert to financial matters, noting repeatedly the incomes of bishops and archbishops, perhaps with some envy. He did not hesitate to break the law and accept gifts of gold and silver from mine owners. He knew that as a priest he was immune to searches by customs officers and other officials. The journey to America not only satisfied his curiosity, but may well have brought him a little fortune.

Comparing al-Mawsuli's accounts with others, a consistent pattern of visits and stops for travellers appears. Visitors followed set routes, saw the same "tourist" attractions, listened to and recorded the same stories, and developed the same views of native populations. Al-Mawsuli read extensively about the Spanish conquest of the Americas and the descriptions of the lands and the peoples; it is not clear when he did that reading, but the ideas that he found there influenced his views, particularly in regard to the Indians. This first Arabic text about America repeats the same views of the Indians as "infidels" and "devil worshippers" as the Spanish sources.[179]

Al-Mawsuli had a good command of Arabic, considering the time and region in which he lived. Although his writing exhibits numerous idiosyncrasies in grammar, vocabulary, and spelling, his Arabic was competent. As a Chaldean Christian, he learned both Syriac and Arabic as his mother tongues; as a priest in the Chaldean Church, he used Syriac in his liturgical and ecclesiastical duties; Arabic was used for all other facets of his life. Al-Mawsuli knew Turkish, too, since that was the language of the Ottoman administration (and the northern part of Iraq was heavily influenced by the Turko-Ottoman legacy).[180] There are numerous Turkish words in the text. Some phrases and terms in his preface are Qura'nic, showing how the Arabic of the Qur'an had become the practiced Arabic of all the religious communities within the world of Arabic-speaking Islam.

Although the date of al-Mawsuli's death is not known, the Russian historian Ignatii Krachkovkii maintains that the Iraqi priest died and was buried in Rome in 1693.

[Note: One manuscript of this account is in the Syriac Bishopric in Aleppo. It is in 369 pages: pages 1–100 constitute the journey, followed by 214 pages of translations from European writers on the discovery of America. This manuscript was edited by Antoine Rabbat in 1906. The other [later] manuscript is at the British Library [MS Oriental 3537]]

Extracts from Al-Mawsuli's Travels in Peru:

…The road was difficult because rain fell day and night for three days. We reached it [the village of Loja] and I rested for a day and a night because of the cold and the heavy rains. On the following day, I left for the mountains, where there are gold mines, to a village called Sullana. For three days, we followed a very difficult path between the mountains. I reached the aforementioned village, which is on top of the mountain and surrounded by the gold mines. I observed all the ways used to extract gold from ore. First, they crush the ore by means of a water mill. Then they rinse the crushed ore and sift out the gold. They then melt it and pour it into discs. I bought four hundred miskals of that gold because not all the mills were operating. After ten days, I wanted to continue my journey, but the priest of the village pointed me to another road, saying, 'There is another and a better road than the one you took. But it is devoid of people and villages. You need to take provisions with you for five days.'

I heeded his advice, and carried with me what I needed, and I took two companions—I mean muleteers—an Indian and a *mestizo*, which means 'of mixed blood', the mother being Indian and the father Spanish.

We followed a rough road for a day and a night. Satan wanted to tempt that mestizo muleteer because he had planned to kill me. But God the exalted exposed his plan at the hands of my servant. So I took his weapons from him and remained wary until we reached three contiguous villages, the first called Basilica, the second Jonjonama, and the third Wakanama. When the villagers who were Indians saw me, they wondered at me, saying, 'How did you travel through these rough paths? Either you are a prophet or a saint.' Their priests are also Indians like them, but the Indians of these regions do not have beards, only a few hairs on their chins. Because I had a full beard, they marvelled at me, saying that I had great courage for having travelled that path.

On the following day, we left for a village called Amotapé. That night, as I was sleeping in my tent, the companions of the aforementioned two [muleteers] plotted to kill me. I had an Indian boy with me who knew Spanish. At night, he had woken up and heard them plotting. Shaking with fear, he ran and woke me up, and reported what he had heard. By God's grace, a mule broke loose that night and fled into the mountains. The two companions of the aforementioned mestizo ran after it all night and returned with it at sunrise. At that point, I took away their weapons from them because I had no weapons myself. And fearing treachery, I took the sword in my hand and called the mestizo and said, 'Kneel down and confess to me how Satan tempted you to such a deed. Tell me the truth.' So he confessed, asking me for forgiveness. After five days, we reached the aforementioned village. Just before entering the village, however, the two traitors ran away, leaving their mules behind, whereupon the village priest came to welcome me. I told him about all that had happened to me. He said, 'God has saved you, because it was in that same path that my brother was murdered.' ...After staying there [a city called Piura] ten days, I left for a village called Illimo. We followed a deserted waterless path, covered with sand, like the earth of Egypt. All the inhabitants of this village were Indians, but their priest was Spanish. Some of the Indians were true Christians, but others were Christians out of fear. On the following day, I went to a city belonging to the Indians called Lambayeque, a big city inhabited by rich Indians and some Spaniards. The bishop's assistant invited me to his house and asked me to celebrate mass on Sunday, and to preach to the Indians in Spanish. I celebrated mass on Sunday, and preached to thirty-five priests and about three thousand souls from the common people. They were greatly enlightened by my preaching and marvelled at me because of my beard and my different vestments. All welcomed me and came up to me for blessing especially because I gave them rosaries and crosses from Jerusalem...

...Some of the friends had offered me a coach to take me to the outskirts of the city [Lima] to view the buildings of the ancient Indians. Among what I saw were Indian graves: during their days of infidelity, the Indians buried their dead above ground, and constructed a very high tomb, two arm lengths in height, one and a half in width and three in length. These tombs were separated from each other, each lying in a different location.

During my stay [at Lima], a violent earthquake struck two leagues out of the city. There was a mountain standing above a running river that, as a result of the earthquake, collapsed into the middle of the river and blocked the water course. Water flooded the ground and destroyed the farms of three villages. At the same moment and hour that the mountain collapsed, an earthquake struck in the aforementioned city of Lima and people fled the city in fear because many houses and some churches collapsed...

Extracts from Al-Mawsuli's Travels in Bolivia:

...Eight days later, I left for the city of Potosi and, for the first part of the journey, I stayed in an Indian village. Instructions had been given to provide me with mules from one village to another and I was charged the same rental fees as the [Spanish] sultan. So I called the sheikh of the Indians and after I had paid him, I told him to fetch me the beasts, insisting that he do so one hour after midnight. But the time went past, the sun rose and the day broke, and he still had not fetched me the beasts. I sent for him and they brought him to me, drunk. I spoke to him in Spanish and he replied in Indian. I ordered him tied to a house post and whipped. On the first blow, he begged to be untied and spoke in Spanish saying that the beasts are tied at his house. So I asked him why he did not speak to me in Spanish until only after he had tasted the lash. He answered, 'We Indians do not cooperate with the Spaniards if they do not whip us.'

...One day, I went to the money mint where piasters, half piasters, and quarters are made. There are forty slaves working there and twelve Spaniards. We saw the piasters piled like a hill on one side, the half piasters on another, and half quarters on another. They were stepping on them the way they walk on dirt. Near this city is the mining mountain that is known all around the world. It has such rich deposits that for the last 140 years an incalculable revenue has been generated from all four of its pits[181]. They have encircled it and descended into its bottom to locate the silver. They have built wooden posts to hold up the mountain from each side so that it will not fall: from the outside it looks solid, but it is hollow inside. Nearly seven hundred Indians labour inside in the digging of ore for people who have bought shares from the sultan. Each miner owns specific Indians who work in his [part of the] mine by order of the [Spanish] sultan who decreed that every Indian village should provide men for the mines.

The law is to take one of every five men, and if the village governors refuse to send these men, the minister dismisses them. When the Indians arrive in Potosi, the governor distributes them to the miners.[182]

[These extracts have been reprinted from *In the Lands of the Christians* with the kind permission of Nabil Matar and Taylor & Francis Books, Inc., and Routledge.]

The Poetry of Basho's Road to the North (1689)
From Basho's *Oku-no-hosomichi* (1702)

Basho (bah-shoh), pseudonym of Matsuo Munefusa (1644-94), Japanese poet, was considered the finest writer of Japanese haiku during the formative years of the genre. Born into a samurai family prominent among nobility, Basho rejected that world and became a traveller, studying Zen, history, and classical Chinese poetry, living in apparently blissful poverty under a modest patronage and from donations by his many students. From 1667 he lived in Edo (now Tokyo), where he began to compose haiku, and which he elevated to the level of serious poetry in numerous anthologies and travel diaries.

Basho was born in 1644 in Ueno, lga Province, part of present-day Mie Prefecture. As a youth, Basho entered feudal service but at the death of his master left it to spend much of his life in travelling about Japan in search of imagery. Thus he is known as a traveller as well as a poet, the author of some of the most beautiful travel diaries ever written in Japanese. Basho is thought to have gravitated toward Kyoto, where he studied the Japanese classics. Here, also, he became interested in the haiku of the Teitoku school, which was directed by Kitamura Kigin.

In 1672, at the age of 29, Basho set out for Edo (modern Tokyo), the seat of the Tokugawa shoguns and *de facto* capital of Japan. There he published a volume of verse in the style of the Teitoku school called Kai-Oi. In 1675 he composed a linked-verse sequence with Nishiyama Soin of the Danrin school. Thereafter, generous friends and admirers made it possible for him to continue a life devoted to poetic composition, travelling and meditation.

In the summer of 1684 Basho made a journey to his birthplace, which resulted in the travel diary *The Weatherbeaten Trip* (*Nozarashi Kiko*). That same year he published the haiku collection entitled *Winter Days* (*Fuyu no Hi*). It was in *Winter Days* that Basho enunciated his revolutionary style of haiku composition, a manner so different from the preceding haiku that the word "*shofu*" (haiku in the Basho manner) was coined to describe it. In 1686 *Spring Days* (*Haru no Hi*) was compiled in Nagoya by followers of Basho, revised by him, and published in Kyoto. The simplicity it exhibits is the result of the methodical rejection of much complication, not the simplicity with which one starts but rather that with which one ends.

In the autumn of 1688 Basho went to Sarashina, in present-day Nagano Prefecture, to view the moon, a hallowed autumn pastime in Japan. He recorded his impressions in *The Sarashina Trip* (*Sarashina Kiko*). Though one of his lesser travel diaries, it is a kind of prelude to his description of a journey to northern Japan a year later. It was at this time that Basho also wrote a short prose account of the moon as seen from Obasute Mountain in Sarashina. *The Journey to Ou* is perhaps the greatest of Basho's travel diaries. A mixture of haiku and *haibun*, a prose style typical of Basho, it contains some of his greatest verses. This work immortalizes the trip Basho made from Sendai to Shiogama on his way to the two northernmost provinces of Mutsu and Dewa (Ou). The diary reflects how the very thought of the hazardous journey, a considerable undertaking in those days, filled Basho with thoughts of death. He thinks of the Chinese Tang poets Li Bo and Tu Fu and the Japanese poets Saigyo and Sogi, all of whom had died on journeys.

In the following year Basho began the journey that would eventually become the material for his major work of prose-and-poetry-and-travelogue, *The Narrow Road to the Far North* (*Oku-no-hosomichi*). Setting out early in the spring of 1689 from Edo with his disciple Kawai Sora, Basho travelled for five months in remote parts of the north, covering a distance of some 1,500 miles. The poet saw many notable places of pilgrimage, including the site of the hermitage where Butcho had practiced Zen meditation. The entire trip was to be devoted to sites with historical and literary associations. He proceeded to Hiraizumi to view ruins dating from the Heian Period. Crossing over to the coast of the Sea of Japan, Basho continued southwest on his journey to Kanazawa, where he mourned at the grave of a young poet who had died the year before, awaiting Basho's arrival. He continued to Eiheiji, the temple founded by the great Zen priest Dogen. Eventually there was a reunion with several of his disciples, but Basho left them again to travel on to the Grand Shrine of Ise alone. Here the account of this journey ends. The work is particularly noteworthy for the excellence of its prose as well as its poetry and ranks high in the genre of travel writing and in the canon of Japanese literature. Basho continued to polish this work until 1694; it was not published until 1702.

[Extract from Basho, Matsuo. *Narrow Road to the Deep North and Other Travel Sketches*. Translated from the Japanese with an introduction by Nobuyuki Yuasa (1966). London: Penguin, 1967. Reprinted with permission from the publishers. Some diacritical marks on names could not be replicated.]

Days and months are travellers of eternity. So are the years that pass by. Those who steer a boat across the sea, or drive a horse over the earth till they succumb to the weight of years, spend every minute of their lives travelling. There are a great number of ancients, too, who died on the road. I myself have been tempted for a long time by the cloud-moving wind, filled with a strong desire to wander.

It was only towards the end of last autumn that I returned from rambling along the coast. I barely had time to sweep the cobwebs from my broken house on the River Sumida before the New Year, but no sooner had the spring mist begun to rise over the field than I wanted to be on the road again to cross the barrier-gate of Shirakawa in due time. The gods seemed to have possessed my soul and turned it inside out, and roadside images seemed to invite me from every corner, so that it was impossible for me to stay idle at home. Even while I was getting ready, mending my torn trousers, tying a new strap to my hat, and applying moxa to my legs to strengthen them, I was already dreaming of the full moon rising over the islands of Matsushima. Finally, I sold my house, moving to the cottage of Sampu for a temporary stay. Upon the threshold of my old home, however, I wrote a linked verse of eight pieces and hung it on a wooden pillar. The starting piece was:

Behind this door
Now buried in deep grass,
A different generation will celebrate
The Festival of Dolls.

It was early on the morning of March the twenty-seventh that I took to the road. There was darkness lingering in the sky, and the moon was still visible, though gradually thinning away. The faint shadow of Mount Fuji and the cherry blossoms of Ueno and Yanaka were bidding me a last farewell. My friends had got together the night before, and they all came with me on the boat to keep me company for the first few miles. When we got off the boat at Senju, however, the thought of the three thousand miles before me suddenly filled my heart, and neither the houses of the town nor the faces of my friends could be seen by tearful eyes except as a vision.

The passing spring,
Birds mourn,
Fishes weep
With tearful eyes.

With this poem to commemorate my departure, I walked forth on my journey, but lingering thoughts made my steps heavy. My friends stood in a line and waved good-bye as long as they could see my back.

I walked all through that day, ever wishing to return after seeing the strange sights of the far north, but not really believing in the possibility, for I knew that departing like this on a long journey in the second year of Genroku I should only accumulate more frosty hairs on my head as I approached the colder regions. When I reached the village of Soka in the evening, my bony shoulders were sore because of the load I had carried, which consisted of a paper coat to keep me warm at night, a light cotton gown to wear after the bath, scanty protection against the rain, writing equipment, and gifts from certain friends of mine. I wanted to travel light, of course, but there were always certain things I could not throw away for either practical or sentimental reasons.

I went to see the shrine of Muro-no-yashima. According to Sora, my companion, this shrine is dedicated to the goddess called the Lady of Flower-bearing Trees, who has another shrine at the foot of Mount Fuji. This goddess is said to have locked herself up in a burning cell to prove the divine nature of her newly-conceived son when her husband doubted it. As a result, her son was named the Lord Born Out of the Fire, and her shrine Muro-no-yashima, which means a burning cell.

It was the custom of this place for poets to sing of the rising smoke, and for ordinary people not to eat konoshiro, a speckled fish, which has a vile smell when burnt.

I lodged in an inn at the foot of Mount Nikko on the night of March the thirtieth. The host of the inn introduced himself as Honest Gozaemon, and told me to sleep in perfect peace upon his grass pillow, for his sole ambition was to be worthy of his name. I watched him rather carefully but found him almost stubbornly honest, utterly devoid of worldly cleverness. It was as if the merciful Buddha himself had taken the shape of a man to help me in my wandering pilgrimage. Indeed, such saintly honesty and purity as his must not be scorned, for it verges closely on the Perfection preached by Confucius.

On the first day of April, I climbed Mount Niko to do homage to the holiest of the shrines upon it. This mountain used to be called Nikko. When the high priest Kukai built a temple upon it, however, he changed the name to Nikko, which means the bright beams of the sun. Kukai must have had the power to see a thousand years into the future, for the mountain is now the seat of the most sacred of all shrines, embracing the entire people, like the bright beams of the sun. To say more about the shrine would be to violate its holiness.

> *It was with awe*
> *That I beheld*
> *Fresh leaves, green leaves,*
> *Bright in the sun.*

Mount Kurokami was visible through the mist in the distance. It was brilliantly white with snow in spite of its name, which means black hair.

Rid of my hair,
I came to Mount Kurokami,
On the day we put on
Clean summer clothes.
     (Written by Sora)

My companion's real name is Kawai Sogoro, Sora being his pen name. He used to live in my neighbourhood and helped me in such chores as bringing water and firewood. He wanted to enjoy the views of Matsushima and Kisagata with me, and also to share with me the hardships of the wandering journey. So he took to the road after taking the tonsure on the very morning of our departure, putting on the black robe of an itinerant priest, and even changing his name to Sogo, which means Religiously Enlightened. His poem, therefore, is not intended as a mere description of Mount Kurokami. The last two lines, in particular, impress us deeply, for they express his determination to persist in his purpose.

After climbing two hundred yards or so from the shrine, I came to a waterfall, which came pouring out of a hollow in the ridge and tumbled down into the dark green pool below in a huge leap of several hundred feet. The rocks of the waterfall were so carved out that we could see it from behind, though hidden ourselves in craggy cave. Hence its nickname, See-from-behind.

Silent a while in a cave,
I watched a waterfall,
For the first of
The summer observances.

A friend was living in the town of Kurobane in the province of Nasu. There was a wide expanse of grass-moor, and the town was on the other side of it. I decided to follow a short cut which ran straight for miles and miles across the moor. I noticed a small village in the distance, but before I reached it rain began to fall and darkness closed in. I put up at a solitary farmer's house for the night, and started again early next morning. As I was plodding through the grass, I noticed a horse grazing by the roadside and a farmer cutting grass with a sickle. I asked him to do me the favour of lending me his horse. The farmer hesitated for a while, but finally, with a touch of sympathy in his face, he said to me, 'Three are hundreds of crossroads in the grass-moor. A stranger like you can easily go astray. This horse knows the way. You can send him back when he won't go any further.' So I mounted the horse and started off, when two small children came running after me. One of them was a girl named Kasane, which means manifold. I thought her name was somewhat strange but exceptionally beautiful.

> *If your name, Kasane,*
> *Means manifold,*
> *How befitting it is also*
> *For a double-flowered pink.*
> (Written by Sora)

By and by I came to a small village. I therefore sent back the horse, with a small amount of money tied to the saddle.

I arrived safely at the town of Kurobane, and visited my friend, Joboji, who was then looking after the mansion of his lord in his absence. He was overjoyed to see me so unexpectedly, and we talked for days and nights together. His brother, Tosui, seized every opportunity to talk with me, accompanied me to his home and introduced me to his relatives and friends. One day we took a walk to the suburbs. We saw the ruins of an ancient dog-shooting ground, and pushed farther out into the grass-moor to see the tomb of Lady Tamamo and the famous Hachiman Shrine, upon whose god the brave archer, Yoichi, is said to have called for aid when he was challenged to shoot a single fan suspended over a boat drifting offshore. We came home after dark.

I was invited out to Komyoji Temple, to visit the hall in which was enshrined the founder of the Shugen sect. He is said to have travelled all over the country in wooden clogs, preaching his doctrines.

Amid mountains of high summer,
I bowed respectfully before
The tall clogs of a statue,
Asking a blessing on my journey.

There was a Zen temple called Unganji in this province. The Priest Buccho used to live in isolation in the mountains behind the temple. He once told me that he had written the following poem upon the rock of his hermitage with the charcoal he had made from pine.

This grassy hermitage,
Hardly any more
Than five feet square,
I would gladly quit
But for the rain.

A group of young people accompanied me to the temple. They talked so cheerfully along the way that I reached it before I knew it. The temple was situated on the side of a mountain completely covered with dark cedars and pines. A narrow road trailed up the valley, between banks of dripping moss, leading us to the gate to the temple across a bridge. The air was still cold, though it was April.

I went behind the temple to see the remains of the Priest Buccho's hermitage. It was a tiny hut propped against the base of a huge rock. I felt as if I were in the presence of the Priest Genmyo's cell or the Priest Houn's retreat. I hung on a wooden pillar of the cottage the following poem which I wrote impromptu.

Even the woodpeckers
Have left it untouched,
This tiny cottage
In a summer grove.

Taking leave of my friend in Kurobane, I started for the Murder Stone, so called because it killed birds and insects that approached it.

I was riding a horse my friend had lent me, when the farmer who led the horse asked me to compose a poem for him. His request came to me as a pleasant surprise.

> *Turn the head of your horse*
> *Sideways across the field,*
> *To let me hear*
> *The cry of a cuckoo.*

The Murder Stone was in a dark corner of a mountain near a hot spring, and was completely wrapped in the poisonous gas rising from it. There was such a pile of dead bees, butterflies, and other insects, that the real colour of the ground was hardly discernible.

I went to see the willow tree which Saigyo celebrated in his poem, when he wrote, 'spreading its shade over a crystal stream'. I found it near the village of Ashino on the bank of a rice-field. I had been wondering in my mind where this tree was situated, for the ruler of this province had repeatedly talked to me about it, but this day, for the first time in my life, I had an opportunity to rest my worn-out legs under its shade.

> *When the girls had planted*
> *A square of paddy-field,*
> *I stepped out of*
> *The shade of a willow tree.*

After many days of solitary wandering, I came at last to the barrier-gate of Shirakawa, which marks the entrance to the northern regions. Here, for the first time, my mind was able to gain a certain balance and composure, no longer a victim to pestering anxiety, so it was with a mild sense of detachment that I thought about the ancient traveller who had passed through this gate with a burning desire to write home. This gate was counted among the three largest checking stations, and many poets had passed through it, each leaving a poem of his own making. I myself walked between trees laden with thick foliage, with the distant sound of autumn wind in my ears and the vision of autumn tints before my eyes. There were hundreds and thousands of pure white blossoms of *unohana* in full bloom on either side of the road, in addition to the equally white blossoms of brambles, so that the ground, at a glance, seemed to be covered with early snow. According to the accounts of Kiyosuke, the ancient are said to have passed through this gate, dressed up in their best clothes.

> *Decorating my hair*
> *With white blossoms of unohana,*
> *I walked through the gate,*
> *My only gala dress.*
> (Written by Sora)

Pushing towards the north, I crossed the River Abukuma, and walked between the high mountains of Aizu on the left and the three villages of Iwaki, Soma, and Miharu on the right, which were divided from the villages of Hitachi and Shimotsuke districts by a range of low mountains. I stopped at the Shadow Pond, so called because it was thought to reflect the exact shadow of any object that approached its shore. It was a cloudy day, however, and nothing but the grey sky was reflected in the pond. I called on the Poet Tokyu at the post town of Sukagawa, and spent a few days at his house. He asked me how I had fared at the gate of Shirakawa. I had to tell him that I had not been able to make as many poems as I wanted, partly because I had been absorbed in the wonders of the surrounding countryside and the recollections of ancient poets...

(Early Summer of the Seventh Year of Genroku Soryu)

Sheikh I'tesamuddin's Wonders of Vilayet

Contributed by Kaiser Haq

From *Shigurf Nama-e-Vilayet* (1765)

This is one of the earliest accounts of the modern West by a non-Westerner. I say "modern" in contradistinction to the medieval West, which had come under the observation of Arab writers. All accounts of "Otherness" are significant, but "modern" ones naturally possess an added relevance for us. This being the age of Western expansion and dominance, the latter are mostly Western works about the non-Western world. Analysis of these, now a sizeable critical industry, invariably reveals their collusion with colonialism. The thesis is valid in the main, but excessive preoccupation with it may prove to be chiefly an outlet for resentments inherited by the post-colonial intellectual. The aim of healthier relations between peoples, which presumably underlies such critical inquiry, will surely be better served if accounts of "Otherness" are considered in a dialogic perspective. At least one critic has voiced the need for this. "I would have liked to learn more about the images of 'races' other than the black—the yellow, for example, or the white as seen by nonwhites," Tzvetan Todorov noted in commenting on contributions to a symposium.[183]

In 1765, after granting the revenue rights of Bengal in perpetuity to the East India Company, the Moghul Emperor Shah Alam II, beleaguered as he was by tenacious enemies, implored the protection of His Britannic Majesty's troops. Since it was not in Robert Clive's power to place British soldiers in the service of a foreign court it was agreed that a letter containing the request would be despatched, together with a present of 100,000 rupees from the Emperor to his British counterpart. The Mission was entrusted to Captain Swinton and at the Emperor's suggestion that an Indian well-versed in Persian should be there so that the letter's contents could be properly explained and interpreted, Mirza Sheikh I'tesamuddin was chosen to accompany him.

Thus began an extraordinary adventure for the Mirza that lasted nearly three years and provided material for a fascinating memoir, though nothing came of the mission. After three weeks at sea the Mirza learned from Captain Swinton that Clive had held back the letter, saying that there was no point in sending it with them as the present intended to accompany it had not yet arrived from the Emperor. Clive had promised Captain Swinton that he would himself follow with the letter and the money. But in England the Mirza discovered that Clive had suppressed the letter and presented the money on his own behalf. The reason for such duplicity was that Clive felt, with good reason, that it was in the Company's interest to prevent any direct contact between the English King and the Moghul Emperor.

Had the mission been successful Indian history probably, and this memoir certainly, would have turned out rather differently. India's fortunes might have fared better and the memoir would have given us a close view of the court of George III, but I think the loss is more than made up by the account of the Mirza's travels in Britain, which he might not have been able to undertake if he had become embroiled in diplomatic activities.

The likely dates of the Mirza's birth and death are 1730 and 1800 respectively. His family claimed descent from the Prophet Mohamed. The claim may or may not be valid. But we do know that the Mirza's family tree goes back to the sixteenth century, and that his ancestors came to India to escape a Mongol invasion of Persia. The family distinguished itself for piety and scholarship, and its scions never lacked respectable employment in the administration and the judiciary.

Most of the Mirza's life as a *munshi* was spent in the Company's employ, but its high point was the brief spell during which he worked for Emperor Shah Alam II. The Emperor conferred on him the title of Mirza, roughly comparable to a knighthood, thus elevating him to the status of a courtier. On his return from Europe the Mirza became a local celebrity and was given the nickname of "Vilayet Munshi", *Vilayet* being the Indian word for Britain and Europe. During his second stint in the Company's employ he was involved in the diplomatic manoeuvres that ended the Mahratta wars. He began writing his memoir, he tells us, at the behest of friends, and to seek distraction from the anarchy all around. This is no doubt an allusion to the war in South India between the Company and Tipu Sultan. He wrote in Persian, the language he knew best, titling his narrative *Shigurf Nama-e-Vilayet*, or *Wonderful Tales about Europe*.

The Mirza lived through the most crucial transition in Indian history. When he was born the East India Company was one among several European trading houses; when he died they were the effective rulers of most of India. Yet he was not a "colonial subject", and this coupled with his elite background makes his memoir unique. He embodies the humane qualities as well as the prejudices of his culture. He is curious about alien cultures, and is a good observer possessed with an engaging descriptive ability. In this he is a refreshing contrast to the introversion that, as V.S. Naipaul points out in relation to Gandhi, often characterizes the colonial subject's response to the West. Equally noteworthy is his comparison of Europe with India, which includes a clear-sighted critique of Indian decadence and a generous acknowledgement of the qualities that have contributed towards European, especially British, ascendancy. His prejudices can be quite embarrassing, and his observations are often skewed by lack of scientific knowledge, but such flaws, especially the latter, generally add a delightful piquancy to the narrative, as do his foibles, like his obsession with halal food. Similarly, it is amusing to note how he absorbs the British prejudice against the French.

The reader will be struck by what we may call his sense of "race". It is worth pointing out that he belongs to a culture with the longest history of colour prejudice. Aryan hordes pouring into India from the second millennium BC latched on the superficial traits differentiating them from the autochthons as indices of human worth. The "twice-born" Aryan of the higher castes was light-complexioned and sharp-featured, the "inferior" low-caste or caste-less Untouchable was dark, blunt-featured, shorter. Despite the inevitable racial intermingling down the centuries colour prejudice persists, and colours the sexual aesthetics of most Indians. None is more aware of subtle differences of shade than the Indian. The Muslim invasions bringing in Arab, Persian, Afghan and Moghul—all lighter-complexioned than the average Indian—reinforced the prejudice, despite the professed egalitarianism of Islam. The Mirza's comments on the darker peoples encountered on the way reveal his prejudice, as does his ecstatic celebration of European womanhood. The White Woman seems to embody the Platonic idea of beauty; she is a paradisiacal *houri*.

The Mirza's original text has never been published. The book that introduced me to him was a complete Bengali translation, *Vilayetnama,* or *Tales of Vilayet* (Dhaka: Muktadhara, 1981), by the late Professor A.B.M. Habibullah. In his preface Professor Habibullah mentions that his translation is based on the two extant manuscripts of the original, one in the British Museum, the other in the Khoda Buksh Library in Bankipur, Bihar, India. An earlier—"abridged and flawed"—translation into English by James Edward Alexander had been published in London in 1827 by John Taylor under the elaborate title of *Shigurf Namah-i-Vilaet* or *Excellent Intelligence Concerning Europe, Being the Travels of Mirza Itesa Modeen*. Professor Habibullah ascribed the portrait of the Mirza reproduced as the book's frontispiece to Northcote, R. A. In 1939 at a conference of the Indian Historical Records Commission Professor Habibullah presented an English translation of the Moghul Emperor's letter to George III, which had somehow survived.

I found Alexander's translation too quaint for modern taste, perhaps the result of the translator's misguided attempt to capture the peculiarities of Persian syntax, and resolved to produce a more readable English version. My Persian unfortunately did not extend beyond a few words, but I realized that working from the Bengali translation I could remain true to the substance of the original, for seven centuries of Muslim rule in India had introduced the conceptual currency of Persian into the Indian vernaculars. Though abridged, Alexander's translation has a few extra passages. Since these are in keeping with the rest there is no reason to doubt their authenticity, and I have included them after editing them in the interests of lucidity. Their existence leads one to believe there were at least two versions of the original text.

[Selected extracts from Mirza Sheikh I'tesamuddin's *Shigurf Nama-e-Vilayet*, 1765, translated into English as *The Wonders of Vilayet*, Leeds: Peepal Tree, 2002, by Kaiser Haq. Contributed by the author with the publisher's permission.]

Chapter V

Vilayet at Last

Our ship anchored a couple of miles from the shore at the French port of Nantes. One of our guns fired a signal, in response to which a pilot boat was sent to guide us to the wharf of the French East India Company. The whole operation took about two hours.

As soon as we docked vendors flocked to the ship bearing fruits, bread, cheese, biscuits and butter. The sailors, who had not seen such fresh fare for six months, regaled themselves on it, and were generally overjoyed at seeing their homeland again. I could well understand their feelings. For six months I too had seen hardly anything besides sea and sky, and like a caged bird I was continually counting the ship's planks to pass time and to keep at bay the terrifying thought that the ocean might have no end. The sight of dry land and human habitation infused new life into my frame.

One thing astonished me. The lower orders among the French are so poor that they cannot afford shoes, and as a substitute wear wooden sandals. They take small blocks of wood and chiselling holes of the appropriate size they slip their feet into them and walk about with a ludicrous shuffle.

There are poor people in England too, but they do not suffer for want of leather boots and socks. Captain Swinton and Mr. Peacock laughed at the sight of the miserable Frenchmen in their comical footwear and said, 'These people are so wretched because they are not industrious like the English. They are very indolent.'

Since an edict of the French king forbids private citizens to import merchandise from the East, Customs officials came on board and stationed guards to make sure that passengers' baggage didn't get mixed up with the Company's cargo. If anyone is caught trying to smuggle in goods, these are confiscated and a penalty imposed. The Captain's mates, a doctor, and a priest, who brought pieces of cotton cloth from Bengal concealed them in their pockets and on their person, tying them round their waists and chests, put on their usual clothes on top, and stole past the guards like thieves. Captain Swinton and Mr. Peacock went to look for lodgings in the town. I had to remain on board for two or three days more, during which time I learned a little about the people of the region and their laws and customs.

Man steals from his own pocket, runs a proverb. I found ready proof of its truth in the behaviour of Captain Swinton and Mr. Peacock. They had brought gold, silver, varieties of cloths and other valuable goods, which they had no difficulty in taking off the ship as the French officials were lenient towards Englishmen. They then entrusted the goods with transporters on the understanding that they would smuggle them into England concealed in consignments of fruits and vegetables.

After sixteen days in Nantes I parted company with Captain Swinton and Mr. Peacock. They set off for England in a fast post-chaise, while I set sail in a sloop. A week later I reached Calais, where I spent two weeks as a house guest of the sloop's Captain. I spent my time in walking about the streets and markets, observing the architecture and way of life of the townspeople, as well as the agricultural practices in the surrounding countryside. Wheat, maize, mustard, lentils, peas, radishes, watermelons, spinach, oranges, grapes, guavas, pears, apples and pomegranates grow much better here than in England. The latter, being further to the north, is subject to severe cold weather and snowfall, which do not conduce to the growth of fruits and vegetables. However, even in France fruits peculiar to the Arab world, like pistachio, and fruits and crops peculiar to India, like rice, *mash kalai* [a kind of pulse], mangoes, coconuts, bananas, aubergines, etc. cannot be seen at all.

The houses in the country are built of stone slabs, with roofs of terra cotta tiles. As the bamboo doesn't grow here the scaffolding for the roofs is built of wood. The poorer classes live on a diet of broth and barley-bread and wear coarse wool or clothes woven from hemp, of which ropes are also spun. Most of them cannot afford leather shoes. Paris, the capital of France, is several hundred miles from either Calais or Nantes. Frenchman and foreigner alike sing high praises of the buildings and gardens of that city, its artistic innovativeness, scientific and technological advancement, the polished manners, cultivation, well-spokenness and wit of its inhabitants. In these respects it far surpasses all other cities in the Firinghee world.

The French claim that they have taught music and horsemanship to the English. Wealthy Englishmen send their children to French schools to polish up their manners and taste. The French say that the present excellence of the English in the arts and sciences, trade and industry, is the result of French education; in the past, when they lacked this education, they were ignorant like the mass of Indians. However, even the French admit that the English have always been outstanding soldiers.

The French say that the lower classes of Englishmen do not go to foreign countries to seek trade or employment because, being stupid and without any skills or business acumen, they would fail to earn a decent livelihood...

＊　＊　＊

From Calais I took a packet boat going to England. It took us a day to reach the small English port of Dover. Customs officials came on board to inspect our luggage and in the trunk of Mrs. Peacock, who was of mixed Portuguese and Indian parentage, they discovered a roll of flowered cotton and another of kincob. As it was a punishable offence to bring these items into the country the boat was seized with everything on board and taken up a narrow canal that came down to the sea. The mouth of the canal was then closed by securing a heavy wooden gate. I disembarked, put up at an inn, and after dispatching a letter to Captain Swinton in London, in which I gave an account of all that had transpired, I occupied myself in sightseeing through the streets and bazaars of the town and its environs.

The English had never seen an Indian dressed as I was. They considered me a great curiosity and flocked to have a look. As I was a foreigner they showed me great kindness and hospitality and after a few days treated me as an old acquaintance. The friendliness of the English and, more particularly, the sight of their lovely women dispelled the sorrow of solitude and cheered me greatly.

One day some people took me to a dance party at the house of .one of their friends. As soon as I entered, the music and dancing stopped. The assembled ladies and gentlemen thronged round me in wide-eyed amazement and examined my robe, turban, shawl and other parts of my costume. They concluded that it was the costume of a dancer or actor and invited me to join the dance. I protested that I had no knowledge of the art of dancing, but they refused to believe me. They said there was nobody on earth who didn't know something of music and dancing. One of the English gentlemen said that as I was newly arrived in England I was perhaps feeling shy to dance with ladies of another race. At this the ladies tittered with amusement. They continued to stare at my clothes and countenance, while I gazed at their astonishing loveliness. How ironic that I, who had gone there to enjoy a spectacle, became a spectacle myself. In such attractive company, I mused, even the wisest are apt to lose their wits. The ladies were lovely as houris; their beauty would have shamed even fairies into covering their pretty faces. I could not distinguish between the brightness of the lamps and the splendour of their appearance. Speechless with admiration, I stood like a statue, and overwhelmed by the glory of Allah's creative power, recited this distich to myself:

> Out of dust he produces a living body,
> And from seed makes a fair face.

Not long after, Captain Swinton and Mr. Peacock came down from London with release orders for our belongings. The packet boat was freed from custody and sent on to London, whither we now travelled by coach. There Captain Swinton took me to his brother's house in Coventry Street, near Haymarket.

Just as I had been depressed by the hardships of the voyage, I now felt elated by the beautiful sights of London town, amidst which my homely face was like a leafless plant in a flowering rose garden. But though I was far from being well-dressed, the English were pleased to receive me, and treated me kindly. It is a sign of the generosity of the English, which I cannot find words to describe or praise. A traveller from abroad is dearer to them than their own life, and they will take great pains to make him happy.

The English had never seen an Indian munshi before, but only lascars from Chittagong and Dhaka, and were consequently unacquainted with the clothes and manners of an Indian gentleman. They took me for a great man of Bengal, perhaps the brother of a Nawab, and came from far and near to see me. Whenever I went abroad crowds accompanied me, and people craned their heads out of windows and gazed at me in wonder. Children and adolescents took me for a curious specimen and ran into their houses crying, 'Look! Look! A black man is walking down the street!'—at which their elders would rush to the door and stare at me in amazement. Many children and small boys took me for a black devil and kept away in fear.

It was the height of summer, so I would go out dressed in pyjama-trousers and a long, loose shirt, with a cummerbund which held a dagger; a shawl thrown over the shoulder; turban; and gilt-embroidered shoes. Many were pleased with my costume, but others thought it was effeminate.

Within a couple of months everyone in the neighbourhood became friendly. The fear which some had felt vanished completely, and they would now jest with me familiarly. The ladies of the bazaar approached me and, smiling, said, 'Come, my dear, and kiss me!'

Chapter X

The Highlands

The Highlands occupy the northern extremity of Scotland. Further to its north is the sea. It is sparsely populated, being infertile and full of mountains and forests. It snows and rains virtually twelve months a year. But this harsh climate doesn't seem to inconvenience the inhabitants, especially the lower orders, who have grown used to it. When a shepherd or farmer feels tired in the course of work, he will spread half of his cloak on the bare ground, and lying down on it, cover himself with the other half and go to sleep. If so much snow collects on the cloak that they feel suffocated, they spring up, give it a shake and lie down again on the snow.

The tails and wool of the sheep are curled like the cotton of a coverlet. For this reason the cold cannot penetrate into their bodies and throughout the year the flocks can be kept out to pasture. When snow covers the ground and grazing becomes impossible, the sheep as well as horses and cows are fed upon hay. Sheep on whose bodies wool is scant grow weak and thin in a severe winter, but such specimens are rare. The grass here is sweet and extremely nutritive for animals. Grams and pulses do not grow in Vilayet, but there is a grain with blackish seeds called corn, which the Scotch eat themselves and also feed their animals.

The Highlanders wear a jacket and a cap, but neither breeches nor boots. The lower part of the body is covered by a skirt called a kilt, but the knee is bare and cotton stockings are worn on the legs. Instead of shoes they wear wooden sandals fastened to the feet with leather straps. They carry a double-edged sword. I was told that their courage was beyond compare. But they are also simple-minded and doltish.

A Highlander who had gone to London was sightseeing about the bazaars, followed by a curious crowd of Englishmen and boys. One of the Englishmen in sport lifted the skirt of the Highlander's kilt from behind. He was overcome with shame at this, but at the same time his wrath was inflamed and with a stroke of his sword he cut off the offender's head. The Police and townspeople surrounded him but could not force him to surrender. He undauntedly stood his ground, prepared either to kill or die. He wounded many people, and on whichever side he charged they fled before him. No one had the courage to approach him, far less seize him. Word of this strange situation eventually reached the King, who sent a courtier to summon him. The Courtier went before him and said, 'His Majesty has sent for you.' On hearing the King's name the Highlander immediately bowed his head and followed the royal envoy. When he appeared in the royal presence the King asked why he had heedlessly murdered a man. The Highlander knelt on one knee, according to the custom of Vilayet, bowed his head and after making obeisance, replied in a respectful tone, 'When that man exposed a shameful part of my body I felt my honour had been ridiculed, and therefore in a state of rightful anger I struck him dead. But when I received your royal summons I hastened to surrender myself to you and I feel proud to have been permitted to kiss your threshold. Otherwise none would have been able to capture me alive.' The King was impressed by this simple and courageous man's defence and pardoned him...

There are amusing stories about the English too, particularly their country people, who are ignorant and stupid. One of them went to town where he was feted by a friend. He greatly relished a sheep's liver kebab, which he had never tasted before, and took down its recipe. Before returning home he went to a butcher and bought a sheep's liver, which he tied in a napkin and carried in his hand. A pie dog came up from behind, snatched the liver, napkin and all, and scampered off. The rustic shouted jeeringly after the dog, 'You silly beast, you've got the raw liver, but the recipe is in my pocket!'...

Such stories only prove the truth that Allah did not create all five fingers equal. There is no country in the world where there are no stupid and ignorant people. In fact, everywhere they are the majority.

Abu Taleb in Africa and Europe
From *Lubbu-s Siyar* (1803)

Dean Mahomed, writing in English, addressed a European audience in a bid to defend "…my countrymen who, I am proud to think, have still more of the innocence of our ancestors, than some of the boasting philosophers of Europe." His contemporary, Mirza Abu Taleb (b. ?1770), writing in Persian (or, rather, Indo-Persian), had another reason altogether for making his accounts available: he wished to "afford a gratifying banquet to his countrymen" by describing the "curiosities and wonders which he saw" and giving "some account of the manners and customs of the various nations he visited."

Abu Taleb wrote during a phase that saw much significant creativity in the Persian language in India—a language that had assumed Indian shape by then, as is attested by the writer of an early contemporary novel, *Nashtar*, who explicitly states that his Persian is the Persian spoken by Indians and not some scholarly or classical variety. This creativity was to culminate in the letters of Asadullah Khan Ghalib in the nineteenth century (which also contain travel descriptions), but within the next 100 years, Persian would disappear as the language of culture and officialese in North and Central India and would be replaced by English. In the late eighteenth and early nineteenth centuries, Persian texts were still being written in India and Abu Taleb's book is by no means the only travel text in Persian from that period. Another interesting travel book, which we have been unable to extract from for reasons of space, was also written by an Indian who travelled to Central Asia: Mir Izzatullah (Meer Izzat Oolah). As such, Abu Taleb's account should be seen as part of a separate literary tradition, much of which has been forgotten or is yet to be recovered. As Rozina Visram points out in *Asians in Britain*, some texts in Persian by Indian travellers in eighteenth-century England, such as Munshi Ismail (1772) and Mir Muhammad Husain (1776), are known only through the works of recent scholars.

In 1797, Mirza Abu Taleb Khan, a minor Indian nobleman, despondent about "professional" and family matters in India, decided to strike out in other directions. Even as the early years of colonization were being consolidated by an increasingly one-way traffic in travel accounts, Abu Taleb set out for Europe. In this he was not altogether unusual. Asians and Africans had travelled to Europe and elsewhere earlier. Some had even left travel accounts, which have been largely—but not completely—ignored by Western scholarship. Abu Taleb himself reports meeting some of these travellers who became absorbed and lost in the "new" continent discovered by them. Like most people of their times, European or non-European, they left no written accounts. But these anonymous or unrecorded travellers should not be overlooked. Abu Taleb's own account informs us of such "colourful" characters as the "Christian" man, Fertekulin, whom he meets in Paris and who reveals that he is actually a Muslim named Syed Mohammed,[184] or Noor Begum, "who accompanied General De Boigne from India."[185] Another of these "well assimilated" characters (how the Social Democrats and liberal Conservatives of today's Europe would have loved them!) was Mrs Ducarrol. Abu Taleb reports that she was "a young Hindoo widow of rank, whom Mr Ducarrol rescued from the funeral pyre of her former husband, and having converted her to Christianity, married her. She is very fair, and so accomplished in all the English manners and language, that I was some time in her company before I could be convinced she was a native of India."[186]

Unlike his older contemporary Dean Mahomed, Abu Taleb started learning English only on his outward journey. By the time he arrived in Ireland, he spoke broken English. He notes that the Irish understood his broken English with greater magnanimity than the English could ever muster: "… after I had resided for a whole year in England, and could speak the language a hundred times better than on my first arrival [in Ireland], I found much more difficulty in obtaining what I wanted than I did in Ireland."[187] He had already been warned of this by his Irish friends, who had noted that the people in England "will not give themselves any trouble to comprehend your meaning, or to make themselves useful to you."[188] More than in his detailed comparisons (which are a combination of acute perception and class-and-culture-related clichés), it is in such incidental remarks that Abu Taleb lays bare the modern structures of power and exploitation, of difference and identity that were still assuming shape in his times. One such remark relates to his sceptical perception of what came to be termed "racial differences": "Many of the English philosophers contend that distance from, or proximity to the sun, does not at all affect the human colour... but if this axiom is true, I cannot comprehend why Europeans should be fair, Ethiopians black, and Indians of swarthy complexions."[189]

To return to the outlines of his journey, Abu Taleb set out from Calcutta in 1797, aboard a vessel bound for Denmark (from which he witnessed the piratical looting of an English vessel by the Danish captain), and after travelling through the Nicobar Islands, Cape Town and St. Helena, disembarked at Cork. From there he sailed to Dublin and a number of other European cities (including London and post-1789 Paris), returning via Greece, Malta, Turkey and Persia in 1803. The greatest period of his travel was spent in residence in London. His account is remarkable for many reasons, among these his attitude to Modernity and Tradition and Science/Rationality and Religion. Both these pairs, often dichotomized explicitly in colonialist writing and implicitly in many post-colonialist texts, are not dichotomized on an East-West axis by him though he is evidently aware and cautiously appreciative of the development of science and technology in Europe.

While a man of his times and clearly in favour of the patriarchal ideology of restricting the movement of women in the name of protecting them, Abu Taleb nevertheless compares Persian and Indian women unfavourably with Turkish women because the latter are allowed "much greater freedom" and "knowledge of the world". In effect, he is in favour of greater liberty and better education for women than what he thinks is available to them in India or Persia. However, he also writes a "vindication of the Liberties of the Asiatic Women"—a discussion that he prefaces with the scoffing remark that "in respect of [liberty] the English consider their own customs the most perfect in the world."[190]

Perhaps the matter is best illustrated by quoting from Abu Taleb's defence of "the Liberties of Asiatic Women", which is largely a defence of the *zenana*. He makes some telling points whose purport he is sometimes incapable of realizing, for example when he points out that the liberty of daughters to avoid "arranged marriages" in Europe "is merely nominal, as, without the will of the father and mother, the daughter's choice is of no avail."[191] He also points out that Asian women (of his time) enjoyed superior rights in the case of divorce as they kept the daughters, while in England, the mother "has to abandon all to the father." Finally, he defends the *zenana* by putting it in a more complex cultural context: "The notions which European women have, that the women of Asia never see a man's face but their husband's and are debarred from all amusement and society, proceed entirely from misinformation: They can keep company with their husband's and father's male relations, and with old neighbours and domestics; and at meals there are always men and women of this description present; and they can go in their palankeens to the houses of their relations, and of ladies of their own rank, even though the husbands are unacquainted; and also walk in gardens after strangers are excluded; and they can send for musicians, and dancers, to entertain them at their own houses; and they have many other modes of amusement besides these mentioned."[192]

Abu Taleb's discourse on women is, as is evident, replete with patriarchal tropes, though so would be the statements of his European contemporaries. What is interesting, however, is his attempt to defend what he considers unimpeachable in his own culture and his refusal to accept European definitions. In this sense, Abu Taleb is post-colonial far before any kind of political post-colonialism came into being in India: actually, one can argue somewhat pedantically that India had not been formally colonized in 1798 and would not be officially colonized until after the *ghaddar* of 1857. Abu Taleb's discourse, then, reveals the superfluity of the designation "post-colonial" when removed from the field of political studies.

[Extracts from Abu Taleb's *Lubbu-s Siyar* (1803), Trans. from Persian by Charles Stewart in 1814 as *Travels of Mirza Abu Taleb Khan in Asia, Africa and Europe During the Years 1799 to 1803*. Republished by Sona Publications, New Delhi in 1972. All footnotes in the introduction to this section refer to the 1972 edition.]

Cape Town[193]

After some days, I learned that all the passengers, being disgusted with the bad conduct of the captain, had resolved not to return on board again, but to proceed to the Cape Town, and wait there the arrival of some English vessel, in which they might embark for Europe. I was therefore under the necessity either of abandoning my companions, or of incurring a heavy expense by quitting this disgusting ship: and having resolved upon the latter, I went on shore, and took up my residence at the house where the other passengers were staying.

Our landlord, who was called Barnet, was a very smooth speaker, and appeared very polite. He said he was by descent a Scotchman, though born and bred amongst the Dutch. With this person I agreed for my board and lodging at the rate of five rupees a day. His family consisted of his wife, two children, and five slaves; and notwithstanding there were, fifteen of us, including servants, who lodged in the house, they attended minutely to all our wants, and even anticipated our wishes, without any noise, bustle, or confusion.

Some time previous to our arrival at the Cape, it had been taken possession of by the English, and was garrisoned by about 5000 European soldiers, under the command of General Dundas (a nephew of the celebrated Mr. Dundas, one of the principal Ministers of the British Empire), who also acted as Governor during the absence of Lord Macartney. The troops at False Bay were commanded by Captain Collins, on whom I waited, and was received with great attention and politeness. He returned my visit on the following day, and invited me to dine with him. We found a large company assembled, and were entertained in a very sumptuous manner. Although I then understood English but imperfectly, yet the marked attention of Captain and Mrs. Collins and their friends was so flattering, that I never spent a more agreeable day in my life. On taking leave, they requested me to drink tea with them every evening I was disengaged, during my stay at False Bay. From the commanders of the ships of war, Captains Lee and Gouch, I also received the greatest attention. They invited me twice to entertainments on board, and sent their own barges to convey me. Upon entering and leaving the ship, I was saluted by the discharge of a number of pieces of cannon, and was treated in every respect as a person of consequence.

After a short residence with Mr. Barnet, I experienced a very great change in his behaviour. Our table became daily worse supplied, and his conduct was sometimes rude. He one day came and desired I would change my apartment for a smaller one, as he expected more guests, and could put up two or three beds in my room. After I had removed my luggage to another, he then told me that room was pre-engaged, and that I must remove to a third, in which I found a gentleman's trunks, who was gone to Cape Town, and might possibly return during the night. I was much irritated at such conduct, and asked him what he meant. He replied, that he had let me have my lodgings too cheap; and that if I wished to remain there, I must pay him ten rupees (£1.5s) a day. I observed that his behaviour was that of a *blackguard Dutchman* and that I should quit his house the next day. I accordingly made my preparations for proceeding to Cape Town; and although I left his house before sunrise he insisted on my paying him for the whole of that day. He also charged very extravagantly for my washing, and other matters wherein I had employed him. But I was still more provoked at the behaviour of his wife, to whom, on the day of my arrival, I had presented a bag of fine Bengal rice, worth at the Cape forty or fifty rupees; she was in consequence very polite for three or four days, but afterwards totally changed her conduct.

On the 2nd of July I set out for Cape Town, in a coach drawn by eight horses, all of which were driven by one man, and with such dexterity as I have never witnessed. Part of the road was through water up to the horses' bellies; in another place the wheels sank nearly up to the axle-trees in sand; and although we climbed and descended very steep mountains, we were seldom out of a gallop. When we approached within four or five miles of the town, we found the road broad and even, lined on each side with hedges; the country was also well cultivated, and adorned by groves and gardens, with here and there windmills and farm-houses, which much ornamented the scenery. On this road the English and the genteel Dutch families take the air, either on horseback or in carriages, every day from noon till four o'clock.

At the distance of three miles, the town appears very beautiful and superb, and much delights the beholder. The distance from False Bay to Cape Town is a day's journey; but as there are houses for the entertainment of travellers on the road, we had a comfortable breakfast and dinner at the proper hours.

It was nearly dark when we entered the town; and lodgings having been secured for me by one of my ship-mates, I drove directly to Mr. Clark's, the best house of that description in the place.

Two sides of the town are surrounded by mountains; and some of the houses are so near the Table Land, that a stranger is in dread of its falling on them. These mountains are covered with a variety of flowers and sweet herbs, and afford an excellent pasture for cattle; they also abound with springs of delicious water, which not only supply the inhabitants with that indispensable element, but also serve to turn mills, and to irrigate the lands when requisite.

The inhabitants of the Cape frequently form parties of pleasure atop the Table Land; and although several places in the road are so steep that they cannot be ascended without the aid of ropes, the Dutch ladies are so accustomed to climb precipices, that they always accompany the men on these excursions.

On another side of the town is Table Bay; on the shore of which are erected very formidable batteries, sufficient to prevent an enemy from entering it. Some batteries have also been constructed on the land side. In short, the fortifications of this place were so strong, that when the English came to attack the Cape, they found it expedient to proceed to False Bay, and effect their debarkation at that point; they thence proceeded by land, and having with great difficulty clambered over the mountains, made their attack on that side, and thus compelled the Hollanders to capitulate.

The town is about six miles in circumference. A few of the houses are built of stone, but the generality of them are only brick and mortar. The streets are very broad and straight, and paved on each side with large bricks or flag stones. Each street is also provided with one or two channels for carrying off the water, so that even in winter there is scarcely any mud or dirt to be seen. Each side of the street is also planted with a row of trees, which afford an agreeable shade; and along the front of every house is erected a seat of masonry, about a yard high, for the inhabitants to sit on and smoke their pipes in the summer evenings. This custom, which is, I believe, peculiar to the Hollanders, appeared to me excellent.

Nearly in the centre of Cape Town is a large handsome square, two miles in circumference, in which the troops are exercised. Two sides of the square are enclosed with streets of lofty houses, a third is bounded by the Fort, and the fourth faces the sea. The Fort is regular, and much resembles that of Calcutta, but smaller. The bazars are well built, and well supplied with every requisite.

Having said so much of the place, I will now take the liberty of describing the inhabitants. All the European Dutch women whom I saw, were very fat, gross, and insipid; but the girls at the Cape are well made, handsome, and sprightly; they are also good natured, but require costly presents. Even the married women are suspected; and each of the Englishmen of rank had his particular lady, whom he visited without any interruption from the husband, who generally walked out when the admirer entered the house. The consequence was, that the English spent all the money they got; while the Hollanders became rich, and more affluent than when under their own government.

The generality of the Dutchmen are lowminded and inhospitable, neither do they fear the imputation of a bad name, and are more oppressive to their slaves than any other people in the world. If a slave understands any trade, they permit him to work for other people, but oblige him to pay from one to four dollars a day, according to abilities, for such indulgence. The daughters of these slaves who are handsome they keep for their own use, but the ugly ones are either sold, or obliged to work with their fathers. Should a slave perchance save money sufficient to purchase his freedom, they cause him to pay a great price for it, and throw many other obstacles in his way.

I saw a tailor, who was married, and had four children; he was then forty years of age, and had, by great industry and economy, purchased the freedom of himself and wife; but the children still continued as slaves. One of them, a fine youth was sold to another master, and carried away to some distant land; the eldest girl was in the service of her master; and the two youngest were suffered to remain with their parents till they should gain sufficient strength to be employed.

As the female slaves are employed in making the beds, and looking after the rooms of the lodgers, they frequently have opportunities of getting money; great part of which they are, however, obliged to pay to their avaricious owners.

During my stay at the Cape, I suffered great inconvenience from the filthiness and stench of their privies, which they take no pains to keep clean. Neither have they any baths, either hot or cold, in the town; and ablution is quite unknown to the inhabitants.

Dublin

...The barracks of Dublin are very extensive; and there are two handsome parades, well paved and flagged for the exercise of troops in rainy weather.

The public hospitals of this city are numerous, and are admirable institutions. One of these is for the delivery of poor pregnant women; another for the reception and education of orphans; and the third for the maintenance of wounded or worn-out soldiers.

In these countries it is common for persons, when dying, to bequeath estates, or a large sum of money, to endow hospitals, or for other charitable purposes. This custom is truly praise-worthy, and should be accepted as an excuse for those who, during their existence in this world, hoard up their riches, and often deny themselves the enjoyments of life.

In this city there are but two hot baths, the roofs of which resemble large ovens. They are not properly fitted up; and are so small that with difficulty they hold one person; and even then the water does not rise above his middle. Being a case of necessity, I bathed in one of them; but there were not any attendants to assist me; and instead of a rubber, I was obliged to use a brush, made (I hope) of horse's hair,[194] such as they clean shoes with. The fact is, that in winter the people of Dublin never bathe, and in summer they go into the sea or river: these baths are therefore entirely designed for invalids or convalescents.

Dublin can boast but of two public Theatres or play-houses, each of which will contain about 1500 persons. The half of the building which is appropriated to the audience is divided into three parts, denominated, the Boxes, Pit, and Gallery: the first of these is intended for the nobility and gentry, and the second for the tradesmen, and the third for the lower classes of people. The prices of admittance are, five shillings, three shillings, and one shilling. The other half of the building is occupied by the stage, on which the actors exhibit: this is subdivided by a number of curtains and scenes, upon which are painted cities, castles, gardens, forests etc. The whole of the house is well lighted, by candles placed in chandeliers, lustres etc.

In the exhibition which afforded me the greatest amusement, the actors spoke in some barbarous language. One of them represented an Ethiopian magician, called Harlequin, with whom the daughter of a nobleman falls desperately in love: the magician in consequence conveys her, while asleep in her bed, to his own country. Here she is visited by the Queen of the Fairies, and several of her attendants, all of whom descend on the stage in flying thrones: they reproach her for her partiality to such a wretch, and advise her to discard him: she, after shewing evident proofs of her attachment to the magician, yields to their advice, and requests they will assist her to return home. The queen orders one of the attendants to accompany the young lady, and to remain with her as a protection against the power of the magician, and to assist her father and her intended husband. Harlequin, however, contrives to visit his mistress;

and the lovers being soon reconciled, they attempt at one time to escape in a coach, at another in a ship, but are always brought back. At length, in one of the affrays, the father is wounded, and confined to his bed: here he is visited by the Angel of Death, represented by the skeleton of a man with a dart in his hand, who tells him he must either marry his daughter to Harlequin, or accompany him. The father consents of the marriage, which is celebrated with great rejoicing; and thus ends the farce. Another of their exhibitions was named The Taking of Seringapatam: all the scenes in this, were taken from a book recently published, containing an account of the late war in Mysore, and the fall of Tippoo Sultan. The representation was so correct, that everything appeared natural; and the conclusion was very affecting.

I was much entertained by an exhibition of Horsemanship, by Mr. Astley and his company. They have an established house in London, but come over to Dublin for four or five months in every year, to gratify the Irish, by displaying their skill in this science, which far surpasses any thing I ever saw in India.

I was also much astonished on seeing a new invention of the Europeans, called a Panorama. The scene was Gibraltar, a celebrated fort belonging to the English, at the entrance of the Mediterranean Sea, on the coast of Spain. I was led by a dark entrance into the middle of a large room, round which a picture of this famed fortress was hung; but, by some contrivance, the light was so directed, that every object appeared as natural as life. They also exhibited an engagement between an English and a French fleet, in which not only the noise of cannon was distinctly heard, but also the balls flew about, and carried away the masts and sails of the adversaries' ships...

The Irish

I shall here endeavour to sketch the character of the Irish. The greater number of them are Roman-Catholics, or followers of the religion of the Pope; only a small proportion of them being of the religion of the English, whom the former call Dissenters or Philosophers (i.e. Deists or Atheists).

They are not so intolerant as the English, neither have they the austerity and bigotry of the Scotch. In bravery and determination, hospitality and prodigality, freedom of speech and open-heartedness, they surpass the English and Scotch, but are deficient in prudence and sound judgement: they are nevertheless witty, and quick of comprehension. Thus my land lady and her children soon comprehended my broken English; and what I could not explain by language, they understood by signs: nay, before I had been a fortnight in their house, they could even understand my disfigured translations of Persian poetry. When I was about to leave them, and proceed on my journey, many of my friends appeared much affected, and said: 'With your little knowledge of the language, you will suffer much distress in England; for the people there will not give themselves any trouble to comprehend your meaning, or to make themselves useful to you.' In fact, after I had resided for a whole year in England, and could speak the language a hundred times better than on my first arrival, I found much more difficulty in obtaining what I wanted, than I did in Ireland.

In Dublin, if I happened to lose my way, and inquired it of any person, he would, immediately on perceiving I was a foreigner, quit his work, and accompany me to the place where I wished to go. One night, as I was going to pay a visit at a considerable distance, I asked a man, which was the road. He instantly accompanied me; and when we arrived at a particular spot, I knew where we were, and, having thanked him for the trouble he had taken, said I was now perfectly acquainted with the remainder of the road, and begged he would return home. He would not consent; but, after we had gone some distance further I insisted upon his leaving me, otherwise I should relinquish my visit. He apparently complied; but I could perceive, that, from his great care of me, he still followed. Being arrived at the door of my friend's house, I waited for some time, that I might again have an opportunity of thanking him; but as soon as he saw that I had reached a place of security, he turned round, and went towards home.

The Irish, by reason of their liberality and prodigality, seldom have it in their power to assist their friends in pecuniary matters: they are generally in straitened circumstances themselves, and therefore cannot, or do not aim at the comforts or elegance of the English: neither do they take pains to acquire riches and honours like the Scotch, by limiting their expenses when in the receipt of good incomes, and paying attention to the Great. In consequence of this want of prudence, they seldom attain to high dignities, and but few of them, comparatively, make much progress in science.

Their great national defect, however, is excess in drinking. The rich expend a vast deal in wine; and the common people consume immense quantities of a fiery spirit, called whiskey, which is the peculiar manufacture of this country and part of Scotland.

One evening that I dined in large company we sat down to table at six o'clock: the master of the house immediately commenced asking us to drink wine, and, under various pretences, replenished our glasses; but perceiving that I was backward in emptying mine, he called for two water glasses, and, having filled them with claret, insisted upon my taking one of them. After the table-cloth was removed, he first drank the health of the King, then of the Queen; after which he toasted a number of beautiful young ladies with whom I was acquainted, none of which I dared to refuse. Thus the time passed till two o'clock in the morning; and we had been sitting for eight hours; he then called to his servants to bring a fresh supply of wine. Although I was so much intoxicated that I could scarcely walk, yet on hearing this order, I was so frightened, that I arose, and requested permission to retire. He said he was sorry I should think of going away so soon; that he wished I would stay till the wine was finished, after which he would call for tea and coffee. I had heard from Englishmen, that the Irish, after they get drunk at the table, quarrel, and kill each other in duels; but I must declare that I never saw them guilty of any rudeness, or of the smallest impropriety... [Proceeds to discuss caricatures]...

For some time after my arrival in Dublin, I was greatly incommoded by the common people crowding round me, whenever I went out. They were all very curious to see me, but had no intention of offending me. Some said I must be the Russian General, who had been for some time expected; others affirmed I was either a German or Spanish nobleman; but the greater part agreed that I was a Persian Prince. One day, a great crowd having assembled about me, a shopkeeper advised me walk into his house and to sit down till they should disperse. I accepted his kind invitation, and went into the shop, where I amused myself by looking at some penknives, scissors etc. The people however thronged so about his windows, that several of the panes were broken; and crowd being very great, it was in vain to ask who had done it.

About a fortnight after my arrival, there fell a very heavy shower of snow. As I had never before seen any thing of the kind, I was much delighted by it. The roofs of the houses and tops of the wall were soon covered with it, and in two or three days the fields and mountains, as far as the eye could reach, became a white surface. During the time it continued to snow, the cold was not very great; but when it ceased, notwithstanding I had all my doors and windows shut, and had three blankets on my bed, I felt the frost pierce through me like an arrow. The fire had scarcely any effect on me; for while I warmed one side, I was frozen on the other; and I frequently burned my fingers before I was aware of the heat. At length I discovered, that the best remedy was walking; and during the continuation of the frost, I walked every day seven or eight miles. I was apprehensive that my health would have suffered from the severity of the climate; but, on the contrary, I had a keen appetite, and found myself every day get stronger and more active.

I recollect that in India, when I only wore a single vest of Dacca muslin, if I walked a mile I was completely tired; but here, when my clothes would have been a heavy load for an ass, I could have run for miles without feeling the smallest fatigue. In India, I slept daily seven or eight hours, at different times, without feeling refreshed; but during the two months I remained in Ireland, I never slept more than four hours any night, and yet I never felt an inclination to lie down in the day time...

Indian Women in London

[Extracted from a section that describes Abu Taleb's daily activities in London, including the writing of poetry, and a visit to Greenwich, contains complimentary accounts of the Freemasons, the Royal Library and the British Museum, as well as a seven cubit tall Irish "Giant", and a less complimentary account of London poverty.—Ed.]

...During my residence in London, I had the good fortune to form an acquaintance with two or three Hindoostany ladies, who, from the affection they bore to their children, had accompanied them to Europe. The most distinguished of these was Mrs. Ducarrol. It is generally reported that she was a young *Hindoo* widow of rank, whom Mr. Ducarrol rescued from the funeral pile of her former husband, and having converted her to Christianity, married her. She is very fair, and so accomplished in all the English manners and language, that I was some time in her company before I could be convinced she was a native of India. This lady introduced me to two of three of her children, from sixteen to nineteen years of age, who had every appearance of being European.

I visited Noor *Begum*, who accompanied General De Boigne from India. She was dressed in the English fashion, and looked remarkably well. She was much pleased by my visit, and requested me to take charge of a letter for her mother, who resides at Lucknow.

When General De Boigne thought proper to marry a young French woman, he made a settlement on the *Begum*, and gave her the house in which she resides. She has two children, a boy and girl, of fifteen and sixteen years of age, who, at the time of my visit, were at school, but always spend their holidays with her.

I have before mentioned, that one of the objects I had in view, in coming to Europe, was to instruct young Englishmen in the Persian language. I however met with so little encouragement from the persons in authority, and had so many other engagements to amuse me, that I entirely relinquished the plan...

Machines

In England, labour is much facilitated by the aid of mechanism; and by its assistance the price of commodities is much reduced: for if, in their great manufactories, they made use of horses, bullocks, or men, as in other countries, the price of their goods would be enormous. It is impossible, without the aid of drawings or plates, to describe the mode and the various uses to which it is applied: I shall however mention a few of the instances, that some general idea may be formed of the subject. I shall only add, that the English are so prejudiced in favour of this science, that they often expend immense sums, and frequently fail two or three times, before they succeed in getting the machinery of any extensive work in order. The French, on the contrary, although good mathematicians, are content with manual labour, if any difficulty occurs in erecting the machinery.

[There follows a long and at times detailed description of various machines and manufacturing processes, and occasional comparisons of the "manufacturing skills" of various European lands.—Ed.]

...On entering one of the extensive manufactories in England, the mind is at first bewildered by the number and variety of articles displayed therein: but, after recovering from this first impression, and having coolly surveyed all the objects around, every thing appears conducted with so much regularity and precision, that a person is induced to suppose one of the meanest capacity might superintend and direct the whole process. Whatever requires strength or numbers is effected by engines; if clearness of sight is wanted, magnifying glasses are at hand; and if deep reflection is necessary to combine all the parts, where by to insure a unity of action, so many aids are derived from the numerous artists employed in the different parts of the work, that the union of the whole seems not to require any great exertion of genius. Thus, in all kinds of clock-work, the wheels, chains, springs, etc. are made by different artists, and only require a person who is conversant in the business to select and put the pieces together...

The defects of the English [abridged]
The first and greatest defect I observed in the English, is their want of faith in religion, and their great inclination to philosophy (atheism). The effects of these principles, or rather want of principle, is very

conspicuous in the lower orders of people, who are totally devoid of honesty. They are, indeed, cautious how they transgress against the laws, from fear of punishment; but whenever an opportunity offers of purloining any thing without the risk of detection, they never pass it by. They are also ever on the watch to appropriate to themselves the property of the rich, who, on this account, are obliged constantly to keep their doors shut, and never to permit an unknown person to enter them. At present, owing to the vigilance of the magistrates, the severity of the laws, and the honour of the superior classes of people, no very bad consequences are to be apprehended; but if ever such nefarious practices should become prevalent, and should creep in among the higher classes, inevitable ruin must ensue.

The second defect, most conspicuous in the English character, is pride, or insolence. Puffed up with their power and good fortune for the last fifty years, they are not apprehensive of adversity, and take no pains to avert it. Thus, when the people of London, some time ago, assembled in mobs on account of the great increase of taxes and high price of provisions, and were nearly in a state of insurrection,—although the magistrates, by their vigilance in watching them, and by causing parties of soldiers to patrol the streets day and night, to disperse all persons whom they saw assembling together, succeeded in quieting the disturbance,—yet no pains were afterwards taken to eradicate the evil. Some of the men in power said, it had been merely a plan of the artificers to obtain higher wages (an attempt frequently made by the English tradesmen); others were of opinion that no remedy could be applied; therefore no further notice was taken of the affair. All this, I say, betrays a blind confidence, which, instead of meeting the danger, and endeavouring to prevent it, waits till the misfortune arrives, and then attempts to remedy it. Such was the case with the late King of France, who took no step to oppose the Revolution, till it was too late. This self-confidence is to be found, more or less, in every Englishman: it however differs much from the pride of the Indians and Persians.

Their third defect is a passion for acquiring money, and their attachment to worldly affairs. Although these bad qualities are not so reprehensible in them as in countries more subject to the vicissitudes of fortune, (because, in England, property is so well protected by the laws, that every person reaps the fruits of his industry, and, in his old age, enjoys the earnings of economy of his youth,) yet sordid and illiberal habits are generally found to accompany avarice and parsimony, and, consequently, render the possessor of them contemptible: on the contrary, generosity, if it does not launch into prodigality, but is guided by the hand of prudence, will render a man respected and esteemed.

The fourth of their frailties is a desire of ease, and a dislike to exertion: this, however, prevails only in a moderate degree, and bears no proportion to the apathy and indolence of the smokers of opium of Hindoostan and Constantinople; it only prevents them from perfecting themselves in science, and exerting themselves in the service of their friends, upon what they choose to call trivial occasions. I must, however, remark, that friendship is much oftener cemented by acts of courtesy and good-nature, than by conferring permanent obligations; the opportunities of doing which can seldom occur, whereas the former happen daily. In London, I had sometimes occasion to trouble my friends to interpret for me, in the adjustment of my accounts with my landlord and others; but, in every instance, I found that, rather than be at the trouble of stopping for five minutes longer, and saying a few words in my defence, they would yield to an unjust demand, and offer to pay the items I objected to at their own expense: at the same time, an aversion to the employment of interpreter or mediator was so conspicuous in their countenance, that, latterly, I desisted from troubling them. In this respect I found the French much more courteous; for if, in Paris, the master of an hotel attempted to impose on me, the gentlemen present always interfered, and compelled him to do me justice.

Upon a cursory observation of the conduct of gentlemen in London, you would suppose they had a vast deal of business to attend to; whereas nine out of ten, of those I was acquainted with at the west end of the town, had scarcely any thing to do. An hour or two immediately after breakfast may be allotted to business, but the rest of the day is devoted to visiting and pleasure. If a person calls on any of these gentlemen, it is more than probable he is told by the servant, his master is not at home; but this is merely an idle excuse, to avoid the visits of people, whose business they are either ignorant of, or do not wish to be troubled with. If the suppliant calls in the morning; and is by chance admitted to the master of the house, before he can tell half his story, he is informed, that it is now the hour of business, and a particular engagement in the city requires the gentlemen's immediate attendance. If he calls later in the day, the gentleman is just going out to pay a visit of consequence, and therefore cannot be detained: but if the petitioner, unabashed by such checks, continues to relate his narrative, he is set down as a brute, and never again permitted to enter the doors. In this instance, I again say that the French are greatly superior to the English; they are always courteous, and never betray those symptoms of impatience so conspicuous and reprehensible in the English character ... [Lengthy extract left out.—Ed.]

Their seventh defect is a luxurious manner of living, by which their wants are increased a hundred-fold. Observe their kitchens, filled with various utensils; their rooms, fitted up with costly furniture; their side-boards, covered with plate; their tables, loaded with expensive glass and china; their cellars, stocked with wines from every quarter of the world; their parks, abounding in game of various sorts; and their ponds, stored with fish. All these expenses are incurred to pamper their appetites, which, from long indulgence, have gained such absolute sway over them, that a diminution of these luxuries would be considered, by many, as a serious misfortune.

The eighth defect of the English is vanity, and arrogance, respecting their acquirements in science, and a knowledge of foreign languages, for, as soon as one of them acquires the smallest insight into the principles of any science, or the rudiments of any foreign language, he immediately sits down and composes a work on the subject, and, by means of the Press, circulates books which have no more intrinsic worth than the toys bestowed on children, which serve to amuse the ignorant, but are of no use to the learned. This is not merely my own opinion, but was confirmed to me both by Greeks and Frenchmen, whose languages are cultivated in England with more ardour than any other... [Extract left out.—Ed.]

...If the English will take the trouble of reading ancient history, they will find that luxury and prodigality have caused the ruin of more Governments than was ever effected by an invading enemy: they generate envy, discord, and animosity, and render the people either effeminate, or desirous of a change. To these vices may be ascribed the subversion of the Roman Empire in Europe, and the annihilation of the Moghul government in India.

Their final defect is a contempt for the customs of other nations, and the preference they give to their own; although theirs, in fact, maybe much inferior. I had a striking instance of this prejudice in the conduct of my fellow-passengers on board ship. Some of these, who were otherwise respectable characters, ridiculed the idea of my wearing trowsers, and a night-dress, when I went to bed; and contended, that they slept much more at their ease by going to bed nearly naked. I replied, that I slept very comfortably; that mine was certainly the most decent mode; and that, in the event of any sudden accident happening, I could run on deck instantly, and, if requisite, jump into the boat in a minute; whilst they must either lose some time in dressing, or come out of their cabins in a very immodest manner. In answer to this, they said, such sudden accidents seldom occurred, but that if it did happen, they would not hesitate to come on deck in their shirts only. This I give merely as a specimen of their obstinacy, and prejudice in favour of their own customs.

In London, I was frequently attacked on the apparent unreasonableness and childishness of some of the Mohammedan customs; but as, from my knowledge of the English character, I was convinced it would be folly to argue the point philosophically with them, I contended myself with parrying the subject. Thus, when they attempted to turn into ridicule the ceremonies used by the pilgrims on their arrival at Mecca, I asked them, why they supposed the ceremony of baptism, by a clergyman, requisite for the salvation of a child, who could not possibly be sensible what he was about. When they reproached us for eating with our hands; I replied, 'There is by this mode no danger of cutting yourself or your neighbours; and it is an old and a true proverb, "The nearer the bone, the sweeter the meat": but, exclusive of these advantages, a man's own hands are surely cleaner than the feet of a baker's boy; for it is well known that half the bread in London is kneaded by the feet.' By this mode of argument I completely silenced all my adversaries, and frequently turned the laugh against them, when they expected to have refuted me and made me appear ridiculous... [Extract left out.—Ed.]

Many of these vices, or defects, are not natural to the English; but have been ingrafted on them by prosperity and luxury; the bad consequences of which have not yet appeared...

Driss Ben Driss Al-Amraoui: Moroccan Ambassador to Europe

Contributed by Sadik Rddad

From *Tuhfat al Malik al Aziz Bimamlakat Bariz*

It is not until recently that Moroccan travellers to Europe, for a long time ignored by academic scholarship, came to receive some critical attention. In fact, the Moroccan image of the West is no less deserving of study than orientalist views of Morocco. In his seminal work, *The Muslim Discovery of Europe*, Bernard Lewis admits that "the reader of the Moroccan and Ottoman Embassy reports of the seventeenth and eighteenth centuries cannot but be struck by the superior quality of Moroccan reporting of Europe."[195] He goes on to point out the qualitative merit of their accounts: "The Moroccan envoys show an interest in European affairs extending beyond the surface movements of personalities and events. They seek and obtain often good information about political and religious as well as commercial and military affairs."[196]

Yet, in spite of the depth, accuracy and importance of Moroccan travel literature relating to Europe as well as its indispensability as an alternative voice in the process of understanding and completing European history and culture, the Moroccan has usually been represented rather as a "silent interlocutor" and barbarous Other. The aim of translating and presenting this excerpt from al-Amraoui's embassy report is to contradict the Western claim that the natives are "silent interlocutors" and that they "cannot represent themselves." His account is a counterproductive and "counterpuntal" re-narration of Moroccan history, culture, religion and world view. Although the basic purpose of al-Amraoui's ambassadorial mission to France was to seek first-hand knowledge of Western scientific, technological and military progress that led to its progress and the defeat of Morocco[197], yet at a discursive level, it can be viewed as a native interrogation of "White Mythologies" and of the ideological bases of humanism, enlightenment and historiography.

In Islamic tradition, especially in the Middle Ages, travel to the "House of War"[198] was controversial, met with disapproval and was thus limited. Three main factors, however, imposed Moroccan embassy exchange with "infidel countries" and justified their violation of the Islamic tradition. First, the defence of the Moorish minority in Spain in the reign of Philip III. Ahmed ibn Quassim al Hajari's *Näsir al-dîn 'älä al-qawm al-kâfirîn*[199] is an excellent example of this type of writing. Second, the difficult endeavour to ransom Moroccan captives and manuscripts[200] in Christian lands. Ambassador al Wazir al Ghassani's visit to Spain in 1690-91 and Mohammed Ben Othman al Meknassi's *al-ixirfî fiqaqi al-'assir*, which recounts his journey to Spain (1779-80), are representative of this category of travels. Third and most important is European expansionism. Moroccan diplomatic activity in Europe flourished and accelerated when independent Morocco started to feel the danger of the inevitable advance and extension of European colonial desire into most Islamic countries. The conquest of Algeria in 1830, the crushing defeat of Moroccan troops by the French in the battle of Isly in 1844, together with its defeat in the battle of Tetuan, forced abandonment of the inward-looking policy espoused by Moroccan Sultans, especially king Moulay Sulayman (1793-1822), in favour of an outward and more open attitude towards European powers: France, Britain and Spain. These battles had revealed, among other things, the military weakness and backwardness of Morocco, hitherto veiled by an imaginary power secured by a victorious past: its imperial expansion inside Europe and its unique resistance to and independence from the Ottoman empire. Therefore, numerous embassies were sent to the "House of War" to account for Morocco's backwardness and to find answers to the overwhelming question: why did the West progress? In this context, five major envoys were sent to Europe in the nineteenth century. They are namely, Mohammed al-Safar to France (1845-46)[201], Driss Ben Driss al-Amraoui to France in 1860, Taher Ben Abderrahman al-Fassi to England in 1860, Driss Jaaidi to France, Belgium, England and Italy in 1875, and finally Ahmed al-Kardudi to Spain in 1885.

Immediately after the Spanish invasion of Tetuan, and its impact on the Moroccan economy and on national pride, Moroccan diplomacy witnessed an unprecedented mobilization. King Mohammed Ben Abderrahman sent two concurrent embassies to France and England in 1860.

Al-Amraoui, who concerns us here, set out to France on 17 July 1860. Although his visit was very short (only forty days), he was able to fill his narrative with sensitive and accurate observations about political, military, economic, technological, social and religious life in France. He was highly fascinated by the charismatic Napoleon III and spoke in some detail about the declaration of the Republic, and how he managed to come to absolute power in 1851 after a well-planned military coup. He also showed great interest in the French Parliamentary and judiciary systems. Al-Amraoui's encounter with France came at a time when she was undergoing a technological and scientific revolution. He understood that there lay the talisman and the answer to the superiority of, and imbalance between, the "House of War" and the "House of Islam". He was mainly struck by the highly sophisticated army of France, and by the magic of telegraph and railway that were essential to modern economic and social development. He would, however, remind his Muslim reader that this worldly life is the paradise of the unbelievers. "These people," he thinks, "are not different from us; our minds and theirs are similar. Yet, they sank in worldly attractions, and we have been able, thanks to God, to avoid them and hate their misdeeds and faithlessness."

Al-Amraoui devotes some space in his account to speak about the place of women in French society. As a Muslim, he was amazed by the high esteem and the boundless freedom they enjoyed. His description seems to intertext most of the previous Muslim travels to Christian lands. Consider the Moroccan Ambassador al-Ghazal's depiction of Spanish women almost one century earlier.

...Their dwellings have windows overlooking the street, where the women sit all the time, greeting the passers by. Their husbands treat them with the greatest courtesy. The women are very much addicted to conversation and conviviality with men other than their husbands, in company or in private. They are not restrained from going wherever they think fit. It often happens that a Christian returns to his home and finds his wife or his daughter or his sister in the company of another Christian, a stranger, drinking together and leaning against one another. He is delighted with this and, according to what I am told, he esteems it as a favor from the Christian who is in the company of his wife or whichever other woman of his household it may be...[202]

[Extracts from Driss ben Driss al-Amraoui's *Travels to France*[203] Extracts translated by Sadik Rddad from Driss Ben Driss al-Amraoui, *Tuhfat al.malik al-'azîz bimamlakat bârîz*, Ed. By Zaki M'barek, published by Presses des Etablissements d' Emballage, Tangier, in 1989.]

The palace of Versailles

The city of Versailles is one hour by train from Paris. They insisted that we visit its palace and water fountains. Its palace is bigger than the one in which we met their king in Saint-Cloud. It consists of a vast hall, a church and over forty different rooms. The walls are covered with tableaux most of which represent battle scenes, such as the conquest of Egypt, the conquest of Constantinople, and their battle against Moscow to help the Ottoman Sultan, may God glorify him! We saw marvellous scenes: some warriors were ready to fight; some lay dead and covered with blood, while others were agonising. The war leader is seen pointing and giving orders and advice to his soldiers. The tableaux are as big as the size of humans. The viewer is easily brought to believe that they were real war situations. Another tableau represents the Council they held to declare peace. It features the ministers and representatives of other countries, each wearing national/special costumes. The visitor would have the impression that they were really talking to each other. Near the palace, there is an immense well-organised garden. Its trees produce no fruits, as it is conventionally the case in all house gardens. In it, there are marvellous mechanisms of water-jets that make water come out of the mouths of sculptured stones. What amazed us most was a big fountain that was surrounded by sculptures of four men, four lions, four dolphins, and four horses, out of whose mouths comes fourth coloured ascending water…

They took us on a tour on foot around this immense garden; we visited over thirty different fountains. During all our travel, we have never been so exhausted as we were that day. People were looking at us all the time and were immensely surprised by the way we looked. There were over three thousand of them; men and women. They followed us wherever we went. It was thanks to twenty soldiers that we were able to make our way through waves of human beings. Without them, we would have certainly been killed, for the place was overcrowded. The interpreter told us that he heard two women talking about us; they wondered about what we eat and whether our food is similar to theirs. One of the visitors overheard them and told them that we are man-eaters, and that our Sultan gives us everyday a woman as a gift to eat. They were really astonished at what he said. These crowds of people came to visit that place because it was Sunday. In fact we were not really fascinated with what we have seen, for water is much more abundant in our country and playing with it is useless.

We had no fun that day; we were so exhausted that we regretted having accepted their invitation to visit that place. The person who was in charge of that place informed us that they have there the portrait of a Moroccan Ambassador sent by king Moulay Ismail, May God bless his soul, to King Louis XVI. His name was Abdallah Ben Aisha R'bati. During his visit, he saw the daughter of the king; he never saw such beauty in his country. He told the ministers of his intention to ask her hand for Moulay Ismail. He was advised in the most courteous way that he would better not tell the king of this. They also informed us of the visit of another Ambassador from Morocco over fifty years before, and that his name was Hajj Driss Ben Driss El Fassi.

The Playhouse
This is a place where they present different games, acrobatics, horse-ride, magic, dance, poetry reading, story telling, and quizzes in their

language. They also perform plays to criticise the government and to expose the vices and follies of the people. Although these are just humorous and futile performances, yet people from all walks of life— the poor and the rich, noble and ordinary men—are so crazy about them that they pay a considerable amount of money to watch them. In every playhouse there are special seats that are said to be reserved for the king and his wife. They also have special performances for the king, which they call 'The Royal Comedy.' Whenever he feels like watching a specific game or play, he summons actors to perform it for him. I used to laugh at such things because I deemed them as trivial and worthless. It was not until I came across the Egyptian Sheikh, Rifaat's statement that these are serious matters presented in a comic and non-serious form that I started taking them seriously. Concerning horseplay and acrobatics, they are visibly serious matters, while dance and music relieve the heart and cheer up the soul. Doctors and wise people pointed out that music has an impact on the soul, so much so that some diseases can be cured by means of music. Tales and poetry temper morality and behaviour, reveal the mysteries of the world, and teach about war strategies and tactics. I learnt that Moulay Ismail, may God bless his soul, wrote numerous copies of tales known as *al-azaliya* and *al-fidawiyyah*[204] and distributed them among his army leaders. These tales teach them a great variety of war tactics, fighting techniques, when to attack and when to withdraw as well as adventure, bravery, and the best arrangement of the conditions of peace agreement and truce. Those soldiers who cannot learn by heart parts of the '*al Fidawia*' can by no means be members of the free soldiers known as '*al-Bukhari Slaves*.' As for the quizzes, and the questions and answers, it is clear that they help sharpen the memory and improve the mind. They also teach children the art of conversation, how to choose their words, and what to say, when to say it and when to be silent... they invited us to attend one of the shows, featuring dancing and singing, but we apologised. On the one hand, we don't understand their songs, and whatever we can't understand we can't taste; on the other hand, our religion prohibits us to watch women dance. We did however attend horseplay and a magic show...

Had I given way to my pen to describe in detail all the worldly temptations I saw in their country, I would have never been able to stop writing, or would have been driven into undesirable length.

But all such things are but chattels of deception, transient worldly illusion and mirage, which are useful to know but abandon. God saved the faithful believers from the various temptations and futilities of this ephemeral world, and He shall cast His wrath on, and send to everlasting hell, those who went astray and disobeyed Him. These people are not different from us; our minds and theirs are similar. Yet, they sank in worldly attractions, and we have been able, thanks to God, to avoid them and hate their misdeeds and faithlessness. No man with a mind in his head can in fact be satisfied with their life conditions. It suffices to refer to the liberal and sinful behaviour of their women, and the latter's authority and superiority to men to show how low and disgraceful their life is.

French Women

French women go out unveiled and plunge in the world of sin and prostitution, and nobody can prevent them from doing whatever they wish. Men's obedience to women and the latter's liberty is so well known that they say: 'Paris is the paradise of women and the hell of horses.' The wife is sovereign at home; her husband obeys her. It is part of their traditions that the wife receives guests, takes care of them and talks with them whether they are men or women. The husband is expected to courteously follow her orders, and if ever he shows any dissatisfaction with her, he is considered as impolite and savage. We learnt that the majority of women give in to vile immoral deeds, and that jealousy is very rare among men. A wife can take the hand of another man in the presence of her husband who wouldn't react or show any sense of irritation. He would even ask his neighbour or his friend to accompany her to a recreational area or a show if he is busy. Husbands don't question the behaviour of their wives even when they hear rumours about their misdemeanour.

In fact there are laws that regulate marital relationships. For example, if a husband surprises his wife with another man, he has to present the proof of her adultery to the judge, and has to determine its nature. If the man is found in her house, he is sent to prison and is forced to pay a certain fine; the husband has the right to divorce her if he wishes to without having to give her alimony. But if she is caught at the man's place, he is acquitted and her husband is free to divorce her. But if he divorces her without any proof, he is charged with alimony as long as she is alive, and is never allowed to marry another woman unless she dies. Again, a man is not allowed to marry two wives even if he is a king; and this is one of the reasons why men are not jealous and why their wives are granted so much freedom, which they exploit to give in to their sexual desires. Prostitution is not considered as a vice in this country. Married men, however, are blamed for it, while those who are single are proud of it and speak about it publicly. It is said that there are thirty thousand prostitutes in Paris. Each of them gets hold of an official permission to practice her profession, and is required to abide by the laws that regulate prostitution. The parents have no right on their daughters when they are eighteen, and are thus unable to prevent them from practicing prostitution. They have certain customs that are so despicable and disgraceful that it is preferable not to hear about them, and a writer would better not talk about them. I have just pointed out to some of them in order to enlighten the ignorant and have the attention of those who are carefree.

Blyden: A Pan-Africanist's Voyage to Palestine
From *From West Africa to Palestine* (1873)

Born into an Ibo family in 1832, Blyden spent his early years living in St. Thomas, Virgin Islands and Venezuela. After studying theology and entering the clergy in 1851, Blyden settled in Liberia, where he believed that he could work to "enhance African culture". Blyden died in Freetown, Sierra Leone, in 1912.

He expressed pan-African ideas in his sermons and speeches, as well as in articles for Liberian, British and American publications. In many of these texts he argues that the African race could only advance if Europeans kept at a distance. His sense of "African uplift", as he called it, was based on the repatriation of Africans who had been geographically displaced by slavery. Some of these concepts are expressed in his 1887 book, *Christianity, Islam and the Negro Race,* which also expresses the need to teach Islamic thought in Africa as a way of promoting industry and education.

His interest in Islam led him to study Arabic, and in 1866 he travelled to Egypt and Lebanon, where he perfected his knowledge of the language. He published a narrative of this trip in 1873, in which he describes the well-known tourist attractions that he visited *en route* to Lebanon. This travel narrative does not only give us Blyden's touristic forays, but also gives us insightful observations into Middle Eastern culture. For example, he writes long descriptions on the different cultural and religious practices of the Middle East, concluding that "there seems to be remarkable unanimity among the principle sects—Jews, Christians and Muslims—as to the final destiny of Jerusalem; that God will finally be worshipped on 'that mountain,' and that all the tribes will flow onto it" (145). At other times, Blyden's travel writing takes a less utopic and religious tone. In Egypt, for instance, he is awestruck by the Pyramids (and by Egyptian culture in general), and it fills him with pride to note that he is a "descendent of Ham", a race which "contributed to the building of this great civilization" (138). To draw a line between himself and his Egyptian ancestors, he engraves the word "Liberia" into one of the Pyramids. And, finally, while in Lebanon, Blyden comments on the cultural practice of women's veiling. His descriptions of veiling are interestingly ambivalent. On the one hand, he refers to it as a "primitive" custom, which transforms women into "sheeted ghosts"; on the other hand, though, he sees the veil as a "graceful" garb that is more attractive than the European bonnet. Such comments remind us of recent studies of ambivalence in postcolonial theory.

[Extracts from Edward Wilmot Blyden's *From West Africa to Palestine* (1873), originally written in English]

. . . On the 10th July, at seven a.m., we anchored in the harbour of Alexandria. I now had before me the renowned land of Egypt. How shall I describe the emotions with which the first sight of this ancient country inspired me? How shall I select and reproduce in an order intelligible to others the thoughts which, in rapid succession, passed through my mind?

I was prepared to find a large harbour, but was greatly surprised at the presence of so large a number of vessels from nearly all parts of the world, and of three or four splendid steam corvettes belonging to the Egyptian government.

I saw in the distance the site of the ancient Pharos, the first great lighthouse constructed in the Mediterranean, and one of the seven wonders of the world. Immediately before me lay the city built by Alexander the Great. When Alexander boasted that he would here build an emporium of commerce that would surpass Tyre, which he had destroyed, and attract the shipping of the world, he little dreamed that the day would come when the most important operations carried on in this city would be by vessels from powerful nations of the west; some of them inhabiting countries then unknown to maritime enterprise. The history of Alexandria since his death had more than realized the dream of the world's conqueror.

About an hour after we anchored a steam-tug came alongside the

Nyanza, and took off those passengers and their effects who had taken through tickets for India, China, Japan, and Australia. So far as I was concerned the responsibility of the P. & O. Company ceased on the arrival of the steamer at Alexandria. I was therefore obliged to hire a boat to take me ashore. On landing I was very near losing my baggage, amid the wonderful crowd of men and beasts by which I was beset—Negroes, Arabs, Turks, donkeys, camels—in terrifying rivalry for my trunks. I was not disposed to allow anyone to touch my baggage until I could decide upon my destination. At length an Arab, calling himself Hamad, and representing himself as a professed dragoman, came to my assistance, and relieved me of the disagreeable pressure. He assisted me in passing through the Custom House, which was a small affair. I then hired a carriage, and had myself conveyed with my baggage to the United States Consulate-General, where, after exhibiting a letter of introduction from Mr. Adams, the American minister in London, I was most kindly received by Mr. Hale, the Consul-General, a very polite and well-educated gentleman from New England.

Learning from Mr. Hale that the next railway train from Cairo that day would start in about an hour's time, I deposited my baggage in his office, and taking a letter from him to the United States Consul at Cairo, I hastened to the railway station; and, arriving just in time to get a ticket and procure a seat, I was borne whirling up the valley of the Nile at the rate of thirty miles an hour.

I looked at my ticket, and found that it was printed in Arabic characters. I felt a strong desire to retain it as a curiosity, but was obliged to give it up at the end of the journey…

Half an hour after crossing the river, we caught a view of the pyramids in the distance. Here was opened to me a wide field of contemplation, and my imagination was complete 'master of the situation.' Though we were in an exposed plain, and my companion complained of the intense heat, I did not notice it, so eager was I to gain the pyramids, which seemed further and further to recede the longer we rode towards them. We saw them for three hours before we came up to them.

Just before reaching the pyramids we passed a small village of Arabs, who make their living, for the most part, by assisting travellers to 'do' the pyramids. About a dozen of them rushed out as they saw us approaching, with goblets of water, pitchers of coffee, candles, and matches, and engraving knives. The water was very acceptable. I looked at the other articles, and wondered what could be the object of them.

The pyramids stand apparently on a hill of sand, on the borders of the Libyan Desert. We had to ascend a considerable elevation—about 130 feet—before getting to the pyramid of Cheops. In the side of this apparent hill of sand, extending from the pyramids of Ghizeh to the smaller pyramids of Abusir and Sakarah, about two miles, are excavated tombs. The pyramids then are at the extremities of an immense city of the dead; they, themselves forming the imperishable tombs of the mighty monarchs who constructed them.

On reaching the base of the great pyramid I tried to find the shady side, but it was impossible to find any shade. On the north side there were several large stones, taken out at the base—leaving huge spaces. Into one of these Ibrahim, myself, and our donkeys entered and sheltered ourselves. The Arabs crowded about us, and kept asking question after question, suggesting the pleasure we should enjoy in ascending to the top, and the advantage to be reaped by visiting the interior. But I paid very little attention to them. They addressed me in broken English, French, and Italian. Other thoughts were crowding my mind. I thought of the continuous fatigue I had undergone, without eating anything, sustained only by the object I expected to attain in front, viz., a close inspection of the pyramids. And now that I had gained my point, and sat down to rest under the shadow of a great rock, I could not help feeling that my effort was, after all, but a forcible type of our experience in one-half the pursuits we follow through life. My enchanting dreams and fancies left me completely, as heated, and weary, and hungry, I sat down to rest. How speedily that most cursory experience of the reality often levels to the dust all the mountains built up by the imagination!

Though I cannot say that at the first view of the pyramids they fell below my expectation, still they did not exactly appear what I expected them to be. Their greatness grew upon me as I looked at them. They are something magnificent. (How inadequate that adjective to convey what I meant!)

I had read Longfellow's beautiful description:—

> *The mighty pyramids of stone,*
> *That, wedge-like, cleave the desert airs,*
> *When nearer seen and better known,*
> *Are but gigantic flights of stairs.*

But I had supposed that this was merely poetic and ideal, referring to the layer after layer of stone or brick put up 'by slow degrees, by more and more' in constructing large edifices: I did not imagine that, in reality, the pyramids were built in steps; but they are really 'gigantic flights of stairs'—so that they can be ascended to the very top. Travellers frequently go up…

After gazing in amazement at the outside, I made up my mind, on consultation with Ibrahim as to the safety of the enterprise, to visit the central hall in the interior. Had I known, however, that the performance required so much nerve and physical strength as I found out during the experiment, I should not have ventured. The entrance is first by a very steep and narrow passage, paved with immense stones, which have become dangerously slippery by centuries of use. There are small notches for the toes of those who would achieve the enterprise of entering, distant from each other about four or five feet, showing that they were intended for very tall men who wore no shoes. The modern traveller is obliged to make Hiawathan strides to get the toe of his boot into one of these notches, which are also wearing smooth, so as to make the hold which he gets exceedingly precarious. But for the help of these half-naked, shoeless, and sure-footed Arabs, it would be impossible for Western pilgrims generally to accomplish the feat of visiting the interior. Before entering, the Arabs lighted two candles— an operation which, I confess, somewhat staggered me, as it gave me the idea of sepulchral gloom and ghastliness. I had supposed that the interior of the pyramids was lighted in some way, though I had not stopped to think how. As we had to go down sideways, two attended me, one holding my left and hand and the other my right, so that if one slipped the other would be a support. If we had all slipped at once, it is difficult to imagine what would have been the result. The lighted candles were carried in advance...

Here, then, is a very plain dilemma to which we bring our adversaries. Either Negroes existed in those early days or they did not exist. If they did exist, then they must have had a part in the founding of those great empires; if they did not exist, then they are a comparatively youthful race, whose career is yet to be run; and it is unfair to say that they have not achieved anything in the annals of history, especially considering the obstructive influences, already referred to, which have operated upon their country.

But the conjecture is by no means improbable that the particular type or development of this race, spread along the western coat of Africa, in Upper and Lower Guinea, and from which the American continent has been supplied with servile labourers for the last three hundred years is of comparatively recent origin. And this will account for their wonderful tenacity of life, and their rapid increase, like the youthful and elastic Hebrews of old, amid the unparalleled oppressions of their captivity...

The Sphinx, which I gazed at a long while, is a most impressive spectacle. This colossal and fanciful figure, half human, half animal, the body being that of a lion, was an emblematic representation of the king—the union of intellect and physical power. It was cut out of the solid rock, with the exception of the paws and a portion of the backbone, which are of hewn stone. Its height to the top of the head was sixty-three feet, its length a hundred and forty-three feet, and it measured a hundred and two feet round the forehead. The head-dress is destroyed, and the face is much mutilated, so that the features, which were Egyptian in their character, are scarcely distinguishable. Below its breast and between its paws, which extended fifty feet from the chest, though now covered with sand, stand the remains of a small temple and altar, the incense smoke from which ascended to its expanded nostrils.

The veil is worn constantly by all the native females. It takes the place of the western bonnet altogether; in fact, it is more that the bonnet. Like the turban or tarbush, which is never off the head of the male, the veil is never away from the head of its mistress. In the house and in the street, at the wash-tub or the ironing-table, in the kitchen, at the well, or in the market, the veil is always present. However ragged and filthy, the veil must be on the head or over the face; and frequently other portions of the body are left altogether exposed in order to cover the face. The Druses and Mussulmans are most particular that their women shall be closely veiled; and, through fear of these sects, Jews, Maronites, Greeks, and Protestants keep up the practice. When Protestant females of intelligence are asked why, knowing better, they keep their faces so much concealed, they reply, 'Well, we don't care about being closely veiled; but if we don't veil we are liable to be laughed at or insulted by Druses or Mussulmans.' In the cities the Mohammedan women are wrapped up from head to foot in white muslin, so as to look very much like sheeted ghosts.

But, after all, there is something graceful in the veil as it is worn by most of the Protestant females. No one who has lived in the East any time would like to see the custom of moderate veiling fall altogether into disuse. How it would shock all the feelings of propriety and reverence, even of the most enthusiastic admirer of Western costume, to see a painting of any of the holy women of the Bible in the modern European bonnet and its concomitants!. . .

Jerusalem

Sept. 9th—To-day (Sunday) I had the privilege of worshipping in Jerusalem and on Mount Zion in the English cathedral. Rev. Mr. Barclay read the service, and Bishop Gobat preached, from John xvi., 12-14, a truly evangelical, simple, and instructive sermon. Divine service is also celebrated in this church in the Hebrew and German languages. There is no Sabbath in Jerusalem; business is carried on as on other days by Jews and Moslems, who form the great bulk of the population.[205] I saw camels going to and fro with their loads, and every other form of activity engaged in, showing that the people no longer 'Remember the Sabbath-day to keep it holy.'

September 10th—Early this morning, in company with the Misses Gobat, who have lived in Jerusalem from childhood, and are full of enthusiastic veneration for its sacred scenes, I went out again through the eastern gate, walked along the Garden of Gethsemane with open Bible in hand, trying to identify localities. We ascended for a little distance the Mount of Olives along what is supposed to have been the usual route of our Saviour to and from Bethany to the city. We then descended into the Valley of Jehoshaphat, and went as far as the Pool of Siloam, of which we tasted the waters. There were a few women washing clothes here. We could gain no admittance into the Garden of Gethsemane. It is surrounded by a stone wall about six feet high, and entered by gates, which are always kept locked in the custody of a monk; who was away at the time of our visit. After lingering awhile we entered the city and visited several of the Jewish synagogues. It was now the season of their New Year Festival, and a great many Israelites had come to Jerusalem 'for to worship' from various countries. We spent some time at the Spanish and Polish synagogues. Some of the worshippers seemed deeply in earnest; most, however, looked around and stared at us while repeating their prayers, they all had a singular motion of the body, waving to and fro, while reading or chanting, as if in agony. The females, I noticed, were not admitted into the synagogues, but sat in the passages and on the steps, closely veiled . . .

We reached Bethlehem about three o'clock. The chief place of interest here, is, of course, the Church of the Nativity. This edifice is said to be built over the site where stood the stable in which Christ was born. It is in the shape of a cross, built AD 325, by the Empress Helena. Here were pointed out the spot where the babe was lying in the manger when the shepherds made their visit, the place where the wise men offered their gifts, and numerous other localities connected with the Savior's nativity. We spent about an hour in this church; then, paying a short visit to Rev. Mr. Muller, the German missionary at

Bethlehem, we left the little town around which cluster so many interesting and sacred associations . . .

Winding through some narrow, crooked lanes, we reached another most interesting section of the wall of the ancient temple—the wailing place of the Jews . . .

After the capture of Jerusalem by Adrian, the Jews were excluded from the city, and it was not till the age of Constantine that they were permitted to approach, so as to behold Jerusalem from the neighbouring hills. At length they were allowed to enter the city once a year, on the day on which it was taken by Titus, in order to wail over the ruins of the Temple; but this privilege they had to purchase of the Roman soldiers. They are now permitted to approach the precincts of the temple of their fathers, and bathe its hallowed stones with their tears.

No sight in Jerusalem affected me more than that which presented itself in this retired spot, beneath the massive remains of that ancient building. The usual day for wailing is Friday, but, as this was holiday season, they wailed every day, and I had the opportunity of seeing Jews of both sexes, of nearly all ages, from various paths of the earth, lifting up a united cry of lamentation over a desolated and dishonoured sanctuary. The women, for the most part, sat in silence, and the tears rolled down their cheeks. Some of the young girls, as if embarrassed by the presence of spectators, buried their heads in the cavities between the stones and wept. Old men tottered up to the wall, muttering something with trembling lips, and kissed the mighty stones...

Among such a number of conflicting sects the missionary of the Cross finds indeed hard work. Each sect stands off from the other in menacing attitude. In all the cities, and in some whole sections of country, religious feuds and animosities are fearful in their bitterness. Jerusalem is a city of religious controversy, with all 'its personal alienations, its exasperating imputations, and its appeals to prejudice and passion.' Not unfrequently, at the Church of the Holy Sepulchre, the aid of the Turkish soldiers is invoked to quell the disorders among discordant sects. The Christian world may well pray for the *peace* of the literal Jerusalem.

There is one subject, however, upon which there seems to be remarkable unanimity among the principal sects—Jews, Christians and Moslems—viz., as to the final destiny of Jerusalem; that it is to be the scene of latter-day glories; that the Jews are to be restored to the land of their fathers, and the Messiah is to be enthroned in personal reign in the 'City of the Great King'. And there seems to be something in the locality which makes one feel that Jerusalem is no ordinary place, whether we regard its past or its future. The most materialistic mind cannot visit the city and leave it without profound emotion. It seems difficult for Christians who have resided any time in the city to escape the impression that God will finally be worshipped on 'that mountain,' and that all the tribes will flow unto it. . .

Malabari: A Love-Hate Affair with the British

From *The Indian Eye on English Life or Rambles of a Pilgrim Reformer* (1893)

The number of travel books in English by Indians in the nineteenth century is simply mind-boggling—and more so because the field seems to have largely eluded the gaze of scholars in spite of the fact that the texts are available in English. (Obviously, travel texts were also written in Indian languages in and around the period, and one of them—Abu Taleb's eighteenth-century travel book—has been included here as well, along with Dean Mahomad's more visible account in English from the eighteenth century.)

Some important eighteenth- and nineteenth-century travel texts in English by Indians include Dean Mahomed's *The Travels of Dean Mahomet* (1794), J. Nowrojee and H. Merwanjee's *Journal of a Residence of Two Years and a Half in Great Britain* (1841), Ishuree Dass's account of a voyage to England and America (1851), Bholanath Chanda's *Travels of a Hindoo to Various Parts of Bengal and Upper India* (1869), Keshab Chandra Sen's *Diary in England* (1886), Trailokyanatha Mukharji's *A Visit to Europe* (1889), Nandalal Dasa's *Reminiscences—English and Australasian* (1893), B. M. Malabari's *The Indian Eye on English life or Rambles of a Pilgrim Reformer* (1893), Romesh Chunder Dutt's *Three Years in Europe* (1896), T. B. Pandiyan's *England to an Indian Eye, or, English Pictures from an Indian Camera* (1897) and G. N. Nadkarni's *Journal of a Visit to Europe in 1896* (1903). Also, Pandita Ramabai's Marathi book, *The Peoples of the United States* (1889), needs to be mentioned: it was finally left out from this anthology as it has been recently published as *Returning the American Gaze*, with an excellent introduction by Meera Kosambi. These accounts often share certain features with early twentieth-century travel accounts in English by Indians like B. C. Mahtab (?1908), Meherban Narayanrao Babasaheb (1915), Bhawani Singh (1916), D. F. Karaka (1938) etc.

The texts concern themselves with various matters, ranging from education and culture to trade and commerce and focusing on street life as well as museums and cultural exhibitions. They often display much political awareness and sometimes retain a literary flavour. Their writers position themselves differently on the issue of empire—some view themselves as equal partners and others as subject people—but they often consider matters of class, race and (to employ a subsequent term) "hegemony". Obviously, these texts deserve an anthology to themselves, but the rigours of space have forced us to select only one out of the many listed (and some not listed) above.

The Parsi journalist Behramji M. Malabari's *The Indian Eye on English Life* presents one common version of the Indian's use of travel and travel writing in the colonial period. B. M. Malabari, a Parsi, was already an established journalist, poet and social reformer (author of the important *Notes on Infant Marriage and Enforced Widowhood*, 1884)[206] in Bombay when he visited England: his book, *The Indian Eye on English Life*, seems to suggest that he visited London for the first time in 1890, after many invitation by "friends".[207] Susheila Nasta, however, notes that Malabari "visited Victorian Britain regularly between 1870 and 1890".[208] His book, written in English, was published by Archibald Constable and Company, publishers to the India Office, in 1893.

The book starts with an account of Malabari's Anglophile fascination with London. It describes his journey to the place at a time in 1890 when "literary effort", "political interest" and "social movements" were at a low enough ebb to enable the author to find the time for the trip. Leaving on the Austro-Hungarian steamship, *Imperator*, on which he had procured a single berth and "permission to dine in my cabin and to have my man with me", Malabari arrived in Dover on an unspecified date and left for London by train. Much of the book consists of Malabari's meditations on London life—interspersed with tongue-in-cheek comments on the British and sometimes outright cultural and political criticism—and his short but almost novel-like sketches of events and people like his manservant, nicknamed Crocodile.

London not only comes across in Malabari's narrative as "an 'imperial theatre' where the drama of the ambivalent location of the colonial citizen-subject was played out for the benefit of rulers and ruled alike."[209] It also comes across as a space of contrast and comparison with both scenes in India and those in Europe, across which Malabari also travelled towards the end of his stay. This play of difference and similarity between the so-called colonial periphery and the colonial centre—nuanced by the third axis of continental European cities like Paris or Rome—is present in other travel texts of the age, such as Abu Taleb's Indo-Persian *Lubbu s Siyar*.

"By writing the metropolis through Indian eyes, he [Malabari] was both able to confront his initial Anglophilia as a Bombay Parsi, being seduced like many others who followed him by the imagined attractions of the English 'mother-land', whilst at the same time deconstructing its image, as a journey to an illusion. Malabari carefully maps the social geography of London for his Indian readers, but he also seriously criticizes the contradictory realities of the heart of darkness within the Britain that he encounters," according to Nasta.[210] However, it is interesting to note that the book itself, if Malabari's short preface is to be trusted, was offered not to the Indian reader but "to the British public by a stranger in blood, in creed, and in language."

Of particular interest, as highlighted in the chapter on Malabari in Burton's *At the Heart of the Empire*, is the text as a record of the spatial and cultural contingencies of a privileged colonial subject's masculinity in the late-Victorian period while negotiating the imperial metropole. The selection below intends to point in those directions, while concentrating primarily on Malabari's writings as a traveler—someone negotiating the familiar and the strange within which all travellers have to situate their movements, or at least their description of those movements.

[Extracts from B. M. Malabari's *The Indian Eye on English Life or Rambles of a Pilgrim Reformer* (1893), written originally in English]

From Chapter I

[Bombay to London]

A trip to London has been my dream for years, a hope long deferred. More, indeed, than wish or hope, it has been a faith with me, to be rewarded in the fullness of time. By the end of 1889, I find I have rambled over nearly the whole of the Indian Continent, comparing its past with the present, and catching a glimpse of the future, as afforded by the comparison. What could be more natural for a student of humanity, a pilgrim in search of the truths of life, than that he should now wish for a look at the other world, beyond the seas, whose fortunes are so closely knit with those of his own country? There is so much to learn and to unlearn from contact with a different civilization, more robust and more real, in spite of its "falsehood of extremes."

About 11 a.m., on the first of April 1890, I say good-bye to friends once more. I read the last letters from the contributors to the *Indian Spectator*, kindly undertaken to relieve me of all work. Finally, I am about to drop into my deck–chair when I feel a friendly hand tap me on the shoulder from behind. It is Mr. Patrick Ryan, the Magistrate, heaving and panting. For a minute he cannot speak, though beaming all benevolence. On recovering his breath he explains that he heard of my sudden flight just before starting for Court, that he looked into the Court only to tell the clerks he would be delayed for an hour, and drove up to the harbour as fast as he could. "I dared not let you slip out without a shake of the hand," adds the honest old Irishman. "Who knows? we may never meet again." It is fated, indeed, to be our last parting on this side of the grave. A few months later, while still in England, I hear of Mr. Ryan's death at Poona, under very sad circumstances. Dear old Patrick Ryan! How kind and wise! Wise for every one but himself. Many a time have I consulted him in matters of extreme delicacy. Many a time have I recommended applicants to his unpaid service. He loved to help the needy, by purse and by pen. As a magistrate he was more humane, perhaps, than just, always siding with the helpless and the ignorant, as against the powerful police or unscrupulous limbs of the law. How often he turned away from the Police Inspector with a tactful compliment to his ingenuity, and turning to the accused with pretended severity, dismissed him or her with the remark, "Don't let me see you here again!" He was always for giving "a chance" to the accused, especially where the Police conducted the prosecution; and in not a few cases, I believe, he prevailed upon friendly lawyers to defend the defenceless. No wonder that he was one of the most popular men that ever sat on the bench. Personally he exhibited a rare power of friendship. He volunteered useful advice to me on complicated questions of law and procedure, put me straight on the Home Rule and other political problems, offered to grind for the *Indian Spectator*, and last time I went to the hills he offered to read the proofs for me, so that I could have a real holiday. Poor fellow, what was there between thee and me to lead to this extravagance of friendly regard? And I was denied the solace of watching over thee in thy last moments! Bombay will long remember this warm-hearted official Bohemian, with all his blunderings and improvidence. In his day he is said to have sowed his wild oats rather wildly; and a plentiful crop of them he had to reap. But that was long before my time. I knew only Patrick Ryan, the popular magistrate.

Two minutes after Mr. Ryan's departure the Imperator *weighs* anchor, and for the first time now I feel sure that I have left for the Land of Freedom, the land of my youthful dreams, which holds so much that is precious to me personally, and so much more that is of greater value to the land of my birth.

The *Imperator* is quite a little palace afloat, both as regards size and steadiness. From captain to cabin-boy it has over eighty hands at work day and night; and yet everything in every department goes on with the regularity of a clock. The principle of division of labour is so well maintained, that there is not the slightest friction observable amongst officers or men. Not only is there no grumbling as to overwork, or other kind of work than that contracted for; there is scarcely any ordering about found necessary. Every hand seems to know his own work; its why, when, and how. Every hand goes through the work cheerfully, humming or whistling a tune, or smiling at the onlookers who stand gaping in admiration at some perilous feat he may be performing on the top-mast.

This *esprit de corps* is what strikes one most on board. How much we Indians differ from Europeans in the matter of organization! We hardly understand the word. I doubt if we have it in our vernaculars. At any rate, the spirit seems to have been almost lost to us. What a comprehensive word, this organization! It includes order, discipline, presence of mind—the best form of individual and collective responsibility. Think of a vessel like the *Imperator*, officered and manned by natives of India! What sulks, what shirkings, what disorder, each blaming the other for his own fault! In no respect are we so inferior to Europeans as in that of organized effort. Yet the root-idea of our system of caste is so akin to modern organization! Caste in India was once the most perfect type of organization. Others seem to have borrowed from us both the idea and the institution. How fallen we are from our original selves! Too much credit could not be given to the P.&O. and other Companies for the employment of Indian Lascars. They make capital sailors, and have more than once proved themselves worthy of their salt in times of danger. In fact, the Indian sailor ought to be found equally efficient with the European sailor, and much less expensive; as is known to be the case with the Indian soldier. I do not know of more than two natives who have made capable ship-officers. Most of our coast steamers are officered by natives who know little of navigation, and would be found unfit for work on strange seas. Why don't our educated men take to this branch of the public service? Perhaps they are not alone to blame for the neglect.

And why don't they take more kindly to travelling abroad?...

As to the attitude of caste regarding foreign travel, one cannot deny that it is more or less hostile, and not without reason. Caste loves contentment—to let things alone. Foreign travel brings discontent, under the happiest of circumstances. The priestly law-givers of India were shrewd enough to see the risk; in their day perhaps the evil outweighed the good. We are now living under totally different conditions. If the educated Hindu is sufficiently educated to conciliate the reasonable prejudices of his elders, he has little or nothing to lose from crossing the *Kálápani* ("Black Waters"), and certainly a great deal to gain.

...One evening I salute a lady whom I have been asked to look up, and whose brother has spoken to her about my presence on board. With my usual knack at blundering I go up to the wrong lady—that is, to her maid [German] who modestly explains, "Me comb mit him"—I come with her. Shade of Lindley Murray!—a quadruple murder in a sentence of four words! Here is a clever-looking lady's maid who has been in Anglo-India for some time, and who defies her form of speech with such utter defiance. "Me comb mit him!" Talk of "Babu English" after this. A Babu schoolboy would blush at it. But why blame the poor German maid? There are thousands of English *ladies* and *gentlemen* who cannot speak German or any Indian dialect any better. Is it not curious that the average Englishman, who scorns to pick up foreign languages while travelling, insists upon foreigners speaking to him in English? You observe this everywhere on the continent, as also in India, where hotel-keepers, railway servants, cab-drivers, and others are obliged to accommodate the grumpy islander so far. In no other respect, perhaps, does the imperial instinct of the Anglo-Saxon seem to be more imperiously asserted.

Talking of "Babu English," I should like to know how many Englishmen speak Bengali half so well as Bengalis speak English. How many are the English scholars who handle the language more effectively than, for instance, Sambhu Chunder Mookerji, or Rajendralal Mitra, Kristodas Pal, or Keshub Chunder Sen?...

From Chapter II

[In and about London]

…From Dover to London is an exceedingly pleasant drive, through a country as different as could be from our own. Travelling first-class, one is comparatively safe from fatigue; but he loses little, so far, even when travelling second or third, if he can stand a crowd. The British crowd, in a railway carriage or other public conveyance, is, as a rule, orderly and well-behaved; the presence of women makes it more so. This remark hardly applies to a crowd of holiday-makers abroad. What strikes an Asiatic most, on getting out at Victoria Station, is the noise and bustle around him. Every man and woman—one might say every animal, and even some of the inanimate objects—seem to be full of life. The streets and thoroughfares of London present a sight in this respect, which it is impossible for the stranger to realize save with his own eyes. I happen to have read a good deal about this, but what I actually see here exceeds my anticipation. To "Crocodile" it is all a new world. He stands apart, gaping at the scene in bewildered admiration. The crowds of women in the streets, walking rapidly past, pushing and elbowing every one who stands in the way, all intent on business or pleasure, are a sight not likely to be soon forgotten. For me it is a sight more striking than attractive. After all, a woman's place is at home rather than in the street. Of course, the climate and the conditions of life generally impose this outing upon not a few Englishwomen who are apparently unwilling to rough it in a crowd. But it is none the less painful on that account to see a delicate girl struggling to return home in the midst of a traffic heavier than we see in India during our annual fairs. This traffic is maintained every day by railway trains, running under ground and above ground, by omnibuses, trams, cabs, private carriages, waggons, trucks, hand-barrows, tricycles, etcetera, to say nothing of the immense pedestrian crowds. In the large and more fashionable business quarters, such as Bond Street, Piccadilly, Oxford and Regent Streets, into which the various agencies mentioned above pour vast multitudes every five minutes, and some of which are broad enough, besides the pavements, to hold a row of five carriages abreast, I stand breathless of an evening, watching what goes on before my eyes. Carriages and pedestrians alike seem to have a hair-breadth escape of it now and again. But amid this surging ocean of humanity, the police-constables keep such order, the drivers are so skilful, and the pedestrians so alert, that accidents are very rare indeed. And yet the eye, if it can observe well, may detect a good deal of suffering among the gay or busy crowd. Here is some fashionable cad, nearly driving over a fragile old woman. She rushes, trembling, to the constable's side. There goes a knot of boy-sweepers, running about between carriages and even under them, in order to keep the ground clean. You could not expect greater agility from mice or squirrels. There is more safety, of course, on the pavements. But you are not quite safe here either, from dangers other than trampling. Few respectable women, I find, will venture out into some of these streets towards evening without a guide; so great is the rush therein of the unworthy ones of their sex, of their victims and tyrants. The back parts of not a few streets seem to have been given up to a Godless population, foreign and English. A large percentage of this, I should think, represents virtue first betrayed, and then crowded out, by vice.

What strikes you most about Englishwomen is their look of health, strength, elasticity, all proclaiming a freedom of mind, to begin with. How they walk, and talk, and carry themselves generally! How they rush in and out, saying good-bye with the right hand turned towards themselves, meaning what our women in India always say, "vehela aujo," come back soon! How they kiss one another, and offer their children, even their cats and dogs to be kissed by the friends departing! Does this last ceremony show heart-hunger, or is it affectation? Here they are, half a dozen of them rushing into my omnibus (the Lord have mercy on an unprotected orphan!) squeezing themselves into their seats. I am between two of the prettiest and quietest, feeling a strange discomfort. As the bus hobbles along, I feel my fair neighbours knocking against me every moment. *They* do not seem to mind it at all; it is a matter of course. Why, then, should I cry out against the inevitable? Evil to him who evil thinks. We are all too busy here, reading the paper, chatting about the weather, minding our packages and our toes. Further, I find both my neighbours resting their parasols between them and me on either side. A straw shows how the breeze blows. The breeze that I have just discovered is very refreshing to my soul. I have also noted that respectable Englishwomen rather avoid entering a carriage occupied by men. It is mainly through such experience that I am learning to take a charitable view of ladies sitting on the knees of gentlemen, or gentlemen on the knees of ladies, when three of a family happen to be in one hansom, or more than ten in a railway carriage. These sights, queer as they are, do not offend me now. They would be an eyesore amongst our own people. I myself could hardly bear them at first; but that is no reason why I should judge others in such a matter, before I am well equipped to form a judgment.

I have said above that the average Englishwoman strikes me most by her healthy looks and active habits. But, as usual, there is another side to this picture. One often meets with the anæmic and the consumptive, victims of overwork, starvation, or dissipation, in themselves or their parents. How pathetic is the sight of one of these girls, moving softly like a ghost, with a frame so fragile as to be driven by the wind behind, with a transparent skin and glassy eyes, exhausted by the effort to creep on to the platform, and going directly to sleep in the carriage, with the delicate little mouth half open, as if to allow the breath of life to ebb out without a struggle! It fills me with grief to watch this fair slight being as if in the process of dissolution. And yet I sit there, fascinated by her presence, unmindful of time or distance.

It makes one laugh to hear the English talk of their "fine day," their "lovely, splendid, magnificent, glorious weather." Why, I never saw a whole day in London that could honestly be described as "fine," let alone the hyperboles. One may speak of a "fine" five minutes; a fine half-hour or hour. Nothing beyond that, so far as I could see. As a matter of fact, every five minutes of "fine weather" in London is worth recording in letters of gold.

The Englishman's dress is perhaps as much under the influence of climate as his temper; it is capricious, but not ill-suited to his wants, though one would think it might be made more becoming in some particulars. The Englishwoman's dress is necessarily more complicated, but on the whole it sits well on her, and is better suited to active outdoor movements than is the Indian lady's, as a rule. The tendency in this respect is markedly towards freedom. But it will be many years, I am afraid, before anything like real freedom is reached. The present cumbrous arrangement reminds one of the days of female slavery, when everything was done by their lords to keep women within sight. Englishwomen are advancing rapidly in every direction. But they seem to be slow to improve in the matter of dress. Can this be from their own desire to be easily caught when outstripping the limits of womanly independence? Woman's instinct is said to be sounder than her reason. For my part, I am not ashamed of sympathizing with the movement for a simpler, cheaper, more rational system of dress. It would save many a milliner's bill, many an hour wasted on the daily toilet, many a gap in domestic harmony, and many a bonny English lass from descending to the grave before her time…

From Chapter III

[Life as seen at home]

…To English friends in India, and more so to those in England, who are extra-polite to us, simply because we happen to be strangers, who stoop and bend in order to pat us on the back, I appeal earnestly to treat us more like fellow-subjects. By all means be kind and hospitable to us, as you are to your own people; but, above all, be just and impartial. Treat us as you treat your own brethren. Spare us not if you find us tripping. In a word, do not patronize but befriend us. Give us the right hand to fellowship at school and college, in the highways and byways of public life. Anything more from you we would rather be without. Habitual excess of forbearance is perhaps worse, in the long run, than an excess of severity.

The same equal treatment we ask for in the case of the nation as in the case of individuals. We want the public services to be open to Natives and Europeans alike; to be entered by one common portal, that of competition. We do not want England to send us her superfluous wealth, she has much need of that at home. But we do want her to manage our resources in India as carefully as she manages her own. And the best way to do this, we think, is to associate with yourselves, in the conduct of public affairs, those of us who are competent for it, not by means of patronage—that is, on official sufferance—but by election mainly at the hands of qualified voters. In short, within the measure of our capacity and the circumstances of the country, there should be an approximation in the methods of government between India and England, with equality as the basis both of public administration and personal intercourse.

This, and much more, might be impressed upon the average English politician, if only he could be got at. But the difficulty is to interest him in the affairs of far-off India. His ignorance does not appear to be wilful. India is so large a problem that the majority of Englishmen give it up in despair. Those who are drawn to it by personal ties, or by a more generous attachment, are distracted by the proverbial multitude of counsel. I believe there ought to be a central informing agency in London, untainted by party bias and by pecuniary interest. Anglo-Indians could be of great service in this connection. Some of these doubtless are; I wish there were more. India has little to do with party politics. Conservatives, Liberals, and Radicals, are practically the same to her. Most of them are actuated by honest, if not strictly honourable intentions towards us. But it would be idle to expect the English, as a people, to concern themselves with our affairs, when they have so many of their own to occupy them. Their want of interest is excusable; they make no secret of it. There is hardly any excuse, however, for the ignorance of responsible men who have the governing of India. Theirs is sometimes a compound ignorance, as the Arabian would call it, an ignorance that knows not it is ignorant. My Lord Rattledrone is a good hand at letting in the light of knowledge Indian on the foggy horizon of his peers. Sir Evan

Gossamer may get up a flash now and then to dazzle the Lower House. But when they and I come to close quarters, why do these rulers of India so often think discretion the better part of valour? Where is the need for running away from Indian questions? Take heart of grace, gentlemen, and face your duty. It is no use putting off the evil day. The day will grow more and more evil that way. India is getting on but for the unnatural economic conditions imposed on her by your ignorance. The drain on her resources, perhaps inevitable in the beginning, has been so continuous, that she has hardly enough blood left in her now for healthy circulation. This process of depletion tells most on the peasantry, least able to bear up against it. The heavy expenditure incurred by the military departments, coupled with this perpetual drain of resources, cannot last for ever. The sooner you find a remedy, the better for us both.

As to ruling India by the sword, my dear Colonel Swashbuckler, you ought to know better. How many swords do you keep in India? Sixty thousand?—eighty thousand?—a hundred thousand? And what is the population of India?—two hundred millions. Now, I defy you to cut off two thousand heads with one sword, even in imagination. You will use the armies of the Native States? How much will that swell the number of your swords? And you are shrewd enough to know that blood is thicker than water. Take my advice, dear Colonel; put your sword into a barrel of vinegar. It will improve vinegar and steel alike, and give you time to read up your school books of history again...

From Chapter IV

[Christianity]

...Is it not enough for the man that they contribute towards the maintenance of himself and his church, and patronize them both once a week with their presence? The men seem to be more eager to leave the house of God than to enter it. Once fairly out of its precincts, the average church-goer lapses into his habit of surly or reckless selfishness. His Christianity strikes one as being a religion mainly of flesh, bone, and muscle. It teaches him, more than anything else, how to live, to survive, to make the best of life. At home or abroad, he appears a good deal to be guided by this same muscular principle, to aggrandize, to conquer, and to rule. His life, at its best, is a high fever of humanity from which the divine has been eliminated, or in which, rather, the divine has not yet made a dwelling-place. It makes one wonder at such times if the life and teachings of Christ—Britain's most precious heritage—may not, after all, be thrown away upon a people whose spiritual appreciation is so defective. Are such a people likely to attain to anything like a perfect life, making for peace and righteousness?...

...It is sometimes asked—what has Christianity done for the nations of Europe? Has it softened the hatred of man for man? Has it not, rather, hardened the hatred and perpetuated it; raised war into a merit and a pastime; added vastly to the original selfishness of the race, making sin and vice and crime more easy at home and abroad? These evils, like others, perhaps, that may be suggested, doubtless mark the history and progress of Christian civilization. But why call a religion to account when it is the professors of the religion, not the believers, who are guilty of violating its spirit? The fact is, that the brute in man is still more or less rampant. It breaks out at different times and in different forms, and has to be controlled or subdued by different methods. The struggle has been co-existent with the progress of humanity. It is the struggle between good and evil, as the Zoroastrian would put it. The evil is the material side of our nature, which may or may not have pre-existed our spiritual nature. It is hopeless for man to reconcile the two. Such reconciliation, ready made to hand, would probably defeat the objects of creation.

On the other hand, one need not be a Christian himself to be able to see that Christianity has tended powerfully to humanize one of the least human of the races of man. In its essence, it ought to exercise a threefold influence,—to humanize, to liberalize, to equalize. This, to me, is a very great achievement...

From Chapter V

...Of the infinite variety of sign-boards that adorn the streets of London and other towns, none is more ubiquitous than "Apartments." These are suites of rooms, let out by the week generally, with or without food. Most of the "apartments" speak of a shabby-genteel existence, being kept up by wives, widows, or daughters of broken-down traders, or others who "have seen better days." The landladies try to make both ends meet by taking in lodgers. My experience of "apartments" has been none of the pleasantest. And I believe many other Indian gentlemen, especially students, have had their worst disappointments here. Not a few of the housekeepers trade upon the lodgers' ignorance, pile charge upon charge for things that have never been supplied, or supplied indifferently. Their object is to get as much as they can out of the strangers, and that in the shortest space of time. I have been told of "apartments" that have a skeleton in the cupboard, more hideous than needs to be revealed in this place.

Our second "apartments," for instance, were somewhat of this kind. The landlady was generally in her cups, with a lady lodger who had the knack of mistaking other people's rooms for her own, and of waking others up by delicate knocks at the door and asking after their health. There was a gentleman lodger, too, who dined elsewhere, leaving his room early in the morning and seldom returning till twelve at night. We were served with bad food, worse cooked, and charged at a rate which a first-class hotel might be glad to secure. And though we had a comfortable suite of rooms, with a bath, we were nothing loth when Dr. B—— offered to release us from this fashionable bondage with starvation.

We had a still livelier time of it at Brighton. Dr. B—— and a Panjaubee friend arranged with a lady for a room at there shillings a day, and simple fare for a simple charge. We stayed there two days and a night, "Crocodile" and I myself; and were presented with a bill running over three pounds odd. I paid off the bill, in spite of vehement protests from "Crocodile," and was taken to task by the friends for encouraging fraud. On inquiry we found that this lady was widow of a defunct tradesman. She kept "apartments" during the season at Brighton, and spent the rest of the year in London or the country, as daughter of a gentleman at large.

If the English are a nation of shopkeepers, they are on the whole very honest for the character given them by Napoleon. Not that they have more scruples than others in making the razor that will sell—whether it shaves or no, it is for the buyer to find out. They are shrewd business men, eager to push their wares, to make money and to retire as fast as they can on a competency, to live as gentlemen at large. Small shopkeepers are about the same everywhere.

Dr. B—— buys me a pair of boots, on the express condition that they shall be quiet. But they begin to squeak within a quarter of an hour of the first wear. The worthy doctor thereupon goes up to the shopman and reads him a heart-rending sermon on the evils of selling goods under false pretences. The man listens patiently, and then stammers something like this apology:—"I am very sorry, sir, but if I am to stick to the truth always my master will kick me out. He pays me for *selling* the stock. How can I turn away a customer honestly? And, after all, what do *you* gain by my telling the truth? The next shop will sell you the boots as much with a life. You gain nothing by my truth-telling, while I lose my custom, and very likely my place. The only party that gains is at the next shop; and he gains by telling the same lie for which you condemn me."

Is not there a ring of truthfulness in this false arguing? There is considerable force in it, at any rate. The man undertakes to stop the noise in his boots; and two days after returns them packed in a showy cask, swearing they are "all right." We find, however, he could do nothing to them, save packing them in the case. Having meant them for sale, perhaps he wishes us to keep them for show. The fact is, he cannot afford to tell the truth. It is as much as his place is worth. He is not so much to blame as his employer; and the latter may be less to blame than the public who want cheap things as well as good. Not a little of sharp practice at shops is due to this hankering for bargains.

I buy an umbrella for a guinea, which shows holes innumerable within a week. I want an estimate for a little printing which is to be done sharp, and the estimate sent is three times higher than the price for which I get the job done at a larger press. Such sharp practice is very common in London, especially when you are not on your guard. Look the shopman squarely in the face, and let him understand that you understand him. Again, keep well within the terms of your bargain. If you want just a little more of this or that, you will have just a little too much to pay all round. The Englishman dislikes waiting upon an uncertain customer, and will make him pay "through the nose." The best way to deal with an English rough who is inclined to be vicious, whether at the shop or in the street, is to knock him down before he has the chance of serving you the same way. You may give him your hand when he is down, and he will like you all the more on getting up. On the other hand, if you give him an advantage to start with, you must be prepared for one of the hardest knocks you ever got...

NOTES

1. Quoted by and translated from the Arabic by Tim Mackintosh-Smith in his *Travels with a Tangerine: A Journey in the Footnotes of Ibn Battutah*, pp. 243–44.

2. "The dividing line between fact and fiction, documentation and embellishment, is traditionally elusive [in travel writing]: the extent of Marco Polo's travels, for instance, remains a hotly contested issue." (Clark, p. 2)

3. Pekka Masonen, one of the contributors to this anthology, has drawn my attention to another interesting comparison: the Finnish word for "knowledge" (*tieto*) is related to the Finnish word for "road" (*tie*), thus linking learning to movement and suggesting that learning is a never-ending intellectual journey.

4. "Sedentary travel and travel writing are rigid; sedentary travellers need to 'establish essential difference on a binary frame' and although they may traverse vast distance, no travel need have been undertaken at all. Only nomadic travel, Islam argues, deserves the name of travel in an ethical sense, since it deals with 'encounters with otherness that fracture both a boundary and an apparatus of representation.'"—Mongia, in Khair (ed.), *Amitav Ghosh: A Critical Companion*, Delhi: Permanent Black, 2003, p. 75.

5. See Visram's *Asians in Britain*.

6. See, for instances, the papers in Elsner and Coleman's *Pilgrim Voices*.

7. Pekka Masonen: "When writing my book (which focuses on the development of European historiography of the ancient West African empires of Ghana, Mali, and Songhay), I began to notice references to African travellers made by the 19th-century European explorers, especially in the context of Sudanic Africa. There are many references to West African pilgrims and traders who had visited Northern Africa or Near East, even as far as Constantinople. There are also references to slaves who had managed to return to their homes after being freed by their North African masters. When visiting the city of Kano in Hausaland in 1851, Heinrich Barth, for example, was greeted—in modern Greek—by a Hausa who had spent some twenty years in slavery in Constantinople and had not only learnt the language perfectly, but also adopted Greek manners. Gustav Nachtigal, who left Tripoli in 1869, was told in Bornu in December 1871 that the French and Germans were at war (meaning the Franco-Prussian war which

began in July 1870). T. Edward Bowdich met in Kumasi in 1817 a trader from Jenne who had been to Egypt when Nelson destroyed the French fleet in the battle of Abukir. According to Bowdich, the man could not have invented such a story. These African travellers never wrote down their experiences (as they belonged to oral cultures) and it is difficult to know now what information they passed to their fellow countrypeople. As far as I know, the local oral traditions in the Sudanic Africa do not contain any traces of these travellers. Yet we may say that there were some Sudanic Africans who were interested in the wider world and travelling, and who knew something of what was going on outside their familiar surroundings and wanted to know more. For instance, Muhammad Bello, the caliph of Sokoto, was very interested in the contemporary British policy in India, when he met Hugh Clapperton in 1824." (Private correspondence, July 2003) Also, in his introduction to *In the Lands of Christians*, Nabil Matar effectively dismantles Bernard Lewis's influential claim (in *Islam and the West*) that Arabs and Muslims showed a total lack of "curiosity" towards Europeans in the medieval and colonial periods. Matar goes on to record dozens of Arab travellers to Europe, some of whom left written records.

8.   On the matter of the Chinese, it is interesting to mention a controversial but by no means implausible contention, made by Gavin Menzies in the recently published book, *1421: The Year China Discovered the World*, that the Chinese "discovered" not only Africa but also the Americas and Australia before European explorers. Of course, Africa had never really been lost to Asians and Africans and the (is)land bridge linking Australia to Asia (as well as Arab navigational accounts and routes) indicate that the land mass of Australia was not as lost to Asians as it appeared to have been to European explorers.

9.   Abu Taleb, extracted here, a late eighteenth-century Indian traveller in Europe, makes a sarcastic comment about, to his mind, the English tendency to write down any half-learned fact and cause books to be printed about it.

10.   As Nabil Matar notes in the introduction to *In the Lands of the Christians*, "...for the Renaissance interlocutor... ignorant of the Arab-Islamic heritage of geography and cartography, a well-travelled Muslim seemed an anomaly... Such an opinion has persisted into modern scholarship. In Pagden's two-volume collection of articles, *Facing Each Other: The World's Perception of Europe and Europe's Perception of the World*, there was not a single entry about the 'perception' of or by any of the civilisations of Islam, whether in the Mediterranean Basin, Central Asia or the Indian Subcontinent." (pp. xiii–xiv).

11. Not to mention a special number of *Granta*, reprinted many times, that gave a fillip to contemporary travel writing.

12. Jonathan Swift's *Gulliver's Travels* (1726) can be read as a late but still coeval satire on such accounts of travel, though of course it is a number of other things as well. John Dunton's *A Voyage Round the World*, published only six years before Swift's novel, was even more explicitly a novel that satirized some of the conventions of contemporary travel writing.

13. Both Marco Polo and ibn Battuta had their share of doubters. See also the section on ibn Battuta for an interesting contemporary anecdote regarding the veracity of his accounts.

14. Any attempt to settle this issue of generic identity has to keep in mind the ideological construction of "travel" and "travel writing" in Anglophone discourses, as noted here, and *also* the impact of these constructions on other languages and the resulting internal contradictions: for instance, the Arabic word for modern "tourism", *siyahah*, denoted "mystical travel".

15. This multiplicity of "interests" is also, one may argue, typical of the generic "impurity" that characterizes travel writing in general. If the beginnings of travel and writing about it defy partition and closure, the subsequent history and nomenclature of these two activities remain as difficult to pigeonhole. As Steve Clark has observed, "…the [travel writing] genre presents a problem for academic studies. It seems too dependent on an empirical rendition of contingent events… for entry into the literary canon, yet too overtly rhetorical for disciplines such as anthropology, sociology, geography or history." (1999, p. 2) The genre, if it can be called that, glories in impurity of form and origin: it is fact and fiction, mental and physical, framed by language and often purporting to describe a reality beyond the bounds of that language, historically trans–generic (moving from, say, autobiography or scientific treatise in the past to the novel in recent decades). All these problems of definition are further compounded by the Asian and African context of this anthology.

16. While some of these maps were maps in the modern European sense, others—like the Jain, Hindu and Buddhist pilgrimage maps of the sixteenth and seventeenth centuries—need to be read within an alternative paradigm of cartography and space.

17. Reportedly, in Al-Masudi's map of the world there is a substantial area in "the ocean of darkness and fog" (Atlantic Ocean) which he refers to as the unknown territory, and this has been considered a representation of the Americas by some scholars.

18. One can argue that Columbus is "more" important for the impact of

his "discovery"—conquest, enslavement, colonization, genocide, the rise of modern nation-states based on European patterns etc—but this is a matter of politics and not of the recovery of other routes of travel, which is our concern in this anthology.

19. The earliest extant travel texts on India also predate British colonization by centuries: the Greek Ambassador Megasthenes' account of the great Mauryan Empire (fourth century), the Chinese pilgrims Faxian's (fifth-century) and Xuanzang's seventh-century accounts of largely Buddhist India (extracted here), and an Arab travel diary from 851 AD. Other early travel books include the *Rihla* of the Moorish traveller ibn Battuta (1304-1369), who ranged more widely than Marco Polo (1254-1321) and entered India within a generation of Polo's departure from the land. Travel writing about India in the fifteenth century includes books by the Venetian Nicolo de'Conti and the Russian Athanasius Nikitin and non-European books like the Persian *Matla'-i Sa'dain* by 'Abdu'r-Razzaq. From the sixteenth century onwards, a number of (more visible) European and (later) colonial travel accounts are available, starting with Duarte Barbosa's *A Description of the Coasts of East Africa and Malabar in the Beginning of the Sixteenth Century* and the Latin *Commentarius* of the Jesuit Father Monserrate (who reached Emperor Akbar's court in 1580). However, writing about travel was not exogenous to India before European colonization (in the eighteenth century), though specialized *travelogues*, being a modern phenomenon, might have been. Travel writing is contained in autobiographies like *Babur-Nama*, written by the founder of the Moghul dynasty in the fifteenth century, or biographies like Gul-Badan Begum's (1523-1603) *Humayun Nama*, a history of her brother Humayun's reign in India. (Oral literature and ancient exile-based epics like the *Mahabharata* and the *Ramayana* might also be seen as offering early prototypes of travel writing. Kalidasa's fifth-century *Meghadutam* suggests another literary influence as well.)

20. To avoid stating the obvious, I will offer only one example of the extent of this tendency. The authors of *The Story of English* (a history that is very open to "new Englishes") write that "The Raj *created* an essentially bilingual society [in India]" (360) (my emphasis). Against this prevalent ahistorical perception, one is forced to point out that the educated classes of India were bilingual even before the Raj and the illiterate classes are (mostly) not bilingual even today. There exist in India not only vast regions of, shall we say, monolingualism but also many *other* kinds of bilingualism than the "Indian"-English bilingualism being touted in Europe and, often, by members of the Indian/cosmopolitan bourgeoisie.

21. Of course, we also tend to forget that much (if not most) of Greek culture actually existed in "Asia Minor".

22. This is as true of places of Anglophone interest, like India, as of areas less researched by Anglophone scholars. As Professor Adeeb Khalib, a leading scholar of Central Asian history, put it "there are no doubt many Hajjnamas [accounts of the Hajj pilgrimage] lying around in manuscript repositories in Uzbekistan, but they have not really been explored". (Private correspondence)

23. Tahtawi's *Takhlis al-ibriz ila talkhis Bariz*, which is a critical Islamist's account of French life, based on a visit to Paris around 1830. It includes a long and interesting first-hand account of the Revolution of 1830. The first English translation, *Imam in Paris*, was brought out by Saqi Books (London) only in 2003.

24. It appears than a manuscript translation of the Persian original exists in French in the Bibliothèque Nationale, Paris. It describes 'Abdu 'r-Razzâq's travels from Herat to Calicut and Vijayanagara in South India and back.

25. See Katsu Kokichi: *Musui's Story: The Autobiography of a Tokugawa Samurai*.

26. Readers can refer to Arkush and Lee's *Land Without Ghosts* for many of these extracts, in prose, painting (cartoon in the early twentieth century) or verse such as the lines below from a poem by Huang Zunxian, the Chinese consul-general at San Francisco from 1882 to 1885. Zunxian's long poem records both the experiences and the persecution of Chinese labourers in America and claims for them a status as American "pioneers":

    ...When the Chinese first crossed the ocean,
    They were the same as pioneers...
    ...Dressed in tatters, they cleared mountain forests;
    Wilderness and waste turned into towns and villages...

    Then it records the growing prejudice against the Chinese, and moves on to a criticism of Americans for failing to live up to the ideals of their Declaration of Independence:

    ...Thus, a thousand mouths keep up their clamor,
    Ten thousand eyes, glare, burning with hate...
    ...Those who do not carry passports
    Are arrested as soon as they arrive.
    Anyone with a yellow-colored face
    Is beaten even if guiltless.
    I sadly recall George Washington...
    (Translation by J. D. Schmidt)

27. The extracts from Leo Africanus' book include a section that shows how contextual and easily exchangeable the matter of being "Moorish" or "African" could be for him.

28. Accounts by Asian and African Christians include those by people captured and converted to Christianity (Leo Africanus etc.) and those, like the seventeenth-century al-Mawsuli, who belonged to Arabic Christian communities.

29. There are also nineteenth-century novels in Indian languages that take place in or describe Australia.

30. Which should be seen in a historical context: even European travel writing about the Polar regions is basically a late nineteenth- and twentieth-century phenomenon and thus mostly postdates our period of interest.

31. Nabil Matar's *In the Lands of Christians* presents two seventeenth-century Arab travel accounts of Europe which deal centrally with Muslim prisoners in Europe: one of them written by such a prisoner, converted to Christianity, who was to rise to an important position in Morocco after leaving Europe and returning to Islam.

32. It appears, though the matter is yet to be researched, that while European pilgrimage accounts experienced a boom in the nineteenth century and heavily influenced the development of modern travel writing in European languages, Asian and African pilgrimage accounts lost in visibility (or frequency) in the same period and came to be divorced from the growth of modern literary genres at least in places like India.

33. Is there a difference between the relationship of Muslim, Buddhist and Christian pilgrimage accounts to travel writing? Billie Melman points out (Hulme and Youngs, p. 108) that in Europe "pilgrimage had presented the reverse of travel" because in "Christian dogma and culture, *curiositas*, that is curiosity about the world, is a sin, related to the Original Sin..." Both in Islam and Buddhism this notion of original sin does not dominate: Buddhism has no exact equivalent to the Adam-Eve-Lucifer myth and Islam usually does not put as great a burden on curiosity or Eve for Adam's transgression.

34. Around AD 400, a Chinese monk set out for India in order to collect more books. His (adopted/monastic) name was Faxian, and though he was by no means the first Chinese pilgrim-scholar to visit India, his account remains the earliest such record. About 200 years later, when another Chinese monk, Xuanzang, born in 603, resolved to go to the "western regions" leading to India, his main purpose was to question the sages on points of philosophy and faith. These were pilgrimages that combined curiosity and scholarship with piety and faith.

35. This is another seriously under-explored area, as noted earlier.

36. It is not, however, the only one, as is evident in the section that contains extracts from the autobiographies of two African "Muslim" slaves (ex-slave, in one case) who arrived in the USA in very different ways in the nineteenth century.

37. There are, however, other differences (which I have not focused on in this essay). For instance, Matar notes in his introduction to *In the Lands of the Christians* that European travellers to the Muslim world in the early modern period were often so burdened by "ideological and polemical baggage" and their conviction of Islam as "a false religion", that they "claimed to see what they never encountered"—ranging from Prester John to cannibalism. On the other hand, partly because of Qur'anic acceptance of Christians as a "people of the book" and their own governmental/ecclesiastical functions, Arab travellers to Europe of the same period "described what they saw, carefully and without projecting unfounded fantasies." (p xxxi)

38. It was not unusual for Asians and Africans and, much more rarely, exceptional European travellers to try and critique the Western perception of Oriental—especially Muslim—women as powerless, exploited and oppressed. As early as the eighteenth century, Lady Mary Wortley Montagu—one of those rare European travellers who did not lug around the heavy baggage of cultural superiority—claimed that Turkish women "have more Liberty than we have." (*The Complete Letters of Mary Wortley Montagu*. Vol. I. Ed by R. Halsband. Oxford: Clarendon Press, 1967, p. 328)

39. My personal thanks to Professors Adeeb Khalid, Charles Lock, Pekka Masonen and Nabil Matar for their comments and criticism on reading various drafts of this introduction.

40. Celebrated general who lived in the second century BC, the first Chinese who explored the far regions of the west. He was sent to negotiate treaties in West-Central Asia.

41. "The chair is about seven inches high by a foot square, and the seat of it is wicker-work made of rattan cane. The legs are rounded, and, on the whole, the chair is not heavy."

42. Yijing says elsewhere: "There are strict rules about the six Requisites and the thirteen Necessaries fully explained in the *Vinaya*. The following are the six Requisites of a Bhikshu [mendicant]: 1. The Sanghati, a 'double cloak', 2. the Uttarasanga, the 'upper garment', 3. the Antarvasa, the 'inner garment'. The above three are all called civara. In the countries of the North, these priestly cloaks are generally called kasaya from their reddish colour.... 4. Patra, the bowl, 5. Nisidana, something for sitting or lying on, 6. Parisravana, a water-strainer.

"A candidate for Ordination should be furnished with a set of the six Requisites.

"The following are the thirteen Necessaries: 1. Sanghati, a 'double cloak', 2. Uttarasanga, the 'upper garment', 3. Antarvasa, the 'inner garment', 4. Nisidana, a mat for sitting or lying on, 5. Nivasana, an under garment, 6. Prati-Nivasana (another Nivasana), 7. Sankaksika, a side-covering cloth, 8. Prati-sankaksika (another sankaksika), 9. Kaya-pronchana, a towel for wiping the body, 10. Mukha-pronchana, a towel for wiping the face, 11. Kesapratigraha, a piece of cloth used for receiving hair when on shaves, 12. Kandupraticchadana, a piece of cloth for covering itches, 13. Bhesajapariskacivar, [a cloth for filtering medicine].

43. Ennin divides the first year of his travels according to the Japanese year period *jowa*. The second year he uses both this and the Chinese custom, and afterwards only the Chinese. The Chinese year is numbered according to the era names of the reigning emperor. Kaicheng (836-840) is the last era of emperor Wen Zong's reign (826-840) and Huichang (841-846) the name of Wuzong's only reigning era.

44. One of the five peaks or terraces of Mt. Wutai. Wutai means the five terraces.

45. Manjusri, the bodhisattva of wisdom.

46. Another name for Mt. Wutai.

47. Jiangduxian and Jiangyangxian were subprefectures in the city of Yangzhou.

48. Ibn Jubayr's frequent invocations to God to "restore" cities to Muslim hands should also be seen in the light of a comment by Nabil Matar in the introduction to *In the Lands of the Christians*: 'Western historians find that the only fear in the early modern period was of innocent Europeans who feared the rapacious "Mahometans", completely ignoring the fear the Muslims had of European *nasara*, whose legacy was not only of warfare but of religious persecution.' (p xxvii) While Ibn Jubayr precedes the period being discussed by Matar, we can mark the traces of the fear and repulsion that the Crusades and the *reconquista* were to instill in many Muslims even in these early writings.—Eds.

49. Ian Richard Netton, 1993, pp. 68–69.

50. i.e. from Muslim Spain and North Africa.

51. Baudouin IV (reigned 1174-85).

52. Ibn Jubair, who knew nothing of Scylla and Charybdis, is reminded of the legendary breach of the dyke of Marib, in Southern Arabia.

53. Reference to the proverb of Maidani used, according to tradition, by Mohammad on the conversion to Islam of Abu-Sufyan, the ancestor of the Omayyads: "there is an obstacle between the wild ass and the jump".

54. Quotation, through Maidani, attributable to the pre-Islamic Arabic poet Imru‘-al-Quais.

55. Though they were saved by the intervention of a Christian King, this formula could only be pronounced to a Muslim.

56. Genghis' Empire at this time stretched in the East to Korea and in the West over Central Asia to the Indus and the Caspian Sea.

57. The classic Chinese Feast of the Dragon.

58. A bamboo basket on which hands or feet were rested for ventilation in the hot season.

59. A robe made of fine feathers which resembled the plumage of the crane.

60. This contradicts later accounts by Chinese and Europeans, but is believed to be true and to reflect the Mongol ways before they were "civilized". "Civilization" brought gender segregation.

61. The usual prejudice of a settled people towards nomads; like other pastoral nomads the Mongols had fixed, tribally inherited patterns of movement.

62. See chapter 15.

63. The Chinese word used here is a phonetic transliteration of the Old Turkish word *ordo* meaning "camp" or "palace".

64. One of the four Secretaries of State of Emperor Ogodai mentioned in chapter 4 of the *Brief Account*: one is a Black Tartar, one a Kitan, one a Jurchen, and Chinqai an Uighur. These were the four main groups of the Mongol Empire.

65. In other words it is an alphabetic system of writing with diacritical marks, like Arabic.

66. The Kitan Secretary of State.

67. This, as Amitav Ghosh points out in his preface to this anthology, was and remains a dominant Western myth.

68. i.e. "in the first half, and the second half of the Kaws". This grammatical construction differs from the phrase mentioning the Saba wind.

69. See p. 369.

70. i.e. at right angles to the wind.

71. That is, winds not blowing from the prevailing direction.

72. A corrupt text or something must be missing. Odd days are rarely mentioned only the round tens. Perhaps one should expect something like "although it is sometimes possible up to the 340th day". The Damascus manuscript omits the phrase which follows it but it would have been better to have omitted the preceding phrase.

73. Presumably the north side of the island.

74. The text is not clear here and the reading may be different.

75. Probably the better season, the one used most.

76. This can only mean that the Kaws wind produces a large swell because it begins in the expanses of the outer Ocean, whereas the Saba wind blows on to the Arabian sea from the cultivated land of India.

77. This appears in the margin of the text.

78. It is very difficult to place any date to this. The Turkish dynasty are presumably the Mamlukes and the Beni Ghassan, the Rasulids whose rule in the Yemen came to an end around AH 858 (AD 1454).

79. There must be a mistake or omission in the text here. Presumably when bound for India from Yemen in ibn Majid's time Soqotra was left on one side and in returning from India it was left on the other side.

80. i.e. Pilot guide similar to the *Fawa'id*. The text is in the plural.

81. With a strong SW monsoon wind there is a large swell which continues while the zuhun strikes them at right angles to the swell. The "typhoon" storms appear when the monsoon wind and the swell are much weaker, and only one phenomenon has to be dealt with at one time.

82. Reading "plain, desert", which might also be possibly read as "beloved" but this usually refers to the beloved when angry.

83. Reading with the Damascus manuscript.

84. A quotation from Hadith, Tirmidhi on *'ilm* b. 19 and Ibn Maja on *Suhd*, b. 15. Also used generally as a proverb, see *Majma' al-amthal* (Maidani) Cairo ed. V. I, p. 144 Freytag v. I, p. 385.

85. It appears that the word stands for what is better understood as "matters of honour" in European terms.—Eds.

86. Or "trade".—Eds.

87. Islamic calendar.

88. Holt, p. 7.

89. Holt, p. 6.

90. A military colony established by Frederick II and populated by Muslims deported from Sicily.

91. A Mamluk of Sultan al-Nâsir, he rose to high office until he was disgraced, imprisoned and put to death. He was never able to speak Arabic.

92. Originally a Mamluk of the Amir Balabân al-Tabbâkhî, he won Sultan al-Nâsir's favour and died as governor of Damascus in 1342.

93. Died in his eighties on 16 May 1345, leaving great possessions, which were squandered by his descendants over more than a century.

94. A Mamluk, he died as governor of Safad on 7 August 1342.

95. Chiliad and garrison were units of the defence system.

96. The famous Tang poet (659-744) lived for a time at Moon Lake, southwest of Ningbo.

97. The enigmatical cognomen, Protected Town, is of early date; it is used i.e. by ibn Batuta in the fourteenth century. Babur's tense refers it to the

past. The town had frequently changed hands in historic times before he wrote. The name may be due to immunity from damage to the buildings in the town. Even Chingiz Khan's capture (1222 AD.) left the place well-preserved and its lands cultivated, but it inflicted great loss of men.

98. Here is a good example of Babur's caution in narrative. He does not affirm that Samarkand became Musalman, or (infra) that Qusam ibn 'Abbas went, or that Alexander founded but in each case uses the presumptive past tense, resp. *Bulghan dur, barghan dur, bina qilghan dur,* thus showing that he repeats what may be inferred or presumed and not what he himself asserts.

99. i.e. of [Prophet] Muhammad.

100. i.e. Fat Village.

101. *Ma'lum aimas kim muncha paida bulmish bulghai*; an idiomatic phrase.

102. Abu 'Abdu'l-lah bin Isma'ilu'l-jausi b. 194 AH. d. 256 AH. (810-870 AD.). He passed only a short period of his life in Khartank, a suburb of Samarkand.

103. This though 2475 ft. above the sea is only some 300 ft. above Samarkand. It is the Chupan-ata (Father of Shepherds) of maps and on it Timur built a shrine to the local patron of shepherds. The Zar-afshan, or rather, its Qara-su arm, flows from the east of the Little Hill and turns round it to flow west. Babur uses the name *Kohik Water* loosely; e.g. for the whole Zar-afshan when he speaks (infra) of cutting off the Dar-i-gham canal but for its southern arm only, the Qara-su in several places, and once, for the Dar-i-gham canal.

104. *rud*. The Zar-afshan has a very rapid current. The name Dar-i-gham is used also for a musical note having charm to witch away grief; and also for a town noted for its wines.

105. What this represents can only be guessed; perhaps 150 to 200 miles. Abu-i-fida quotes Ibn Haukal as saying that from Bukhara up to "Bottam" (this seems to be where the Zar-afshan emerges into the open land) is eight days' journey through an unbroken tangle of verdure and gardens.

106. It is still grown in the Samarkand region, and in the nineteenth century a grape of the same name was cultivated in Aurangabad in the Deccan [India].

107. *i.e. Shahrukhi*, Timur's grandson, through Shahrukh. It may be noted here that Babur never gives Timur any other title than Beg and that he styles all Timurids, Mirza (Mir-born).

108. Here still lies the Ascension Stone, the *Guh-tash*, a block of greyish white marble, concerning the date of the erection of the building and meaning of its name.

109. This seems to be the Bibi Khanim Mosque. The author of *Les Mosquées de Samarcande* states that Timur built Bibi Khanim and the Gur-i-amir (Amir's tomb); decorated Shah-i-zinda and set up the Chupan-ata shrine.

110. Cap. II. Quoting from Sale's *Qur'an* (i. 24) the verse is, "And Ibrahim and Isma'il raised the foundations of the house, saying, 'Lord I accept it from us, for Thou art he who hearest and knowest; Lord I make us also resigned to Thee, and show us Thy holy ceremonies, and be turned to us, for Thou art easy to be reconciled, and merciful.'"

111. or, *buland*, Garden of the Height or High Garden. The Turki texts have what can be read as *buldi* but the Z.N. both when describing it and elsewhere write *buland*. *Buldi* may be a clerical error for *bulandi*, the height, a name agreeing with the position of the garden.

112. In the Heart-expanding Garden, the Spanish Ambassadors had their first interview with Timur.

113. The Plane-tree Garden. This seems to be Clavijo's *Bayginar*, laid out shortly before he saw it.

114. The citadel of Samarkand stands high; from it the ground slopes west and south; on these sides therefore gardens outside the walls would lie markedly below the outer fort (*tash-qurghan*).

115. Timur's eldest son, d. 805 AH. (1402 AD.), before his father, therefore. Babur's wording suggests that in his day, the Gur-i-amir was known as the Madrasa.

116. Hindustan would make a better climax here than Samarkand does.

117. These appear to be pictures or ornamentations of carved wood.

118. *i.e.* the Black Stone at Makkah to which Musalmans turn in prayer.

119. As ancient observatories were themselves the instruments of astronomical observation. Babur's wording is correct. Aulugh Beg's great quadrant was 180 ft. high; Abu-muhammad *Khujandi's* sextant had a radius of 58 ft. Jai Singh made similar great instruments in Jaipur, Dihli [Delhi] has others.

120. b. 597 AH. d. 677 AH. (1201-1274 AD.).

121. a grandson of Chingiz Khan, d. 663 AH. (1265 AD.). The cognomen *Ail-khani* (*Il-khani*) may mean Khan of the Tribe.

122. Ilarunu'r-rashi's second son; d. 218 AHM (833 AD.).

123. Mr. Erskine notes that this remark would seem to fix the date at which Babur wrote it as 934 AH. (1527 AD), that being the 1584th year of the era of Vikramaditya, and therefore at three years before Babur's death. (The Vikramaditya era began 57 BC.)

124. This remark may refer to the 34 miles between the town and the quarries of building stone.

125. Steingass, any support for the back in sitting on a low wall in front of a house.

126. *beg u begat, bagh u baghcha.*
127. Four Gardens, a quadrilateral garden, laid out in four plots. The use of the name has now been extended for any well arranged, large garden, especially one belonging to a ruler (Erskine).
128. As two of the trees mentioned here are large, it may be right to translate *narwan*, not by pomegranate, but as the hard-wood elm, Madame Ujfalvy's *'haragatche'*. The name *qara yighach* (*haragatch*), dark tree, is given to trees other than this elm on account of their deep shadow.
129. Now a common plan indeed.
130. *juwas-i-haghazldr (ning) su'i i.e.* the water of the paper-(pulping)-mortars. Owing to the omission from some MSS. of the word *su*, water, *juwaz* has been mistaken for a kind of paper. Kostenko, it is to be noted, does not include paper in his list of modern manufactures of Samarkand.
131. Mine of mud or clay.
132. *qurugh.* Vullers, classing the word as Arabic, Zenker, classing it as Eastern Turki, and Erskine (p. 42 n.) explain this as land reserved for the summer encampment of princes. Shaw (Voc. P. 155), deriving it from *qurumaq*, to frighten, explains it as a fenced field of growing grain.
133. *Cf.* i. 40. There it is located at one *yighach* and here at 3 *hurohs* from the town.
134. *taur.* Cf. Zenker *s.n.* I understand it to lie, as Khan Yurti did, in a curve of the river.
135. 162 m. by rail.
136. *Min Samarkandis aul (or auwal) aichhanda Bukhara chaghiridr ni aichar aidim.* These words have been understood to refer to Babur's initial drinking of wine but this reading is contradicted by his statement (f. 189) that he first drank wine in Harat in 912 AH. I understand his meaning to be that the wine he drank in Samarkand was Bukhara wine. The time cannot have been earlier than 917 AH. The two words *aul aichhanda*, I read as parallel to *aul (baghri qara)* (f. 280) 'that drinking,' 'that bird,' *i.e.* of those other countries, not of Hindustan where he wrote. It may be noted that Babur's word for wine, *chaghir*, may not always represent wine of the grape but may include wine of the apple and pear (cider and perry), and other fruits. Cider, its name seeming to be a descendant of *chaghir*, was introduced into England by Crusaders, its manufacture having been learned from Turks in Palestine.
137. This overstates the time.
138. He is the author of the *Shaibani-nama.*
139. Here *aqar-suiar* might safely be replaced by 'irrigation channels'.
140. *laimi*, which in Afghani (Pushtu) signifies grown without irrigation.
141. It has been suggested that the unusual name Uruch is a Spanish

mispronunciation of the very common Persian name of the time, Ulugh.

142. The 1926 Routledge edition of *Don Juan of Persia* was reprinted by Arno Press in New York in 1973, but there remains very little critical commentary on Don Juan of Persia besides W.E.D. Allen's *Notes of Don Juan of Persia's Account of Georgia* (London: School of Oriental Studies, 1930), and two recent unpublished US dissertations, Linda J. Smith's "Dialogue between Safavid Persia and Europe: Don Juan of Persia's Writing Analyzed" at Illinois State University, 1992, and Bobby Amir Ghaheri's "The Role of Religious Conversion and the Presentation of Historical Debate in the Formation of Geohistorical Theory as seen in 'Relaciones de Don Juan de Persia'" at Ohio State University, 1998.

143. Ferdinand I, Grand Duke of Tuscany, 1587-1609.

144. Sir Anthony Sherley (c. 1565-1635) was one of three sons of Sir Thomas Sherley, all of whom led itinerant and eventful lives. Before his arrival at Shah Abbas the Great's court in 1599, Sir Anthony Sherley had already had his account of buccaneering in the West Indies published by Hakluyt in 1598. His claims to Abbas that he represented Elizabeth I were false, but his declared ability to lobby support for war with the Turks prevailed. After falling out with the Persian embassy in Siena in 1601, he returned to Venice, and in 1605 led an unsuccessful mission from Prague on behalf of the Holy Roman Emperor Rudolf II to Morocco. In 1607, he became a member of the Council of State in Naples, and in 1609, led an unsuccessful Spanish expedition against the Turks. The remainder of his life was spent in Madrid in poverty and obscurity. The Sherleys have been the subject of recent critical attention: see Kenneth Parker's *Early Modern Tales of Orient. A Critical Anthology* (London: Routledge, 1999), pp. 61-82, and Anthony Parr's "Foreign Relations in Jacobean England: The Sherley brothers and 'the voyage of Persia'" in Jean-Pierre Maquerlot and Michele Willems (eds), *Travel and Drama in Shakespeare's Time* (Cambridge University Press, 1995), pp. 14-31.

145. Hippolito Aldobrandini, Pope Clement VIII, 1592-1604.

146. The "Machine" referred to by Don Juan was constructed by Juanelo Turriano in 1565 for Charles V, and could convey 600,000 buckets of water from the river to the city daily.

147. Michael H. Fisher, *The First Indian Author in English*.

148. Austin, Allan D., *African Muslims in Antebellum America*, 1997, p. 4.

149. For instance, in his autobiography, Said consistently refers to Jesus in Qur'anic terms, as the Messiah rather than the son of God.

150. In Senegal.

151. Fayetteville.

152. Sheriff of Cumberland County, of which Fayetteville is the county seat.

153. James Owen (1784-1865), M. C. from North Carolina 1817-19, and afterward president of the Wilmington and Raleigh Railroad and major-general of militia.

154. Bladen County, NC.

155. Italicized in the original translation.

156. John Owen (1787-1841), brother of the preceding, governor of North Carolina from December 1828 to December 1830.

157. Unavailability of the original Arabic text has made it impossible to verify whether the inverted commas—extremely unusual in Arabic until recently—were used by Said or whether they were added by the translator.

158. Probably "Muslim" in the original, as the term "Mohammedan" would be very unlikely in Arabic.

159. [Original note] Barca Gana is alluded to in the *Encyclopaedia Britannica* (Vol V, p. 54) as the general of the Scheik of Bornoo..

160. In 1873, the House of Lords actually had close to 500 members and the Commons 650. The Shah must be giving the number present.

161. This idea, which seems remarkably prescient of the Shah, was repeated some years later by Theodor Herzl, who suggested that Rothschild become King of Israel in return for a sizeable donation. Rothschild gave Herzl the same reply. Interestingly, the Baha'i religion which arose and was first tolerated under the reign of Naser ed-Din but subsequently persecuted, found its refuge in Haifa in Ottoman Palestine, where the founder Bahaullah has his mausoleum and the religion still has its world headquarters.

162. There has been some discussion of the authenticity of the memoirs. It is generally agreed that the broad biographical outlines narrated in the memoir are reliable, though the writer might have exaggerated her own importance in some matters and within the Zanzibar aristocracy. However, the book contains in depth knowledge of Arab life and Zanzibar royal society and, as such, attests to the writer's royal connections at least prior to her elopement.—Eds.

163. A text that ought to be read along with Emily Said-Ruete's book for its discourse on gender is Melek Hanum's *Six Years in Europe* (1873), which unfortunately we could not extract for reasons of space, time and copyright. Melek Hanum grew up in Constantinople, but married a European man (of unspecified nationality), with whom she travelled throughout Europe. While in Europe, she met and fell in love with Kibrizli-Mehemet, whom she agreed to marry despite her hatred of harem life. This marriage soon ended and her husband retained their daughter, at which point Melek Hanum wrote scathing attacks on "the

evils of Islamic society". Unlike Emily Said-Ruete, Melek Hanum's travel writing often condemns harems and women's place in Islamic society. She presents oppressive images of harem life that echo Occidental travel writers' accounts of women in Islam. At times she even turns to idealized images of European domesticity in order to critique and condemn Turkish and Muslim lifestyles. Reading Melek Hanum's book alongside that of Said-Ruete illustrates how women from Muslim cultures can view Europe and Islam from very different perspectives. Indeed, their conflicting positions remind us that travel discourses are never monolithic: what one traveller sees in a culture may be seen very differently by another.

164. Jamal Mahjoub's novel, *The Carrier*, also appears to draw inspiration from the text to narrate the story of another (fictional) Arab traveller.

165. See Introduction to *Al-Abdar's Rihlat al-Abdari,* or *Arrihla al-Maghribia* (*al-Abdari's Travels*, or *The Moroccan Journey*) (Rabat, 1968).

166. Ibn Mohammed al-Abdari, *The Moroccan Journey*, edited with an introduction by Mohammed al-Fassi (Rabat: Ministry of Education, 1968), p. 93.

167. Which has gained for him the dubious accolade of being called the "'disgusted, Tunbridge Wells' of Moroccan travel": see Mackintosh-Smith, *Travels with a Tangerine*, p. 12.—Eds.

168. Albert Hourani, *A History of the Arab Peoples*. p. 129.

169. Said Hamdun and Noël King, *Ibn Battuta in Black Africa*. p. 6.

170. Tim Mackintosh-Smith: *Travels with a Tangerine: A Journey in the Footnotes of Ibn Battutah*, p. 4.

171. It was destroyed in the next century. The ruins are west of Rissani in Tafilelt, on the left bank of the Ziz.

172. There is a difference of a few days or, at times, a couple of years in the chronological accounts of different scholars. Hamdun and King, for example, gloss this date, 753 AH, as 18 February AD 1352.—Anthology Editor.

173. Arab physicians used mercury in the treatment of skin ailments.

174. Editors of ibn Battuta have commented that there is (was?) only one well between Taghaza and Walata, 250 km from the former and 480 km from the latter.

175. There are many references to blind guides in the desert in Arabic literature.

176. The Malinke and Bamana term for a slave of the king sent to supervise or replace a local headman. It was also the title of the head of the king's slaves and chief of his household

177. At least one editor of ibn Battuta has noted that the famous traveller was wrong in considering this a mark of disrespect. It was common

practice.

178. The introduction and the translated extracts have been selected from a longer introduction and a much longer selection from the travels of al-Mawsuli as written and translated, respectively, by Nabil Matar in *In the Lands of the Christians: Arabic Travel Writing in the Seventeenth Century*. The book contains three other (Muslim) Arab accounts of travels in Europe from the seventeenth century. These accounts are as fascinating as that of al-Mawsuli, but had to be left out of this anthology for shortage of space. The editors of this anthology are grateful to Professor Matar and Taylor & Francis Books for permission to reproduce selections from the introduction and the translation. The original texts' convenient anglicized spellings have been retained in this section.

179. See a discussion of this topic in Appendix B of Nabil Matar's *Turks, Moors and Englishmen in the Age of Discovery*.—Eds.

180. Al-Mawsuli's multilinguality does not appear to have been exceptional for his class. Another seventeenth-century Arab traveller, whose account has also been translated and included by Nabil Matar in *In The Lands of The Christians*, was Abdallah Bin Aisha, leader of a Moroccan delegation to France in 1698. While unable to speak French, Bin Aisha was fluent in Arabic, Spanish and English.—Eds.

181. Matar notes that by the time al-Mawsuli visited the mines, the production of silver had declined dramatically from what it had been forty years earlier.

182. Matar: "This is a brief description of the forced labour (*mita*) of the Indians in the mines, first started in 1573. While some Indians worked in the mines, others led the train of pack animals to Arica, where the silver was loaded on ships."

183. Henry Louis Gates, Jr., ed. *Race, Writing and Difference*, Chicago and London: University of Chicago Press, 1986. p. 377.

184. Abu Taleb, p. 219.

185. Abu Taleb, pp. 100-101.

186. Abu Taleb, p. 100.

187. Abu Taleb, pp. 61-62.

188. Abu Taleb, p. 61.

189. Abu Taleb, p. 329.

190. Abu Taleb, p. 342.

191. Abu Taleb, p. 347.

192. Abu Taleb, p. 345.

193. Section headings added by the editors of this anthology.

194. Hog's bristles are an abomination to Mohammedans.

195. Bernard Lewis, *The Muslim Discovery of Europe* (New York and London: W.W. Norton & Company, 1982), p. 118.

196. Ibid.

197. Minister and Ambassador Driss Ben Driss al-Amraoui undertook his visit to France immediately after the quick and humiliating defeat of the Moroccan army by Spain in the Battle of Tetuan in 1859.

198. Up till the nineteenth century, Muslims conventionally refer to Europe as the "House of War" and to all Islamic countries as the "House of Islam".

199. Ahmad al Hajari, *Näsir al-dîn "älâ al-qawm al-kâfirîn*, ed. Mohamed Rizq (Casablanca: Imprimeries Najah al Jadida, 1987)

200. Muslims regarded Arabic manuscripts in Christian hands as captives. Hence the necessity to ransom them. Bernard Lewis tells us that the "high rating accorded to Arabic manuscripts may be seen not so much as an indication of esteem for literature but rather as a desire to rescue Muslim Arabic writings from exile and defilement." *The Muslim Discovery of Europe*, op.cit. p. 117.

201. Mohammed as-Safar's travel narrative is edited and translated from Arabic into English by Susan Miller, *Disorienting Encounters: Travels of a Moroccan Scholar in France 1845-1846*. Miller informs us that in the background to as-Safar's journey "were events which had profoundly upset the Moroccan ruling elite's perception of its own power vis-à-vis the West. Indeed as-Safar's journey was part of an effort to try to correct the imbalance, and to gain insight into what had gone wrong" (p. 4).

202. Quoted by Bernard Lewis, op. cit. p. 288. In her article, "Islamic Imperialism and the Creation of some Ideas of 'Europe'", Jacqueline Kay refers to an ancient joke that "goes back to the First Crusade and is told by the Arabs against the Franks whom they regarded as very lax in the control of their women and generally sexually feeble and decadent." The joke is as follows: "A man comes home to find his wife in bed with another man. He asks this other man what he is doing in bed with his wife, to which the other man replies that he was very tired, overcome with exhaustion, so he had got into bed and fallen asleep. The husband then tells him; 'if this ever happens again, you and I will have a serious quarrel.'" In *Europe and its Others*, Francis Barker *et al.* (eds) Vol. 1 (1984), pp. 59-71.

203. Driss Ben Driss al-Amraoui, *Tuhfat al-malik al-'azîz bimamlakat bârîz,* edited with an introduction by Zaki M'barek (Tanger: Presses des Etablissements d'Emballage, d'Edition et de Distribution, 1989).

204. Medieval heroic romances.

205. He means there is no Christian Sabbath observed; Jews observe it on Saturday.

206. See Sudhir Chandra's "Two Faces of Prose: Behramji Malabari and

Govardhanram Tripathi" in Arvind K. Mehrotra's *A History of Indian Literature in English*. London: Hurst and Co., 2001.

207. See also Antoinette Burton, *At the Heart of Empire*, pp. 152–192.

208. Susheila Nasta, *Home Truths: Fictions of the South Asian Diaspora in Britain*, Hampshire and New York: Palgrave, 2002, p. 20.

209. Antoinette Burton, "Making a Spectacle of Empire: Indian Travellers in Fin-de-Siècle London", *History Workshop Journal*, 42, 1996, p. 128.

210. Susheila Nasta, *Home Truths: Fictions of the South Asian Diaspora in Britain*, p. 20.

SELECT BIBLIOGRAPHY

PRIMARY LITERATURE

Abul Fazl, Allami. *Ain-i-Akbari*. Trans. H. S. Jarrett, Ed. Jadunath Sarkar. New Delhi: Crown Publications, 1988 (reprint).

Abu al-Fidâ. *The Memoirs of A Syrian Prince*. Translated with an introduction by P. M. Holt, Wiesbaden: Franz Steiner Verlag Gmbh, 1983.

Africanus, Leo. *The History and Description of Africa and of the Notable Things Therein Contained, Written by Al-Hassan ibn-Mohammed Al-Wezaz Al-Fasi [alias Leo Africanus], a Moor, Baptised as Giovanni Leone, but better known as Leo Africanus. Done into English in the Year 1600 by John Pory, and now edited, with an introduction by Dr Robert Brown*. Originally published by the Hakluyt Society and reprinted in three volumes by Burt Franklin, Publisher, New York, year not given.

al-Amraoui, Driss Ben Driss. *Tuhfat al Malik al Aziz Bimamlakat Bariz*, edited with an introduction by Zaki M'barek. Tangier: Presses des Etablissements d'Emballage, d'Edition et de Distribution, 1989.

Arkush, R. David and Lee, Leo O. (Trans. and Ed.). *Land Without Ghosts: Chinese Impressions of America from the Mid-Nineteenth Century to the Present*. Berkeley and London: University of California Press, 1989.

Babur, Zahiruddin. *Babur-Nama*. Trans. A.S. Beveridge. London: Sang-E-Meel Publications, 1922. (Also New York: AMS Press, 1922)

Basho, Matsuo. *Narrow Road to the Deep North and Other Travel Sketches*. Translated from the Japanese with an introduction by Nobuyuki Yuasa (1966). London: Penguin, 1967.

Basho: *A Haiku Journey: Basho's Narrow Road to a Far Province*. Trans. and intro. by Dorothy Britton. Tokyo: Kodansha International, 1983.

Baijnath, Lala. *England and India.* Bombay: Jehangir B. Karani, 1893.

Beal, Samuel (Trans. and Ed.). *Si-Yu-Ki Buddhist Records of the Western World* (London, 1884), Delhi: Motilal Banarsidass Publishers, 1994.

Begum, Gul-badan. *The History of Humayun.* Trans. from Persian by Annette S. Beveridge. London: The Royal Asiatic Society, 1902.

Birkeland, Harris. *Nordens historie i middelalderen etter arabiske kilder,* Oslo: ?, 1954.

Bragner, Robert (Trans.). *Piri Reis: Kitab-i Bahriye.* Istanbul: Historical Research Foundation, Istanbul Research Center: 1988.

Chelebi, Evliya. *Narrative of Travels in Europe, Asia, and Africa, in the Seventeenth Century.* Tr. from Turkish by Ritter Joseph von Hammer. London: Oriental Tr. Fund and New York: Johnson Reprint Corporation, 1968.

Collett, Sophia Dobson. L*ife and Letters of Rajah Rammohan Roy.* Ed. D.K. Biswas and P. C. Ganguli, Calcutta: ?, 1962.

Cooper, Arthur (Trans.). *Li Po and Tu Fu.* Penguin, 1973.

Daguan, Zhou (Ta-Kuan, Chou). *The Customs of Cambodia* (1967). Trans. by J. Gilman d'Arcy Paul. Bangkok: The Siam Society, 1993.

Davidson, Robyn (Ed.): *Journeys: An Anthology.* London: Picador, 2001.

Digby, Simon (Ed. and trans.). *Sufis and Soldiers in Aurangzeb's Deccan* (English translation of the Persian manuscript *Malfuzat-i-Naqshbandiyyia,* containing the biographies of two Naqshbandi Sufis). New Delhi: Oxford University Press, 2001.

Dorr, David F. *A Colored Man Round the World: By a Quadroon.* Cleveland: ?, 1858.

Drake, Fred W. *China Charts the World: Hsu Chi-yü and His Geography of 1848.* Cambridge: Harvard University Press, 1975.

Dutt, R. C. *Three Years in Europe.* Calcutta: S. K. Lahiri & Co., 1890.

Efendi, Abbas. *A Traveller's Narrative Written to Illustrate the Episode of the Báb.* Trans. from the Persian. Cambridge: CUP, 1891.

Emin, Joseph. *The Life and Adventures of Joseph Emin, An Armenian, Written in English by Himself.* London: The Author, 1792. (Republished by the Asiatic Society of Bengal, Calcutta, in 1918)

Ennin's Diary: The Record of a Pilgrimage to China in Search of the Law. Translated from the Chinese and annotated by Edwin O. Reischauer. New York: The Ronald Press Company 1955.

Equiano, Olaudah. *The Interesting Narrative of the Life of Olaudah Equiano, Or Gustavus Vassa, The African. Written by Himself* (1789). Leeds: James Nichols, 1814.

Fisher, Michael H. *The First Indian Author in English.* Delhi: Oxford University Press, 1996.

Frodsham, J. D. (Ed.) *The First Chinese Embassy to the West: The Journals of Kuo Sung-t'ao, Liu Hsi-hung and Chang Te-yi.* Oxford: Clarendon Press, 1974.

Gaudefroy-Demombynes, Maurice (Trans.). *Les voyages d'ibn Jobayr.* Paris: Librairie orientaliste Paul Geuthner, 1949-65.

Gibb, H. A. R. *The Travels of ibn Battuta, Translated with Notes.* Cambridge: CUP for the Hakluyt Society, 1958.

Haenisch, Erich; Ts'ung-wu, Yao; Olbrecht, Peter and Pinks, Elizabeth (Trans). *Chinesische Gesandtenberichte über die frühen Mongolen 1221 und 1237.* Wiesbaden: Otto Harrassowitz, 1980.

Hargett, James M. (Ed. and Trans.): *On the Road in Twelfth Century China: The Travel Diaries of Fan Chengda (1126–1193),* Stuttgart: Franz Steiner Verlag, 1989.

Haldar, Rakhal Das. *The English Diary of an Indian Student, 1861–62.* Dacca: The Asutosh Library, 1903.

'Hamdun, Said and King, Nöel (Edited and introduced). *Ibn Battuta in Black Africa.* Princeton: Markus Wiener Publishers, 1994, 1975.

(A) Hindu. *Three Years in Europe.* Calcutta: Thacker, Spink & Co., 1873.

Holt, P. M. (Trans). *The Memoirs of A Syrian Prince: Abu al-Fidâ, Sultan of Hamah (1273-1331).* Wiesbaden: Franz Steiner Verlag Gmbh, 1983.

Hung, William. "Huang Tsun-hsein's Poem 'The Closure of the Educational Mission in America' Translated and Annotated", *Harvard Journal of Asiatic Studies,* No. 18, 1955, pp. 55-73.

Hwui Li, Shaman. *The Life of Hiuen-Tsiang.* Translated with an introduction by Samuel Beal. London: Kegan Paul, Trench, Trübner & Co., 1911.

ibn Khaldun. *Muqaddimah*. Trans. Franz Rosenthal. Princeton: Princeton University Press, 1967.

I'tesamuddin, Mirza Sheikh. *The Wonders of Vilayet*. Trans. by Kaiser Haq. Leeds: Peepal Tree, 2001.

Izzatullah, Mir. *Travels in Central Asia by Meer Izzat Oolah in the years 1812-13*, Trans Cpt. Henderson, Calcutta: ?, 1872.

Jaubert, P. Amedée. *Géographie d'Édrisi*, Recueil de voyages et de mémoire publié par la Société de Géographie, Paris: chez Arthus Bertrand, 1836 (vol. I) and L'imprimerie royale, 1840 (vol. II).

Juan, Don. *Don Juan of Persia*. New York: Arno Press, 1973. (First published by Routledge in 1926)

Khan, Abu Taleb (Trans. from Persian by Charles Stewart, 1814). *Travels of Mirza Abu Taleb Khan in Asia, Africa and Europe During the Years 1799 to 1803*. New Delhi: Sona Publications, 1972.

Kokichi, Katsu. *Musui's Story: The Autobiography of a Tokugawa Samurai*. Translated, with an introduction and Notes, by Teruko Craig. Tucson: The University of Arizona Press, 1988.

Kosambi, Meera. Tr. and Ed. *Returning the American Gaze: Pandita Ramabai's 'The Peoples of the United States' (1889)*. Delhi: Permanent Black (Co-published with Indiana University Press), 2003.

Li ji [Li Chi]. *The Travel Diaries of Hsü Hsia-k'o*. Hong Kong: The Chinese University of Hong Kong, 1974.

Liscomb, Kathlyn Maurean. *Learning from Mount Hua: A Chinese Physician's Illustrated Travel Record and Painting Theory*. Cambridge: CUP, 1993.

Liu, E. *The Travels of Laocan*. Trans. by Yang Xianyi and Gladys Yang. Beijing: Panda, 1983.

Logan, Rayford and Michael R. Winston, Eds. *Dictionary of American Negro Biography*. New York: Norton, 1982.

Lu Yu (Trans. from the Chinese by Chun-shu Chang and Joan Smythe): *South China in the Twelfth Century, a Translation of Lu Yu's Travel Diaries, July 3-December 6, 1170*. Hong Kong: The Chinese University Press, 1981.

Mackintosh-Smith, Tim. *Travels with a Tangerine: A Journey in the*

Footnotes of ibn Battuta. London: Picador, 2001.

— (Ed.). *The Travels of ibn Battuta*. London: Picador, 2002.

Mahomed, Hajee S. S. *Journal of my Tour Round the World*. Bombay: Duftur Ashkara Oil Engine Press, 1895.

Mahomed, S. D. *The Travels of Dean Mahomet, A Native of Patna in Bengal, Through Several Parts of India, while in the Service of The Honourable The East India Company, Written by Himself, In a Series of Letters to a Friend*. Cork: J. Connor and the Author, 1794.

— *Shampooing, or Benefits Resulting from the Use of the Indian Medicated Vapour Bath*. Brighton: The Author, 1822.

Malabari, B. M. *The Indian Eye on English Life or Rambles of a Pilgrim Reformer*. London: Archibald Constable and Company, 1893.

Matar, Nabil (Ed. and Trans.). *In the Lands of the Christians: Arabic Travel Writing in the Seventeenth Century*. First English Translations. New York and London: Routledge, 2003.

Mazoomdar, P. C. *Sketches of a Tour Round the World*. Calcutta: S. K. Lahiri & Co, 1884.

Meskill, John (Trans. and Ed). *Ch'oe Pu's Diary: A Record of Drifting across the Sea*. Tucson: The University of Arizona Press, 1965.

Miller, Susan. *Disorienting Encounters: Travels of a Moroccan Scholar in France 1845-1846*. Berkeley and Los Angeles: University of California Press, 1992.

Mir Muhammad Taqi Mir (Trans., annotated and ed. by C. M. Naim). *Zikr-i-Mir: The Autobiography of the Eighteenth Century Mughal Poet*. New Delhi: Oxford University Press, 1999.

Morris, Ivan, transl. *The Pillow Book of Sei Shonagon*. New York: Columbia University Press and Harmondsworth: Penguin: 1967.

Morrison, G. W. transl., *Wang Wei: Poems*. Hamondsworth: Penguin, 1973.

Mukharji, T. N. *A Visit to Europe*. Calcutta: W. Newman & Co., 1889.

Nijô. *The Confessions of Lady Nij_* (Translated from the Japanese by Karen Brazell). New York: Anchor Books, 1973.

Pandian, T. B. *England to an Indian Eye*. London: Elliot Stock, 1897.

Parekh, C. L. (ed.): *Essays, Speeches, Addresses and Writings on Indian Politics of the Hon'ble Dadabhai Naoroji*. Bombay: Caxton Printing

Works, 1887.

Paul of Aleppo. *The Travels of Macarius: Patriarch of Antioch: written by his Attendant Archdeacon, Paul of Aleppo, in Arabic.* Trans by F. C. Belfour. London: Oriental Translation Committee, 1826–36.

Polo, Marco. *The Travels* (The translation of William Marsden in the revised version by Thomas Wright). Cologne: Könemann, 1996.

Prince, Nancy. *A Narrative of the Life and Travels of Mrs. Nancy Prince.* 1850. Reprinted in *Telling Travels: Selected Writings by Nineteenth-Century American Women Abroad.* Ed. Mary Suzanne Schriber. DeKalb: Northern Illinois UP, 1995, pp. 114-29.

Rajan, Chandra. (Trans. and Ed). *Kalidasa: The Loom of Time.* New Delhi: Penguin, 1989.

Ram, Jhinda. *My Trip to Europe.* Lahore: Mufid-i-am Press, 1893.

Reischauer, Edwin O. *Ennin's Diary: The Record of a Pilgrimage to China in Search of the Law.* New York: The Ronald Press Company, 1955.

Rudolph, S. H. and Rudolph, L. I. with Mohan Singh Kanota (ed.): *Reversing the Gaze: Amar Singh's Diary, A Colonial Subject's Narrative of Imperial India.* New Delhi: Oxford University Press, 2000.

Ruete, Emily. *Memoirs of an Arabian Princess.* Translated from the original German. Translator unknown. Princeton: Markus Wiener Publishers, 2000.

Salesse, Bernadette (trans.). *Journal de voyage en Europe du Shah de Perse Nâser ed-Din Qâjâr.* Paris: Sindbad/Actes Sud, 2000.

Sastri, K. A. Nilakanta (Ed.). *Foreign Notices of South India from Megasthenes to Ma Huan.* Madras (Chennai): University of Madras, 1972.

Satthianadhan, S. *Four Years in an English University.* Madras: Srinivasa, Varadachari & Co., 1893.

— *A Holiday Trip to Europe and America.* Madras: Srinivasa, Varadachari & Co., 1897.

Wu Cheng'en: *The Journey to the West*, vol. 1-4. Trans. and ed. by Anthony C. Yu. Chicago: The University of Chicago Press, 1980-84.

SECONDARY LITERATURE

Abu-Lughod. *Before European Hegemony: The World System AD 1250–1350.* Oxford: OUP, 1989.

Adi, Hakim. *West Africans in Britain 1900-1960.* London: Lawrence & Wishart, 1998.

Austin, Allan D. *African Muslims in Antebellum America.* New York: Routledge, 1997.

Bayly, C. A. *Empire and Information: Intelligence Gathering and Social Communication in India 1780-1870.* Cambridge: CUP, 1996.

— *The Birth of the Modern World,* 1780-1914. Malden, USA and Oxford, UK: Blackwell Publishing, 2004.

Birkeland, Harris. *Nordens historie i middelalderen etter arabiske kilder,* Oslo: ?, 1954.

Brah, Avtar. *Cartographies of Desire: Contesting Identities.* London: Routledge, 1996.

Burton, Antoinette. "Making a Spectacle of Empire: Indian Travellers in Fin-de-Siècle London", *History Workshop Journal,* 42, 1996.

— *At the Heart of the Empire: Indians and the Colonial Encounter in Late-Victorian Britain.* Berkeley and London: University of California Press, 1998.

Butor, Michel. "Travel and Writing", *Mosaic* 8.1, 1974, p. 1-16.

Buzard, James. *The Beaten Track: European Tourism, Literature, and the Ways to "Culture" 1800-1918.* Oxford: OUP, 1993.

Casson, Lionel. *Travel in the Ancient World.* London: George Allen & Unwin Ltd, 1974.

Clark, Steve (Ed.): *Travel Writing and Empire: Postcolonial Theory in Transit.* London and New York: Zed Books, 1999.

Clifford, James. "Notes on Travel and Theory", in *Travelling Theory: Travelling Theorists.* Inscriptions 5, 1998.

— *Routes: Travel and Translation in the Late Twentieth Century.* Cambridge, MA and London: Harvard University Press, 1997.

Coleman, Simon and Elsner, John. *Pilgrimage Past and Present: Sacred Travel and Sacred Space in the World Religions.* London: British Museum Publications Ltd, 1995.

— (Ed.). *Pilgrim Voices: Narrative and Authorship in Christian Pilgrimage*. New York and Oxford: Berghahn Books, 2002.

Dalrymple, William. *White Mughals*. Delhi: Penguin, 2002.

Das, Sisir Kumar. *Indian Ode to the West Wind: Studies in Literary Encounters*. Delhi: Pencraft International, 2001.

Desai, Rashmi. *Indian Immigrants in Britain*. Oxford: OUP, 1963.

Dixon, Conrad. "Lascars: The Forgotten Seamen", in R. Ommer and G. Panting (eds.): *Working Men Who Got Wet, Proceedings of the Fourth Conference of the Atlantic Canada Shipping Project, 24-26 July 1980*. Maritime History Group, University of Newfoundland, 1980.

Dougherty, Michael. *To Steal a Kingdom: Probing Hawaiian History*. Waimanalo, Hawaii: Island Style Press, 1992.

Drake, Fred W. *China Charts the World: Hsu Chi-yü and His Geography of 1848*. Cambridge: Harvard University Press, 1975.

Edwards, Justin D. *Exotic Journeys: Exploring the Erotics of U.S. Travel Literature, 1840-1930*. Hanover, NH: University Press of New England, 2001.

Fisher, Michael H. *The First Indian Author in English*. Delhi: Oxford University Press, 1996.

Frow, John. "Tourism and the Semiotics of Nostalgia", *October* 57, 1991, p. 123-151.

Fogel, Joshua A. *The Literature of Travel in the Japanese Rediscovery of China, 1862-1945*. Stanford: Stanford University Press, 1996.

Fussell, Paul. *Abroad: British Literary Travelling Between the Wars*. New York: OUP, 1980.

Gilroy, Paul. *The Black Atlantic: Modernity and Double Consciousness* (1993). London and New York: Verso, 1999.

Gray, Basil. *The World History of Rashid al-Din*, A Study of the Royal Asiatic Society Manuscript. London: Faber & Faber, 1978.

Grewal, Inderpal. *Home and Harem: Nation, Gender, Empire, and the Cultures of Travel*. Durham, NC and London: Duke University Press, 1996.

Gruesser, John C. "Afro-American Travel Literature and Africanist Discourse", *Black American Literature Forum* 24.1, Spring 1990, p. 5-20.

Holland, Patrick and Huggan, Graham. *Tourists with Typewriters: Critical Reflections on Contemporary Travel Writing.* Ann Arbor: University of Michigan Press, 1998.

Hourani, Albert. *A History of the Arab Peoples* (1991). London: Faber and Faber, 1992.

Hwui Li, Shaman. *The Life of Hiuen-Tsiang.* Translated with an introduction by Samuel Beal. London: Kegan Paul, Trench, Trübner & Co., 1911.

Innes, C.L. *A History of Black and Asian Writing in Britain 1700-2000.* Cambridge: Cambridge University Press, 2004. Irele, F. Abiola and Gikandi, Simon. *The Cambridge History of African and Caribbean Literature* (2 Volumes), Cambridge: CUP, 2004.

Islam, Syed Manzurul. *The Ethics of Travel: From Marco Polo to Kafka.* Manchester: Manchester University Press, 1996.

Jaubert, P. Amedée. *Géographie d'Édrisi, Recueil de voyages et de mémoire publié par la Société de Géographie,* Paris: chez Arthus Bertrand, 1836 (vol. I) and L'imprimerie royale, 1840 (vol. II).

Kabbani, Rana. *Europe's Myths of Orient.* Bloomington: Indiana UP, 1986.

Kaplan, Caren. *Questions of Travel: Postmodern Discourses of Displacement.* Durham, NC: Duke UP, 1996.

Khair, Tabish. *Amitav Ghosh: A Critical Companion.* Delhi: Permanent Black, 2003.

—— "Remembering to Forget Abu Taleb", *Wasafiri,* No 34, London, Autumn 2001, 34-38.

Kumar, Amitava. *Passport Photos.* Berkeley and London: University of California Press, 2000.

Leask, Nigel. *Curiosity and the Aesthetics of Travel Writing, 1770-1840.* Oxford: OUP, 2002.

Leed, Eric. *The Mind of the Traveler: From Gilgamesh to Global Tourism.* New York: Basic Books, 1991.

Lewis, Bernard. *The Muslim Discovery of Europe.* New York and London: W.W. Norton & Company, 1982.

Lewis, Reina. *Gendering Orientalism: Race, Femininity and Representation.* New York: Routledge, 1996.

Liscomb, Kathlyn Maureen. *Learning from Mount Hua: A Chinese Physician's Illustrated Record and Painting Theory*. Cambridge: CUP, 1993.

Logan, Rayford and Michael R. Winston, Eds. *Dictionary of American Negro Biography*. New York: Norton, 1982.

MacCannell, Dean. *The Tourist: A New Theory of the Leisure Class*. New York: Schocken, 1976.

Matar, Nabil. *Turks, Moors, and Englishmen in the Age of Discovery*. New York: Columbia University Press, 1999.

Markovits, Claude. *The Global World of Indian Merchants 1750-1947: Traders of Sind from Bukhara to Panama*. Cambridge: Cambridge University Press, 2000.

Masonen, Pekka. "Leo Africanus: The Man with Many Names", *Al-Andalus-Magreb. Revista de estudios árabes e islámicos y grupo de investigación al-Andalus-Magreb,* viii-ix, fasc. 1 (2000-2001), pp. 115-143.

McClintock, Anne. *Imperial Leather: Race, Gender and Sexuality in the Colonial Context*. New York: Routledge, 1995.

Miller, Susan. *Disorienting Encounters: Travels of a Moroccan Scholar in France 1845-1846*. Berkeley and Los Angeles: University of California Press, 1992.

Mills, Sara. *Discourse*. New York: Routledge, 1997.

— *Discourses of Difference: An Analysis of Women's Travel Writing and Colonialism*. New York: Routledge, 1991.

Miyoshi, Masao. *As We Saw Them: The First Japanese Embassy to the United States (1860)*. Berkeley: University of California Press, 1979.

Montgomery, James A. "Ibn Fadlan and the Russiyah", *Journal of Arabic and Islamic Studies* 3, 2000, pp. 1-26.

Nasta, Susheila. *Home Truths: Fictions of the South Asian Diaspora in Britain*, Hampshire and New York: Palgrave, 2002.

Netton, Richard Ian (Ed.). *Golden Roads: Migration, Pilgrimage and travel in Mediaeval and Modern Islam*. Richmond (UK): Curzon Press, 1993.

— "Basic Structures and Signs of Alienation in the Rihla of ibn

Jubayr", in Netton, Richard Ian (Ed.): *Golden Roads: Migration, Pilgrimage and Travel in Mediaeval and Modern Islam*. Richmond (UK): Curzon Press, 1993, pp. 57-74.

Oliver, Douglas L. *The Pacific Islands*. New York: Doubleday, 1968.

Osborne, Thomas J. *Annexation Hawaii: Fighting American Imperialism*. Waimanalo, Hawaii: Island Style Press, 1998.

Osterhammel, Jürgen. *Colonialism*. Trans. From German by Shelley L. Frisch. Princeton: Markus Weiner Publishers and Kingston: Ian Randle Publishers, 1999 (1995).

Pagden, Anthony. *Facing Each Other: The World's Perception of Europe and Europe's Perception of the World*. Brookfield, USA: Ashgate, 2000.

Phillips, Mike and Phillips, Trevor. *Windrush: The Irresistible Rise of Multi-Racial Britain*. London: HarperCollins, 1998.

Phillips, Mike. *London Crossings: A Biography of Black Britain*. London: Continuum, 2001.

Pratt, Mary Louise. *Imperial Eyes: Travel Writing and Transculturation*. London and New York: Routledge, 1992.

Raby, Peter. *Bright Paradise. Victorian Scientific Travellers*. London: Pimlico Books, 1996.

Ratzel, Friedrich. *Politische Geographie*. Munich: R. Oldenbourg, 1879.

Rauchenberger, Dietrich. *Johannes Leo der Afrikaner. Seine Beschreibung des Raumes zwischen Nil und Niger nach dem Urtext*, Wiesbaden: Orientalia Biblica et Christiana 13, 1999.

Rediker, Marcus. *Between the Devil and the Deep Blue Sea: Merchant Seamen, Pirates and the Anglo-American World*. Cambridge: CUP, 1987.

Reischauer, Edwin O. *Ennin's Travels in T'ang China*. New York: The Ronald Press Company, 1955.

Rennie, Neil. *Far-Fetched Facts: The Literature of Travel and the Idea of the South Seas*. Oxford: Clarendon Press, 1995.

Rice, David Talbot (edited by Basil Gray). *The Illustrations to the "World History" of Rashid al-Din*. Edinburgh: Edinburgh University Press, 1976.

Rodinson, Maxime. *Europe and the Mystique of Islam*. Trans. from French by Roger Veinus. London: I. B. Tauris & Co. Ltd, 1988.

Rubiés, Joan-Pau. *Travel and Ethnology in the Renaissance: South India Through European Eyes, 1250-1625.* Cambridge: CUP, 2000.

Said, Edward. *Orientalism.* New York: Vintage, 1978.

Sarup, Madan. "Home and Identit", *Travellers' Tales: Narratives of Home and Displacement.* Ed. George Robertson *et al.* New York: Routledge, 1994, pp. 93-104.

Sastri, K. A. Nilakanta (Ed.). *Foreign Notices of South India from Megasthenes to Ma Huan.* Madras (Chennai): University of Madras, 1972.

Shirane, Haruo. *Traces of Dreams: Landscape, Cultural Memory, and the Poetry of Basho.* Stanford: Stanford UP, 1998.

Speake, Jennifer, Ed. *Literature of Travel and Exploration: An Encyclopedia* (Three-volume set). London: Routledge, 2003.

Spivak, Dawnine. *Grass Sandals: The Travels of Basho.* New York: Atheneum, 1997.

Spurr, David. *The Rhetoric of Empire: Colonial Discourse in Journalism, Travel Writing and Imperial Administration.* Durham, NC: Duke UP, 1993.

Stafford, Barbara Maria. *Voyage into Substance: Art, Science, Nature, and the Illustrated Travel Account, 1760-1840.* Cambridge: CUP, 1984.

Stagl, Justin. *A History of Curiosity: The Theory of Travel 1550-1800.* Chur (Switzerland): Harwood Academic Publishers, 1995.

Strassberg, Richard E. *Inscribed Landscapes: Travel Writing from Imperial China.* Berkeley: University of California Press, 1994.

Thapar, Romila. *Sakuntalâ: Texts, Readings, Histories.* New Delhi: Kali for Women, 1999.

Torgovnick, Marianna. *Gone Primitive: Savage Intellects, Modern Lives.* Chicago: University of Chicago Press, 1990.

Tibbetts, G. R. *Arab Navigation in the Indian Ocean before the Coming of the Portuguese,* Oriental Translation Fund Series, vol. XLII, London: Royal Asiatic Society of Great Britain and Northern Ireland, 1971.

Van Den Abbeele, Georges. *Travel as Metaphor from Montaigne to Rousseau.* Minneapolis: University of Minnesota Press, 1992.

Van Sertima, Ivan. *The African Presence in Ancient America: They Came*

Before Columbus. New York: Random House, 1976.

Visram, Rozina. *Ayahs, Lascars and Princes.* London: Pluto Press, 1986.

— *Asians in Britain: 400 Years of History.* London and Sterling (USA): Pluto Press, 2002.

Waley, Arthur. *The Real Tripitaka and other Pieces.* London: Unwin Brothers Ltd. 1952. Part two: Ennin and Ensai, 9p. 131-168.

Ward, Julian: *Xu Xiake 1857-1641: The Art of Travel Writing.* Copenhagen: Curzon Press, 2001.

Watters, Thomas (Edited after his death by T.W. Rhys Davids and S. W. Bushell). *On Yuan Chwang's Travels in India 629-645 A.D.* London: Royal Asiatic Society, 1904.

Woods, Gregory. "Fantasy Islands: Popular Topographies of Marooned Masculinity", *Mapping Desire: Geographies of Sexualities.* Ed. David Bell and Gill Valentine. New York: Routledge, 1995, pp. 126-48.

Yared, Nazik Saba (Trans. from the Arabic by S. D. Shahbandar). *Arab Travellers and Western Civilisation.* London: Saqi Books, 1996.

Zhiri, Oumelbanine. *L'Afrique au miroir de l'Europe: fortunes de Jean-Léon l'Africain à la Renaissance*, Geneva: Travaux d'Humanisme et Renaissance, no. 247, 1991.

INDEX